Company Financial Reporting:

Issues and Analysis

The Nelson series in accounting and finance

Consulting editor
John Perrin, Professor and Director of the Centre
for Industrial, Economic and Business
Research, University of Warwick

In memory of JB, a dedicated reader of financial reports.

T A Lee
University of Edinburgh

Company
Financial Reporting
Issues and Analysis

Nelson

Thomas Nelson and Sons Ltd
Nelson House   Mayfield Road
Walton-on-Thames   Surrey KT12 5PL
P.O. Box 18123   Nairobi   Kenya
116-D JTC Factory Building
Lorong 3   Geylang Square   Singapore 1438

Thomas Nelson Australia Pty Ltd
19–39 Jeffcott Street   West Melbourne   Victoria 3003

Nelson Canada Ltd
81 Curlew Drive   Don Mills   Ontario M3A 2R1

Thomas Nelson (Hong Kong) Ltd
Watson Estate   Block A   13 Floor
Watson Road   Causeway Bay   Hong Kong

Thomas Nelson (Nigeria) Ltd
8 Ilupeju Bypass   PMB 21303   Ikeja   Lagos

First published in Great Britain by
Thomas Nelson and Sons Ltd, 1976

Reprinted 1979, 1980

0 17 771027 6
NCN 5710 41 4

Printed and bound in Great Britain at
The Camelot Press Ltd, Southampton

Contents

Preface   viii

Introduction   xi
  Financial information and the public interest   xi
  Financial information and the company   xii
  Financial information and the accountant   xii
  The purpose of the text   xiii

1 The Nature of Companies and Their Financial Reports   1

  Introduction   1
  The nature and form of companies   1
  Company share capital   1
  Public and private companies   2
  Holding and subsidiary companies   3
  Regulating company behaviour   3
  The need for financial information   3
  Annual financial reports   4
  Financial reporting concepts   6
  The concept of income   7
  The concepts of capital and value   8
  The balance sheet   8
  The income statement   13
  The funds statement   16
  The relationship between the annual financial statements   18
  Other sources of reported information   18
  Other sources of information   19
  The audit function   19
  Concluding remarks   20

2 The History and Development of Company Financial Reporting   23

  The pre-limited company era   23
  The railway example   23
  The legislative development of company financial
    reporting: 1844-1900   25
  The legislative development of company financial
    reporting: 1900-1948   27
  Case law and the development of company financial
    reporting   30

History and development of accounting standards   32
Conclusions   34

3 **Present-day Requirements for Company Financial Reporting**   37

The current legal requirements for annual reporting   37
The current legal requirements for prospectuses   42
The current professional requirements   43
The requirements of the Stock Exchange   44
The requirements of the Panel   45
Concluding remarks   46

4 **The Objectives, Uses and Users of Company Financial Reports**   48

Introduction   48
The concepts of utility and relevance   49
The general purpose approach   49
Management and company financial statements   50
Accountability and company financial statements   51
Investment decisions and company financial statements   52
Loan decisions and company financial statements   59
Other uses of company financial statements   59
The quality of company financial reports   61
General or specific-purpose information?   63

5 **The Production of Company Financial Reports**   70

Introduction   70
Producing company financial reports   70
Data processing   71
The nature of data processing   71
Data collection   72
Information processing   72
Communicating the processed information   77
The audit of communicable accounting information   80
Summary   83

6 **Issues and Problems in Company Financial Reporting**   87

Introduction   87
The valuation issue   87
The monetary unit problem   94
The flexibility problem   99
The communications problem   113

7 **Further Issues and Problems in Company Financial Reporting**   121

The problem of satisfying user needs   121
Problems for the auditor   131

8 **The Context for Using Company Financial Reports**   142

Introduction   142
Report analysis and decisions   142
The nature of decisions   143

Report analysis objectives   144
Types of decision   145
The Use of Financial Information by Investors   147
Criteria for analysed data   149
The investment example   150
Fundamental analysis   152
Technical analysis   163
Conclusions   170

9 The Nature of Financial Ratios   **175**

Introduction   175
Objectives of financial ratios   176
Criteria for financial ratios   177

10 The Computation and Use of Financial Ratios   **184**

Introduction   184
A note on company taxation   186
Financial ratios reflecting profitability   188
Financial ratios reflecting liquidity   197
Financial ratios indicating financial structure and
    performance   205
A summarized profile of the company   212
An alternative approach to financial ratios   215

EPILOGUE   **222**

Introduction   222
The user of company financial reports   222
The present state of play in financial reporting   223

APPENDIX: Analysis of Disclosure Provisions Affecting
Company Financial Reports   **226**

INDEXES   **235**

Preface

Accounting is essentially a practical exercise concerned with the measurement and communication of useful financial information. It is also a highly complex and technical process requiring, in most instances, the professionalism of an experienced accountant to produce and report on the required data in a meaningful way. Many would also argue that accounting reports, because of their technical nature, require the professionalism of an experienced financial analyst in order that they be used meaningfully.

Whatever the merits of these arguments and assumptions, it is clear that reported accounting information is an extremely important element in economic decision making, and that it requires to be measured and reported in the best way possible. But what is the 'best way possible' and what are the major problems to be overcome before the 'best way possible' is achieved? As I am not aware of any existing text which fully answers these points, the purpose of this book is to explore in depth the main issues of financial reporting, delineating the major problems and offering what appear to be reasonable and suitable answers.

The text is written within the context of company financial reports because I believe these to be the major source of formal financial information about companies available to investors and other interested parties. While the context is essentially British in terms of the legal and fiscal environment, the text maintains a neutrality which should enable non-British readers to follow it without difficulty. After all, the problems associated with producing and using company financial reports are nct uniquely British.

If the reader searches the relevant literature of accounting, he will find that the topic of financial reporting is usually treated in a fragmented way rather than as a complete package. For example, there are textbooks on financial accounting practice which broadly discuss the nature of financial reporting but concentrate on the purely mechanical problems of producing the data to be contained in them. Similarly, there are books on accounting theory which discuss at length particular financial reporting problems without fully discussing the context in which financial reports are used. There are also books which describe in detail the process of analysing financial reports but fail to convey to the reader the fundamental measurement and communication problems underlying the analysable data. In other words, the interested student of company financial reporting can find its problems and solutions are covered in different parts of various texts. Rarely, if ever, are they discussed completely within one text. Hopefully, this text attempts to remedy this situation.

I have divided the text into two distinct parts. The first part (that is, Chapters 1 to 7 inclusive) deals with the nature and problems associated with measuring and communicating accounting data in company financial reports. I would hope that this gives the interested reader what I believe to be a necessary understanding of the strengths and weaknesses of these reports — that is, necessary in the sense that reports cannot be meaningfully used unless such an understanding exists. The second part (that is, Chapters 8 to 12 inclusive) deals with the use which can be made of reported information and discusses this within the context of the different needs of various users.

It is always tempting when writing on accounting matters to get involved in the detailed mechanics of computing reportable data. Indeed, in many instances, it is not only tempting but also necessary. Accountants and related professionals must at some stage in their education learn these basic skills. However, once they have been learnt, there appears to be little virtue in pursuing the matter endlessly, especially if in so doing it is likely to obscure fundamental arguments and points for debate which are of deep concern to both the consumer and producer of reported accounting information. Thus, this text examines the nature, structure and problems of company financial reporting without getting bogged down in such things as double-entry bookkeeping — despite its arithmetical elegance. This does not mean that the text is devoid of figures — this is neither possible nor desirable. Instead, I have attempted to give the reader figure work whenever this is necessary to develop, explain or examine an argument or a problem. For this reason, I hope the arguments and discussions are clearer than they might otherwise be.

Arguably the largest single problem in writing a text is to clearly, honestly and realistically assess the potential readership. This is never an easy task but I hope I am being fair when I suggest that it should be capable of extensive use by the following groups:

(a)   University and Polytechnic undergraduate students seeking a detailed study of the company financial reporting system, either at first or second year level, as part of their overall study of financial accounting matters.
(b)   Professional accountancy students undertaking foundation or graduate conversion courses.
(c)   Students in professions which are major users of published accounting information — for example, trainee bankers, stock-brokers, and investment analysts and managers.

In each of these groups, the students concerned should, at some stage in their course, require to study the company financial reporting system in depth — not only to understand what the information is and how it is measured and used, but also to appreciate the context in which it is measured and used and the related problems and difficulties which arise. In addition, because the text concentrates to a considerable extent on the users of company financial reports, it should be of interest to students who are required to study investment and financial management as well as financial accounting.

In other words, because of its lack of emphasis on the purely mechanical aspects of the accounting process (which are well covered elsewhere in a large number of texts), I believe this to be a text which can be meaningfully used by non-accounting specialists as well as by would-be professional accountants. Whether the reader is intending to specialize in the preparation of reportable accounting information, or whether he is intending to specialize in its analysis and interpretation, this text should cope with both needs. The ability to compute accounting figures is one thing — the ability to understand fully the problems inherent in the measurement, communication and use of these figures is another. I feel strongly that students should be fully aware of these problems whether they be student accountants, bankers, analysts or stockbrokers.

Finally, it would be wrong to omit any acknowledgement of the various people who have undoubtedly aided me in producing this book. My grateful thanks go to the following:

To Tom Robertson for contributing what is an extremely useful and clear checklist of legal, professional and regulatory provisions covering company financial reporting in the U.K. Condensing all the relevant material into such a few pages is a remarkable feat.

To Mick Glautier, John Perrin and Tom Robertson for reviewing original drafts of the manuscript, and for making many useful suggestions for improvement which have undoubtedly added to any merits the book may now have.

To Ken Fox and Peter Ford of Nelson who, always to my utter amazement, manage to convert a mass of original and amended typescript into the text you are now reading.

To Chris Nash for producing such a clear original manuscript within an almost impossible deadline.

To my ever-patient wife, Ann, who has, yet again, put up with the selfishness, temper and idiosyncrasies of an expectant author.

And, finally and with feeling, to successive Chancellors of the Exchequer who have made it entirely necessary for me to write this book.

Any faults remaining in the book are undoubtedly mine.

T. A. LEE

Author's Note:

The problem with writing a text in any area of rapid change is that at some time the writing has to stop and the publishing begin. In this case, the text was in press when a number of important writings were made public. Particularly, readers' attention is drawn to the Accounting Standards Steering Committee's *The Corporate Report* which reviews the objectives and uses of reporting, as well as the main measurement problems, and advocates the publication of several reports supplementary to the existing structure of historic cost and inflation-adjusted historic cost financial statements. (This is especially pertinent to Chapters 4, 6 and 7 of this text.) In addition, the government-sponsored Sandilands Committee has produced its *Inflation Accounting*, in which it reviews the various income and value models in the context of user needs, recommending the abandonment of historic cost and inflation-adjusted historic cost statements; and, instead, the reporting of data in a form of replacement cost accounting which uses revaluations, market prices and specific indices, as well as realisable values and economic values where relevant. (This report is also pertinent to Chapters 4, 6 and 7 of this text.) Finally, it should be noted that *Statement of Standard Accounting Practice 9*, 'Stocks and Work in Progress' supports the lower of cost and net realisable value basis, with cost defined as expenditure incurred in bringing stock and work in progress to its present location and condition; and *Statement of Standard Accounting Practice 10*, 'Statements of Source and Application of Funds', now advocates the reporting of historic cost-based funds statements by quoted companies.

Introduction

Financial Information and the Public Interest

'When a student is told the result of a test, a golfer sees his ball fall into the rough, or a pieceworker gets his pay packet he is getting knowledge of results. There are few actions which have no perceptible result and in most cases knowledge of results is important to the performer and will effect his future behaviour.'[1]

Knowledge of results and its effect on human behaviour are essential themes of a text concerned with the issues and problems associated with the production, communication and use of financial accounting information. The reasoning behind this proposition is not obscure, but neither is it simple, as the following paragraphs will reveal.

Business activity has developed over the years within the so-called free-enterprise system, with differing degrees of risk being taken by the various suppliers of capital. As business enterprises have multiplied, in number and size, the supply of capital and the related risk-taking have increased correspondingly. Inevitably, this has created a considerable public interest in business activity, not just in terms of shareholders, lenders and creditors, but also including employees, customers, the 'news' media, regulatory bodies of various kinds and government. This public interest has caused business enterprises to accept social as well as economic, financial and legal responsibilities, and has created, as a consequence, a growing need for the communication of information to account for results which are of considerable interest to a wide range of individuals and organizations. In particular, there is an obvious need for reliable information which they can use to acquire an essential knowledge of the way in which business enterprises are 'behaving' in relation to the public interest. By perceiving enterprise behaviour through communicated information, interested parties can use this knowledge to amend or adapt their own behaviour vis-à-vis the enterprises concerned.

One of the most significant aspects of the information systems of business enterprises in a developed economy is that which concerns the production and communication of financial data, particularly that describing enterprise profitability and financial position. This information has obtained such a place of eminence because it attempts to portray the economic resources of the enterprises and the financial results which have been achieved by its management when these resources have been put to use. It attempts to reveal how effective management has been in resource utilization as well as the financial rewards available to compensate for the risks taken by the various suppliers of capital. The importance of this information to these risk-takers increases the more they are divorced from the relevant resource management; the gap between the supplier and manager of capital creates a lack of knowledge of enterprise affairs which needs to be bridged by the periodic supply of formal financial information. Once supplied with this information, the risk-takers are better informed to make decisions and take action concerning their involvement or interest in the enterprise, and this is obviously beneficial to the efficient working of the free-enterprise system.

Financial Information and the Company

The vehicle for a substantial portion of business activity in a free-enterprise economy is the limited liability company, and the need for formal financial information about enterprise affairs is seen clearly within the corporate structure of relationships and interests. Capital is provided to these entities by shareholders, lenders and, at least on a short-term basis, creditors. Depending on the nature and size of the companies involved, these 'investors' may terminate their 'investments' by realization – either through sale on an open or restricted market, or by termination of a contractual agreement. The most long-term and risky investment is recognized generally as that of the shareholder, and in most developed countries operating under largely free-enterprise principles, this is also recognized legally or governmentally by provisions requiring corporate managements to produce and communicate periodic financial information to shareholders. The relevant financial reports containing this information are therefore the main vehicle by which management communicates to corporate ownership. However, owing to the complexity of the corporate financial structure, more and more individuals and institutions have increasingly become concerned with gaining a knowledge of enterprise profitability and financial position, and this has meant that company financial reports to shareholders have come to enjoy a much wider audience.

Financial Information and the Accountant

Largely because of the significant expansion in corporate business activity and its related financial reporting function, the accountancy profession has assumed the considerable responsibility for producing and reporting the required financial accounting information. Although in most countries where corporate financial reports are produced, the legal responsibility for regularly presenting these statements is with company management, it is accountants who are concerned with producing the relevant information on management's behalf, subject to certain prescribed and acceptable standards of measurement and communication. Accountants are also responsible for examining and giving an opinion on the quality of reported information, in their capacity as auditors. The role of the accountant in providing reliable financial information is therefore an important one, and one which is not only onerous but complex. It has been ably described by Morison as follows:

'. . . an accountant is an artist. He finds a subject; he studies it; he must be moved; and then he endeavours to portray his subject faithfully. The main principle involved is one of truth . . .

'The anology of a picture is helpful . . . Accounts present a picture of economic facts. Pictures are drawn by human beings, and therefore vary. There may be many pictures of the one object, each of them true, each life-like and each different; consider a miniature, a presentation portrait, a holiday snap, a caricature. We do not condemn the activity of portraiture because different artists present different views of the same thing; indeed, we only condemn it when they do conform to a single imposed view.

' "Truth sits at the top of a mountain", it has been wisely said, "and there are many ways up." '[2]

The main aim of the accountant is therefore to ensure that the public (that is, the interested public) has the benefit of the best financial reports which can be devised. No accountant would challenge such an objective, but, as the accountancy profession has found over the years, the production of the 'best' financial reports possible is an extremely difficult task which can attract a great deal of criticism and debate.[3] As Morison has concluded:

'The proper nature of accounting is a difficult question, and difficult questions do not admit easy answers — or perhaps any answers. It is for that reason wholly proper to go on asking them. All we can reasonably hope for is the clarification of minds. . . .'[4]

The Purpose of the Text

The above introductory comments are given as a prologue to a description of the nature and purpose of this text. It is concerned essentially with the production, communication and use made of the accounting information contained in the periodic financial reports of companies to their shareholders. As such, it is not so much concerned with the techniques and practices employed by the accountant as with the fundamental issues and problems of principle which affect the measurement of information (from the point of view of the reporting accountant) as well as its use (from the point of view of the individual or institution receiving it). There are many such problems and issues of vital importance in a situation where reliable information for decision-making and other activities is limited, and where its highly technical nature may well be a constraint to its usefulness. They can be divided into the following two identifiable categories.

Issues and problems of a technical nature

For purposes of this text, these may be defined as those relating to the organization of accounting numbers in such a way as to produce useful and reliable accounting messages relating to the financial affairs of companies. They therefore involve the various standards and conventions which are, or could be, adopted in both the production and use of corporate financial reports. However, it should be noted that the explanations and discussions which will follow are in no way intended to equip the reader with an ability to account. The sole purpose is to educate the reader to give him a basic understanding of the technical issues and problems involved in corporate financial reporting.

Issues and problems of a behavioural nature

Accounting information exists to influence human behaviour and can, in turn, be influenced by human behaviour.[5] As such, the production and use of corporate financial reports create a series of issues and problems which relate to the human behaviour aspect. These behavioural points will be fully covered where appropriate, and what empirical evidence is available will be looked at.

Thus, the text can be divided into two distinct parts: the production and communication of accounting information; and the use made of the relevant reports. Each part contains technical and behavioural problems, and these will be separately identified at appropriate stages. First of all, however, the reader will be given an outline of the history and development of the corporate financial reporting system, together with a description of its present form. This will be stated within the UK context but the main steps can be seen in similar developments in the United States and the Commonwealth.

Suggested Discussion or Essay Topics

1. How would you explain the role of the accountant, and what do you consider his contribution to be to the individual company and the community at large?

2. The provision of financial information is essential to the maintenance of the corporate private-enterprise system. Discuss.

3. Published financial information serves to protect the public interest in company activity. Comment on the validity of this statement.

4. The reporting of financial information is more than a matter of measuring accounting data. Discuss.

References

1. J. Annett, *Feedback and Human Behaviour*, Penguin Books, 1969, p.11.

2. A. M. C. Morison, 'The Role of the Reporting Accountant Today—I', *Accountant's Magazine*, September 1970, p. 410.

3. See, e.g., H. Ross, 'The Current Crisis in Accounting', *Journal of Accountancy*, August 1967, pp. 65-9.

4. A. M. C. Morison, 'The Role of the Reporting Accountant Today—II', *Accountant's Magazine*, October 1970, p. 476.

5. T. A. Lee, 'Psychological Aspects of Accounting', *Accounting and Business Research*, Summer 1972, pp. 223-5.

1

The Nature of Companies and Their Financial Reports

Introduction

The purpose of this chapter is to explain, in general terms, the nature, structure and form of company financial reports in widespread use today. The intention is therefore to familiarize the reader with the type of accounting information which describes, in aggregate terms, the financial affairs and conduct of companies. With this background, it is hoped that he will be in a position to follow the subsequent discussions of the issues and problems surrounding the production and use of such information.

The Nature and Form of Companies

Lillie has defined a company as follows:

'A company is an association of persons formed for the purpose of carrying on some business or undertaking, in the name of the association, each member having the right, subject to the regulations governing the administration of the association, to transfer his interest therein to any other person.'[1]

This definition embodies the main characteristics of companies — first, that they have a legal personality and existence separate from their owners; secondly, that their identity is not affected by changes in their owner membership, thereby giving them a theoretically perpetual life; and, thirdly, that they can enter into contractual and other relationships with third parties, through their employees and elected officials and managers, without necessarily having to refer to their owners. Therefore, although similar in certain respects to partnerships, they allow for two factors which partnerships cannot entertain: separation of ownership from management; and consequential permanency of life.

Companies can be divided into two main categories: those with limited liability and those with either unlimited or guaranteed liability. As discussions on corporate financial reports normally refer to the former category, this text will concentrate on it to the exclusion of the other. The term 'limited liability' can be defined as limiting the liability of the owners of a company for its debts to an amount not exceeding the capital they have contracted to subscribe to it. This capital is normally in the form of units of a certain monetary denomination called shares, and consequently the capital of companies is described as 'share capital'.

Company Share Capital

There are several types of share which a company can have, and to which its owners (termed 'shareholders') can subscribe. Each type has certain rights attached to it – that is, rights relating to voting, dividends and capital repayments. Preferred shareholders hold *preference share* units and are usually entitled to dividends as a fixed percentage of capital before dividends to other classes of share are determined; repayments of capital prior to repayment of other classes of share capital; but no right to vote on company matters. However, if a company's memorandum and articles of association do not provide for prior repayment of capital, all shareholders, whether or not their shares are preferential, are entitled, *pari passu,* to a return of the surplus assets on a liquidation. Similarly, a company's memorandum and articles may not restrict voting rights, in which case preference shareholders are not so prohibited.

Ordinary shareholders hold *ordinary share* units which may or may not have voting rights attached, and which have no right to any prescribed level of dividends. Their dividends depend entirely on profitability and the availability of cash, and are determined after any prior rights of preference shareholders have been satisfied.

In certain circumstances, a company may also have *deferred shares,* which usually have similar rights to ordinary shares but which can only be satisfied after preferred and ordinary rights have been satisfied. Again, in certain circumstances, preference shareholders may have cumulative rights to dividends; that is, if preference dividends cannot be paid in any period because of financial constraints, the right to receive them can be carried forward indefinitely until they can be satisfied. All shareholders normally have the additional right to receive, on an annual basis, financial reports from their companies which describe their recent financial progress and position.

Companies can be financed in ways other than by subscription to share capital. Medium-term finance can be obtained from loans made to a company in the form of debenture stock. These loans are often governed by the provisions of a trust deed stipulating *inter alia* the appointment of trustees to administer the loan; a fixed rate of interest to be paid before any dividend distributions are made; a similar right regarding capital repayments; and (not in every case) security of repayment by a legal charge on all or certain of the assets of the company. Voting rights are not normally given to such loans. Short-term finance is given to companies in the normal course of business through bank loans and overdrafts and credit facilities from their suppliers of goods and services.

Public and Private Companies

Companies in the United Kingdom can be divided into two further categories: public and private companies. Such a distinction mainly concerns the transferability of a company's shares, and the number of its shareholders. All companies must have more than two shareholders, but public companies must have more than seven. On the other hand, ownership of a private company is limited to no more than fifty shareholders (excluding past and present employee members). In addition, private companies must have restrictions on the transferring of shares from one person to another (not the case with public companies) and have no right to make public issues of shares (which is the case with public companies). A public company which has transferability of shares, and makes public issues of shares, can seek a quotation on a recognized stock exchange, thereby increasing the marketability of its shares by having quoted purchase and selling prices, and being transferable through registered stockbrokers.

Holding and Subsidiary Companies

The classification of companies can be extended in one further direction which relates to the financial and managerial relationships which can exist between companies. The shareholders of a company in most circumstances appoint a board of directors to manage financial and business affairs on their behalf. One of the courses of action open to a board so appointed is to develop and expand the company by acquiring or controlling other companies. This can be done by purchasing more than one half of the share capital of another company, or by becoming a shareholder in it and controlling the composition of its board of directors. In other words, companies can be acquired or controlled without having to purchase their individual assets and liabilities. The controlling company is called the 'holding' company, and the controlled one is called the 'subsidiary' company. A 'group' is the term commonly given to the aggregate entity, the holding company and its subsidiary.

The holding-subsidiary company relationship can become extremely involved with subsidiary companies acquiring other companies in a chain of suitable share purchases. In many instances, a holding company may control a so-called sub-subsidiary company without owning more than one half of its share capital. For example, if Company A owns 80 per cent of Company B's capital; and Company B owns 60 per cent of Company C's capital; then Company A effectively owns 80 per cent x 60 per cent or 48 per cent of company C − apparently a non-controlling interest. But, because A controls B, and B controls C, A is deemed to control C, despite the less than one half holding.

Regulating Company Behaviour

In most developed countries, the activities of limited liability companies are strictly controlled by statutory or governmental regulations. There may also be a number of institutionalized regulations. In the United Kingdom, all private and public companies are regulated at present by the provisions of the Companies Acts 1948 and 1967; quoted companies are also regulated by the provisions of the Stock Exchange; and, in certain circumstances, companies come under the jurisdiction of the City Panel on Takeovers and Mergers. (The detail of these provisions will be discussed at various stages in this book.)

UK companies are also required to adhere to certain internal regulations governing their conduct. These are legally required of each company, and take the form of its Memorandum and Articles of Association. The Memorandum is mainly concerned with the name, registered office, limited liability and trading objectives of the company. The Articles contain more detailed regulations relating to rights of shareholders, transferability of shares, powers and duties of directors, financial statements, dividends and general meetings.

The Need for Financial Information

The fundamental nature of the limited liability company, particularly the separation of management from ownership and its assumed indefinite life, creates the requirement that its shareholders should obtain some measure of protection from possible unscrupulous managers who may be tempted to exploit the gap which exists between the two groups; to their advantage, but to the disadvantage of the shareholders. This problem has been recognized for many years in most countries where limited liability companies exist, and the solution prescribed has generally been the regular provision of periodic financial information for shareholders. In the United Kingdom, this is provided for by the regulations contained in the Companies Acts 1948 and 1967, which state that shareholders should be given annual financial statements relating to company profitability and financial position. In addition, if the companies concerned are regulated by the Stock Exchange, their shareholders will receive interim summary financial statements of profitability and financial position during the period between receipt of the annual statements. The City Code on Takeovers and Mergers also requires companies (mainly quoted public companies) to provide shareholders with sufficient financial information with which to assess and decide upon the financial and other arrangements connected with a proposed takeover or merger with which their companies are involved.

Thus, shareholders and, additionally, debenture holders, are provided with regular financial information intended to increase their knowledge of their company's business and financial affairs. Because annual financial statements are legally required to be filed with the Registrar of Companies, such information effectively becomes public information and allows other interested persons and institutions to gain access to data about a company's financial progress and position.

Annual Financial Reports

At least once every year, UK companies are legally required to present to their shareholders information of their annual financial results. This normally takes the form of a comprehensive report which can be divided conveniently into several distinct sections: (a) the chairman's report or operational review, (b) the directors' report, (c) the financial statements, and (d) statistical and other data.

The chairman's report

The chairman's report is included in the financial reports of most companies, although, in the United Kingdom, it is not legally required to be presented. Its contents are mainly non-quantitative and normally include a review of the year's operations and financial results; particular comments on important projects or parts of the company; news of new developments; and comments on the progress of the company within the economic, social and political environments prevailing. The importance of the chairman's report has been emphasized by Slater:

> 'We always read the Chairman's Statement over several years in considerable depth. It is often a good way of judging the calibre of management as the hopes expressed in earlier years quite often do not come to fruition and one can get a good idea from the Chairman's Statement as to how the individual sections of the business are performing or have performed over a period. The Chairman's remarks on the company's future profits and prospects are studied very closely as these are sometimes the only guide to current trading and to the future.'[2]

The contents of the chairman's report are not subject to any verification or attestation by the company's independent auditor. The quantity and quality of the information contained in it will therefore very much depend on the attitude and expertise of the chairman concerned. Some chairmen are less communicative than others, the main fear being the disclosure of information which may be beneficial to a competitor or to a potential acquirer of the company concerned.

The directors' report

The directors' report is a legally required statement in the United Kingdom, where the board of directors of companies must give annual information to their shareholders on such matters as the principal activities of the company concerned; significant changes in its assets; details of share and loan issues, material interests of directors in company contracts; company turnover from trading; political and charitable donations; dividend recommendations; details of company exports; names of directors; numbers of company employees; and directors' holdings in share and loan capital. Thus, in this statement, shareholders are not only given significant financial information, they are also kept reasonably well informed about their directors' affairs in relation to the company. As with the chairman's report, there is no legal obligation to have this information attested by the company auditor, although, in practice, auditors do verify the accounting figures contained in the report without specifically reporting on them to the shareholders.

The financial statements

The financial statements which company directors are legally required to present to their shareholders are, in general terms, the profit and loss account (hereafter termed the income statement) and the balance sheet. For a single reporting company, the income statement and balance sheet are regarded as sufficient, but for a company which owns or controls other companies, the situation is somewhat more complex. A holding company is required to produce an income statement and balance sheet relating to its own financial affairs and trading activity, but it must also present an income statement and balance sheet reflecting the aggregate affairs and activity of the group of companies as a whole. These latter financial statements are usually described in the United Kingdom as the consolidated income statement and the consolidated balance sheet. In practice, owing to the accounting techniques of consolidation, it is possible to present the income statement information of a holding company and its group in one statement.

Thus the normal practice with a group of companies is to present a consolidated income statement (which incorporates that of the holding company), a holding company balance sheet and a consolidated balance sheet. The information contained in these essential statements is legally required to be 'truthfully' and 'fairly' reported, and must be verified and attested by an independent professional accountant (or firm of accountants) appointed as company auditor. The auditor's report should be attached to the reported financial statements. (The precise nature and content of these financial statements, together with the audit report, will be discussed separately later on pages 8-20.)

The last category of data in the typical company financial report concerns a hodge-podge of miscellaneous items which companies report voluntarily. Practice varies considerably from company to company, but mainly concerns descriptions of company activities and trends of financial results over a number of years. In addition, many companies now publish a further financial statement in this category. This is the funds statement (variously described as the sources and uses of funds statement, or the source and application of funds statement) which supports the income statement and balance sheet, and describes the periodic changes in the information contained in the latter statement.

Financial Reporting Concepts

The above brief description of company financial reports, which will be elaborated on later in this chapter, reveals a major source of financial information which is available to company shareholders at the present time. As Chapter 2 will reveal, it is a system which has been subject to a great deal of change over the years, despite being based on several concepts and conventions which have remained virtually unaltered during the same period.

First, financial reports are essentially historical documents, describing the financial results of past company activity. Because of inevitable delays in gathering together the necessary accounting data, the information contained in a financial report is often much out of date when compared with the present situation of the company concerned.

Secondly, financial reports have always been, and still are, intended primarily for existing company shareholders. They must also be received by debenture holders irrespective of the provisions of their trust deed, but so far as other interested third parties are concerned, the statements are not legally intended for them. Despite this constraint, these latter persons can make use of them, particularly since they constitute the primary information source about companies and are available to the public through the Registrar of Companies.

Thirdly, because of the fundamental nature of accountants and accounting, coupled with experiences throughout the history of company financial reporting, the so-called conservatism convention is an essential foundation to existing reporting practices. That is, when measuring and communicating accounting data, accountants normally adopt a reasonable caution, particularly when there is an obvious amount of uncertainty and subjectivity involved in determining the figures concerned. This particular accounting approach has been adopted in practice for many years, and has resulted in the application of two further principles of accounting: (a) the historic cost valuation basis, whereby the accounting information contained in the reported financial statements is measured, in most instances, on the basis of the actual cost of the transactions concerned; and (b) the realization principle where, because of the historic cost basis, no cognisance is usually taken of profits or gains earned by the company until such time as they have been realized either in cash or near-cash terms. In other words, increases in the value of the resources of the company are not normally accounted for until such time as these resources are realized. Somewhat in contradiction to this, however, value decreases tend to be accounted and reported before the point of realization, presumably because of the conservatism convention.

And finally, wherever possible, accountants have attempted to measure the accounting information reported by companies as objectively as possible. Financial reports, as previously mentioned, are often the only formal financial communication between ownership and management, and therefore their credibility is especially important to their users. By ensuring that the information is based, as much as possible, on objective and verifiable evidence, the accountant attempts to maximize its credibility. In most developed countries, this concept of information credibility is supported in practice by the audit function — that is, the employment by the company of an independent and usually professionally qualified accountant (or firm of accountants) to examine and report on the quality of the reported information.

The Concept of Income

The term 'income' is used throughout this text and is synonymous with the alternative terms of 'profit' and 'earnings' so often used in accounting practice. It is felt that it is the one term likely to be accepted by all readers, for the term 'profit' has a particular accounting meaning which is materially different from the meaning given to it by, say, economists. 'Income' is an all-embracing term, capable of including all elements of gain or value increases.

At the present time, as for many years, the corporate financial reporting function has been centred around the concept of income. For example, the importance of income within the business context is evidenced by its existence as a major business management objective: the maximization of profitability. Although this objective may not now have the same degree of support as it once had, owing to other economic, political and social matters achieving an increased importance to companies and their managers,[3] it is clear that it is still regarded by investors and other interested parties as an essential indicator of enterprise success or failure.[4] It is a useful yardstick of how well or badly company management has performed on behalf of its ownership, and it can therefore be used as a major means of evaluating the soundness or otherwise of an investment in it.

In traditional accounting terms, income is a periodic measure of the difference between an aggregate of the revenues received from the 'sale' of goods or services by a company and a corresponding aggregate of the various costs incurred by it in order to make these sales. In this sense, the net figure, which is reported in the income statement, is a distillation of many significant events and factors which have taken place during a designated period. The accountant will therefore usually define income as a financial gain arising from business activity and transactions. As such, and ignoring new contributions of capital or equivalent withdrawals, the effect of income is to increase the economic resources of a company (assuming, of course, a stable price level). It can thus be identified, subject to the previously mentioned qualification, as equivalent to the periodic increase in the net wealth of the company concerned.[5] However, much depends on how wealth is defined for reporting purposes, and particularly on how it is valued. Suffice to say at the present stage of the discussion that the value placed upon company resources, and thus on capital, determines the level of reported income, and that differing values will give differing income figures.

The Concepts of Capital and Value

Having stated that accounting income is a residual and temporal measure, indicative of company operational success or failure, which in some way is related to capital and capital value, it is important to state what is meant by capital and value.

During its lifetime, a company will spend money to acquire various goods and services essential to its business activity and, indeed, to its ultimate survival. Thus, it buys stocks of goods, pays for wages and overheads, purchases plant and machinery and so on. It finances these acquisitions with monies received from shareholders and lenders, by credit facilities afforded to it by suppliers, and by earning income from trading which can be 'ploughed back' into the business. Much of the expenditure (for example, on goods, wages and overheads) can be attributed immediately to the measurement of periodic income, being set off or matched against relevant revenues from sales. The remainder, however, is of more long-term benefit to the company, representing resources which it requires to trade or manufacture (for example, buildings, plant or motor vehicles). The aggregate value of these resources, minus any loans and other medium and short-term financing, is equivalent to the measure of shareholders' capital in the company (that is, original subscribed capital plus income retained in the business). This is often described as shareholders' equity, and appears as such in the reported balance sheet.

The importance of value in the measurement of capital can now be seen more clearly. First, the distinction between expenditure of a long-term nature and that which can be matched immediately against sales revenues is vital to the determination of shareholders' capital and periodic income. Secondly, the value placed upon the resources designated as having long-term use to a company will determine the value of its shareholders' capital. Consequently, as measured income is a product of the periodic change in the value of such capital, then it, too, depends greatly on the values placed upon the underlying resources. It is therefore with these problems of resource valuation, capital valuation and income measurement that the corporate financial accounting and reporting function has to cope.

The Balance Sheet

The traditional company balance sheet is a statement of the resources of a company mainly valued on the basis of their original transacted cost, compared with the means by which they have been financed by its shareholders, lenders, suppliers and income retentions. It is therefore a report on its financial position at one particular point in time — a still photograph of company financial affairs, expressed in accounting terms. Thus, at the end of each financial reporting period, a company will own certain resources capable of being measured in accounting terms; owe certain sums of money given to it by way of loan or credit; and have its shareholders' interests represented by subscribed capital and retained income. The measured resources represent the various ways in which the funds made available to a company have been employed by it, and the amounts owed, together with shareholders' equity, represent the sources of funds which have been so employed. By definition, therefore, the employment and sources of funds must equate, and this is represented by the indentity $A = L + E \ldots (1)$; where A = the assets or resources of the company which have been accounted for; L = the liabilities or amounts owed by the company; and E = shareholders' equity in the company.

This then is the basic financial relationship which is reflected in every reported balance sheet.

The nature of assets

'Assets represent expected future economic benefits, rights to which have been acquired by the enterprise as the result of some current or past transactions.'[6]

In other words, transactions which give rise to the right to expect some future economic benefit from 'properties' of one sort or another can be classified as assets of the company. If there is no likelihood of future benefits to be derived from them, they cannot be classified as assets and any relevant expenditure thereon should be matched against sales revenues when determining periodic income.

Assets can be tangible (for example, plant, machinery, stocks of goods and cash) or intangible (for example, goodwill represented by such factors as the skills of managers and workers, or a reputation for high-quality products; as well as patent rights, trademarks and copyrights). However, for accounting purposes each must have been part of a past business transaction which can be accounted for. In other words, although a company may benefit from the use of public roads, it cannot regard them as reportable assets because they have not been purchased directly by it and there is no exclusive right to the economic benefits involved. Similarly, a company may have considerable goodwill which it has built up over the years, but unless it has formally purchased it from a third party, it would not normally be accounted for.

Fixed and current assets

Assets are usually divided into two main categories for reporting purposes: fixed assets and current assets. Fixed assets are those held for use rather than for resale: assets which the company holds in order to receive economic benefits from their use in manufacture or trade. These would include land, buildings, plant, machinery, motor vehicles and office equipment. They are normally accounted for in terms of their original historic cost, although account is taken of the gradual expiry of their service potential from use and obsolescence. This takes the form of reductions in the original costs, which are then charged against sales revenues when measuring periodic income. This expense, which represents the partial expiry of the usefulness of fixed assets, is termed depreciation. The accounting treatment involved is simply an allocation and charge to income of the original cost of the fixed assets concerned over their useful life. Fixed assets are therefore normally described in the balance sheet at their original cost minus any depreciation written off against sales revenues. Occasionally, companies find it necessary to revalue certain fixed assets, such as land and buildings, in which case they will be reported in the balance sheet at the revalued figure.

Current assets are those assets held by the company for resale, and are therefore either in the form of cash or resources which can reasonably be expected to be converted into cash in the near future. Included in this category would be stocks of goods (including any work in progress), debtors (amounts owed by credit customers), short-term investments of cash surplus to requirements, and bank balances. In the case of stocks, the normal valuation basis is original cost, although damaged or obsolete stock is often included at its realizable value. Debtors are usually recorded at their expected realizable value minus any allowances for bad or doubtful debts, but investments may well be expressed in original cost terms.

In certain instances, companies find it difficult to classify particular assets as either fixed or current. A frequent example is the intangible asset, goodwill, which, if it has been acquired from a third party, can be treated as a fixed asset, but equally can be disclosed in the balance sheet under a separate category which is neither fixed nor current.

Thus, taking the left-hand side of identity (1) above, it can now be expanded as follows: $A = F + C + O \ldots (2)$; where F = fixed assets; C = current assets; and O = assets not classified as fixed or current.

Liabilities

'Liabilities are obligations to convey assets or perform services, obligations resulting from past or current transactions and requiring settlement in the future.'[7]

In other words, they are accounting measurements intended to represent amounts owing to persons and bodies outwith a company, other than its shareholders. They can be divided into two main categories: current liabilities (representing amounts due for repayment in the relative short-term; for example, credit suppliers (termed creditors), bank overdrafts, dividends proposed, and taxation liabilities); and medium to long-term liabilities (representing amounts which will require to be repaid over a relatively long period of time; for example, mortgages and debentures). Liabilities such as these are accounted for in terms of the amounts arising from the original transactions concerned.

Thus, expanding the right-hand side of identify (1) above: $L = S + M \ldots (3)$; where S = short-term or current liabilities; and M = medium and long-term liabilities.

Shareholders' equity

'Owners' equity is represented by the amount of the residual interest in the assets of an enterprise.'[8]

In other words, when deducting the liabilities of a company from its aggregate assets, the net figure is representative of the shareholders' interest in it. This interest is composed of the share capital attributable to the various classes of shareholders, together with income which has been retained rather than distributed by way of dividend to the shareholders. Share capital is normally measured on the basis of monies received from shareholders. It may, however, have been augmented by the translation of income retained in the company into shares; in other words, by bonus shares issued to shareholders without further payment on their part. It may also include share issues made in exchange for the acquisition of, or merger with, other companies; in other words, when companies or business assets are acquired or merged, the transaction may be satisfied by the issue of shares in the acquiring company, rather than by payment by cash. Share capital figures disclosed in the balance sheet may not represent the full amount due to be subscribed by shareholders. Shares are often issued to shareholders as partly paid up, the remaining monies due being receivable at a later date.

Retained income which forms part of shareholders' equity consists mainly of undistributed income which has been realized as part of operational and trading activity. It may also include, however, other realized gains from the sale of assets such as land and buildings or investments, or unrealized gains resulting from the revaluation of certain assets of a similar nature.

Thus, again expanding the right-hand side of identity (1): $E = I + R$ ... (4); where I = issued share capital; and R = aggregate retained income.

Identity (4) can be further expanded if it is recognized that the figure for retained income is, in fact, composed of two elements: retained income of the current period to which the balance sheet refers, and aggregate retained income of previous periods. Thus, $E = I + R' + R''$ ... (5); where R' = retained income of the current period; and R'' = retained income of the previous periods.

The expanded identity

Taking the opening identity (1) of $A = L + E$, this can now be re-expressed, in light of the above comments, as $F + C = S + M + I + R' + R''$ ... (6).

This, then, is a simplified model of the company balance sheet, and it is usually found that the accounting data contained in such a financial statement fall into these various categories. It need not, of course, be presented in a form equivalent to identity (6), as this can be rearranged without interfering with the basic relationship. For example, it could be $F + (C - S) = M + I + R' + R''$ ... (7). (In this case, short-term liabilities are set against current assets to produce a net current assets aggregate which can be used as a measure of a company's liquidity position – the net figure is often termed working capital). Or it could be $F + (C - S) - M = I + R' + R''$ ... (8). (In this case, the emphasis is entirely on the interests of the shareholders in the company – that is, reflecting the net assets which support the interests of ownership.)

Illustration 1 represents the balance sheet of a single company. It is presented in summary form, and is not intended to comply with the legal requirements for disclosure which will be discussed later.

Illustration 1. *Outline balance sheet.*

AB Ltd
As at 31 July 19XX

	£	£		£	£	£
Shareholders' Equity			*Fixed Assets*	Cost	Aggregate	
Share capital issued		30,000			depreciation	
Retained income		14,000				
		44,000	Buildings	10,000	4,000	6,000
Long-term Liability			Plant	4,000	2,000	2,000
Debenture loan		10,000		14,000	6,000	8,000
Current Liabilities			*Investment*			
			In subsidiary			
Creditors	3,000		company			14,000
Taxation	6,000		*Current Assets*			
Dividends	3,000	12,000	Stock		12,000	
			Debtors		18,000	
			Bank		14,000	44,000
		66,000				66,000

The only items in Illustration 1 which require further comment are (a) the presentation of fixed assets, disclosed at their original cost minus any depreciation which has been charged against sales revenue in determining periodic income (the net figures represent the unallocated costs of the fixed assets which are intended as a measure of their anticipated future service potential to the company); and (b) the investment in a subsidiary company (this figure represents the financial cost of acquiring shares in another company so as to control it).

The group balance sheet

The reporting treatment applicable to a group of companies is illustrated in Illustration 2. A group balance sheet is presented by taking the balance sheet of the holding company (the figures are as in Illustration 1) and substituting the net assets of the subsidiary at the same reporting date for the figure for 'investment in subsidiary company'. The result is to inflate each of the main balance sheet categories by the appropriate subsidiary company figures. In addition, if the cost of acquiring the subsidiary includes a figure representing its purchased goodwill, then this will also be incorporated in the group balance sheet.

Illustration 2. *Outline group balance sheet.*

AB Ltd and subsidiary company
As at 31 July 19XX

	£	£		Cost	Aggregate depreciation	£
Shareholders' Equity			*Fixed Assets*			
Share capital issued		30,000				
Retained income		22,000				
		52,000	Buildings	12,000	4,000	8,000
Long-term Liability			Plant	7,000	2,500	4,500
Debenture loan		10,000		19,000	6,500	12,500
Current Liabilities			*Goodwill*			1,000
Creditors	6,000		*Current Assets*			
Taxation	6,500		Stock		18,000	
Dividends	3,000	15,500	Debtors		26,000	
			Bank		20,000	64,000
		77,500				77,500

It is not the intention of this book to explain in detail the accounting practices necessary to the production of a consolidated or group balance sheet. However, a number of comments seem pertinent in light of the above illustration.

(a)   The figures for fixed assets, current assets, long-term liability and current liabilities are inclusive of data relevant to the subsidiary company.

(b)   The goodwill figure is that part of the cost of the holding company's investment in its subsidiary representing intangible resources taken over by it. (In certain instances, it can also represent under-valuations of tangible assets taken over, these value changes being unrecorded in the records of the subsidiary company.)

(c)   Share capital is the share capital of the holding company. Owing to the inclusion of the subsidiary company's net assets in the group balance sheet, it is not necessary to include its share capital as well.

(d) The retained income figure includes the aggregate retained income of the subsidiary company belonging to the holding company since the date of its acquisition of the subsidiary.

(e) The above illustrations have assumed that the subsidiary is 100 per cent controlled. If control was less than 100 per cent, because not all of the share capital had been acquired, then the group balance sheet would reflect this by disclosing that part of the subsidiary company's share capital and retained income figure not belonging to the holding company. This would be shown as a group 'liability', presented between 'Shareholders' Interests' and 'Long-term Liabilities', and usually described as 'Minority Interest in Subsidiary Company'. ·

Summary

Summarizing therefore on the company balance sheet, it is clear that it is a statement of financial position, expressed at one particular point of time, and measured in mainly historic cost terms. It is in no way a statement of the present value or market value of a company (or group of companies) as a whole, nor can it be said to be indicative of the market value of shares in the company. It is a record of past transactions giving rise to resources of use to the company in the future, coupled with a statement of the means by which these transactions have been financed.

The Income Statement

In one sense, despite its current importance to investors and other interested parties, the income statement is simply a more detailed report on one particular aspect of the balance sheet — that is, the retained income figure. It is a description and an analysis of the periodic movement in the retained income figure from one balance sheet date to the next. In other words, it explains the composition of item R' in identity (8) above (page 11).

The traditional accounting income identity.

Traditional accounting income can be identified as $R' = s - c - t - d$; where s = sales revenues recognized and accounted for; c = various costs relevant to these sales which have been matched with them; t = taxation on the surplus arising from the matching of s and c; and d = dividends paid and proposed to be paid to shareholders.

Sales revenues (s) represent monies which have been received, or are about to be received, during the specified period from customers in return for goods and/or services from the company. In certain instances, sales may be recognized before the goods and services are complete or delivered to customers, as in the case of long-term contracts in the engineering industries. However, the normal practice is to recognize sales revenues only when there has been a realization or near-realization in cash terms.

Matched costs (c) are those items of expenditure which can be realistically related to the sales revenues recognized. They include the cost of goods and/or services sold (that is, in terms of raw materials, wages, overheads), as well as interest payments on loans, directors' remuneration, audit fees and so on. They also include depreciation written off fixed assets during the period.

The resultant surplus (s-c) represents income from trading operations, and is used as the basis for computing the company's corporation tax liability. Once the latter figure is computed by applying existing tax laws and rules to the basic operating surplus figure, it is incorporated in the income statement as a deduction from trading income. The 'income after tax' figure is then used as a basis for determining the level of dividends to be distributed to shareholders. The preference dividend (if any) is a fixed percentage of the appropriate share capital, whereas the ordinary or deferred dividends are percentages of capital which depend on the availability of measured income and cash resources. The computed dividends are deducted from the 'income after tax' figure, leaving a net figure of retained income for the period.

The income statement can therefore be regarded as a report of the ways in which the measured operational surplus for the period was appropriated, partly to the government by way of tax; partly to the shareholders by way of dividend; the remainder being retained in the company to allow for the necessary maintenance and expansion of its business activity. Illustration 3 outlines the main components of such a statement (assuming no subsidiary companies in the first instance).

Illustration 3. *Outline income statement.*

AB Ltd
Year to 31 July 19XX

	£	£
Sales revenues		129,000
Less: cost of sales		
raw materials	65,000	
wages	33,000	
overheads	11,000	
loan interest	1,000	
depreciation	2,000	112,000
Trading income before tax		17,000
Less: taxation		6,000
Income after tax		11,000
Less: dividends		3,000
Income retained for the period		8,000
Add: income retained in previous periods		6,000
Aggregate income retained		14,000

Income statement characteristics

The following comments support the outline statement in Illustration 3:

(a)   The income statement is a dynamic report in the sense that it discloses information of business activity over time. The balance sheet, on the other hand, is a static report reflecting a position at one point of time — that is, the ending date for the income statement's reporting period.

(b)   The presentation in the illustration of income information is usually in a vertical format, as in the illustration, although it is entirely permissible to present it in a two-sided format (as in the balance sheet illustrations). The same might equally apply to the balance sheet, the style adopted depending entirely on the individual preferences of the accountants involved in the presentation.

(c) The extent of disclosure of income-orientated information is normally in practice fairly restricted. The usual approach is to commence the income statement with the figure for trading income before tax, this being supported by notes on certain items — such as depreciation — which have been recognized in measuring it.

The group income statement

Illustration 4 relaxes the assumption of no subsidiary companies, and shows the income statement for a group of companies in outline. As in Illustration 3, existing legal disclosure requirements have been ignored meantime.

Illustration 4. *Outline group income statement.*

AB Ltd and subsidiary company
Year to 31 July 19XX

	£	£
Sales revenues		160,000
Less: cost of sales		
raw materials	81,000	
wages	36,500	
overheads	14,000	
loan interest	1,000	
depreciation	2,500	135,000
Trading income before tax		25,000
Less: taxation		6,500
Income after tax attributable to the holding company		18,500
Less: dividends		3,000
Income retained for the period		15,500
Add: income retained in previous periods		6,500
Aggregate income retained of which:		22,000
Retained in the holding company		14,000
Retained in the subsidiary company		8,000
		22,000

The consolidation procedures involved in producing a group income statement are similar in principle to those involved in producing the equivalent balance sheet;' namely, the aggregation of similar data and the specific highlighting of group data which, in fact, 'belongs' to the holding company. In this respect, two specific comments should be made:

(a) The normal practice in the United Kingdom is to combine the data from the holding company's income statement with that from subsidiary company statements in such a way that there is no need to produce a separate holding company statement; thus, the disclosure of the headings 'income attributable to the holding company' and 'income retained in the holding company'.

(b) Following on from (a), the requirement to disclose the holding company's periodic and retained income involves the recognition of income attributable to minority interests (if any). The illustration has assumed that no minority interests exist, but if they had, then there would have been a deduction from the 'income after tax' figure representing the proportion of it belonging to minority interests.

The Funds Statement

In addition to the traditional income statement and balance sheet, companies are increasingly presenting a further statement in the annual financial report; that is, the funds statement.[9] Usually described in the United Kingdom as the source and application of funds statement,[10] it reveals the periodic inflow and outflow of funds of a company. As such, it is composed of the periodic movements in balance sheet items — that is, changes in that statement from one reporting date to the next. It can therefore be described in notation form, using the balance sheet identity previously described in this chapter, i.e. $\Delta F + \Delta C = \Delta S + \Delta M + \Delta I + \Delta R$; where Δ = the measured movement in each item over a defined period n to $n + 1$.

The construction of the funds statement thus involves identifying and measuring these periodic movements and arranging them in a sensible report form. So far as measurement is concerned, it can be seen that ΔR is, to a large extent, already explained in terms of the income figures disclosed in the income statement. The other periodic movements, however, are not disclosed in the income statement and are not revealed directly in the balance sheet, which, by definition, is static rather than dynamic. The balance sheet is therefore intended to reflect the end result of these movements, and the income statement describes only one particular change. The funds statement is intended to fill this informational gap, and its main objective can be described as:

'To summarise the financing and investing activities of the entity, including the extent to which the enterprise has generated funds from operations during the period, and to complete the disclosure of changes in financial position during the period.'[11]

It therefore supplies answers to questions which investors and other interested parties may ask of the company and which are related to the new sources of finance it has obtained during the period and the various ways in which these additional funds have been employed.

Presentation of funds data can take several forms, there being in practice no generally accepted format. For example, the various sources and uses of funds can be reconciled to the periodic movement in cash balances or to the periodic movement in working capital (current assets minus current liabilities). Alternatively, the statement can simply equate total sources with total uses. In addition, practice varies as to the amount of funds data included in the statement — some companies give a great deal of information relating to all the financial events they have been concerned with (including those of a non-cash nature, such as the acquisition of a subsidiary company for shares or loan stock); whereas others give relatively little but concentrate on, say, cash transactions. The problems and issues associated with this will be discussed later in the book, but meanwhile, Illustration 5 is intended to describe an outline funds statement.

Illustration 5. *Outline funds statement*

AB Ltd
Year to 31 July 19XX
Source of funds

	£	£
Sources generated within the company:		
Income after tax		11,000
Depreciation		2,000
		13,000
Proceeds of disposal of fixed assets		1,000
Reduction in levels of:		
Stock	5,000	
Debtors	2,000	7,000
		21,000
Sources generated outside the company:		
Issue of ordinary shares	10,000	
Debenture loan	5,000	15,000
		36,000
Use of funds		
Maintenance and expansion of business operations:		
Purchase of fixed assets		3,000
Acquisition of subsidiary company		8,000
		11,000
Repayment of financial obligations:		
Decrease in level of creditors	6,000	
Short-term loan	10,000	16,000
Dividend to shareholders		3,000
		30,000
Increase in bank balance		6,000

It can be seen from the presentation in the illustration that a suitable reconstruction of the figures would produce a funds statement which emphasized the change in working capital; that is, by the aggregation and netting of stock, debtor, creditor and bank figures. Likewise, the example has disclosed funds movements for the holding company only. A group funds statement could be prepared by incorporating the appropriate subsidiary company figures in each of the categories instead of disclosing the acquisition cost only.

One further point should be mentioned, and this concerns the periodic change in fixed assets. It is composed of three elements: the cost of assets purchased, the sale proceeds of assets realized, and the depreciation written off the original cost during the period. Each such element requires to be treated differently: the purchase as a use of funds, the sale as a source of funds, and the depreciation write-off as a source of funds since it is equivalent to income retained in the company.

The Relationship between the Annual Financial Statements

The balance sheet, the income statement and the funds statement form the basis for informing shareholders and other interested parties regularly of the financial affairs of companies. As such, they have a significance which is recognized throughout the business world. They are not all subject to legislative provisions; the funds statement, for example, is not subject to such regulations in many countries. Thus the degree of emphasis placed on them can vary considerably.

Generally speaking, the income statement is usually given primary emphasis because it is an important indicator of company success or failure. The balance sheet and funds statement therefore appear to be regarded as 'back-up' statements, giving additional information for assessing the 'quality' of companies and their income. However, it must be remembered that the three statements are very much related to one another; the balance sheet reveals the 'end result' of company operations and activity over a defined period of time; the funds statement analyses how that 'end result' came about through the receipt and use of funds of various kinds; and the income statement analyses the source of funds derived from operational activity. It is therefore quite wrong to regard any one statement as more important than the other two. Each has its role to play in informing its user, and the latter person cannot possibly obtain an overall picture of a company's financial progress and position without referring to all three statements. They are complementary rather than competing or exclusive alternatives.

Other Sources of Reported Information

It should be made clear at this stage that the annual company financial report is not the only source of reported information about a company available to its shareholders and other interested parties. Besides their annual reports, stock exchange quoted companies in the United Kingdom are required, as a condition of their quotation, to deliver to their shareholders an interim report of profitability and financial position. This report usually covers the six-month period since the last annual report, and is given in summary form only. In addition, it is not subject to independent audit. The aim of these reports is to provide shareholders with up-to-date information about their companies so as to alleviate the disadvantage of the significant time lag between annual reports. It should be noted that the provision for this type of financial information does not usually extend beyond quoted companies in the United Kingdom, though the practice is much more extensive in the United States.

In addition to the aforementioned interim source of information — which is by definition historical in nature — company shareholders are provided occasionally with information of a predictive nature. This occurs when company management produces data relating either to an issue of new shares (UK company law requires that a prospectus be published if the shares are being offered to the public) or on an acquisition or merger with another company or companies (in the United Kingdom there are strict quasi-governmental or professional regulations covering such activities). The financial reports presented in these relatively infrequent situations usually contain historical summaries of profitability and financial position, but may also contain forecast data relating particularly to trading income. These predicted data are obviously far less objective than historic data, but are normally covered by a report on their quality by an independent accountant.

Other Sources of Information

It would be wrong to leave the reader with the impression that the only financial information available is that contained in the required annual, interim or *ad hoc* reports produced by companies. There are, in fact, several other sources to be mentioned, some of which make use in part of reported company information.

(a) There is the analysed information provided by organizations such as Moodies and Exchange Telegraph which is based on company financial reports. These analysed and summarized data are extremely comprehensive and give an in-depth summary of the past financial record of companies.

(b) Companies frequently give interviews to investment analysts, who then produce up-to-date reports which are either circulated to very large investor clients (normally, institutions such as unit trusts, pension funds, investment trusts and insurance companies) or to stockbrokers who, in turn, produce summary reports for their investing clients. This form of information system is usually intended to update the formal reported historic data in company financial statements.

(c) Information about company activity can be contained either in advertisements or public relations material. Because of its general nature, it is not always of immense use to investors and others, although it should be noted that the lack of such information may indicate that the company concerned wishes to maintain a low public profile because of financial or other difficulties.

(d) There is a great deal of economic and industrial information available to aid the user. This information, usually in aggregate statistical form, is inevitably historical in nature, and is contained in various industry and trade journals, including those of government departments. This type of information is useful in building up a picture of a particular industry's position and state of affairs. It therefore helps to provide an essential background to a similar type of assessment of an individual company.

The Audit Function

Much of the formally reported financial information from companies in the United Kingdom and similar countries is required to be examined and reported on by a suitably qualified independent accountant. This is the so-called audit function, and the independent accountant is described as the auditor. In practice, the auditor is normally not an individual but a firm of professionally qualified accountants. The aim of the audit (at least so far as concerns annual financial statements) can be summed up as follows:

'The company audit is concerned with the creation of rational belief and confidence in the accounting information contained in the company's annual profit and loss account and balance sheet. The audit is conducted on behalf of the shareholders in order that they may use the information in investment decisions without doubting its reliability or validity. Because the quality of the information is attested in this way, the audit should also be of benefit to other users of the financial statements.'[12]

Thus, the auditor attempts to lend credibility to the reported information by examining and verifying the way in which it has been produced and reported.

Hopefully, this process gives its potential users greater confidence in its quality, and will encourage them to use it without suspicion. The auditor's comments on the information are contained in a formal report which, in the United Kingdom, takes the following form:

'In our opinion, the financial statements set out on pages X to XX together give a true and fair view of the state of affairs of the company at 31 December 19XX and of its income for the year ended that date and comply with the Companies Acts 1948 and 1967.'

Three factors should be noted from the above brief description of the company audit: (a) the auditor is not a paid employee of the company (he is independent of it); (b) his report is an expression of opinion (this is inevitable owing to the many problems inherent in the production of financial statements); and (c) the auditor is not responsible for producing the information – only for examining and reporting on its quality (he may, however, in certain instances, be employed by the company to produce the information, but this is not part of the audit function; in the United Kingdom it is company management which is solely responsible for the production and quality of the information).

Concluding Remarks

This chapter has been concerned mainly with providing the reader with a necessary foundation knowledge of companies and their financial statements. It has ignored the detailed legal and other provisions regulating their conduct. These, however, will be discussed in Chapter 3. Meantime, in Chapter 2, the emphasis is on the development of corporate financial reporting, particularly within the UK context.

Suggested Discussion or Essay Topics

1. A major disadvantage of the limited liability company is its potential to separate ownership from management. Explain.
2. Distinguish between share and loan capital in a limited company.
3. What are the essential differences between public and private companies in Britain?
4. Compare and contrast holding companies, subsidiary companies and groups of companies. What implications do they have with regard to company financial reporting?
5. The concept of the limited liability company creates a need for financial information. Why?
6. The annual financial report of a company is the single most important source of information about a company. Discuss the validity of this statement.
7. Distinguish between the directors' report and the chairman's report.
8. Explain the apparent dichotomy between the historical nature of the company annual financial report and the concern for the future of the company which is said to be held by shareholders and other interested persons.
9. The concept of income is no more than a man-made conventional symbol or indicator of economic conduct. It is not based on any known natural laws. Discuss the significance of these statements, explaining, in general terms, the nature of the traditional accounting measures of income which are contained in company financial reports.
10. Income cannot exist without capital, and capital depends entirely on the process of valuation. Explain within the context of company financial reporting.
11. The balance sheet is a valuation statement. Comment.

12. Explain the importance of assets in financial reporting. Are all assets of the company capable of being measured and disclosed in its annual financial report?

13. What is meant by the term shareholders' equity?

14. Distinguish between fixed and current assets. What is the relationship between current assets and current liabilities.

15. What is the income statement intended to describe? In what way does it differ from the balance sheet? What is the fundamental relationship between these documents?

16. A knowledge of the future is essential to the proper measurement of past income and financial position. Comment.

17. Highlight the main differences between the financial statements of a single company and the financial statements of a group of companies. What is the most important reason for producing consolidated financial statements?

18. What purpose is served by the funds statement? How does it relate to the income statement and balance sheet?

19. The audit function is a fundamental prerequisite to the existence of a free capital market. Discuss this statement with particular reference to annual financial reports.

Notes and References

1 J. A. Lillie, *The Mercantile Law of Scotland,* Longmans Green, 1956, p. 316.

2. J. D. Slater, 'The Acquirer's View, in *What is Profit?',* The Institute of Chartered Accountants in England and Wales, 1970, p. 61.

3. T. W. McRae, 'The Behavioural Critique of Accounting', *Accounting and Business Research,* Spring 1971, pp. 86-7.

4. R. Ball and P. Brown, 'An Empirical Evaluation of Accounting Income Numbers', *Journal of Accounting Research,* Autumn 1968, p. 176.

5. K. MacNeal, *Truth in Accounting,* Scholars Book Co., 1970 reprint, p. 295.

6. R. T. Sprouse and M. Moonitz, 'A Tentative Set of Broad Accounting Principles for Business Enterprises', *Accounting Research Study 3,* American Institute of Certified Public Accountants, 1962, p. 8.

7. ibid.

8. ibid., p. 9.

9. For a more detailed description of the funds statement, see T. A. Lee, 'The Funds Statement', *Research Series 5,* The Institute of Chartered Accountants of Scotland, 1974, esp. pp. 4-19.

10. ibid., p. 43.

11. 'Reporting Changes in Financial Position', *Accounting Principles Board Opinion No. 19,* American Institute of Certified Public Accountants, 1971, *reproduced in Accountancy,* June 1971, pp. 69-72, at p. 70.

12. T. A. Lee, *Company Auditing: Concepts and Practices,* Gee & Co., revised edition, 1974, p. 18.

Selected Bibliography for Chapter 1

NOTE: This and the remaining bibliographies at the end of each chapter are intended to give the interested reader an opportunity to explore the relevant topics beyond the limits imposed by the writer. However, the selection of additional reading material to support such general introductions has not been easy, and it should be noted that the following references are only some from among a great many which could have been chosen.

Arthur Andersen & Co., *Objectives of Financial Statements for Business Enterprises,* Arthur Andersen & Co., 1972, pp. 1-4. The role of financial statements generally.

F. Bailey, *Current Practice in Company Accounts,* Accountancy Age Books, 1973, pp. 1-21. An introduction to the structure of annual financial statements.

H. W. Bevis, 'The Accounting Function in Economic Progress', *Journal of Accountancy,* August 1958, pp. 27-34. The role of accounting and accountants generally.

R. J. Briston, *The Stock Exchange and Investment Analysis,* Allen & Unwin, 1974, pp. 245-86. A general introduction to the sources of information available to the investor.

J. L. Carey, *Getting Acquainted with Accounting,* Houghton Mifflin, 1973. The nature of accounting (pp. 1-9); the financial reporting function (pp. 29-41); and the audit function (pp. 55-67).

V. Earl, 'Sources of Information', *Accountancy,* November 1973, pp. 92-6. Sources of information for the investor.

G. A. Lee, *Modern Financial Accounting,* Nelson, 1973, pp. 242-88. A detailed practical account of companies and their financial statements.

T. A. Lee, *Company Auditing: Concepts and Practices,* Gee & Co., 1974, revised edition, pp. 1-20. The need for financial information, the financial reporting function, and the audit function.

T. A. Lee, *Income and Value Measurement,* Nelson, 1974, pp. 5-15. An overall explanation of the nature of income, capital and value.

M. Moonitz, 'The Basic Postulates of Accounting', *Accounting Research Study 1,* American Institute of Certified Public Accountants, 1961, pp. 8-20. The environment of accounting.

A. M. C. Morison, 'The Role of the Reporting Accountant Today–1', *Accountant's Magazine,* September 1970, pp. 409-15. The nature of accounting and auditing.

G. Naylor, *Guide to Shareholders' Rights,* Allen & Unwin, 1969. Content indicated by the book's title.

R. H. Parker, *Understanding Company Financial Statements,* Penguin Books, 1972, pp. 9-35. The nature and structure of company financial statements.

2 The History and Development of Company Financial Reporting

The Pre-Limited Company Era

The formation of companies by joint subscription for shares has a history which is well over 350 years old. The need to provide large amounts of money to finance extensive trading and commercial operations created, for example, the East India Company (in 1600), the Hudson's Bay Company (in 1670) and the Bank of England (in 1694). These unlimited liability companies were formed either by special Act of Parliament or by Royal Charter, without managerial accountability to ownership by means of published financial statements. This created opportunities for fraud and embezzlement, and managers speculated and lost vast sums of money belonging to shareholders.

Thus, in 1719, the Bubble Act[1] was introduced, limiting any form of partnership to six members in the hope that this would reduce the incidence of financial mismanagement. The success of the Act in this respect is difficult to ascertain. Certainly, it did not provide for adequate measures of control which might have protected the interests of owners and creditors. In 1825 it was repealed and a maximum limit of twenty members was then placed on partnerships.

This notwithstanding, there were at the time a number of factors influencing governments to allow a more diffuse ownership in business enterprises, and these included the rapidly increasing industrialization of the United Kingdom; and, particularly, the development of railway systems in the first half of the nineteenth century. These changes were creating an ever-growing need for funds to finance the cost of the ventures concerned. They also created an immediate need to provide measures with which legally to protect the providers of the finance from unscrupulous management. In other words, as Littleton and Zimmerman[2] concluded, the problem was to encourage investment in private enterprise while, at the same time, adequately protecting the investors.

The Railway Example

An excellent way of highlighting the movement towards the provision of adequate legal protection for investors and other persons involved with companies is to examine the development of railway accounting.[3] The Railway Age in the United Kingdom occurred between 1830 and 1870, and for the first time, the world saw the emergence of multi-million-pound enterprises, with large numbers of lay shareholders. It was a period of some chaos, but from it came the basis for the present-day system of corporate financial reports.

The significance of railways in economic development came to fruition with the opening of the Liverpool and Manchester Railway in 1830. Following this, other railway lines were opened by companies incorporated by Acts of Parliament, particularly in the 1830s and 1840s. These Acts of Parliament (one for each railway company) gave the authority to build the line concerned and also to raise funds to meet the costs of construction. Interestingly, most of these private Acts required accounting records to be kept, but made no provision for published financial statements or audits (e.g. section 56, Stockton and Darlington Railway Act 1821).[4] In other words, not only were shareholders not provided with financial statements, they were even denied the right to examine whatever accounting records the companies did keep.

Gradually, however, the Acts took greater cognisance of investor needs, and the provision of formal accounting could be evidenced — for example, the Great Western Railway Act 1835 provided for the presentation of half-yearly financial statements at the appropriate general meetings of shareholders. The numerous enactments were eventually consolidated into the Companies Clauses Consolidation Act 1845, which *inter alia* provided that:

'On the books being so balanced an exact balance sheet shall be made up, which shall exhibit a true statement of the capital stock, credits, and property of every description belonging to the company, and the debts due by the company at the date of making such a balance sheet, and a distinct view of the profit or loss which shall have arisen on the transactions of the company in the course of the preceding half-year.'[5]

The balance sheet was examined by at least three directors, signed by the chairman or his deputy and produced at general meetings, but it was not circulated to every shareholder. There was also provision for an audit by a shareholder who was not to be an officer of the company. The balance sheet was then required to be sent to the government department dealing with railways.

This therefore was the situation existing by the mid 1840s. The public could subscribe to these companies and were, in turn, given some measure of protection by the receipt of an audited balance sheet. But, as Lee[6] has pointed out, these provisions did not apply to companies incorporated before 1845. On the face of it, however, the accounting and reporting provisions at least for post-1845 railway companies, appear to satisfy the conditions of stewardship laid down by Bird:

'Every steward is held accountable to the person or body which entrusted resources to him, whether the latter is a "superior steward" or the ultimate owner. Accountability places two obligations upon a steward; he must render an "account" of his dealings with the stewardship resources, and then he must submit to an examination (usually known as an "audit") of that account by or on behalf of the person or body to whom he is accountable.'[7]

Nevertheless, the stewardship-orientated railway accounting of the mid-1800s must be treated with a great deal of caution, for the following reasons: (a) shareholders were required to be provided with a balance sheet only, while there was no corresponding provision for an income statement; (b) the balance sheet provided was not widely circularized to shareholders, inspection having to take place at the company's registered office; (c) there were no generally accepted standards of accounting available to ensure that published information had been properly measured (the main controversy of the time concerned the treatment of expenditure — what should be matched against sales revenues when determining periodic income, and what expenses should be treated as assets for balance sheet purposes);[8]

and (d) auditing standards were extremely poor since few auditors were professionally qualified accountants.[9] In other words, there still remained a great deal of latitude in company accounting and reporting; much was left to the discretion of company directors, thereby increasing the chances of abuses of shareholder rights. Shareholders in railway companies were not therefore in a particularly strong position to protect their interests.

The Regulation of Railways Act 1868 attempted to remedy this, especially with regard to the accounting treatment of expenditure. Prior to this Act, the major abuse in railway accounting and reporting was undoubtedly the arbitrary treatment and classification of expenditure in such a way as to overstate income in bad financial years, and understate it in good years; this being done in either case to justify the payment of certain levels of dividends to shareholders. As Pollins has stated:

> 'However, there is some evidence to suggest that many railway directors as well as shareholders wished to have regular rather than fluctuating dividends, and the entries in the final accounts may very well have been influenced by the desire for a record of stable earnings and dividends. The fact that many items appearing (or not appearing) in the revenue accounts involved personal judgments, and that there was not yet a generally accepted body of accounting doctrine, made it easy for the preparation of the final accounts of even the most conscientiously conducted company to be influenced by considerations of management policy.'[10]

In other words, the poorly developed system of accounting and reporting for these early railway companies provided opportunities for their directors to manipulate reported income to justify payment of dividends, and at the worst extreme, dividend payments were made when income did not really exist to justify them (high dividends being paid to attract more investors to provide funds to alleviate financial difficulties caused by poor or fraudulent management). The 1868 Act provided for the publication and filing with the Board of Trade of detailed accounting statements. including a revenue account (an early form of income statement) and balance sheet in prescribed forms. In particular, the Act required the distinction between depreciable and non-depreciable assets, and created an accounting uniformity amongst railway companies which had not existed previously.[11]

Summarizing, therefore, on the example of railway development, it is clear that the need for investor protection through the provision of relevant accounting information was recognized reasonably early, but the relative lack of acceptable accounting standards, coupled with inadequate legal regulations, allowed unscrupulous managements to abuse the system at will if they so desired. Consequently, by the 1860s, there was an obvious need not only to tighten up the related law, but also to introduce a consistency and uniformity in railway accounting and reporting practices.[12]

The Legislative Development of Company Financial Reporting, 1844-1900

As already indicated, companies had existed in the United Kingdom for some time prior to the mid-1850s. The effects of the Industrial Revolution, with its emphasis on mechanization, manufacturing and the factory system, had given rise to the ever-increasing need of companies for finance from the public. This came in part from subscriptions from shareholders, but a great deal also came from bankers, lenders and creditors. As Lee[13] has pointed out, the failure of less formally structured partnerships was caused, in part, by a lack of sufficient finance, and business enterprises were therefore looking more widely to the public for the necessary funds.

Incorporation by registration (as distinct from formation by Act of Parliament) was introduced by the Joint Stock Companies Act of 1844. Edey and Panitpakdi[14] describe its relatively modern outlook, for example, the provisions for accounting records to be kept; the presentation of a balance sheet to each ordinary meeting of shareholders; the balance sheet normally to be sent to shareholders before such meetings; and the audit of the records and balance sheet. Unfortunately, however, the Companies Bill 1844 provision to present half-yearly income statements to shareholders was not incorporated in the 1844 Act.[15] No legal prescription existed regarding the form of the balance sheet, nor was there provision for incorporating companies with limited liability. The main aim of these provisions was therefore limited, as has been summarized by Edey and Panitpakdi:

'(a) To provide the creditors and shareholders of companies with statements of assets and liabilities that would give indications of the solvency of the companies, and (b) in the case of some classes of companies to prevent actual and potential shareholders or creditors from being misled as the result of dividend distributions made out of capital — which, in effect, means made at the expense, in some sense, of the future of the company without this fact being known.'[16]

The lack of adequate disclosure and auditing provisions in the 1844 Act (for example, auditors were not required to be professionally qualified accountants) was not remedied by the subsequent Joint Stock Companies Act 1855, which did, however, introduce the concept of limited liability. As a result, shareholders of limited companies could only lose what they had invested in them. This particular idea was brought into being because it served as a warning to creditors and lenders not to over-extend their credit and lending facilities to companies.[17] In other words, limited liability was no more than a governmental move to curb the abuses then taking place in the corporate sector.

The 1844 and 1855 Acts were eventually consolidated into the Joint Stock Companies Act 1856, with one important amendment: the compulsory reporting and audit provisions were omitted. Edey and Panitpakdi[18] postulated that this was because of a feeling that such arrangements should be made privately between shareholders and directors if they were felt to be necessary. Thus, at a stroke, the legislative development of company reporting was arrested. However, Table B of the 1856 Act, containing model articles of association, contained voluntary reporting and auditing provisions for companies if this was felt necessary. These included[19] *inter alia* the keeping of proper accounting records (details of these were given); the presentation to an annual general meeting of an annual income statement (details of the contents of which were stipulated); a similar provision for a balance sheet; and the communication of these reports to shareholders at least seven days before the relevant general meeting. In addition, there were audit provisions relating to the published financial statements — that is, they were to be examined and a report was to be given on the balance sheet in particular:

'The auditors shall make a Report to the Shareholders upon the Balance Sheet and Accounts, and in every such Report they shall state whether, in their opinion, the Balance Sheet is a full and fair Balance Sheet, containing the particulars required by these Regulations, and properly drawn up so as to exhibit a true and correct view of the State of the Company's Affairs. . . .'[20]

Table B also contained a standard form of balance sheet for the guidance of company directors and accountants. No similar provision existed for the income statement. This, then, was the corporate financial reporting situation that was to remain until 1900 for the majority of companies (banks and insurance companies had minimum accounting provisions reintroduced long before 1900): that is, a policy of no state interference in such matters through legislation.

There are two other events worth noting before 1900. First, all company laws (that is, for all types of companies) were consolidated into the Companies Act 1862, which contained, in its Table A, model reporting and auditing provisions similar to those in the 1856 Act. And secondly, there were several attempts between 1862 and 1900 to reintroduce compulsory reporting provisions, mainly as a consequence of the growing importance of the company in economic activity and of the market in company shares.[21] However, in 1900, a new Companies Act was introduced. There were no provisions for compulsory accounting and reporting, but an annual audit of accounting records and the balance sheet was required for all companies along the lines contained in Table B of the 1856 Act and Table A of the 1862 Act. Perhaps the reluctance to publish financial statements compulsorily is summed up best by Lee:

'The practices, and resistance to the introduction of compulsory publication of accounts, were sympathetic of the old entrepreneurial attitude — shared by many directors, especially of old-established "family" firms which had been converted to companies — that a businessman's accounts were his private concern, that outsiders had no right to pry into them, and that availability of information would help his competitors.'[22]

Therefore, although many companies did in fact produce financial statements for their shareholders prior to the early 1900s, little doubt exists that the present system of reporting owed little to its inauspicious beginnings in the mid to late nineteenth century.

The Legislative Development of Company Financial Reporting, 1900-1948

It is quite clear that the philosophy behind financial reporting practices prior to 1900 was one of maintaining as much secrecy about corporate affairs as company managements regarded as necessary. The informational needs of shareholders, creditors and lenders were apparently pushed into the background; management was left to manage; and, unless company directors felt inclined to do otherwise, shareholders were deprived of formal information concerning profitability and financial position. Indeed, even in situations when financial information was communicated to shareholders, this normally centred around a summarized balance sheet providing a listing of various assets and liabilities which equated with shareholders' equity. The income statement, if one was produced, was simply a disclosure of income available for distribution, dividends paid and income retained in the company. Any income figure disclosed was intended as a statement of what the directors regarded as the maximum dividends which could be distributed. In other words, the objective of company financial reporting at the time was to justify the level of dividends paid to shareholders and to provide creditors with an assurance that the company was solvent, properly managed financially, and not overdistributing income to their detriment.

This particular approach was recognized formally in the Companies Act 1907 when all companies, with the exception of private companies, were required to produce an annual audited balance sheet. No particular format was prescribed, nor were there specific regulations dealing with the content of these statements. The emphasis remained apparently very much on creditor protection rather than providing information for shareholders in general, and investment decision-making in particular. There were still no formal arrangements regarding professional qualifications for auditors. The Companies Act 1908 then consolidated all previous enactments.

The idea that company shareholders should only be interested in the market price of their shares, and the level of their dividends, persisted for many years, with only public company shareholders being guaranteed the supply of regular information. Even then, the information was limited to a summary balance sheet which hid as much as it revealed owing to the accounting manipulation that took place in its production. It was regarded as a virtue to understate the financial position and profitability of the company in good years by writing down the value of assets considerably; and to do the reverse in bad years. This use of so-called 'secret reserves' was widely practised prior to the 1930s and was regarded as necessary to the creation of financial stability for the benefit of creditors and lenders. The neglect of shareholders' interests in this respect is usefully illustrated by Hannah[23] in his study of takeover bids prior to 1950. Commenting on the relative lack of takeover bidding in the inter-war period (partly because of the concentration of shareholdings either in private family hands or in large blocs controlled by company directors), he reveals that bids were normally made through the board of directors without reference to shareholders. He quotes one accounting authority of the day in this respect:

'This was the usual form of merger between two quoted companies and it therefore seemed quite natural for an accountant to insist in 1925 that "the negotiations must obviously be conducted by the Directors. In order to preserve proper secrecy, it is not possible for the Directors to acquaint the shareholders of the matter." Almost invariably, the shareholders were passive agents in the decision-making process, and the history of their attempts to thwart the decisions of directors and achieve a better bid price is largely a study of failure.'[24]

In addition, as Hannah has pointed out, the quality of reported information was poor when it *was* made available to shareholders:

'One tentative explanation of the failure of contested direct bidding to emerge in its modern form is the quality of information available to shareholders and potential bidders in the inter-war years. . . . Neither balance sheets nor profit and loss accounts gave adequate indications either of assets and liabilities or of trading profits. For a variety of reasons — commercial secrecy, preservation of credit status, reduction of trade union wage pressure, discouragement of new entry — directors sometimes published figures which understated or overstated the true position of their company. The imperfect state of the law relating to company accounts, and in particular to secret reserves and holding company accounts, allowed common resort to such malpractice.'[25]

In other words, the period following the 1908 Act saw the limited publication of financial information on a compulsory basis, and the possibility of manipulated information being presented in published reports. There had therefore been little advance in this respect since the Joint Stock Companies Act 1844. There was a feeling that shareholders were content if they knew that their capital was being kept intact, and that their dividends were being maintained.[26] Shareholders were regarded very much as sleeping partners in companies, and in any case, the majority of companies were family businesses with shares closely controlled by persons who were also directors (Board of Trade statistics reveal that, by 1930, there were 16,263 public companies and 95,598 private companies).

The above notwithstanding, the consolidating Companies Act 1929 introduced one important change, at least for public companies. It required them to present an annual income statement to their shareholders. There was no guidance given regarding its, or the balance sheet's, contents, nor was it required to be audited. In fact, it was a very small step in the direction of providing adequate financial information for shareholders and other interested persons. It should be stated that, despite the gradual mergering of companies into larger entities during the inter-war years, as described by Hannah,[27] there was no legal provision for the publication of consolidated financial statements reflecting the profitability and financial position of groups as a whole. This obviously helped to mask the state of affairs of companies considerably, as only the financial results of the holding company needed to be disclosed.

The 1930s and 1940s, however, witnessed a considerable increase in the number of companies and a consequential increase in share ownership. In 1939, there were 13,920 public companies and 146,735 private companies. By 1949, these figures had changed to 12,075 and 231,443, respectively. The need to review safeguards for company investors was recognized governmentally, and in 1943 the Cohen Committee on Company Law Amendment was formed. The Committee sat for two years, and its report, published in 1945, resulted in the consolidating Companies Act 1948 which radically changed the legal requirements for financial reporting, and which now forms the basis for present-day company financial statements. The main changes in the 1948 Act can be summarized as follows:

(a)   Every company was required to present annually to its shareholders an income statement and balance sheet, both of which had to be audited and reported on.

(b)   The Eighth Schedule of the Act contained a list of items of information which every company was required to disclose, where relevant, in its financial statements. In other words, this was the introduction of a legally enforceable minimum disclosure level, although companies (for example, in banking and insurance) were exempted from certain of the provisions because of the nature of their business.

(c)   Holding companies were required to present to their shareholders consolidated financial statements for the group as a whole. These statements were to be subject to audit and were also subject to the minimum disclosure requirements.

(d)   Company auditors were required to be professionally qualified accountants except in the case of the small family company, defined as an exempt private company.

(e)   The auditor's rights, duties and powers were clearly laid down in the Act.

In particular, he was required to give an opinion on the truth and fairness of the reported information.

The 1948 Act therefore gave companies the basis with which to provide share-holders and other interested persons with meaningful information about their financial affairs.

Case Law and the Development of Company Financial Reporting

Arguably, some of the most significant developments in company accounting and reports took place in the courts of law — that is, particularly during the period from about 1890 to 1930. All of these cases concern the measurement and reporting of periodic income, and especially its relationship to the payment of dividends. The reason for this phenomenon was undoubtedly the lack of guidance on these matters in company law, and the lack of a generally acceptable common body of accounting knowledge (this latter point will be dealt with in detail in the next section).

Relatively early in the history of the limited company, it was decided that dividends should not be paid out of subscribed capital[28] — that is, dividends should only be paid out of surpluses over and above the share capital subscribed to the company. However, with that principle established, there remained the problem of putting it into practice; particularly with regard to the calculation of distributable income elements. A number of cases were decided over the intervening years, each of which presumably had an important influence on accounting practice. The following comments relate to the most significant of these cases.

In *Lee* v. *Neuchatal Asphalte Co. Ltd* (1889) 41 Ch. 1, it was held that a company, empowered to do so by its articles of association, may distribute dividends with-out providing for depreciation of its wasting assets. (A wasting asset, in this context, is one which is being depleted through extraction; for example, as in mines and quarries.) In other words, distributable income could be calculated before deducting such depreciation. The judge, in fact, stated: 'There is nothing in any of the Companies Acts prohibiting anything of the kind. . . . It has been judicially and properly left to the commercial world to settle how the accounts were to be kept.'

In *Bolton* v. *Natal Land and Colonisation Co., Ltd* (1892) 2 Ch. 124, it was held that a company can declare a dividend out of current income without providing for losses caused by exceptional reductions in the value of assets such as land. In other words, it was proper to pay dividends out of trading income before providing for infrequent reductions in asset values.

In *Lubbock* v. *The British Bank of South America* (1892) 2 Ch. 198, it was held that a gain made on the sale of part of a company can be distributed as a dividend, if the articles of association do not prohibit it. Thus, an element of non-trading income was held to be distributable to the shareholders.

In *Verner* v. *General and Commercial Investment Trust Ltd* (1894) 2 Ch. 239, it was held that, as in the *Bolton* case above, an investment trust company can distribute income before providing for decreases in certain asset values.

In *Wilmer* v. *McNamara and Co., Ltd* (1895) 2 Ch. 245, it was held that a company can declare a dividend out of current income without providing for the deprecia-tion of fixed assets. This case hinged on whether depreciation of goodwill and leased property was to be regarded as expenditure which should be deducted from sales revenues in determining distributable trading income. It was held not to be.

In *Foster* v. *The New Trinidad Lake Asphalte Co., Ltd* (1901) 1 Ch. 208, it was held that a realized gain on an asset taken over by a company at its formation is not distributable income, unless such a surplus remains after a revaluation of all other company assets. This decision seems to be contrary to the previous judgement in the *Lubbock* case above.

In *Bond* v. *Barrow Haematite Steel Co., Ltd* (1902) 1 Ch. 353, it was held that preference shareholders cannot compel directors to pay a dividend without retaining income in the company when the articles of association demand that such retentions be made. This judgement comes nearest to the modern practice of prudent financial management by retaining a proportion of available income before declaring dividends to shareholders.

In *Ammonia Soda Co.* v. *Chamberlains* (1918) 1 Ch. 266, it was held that it is not necessarily illegal for the directors of a company to pay dividends out of current income without taking cognisance first of past aggregate losses. In other words, if the value of shareholders' equity in the balance sheet is less than that originally subscribed because of cumulative losses, it is still proper to pay dividends out of current income rather than out of any surplus left after deducting past losses from current income. The judge in this case stated: 'In my opinion this alleged restriction has no foundation in law. . . . I am, of course, far from saying that in all such cases dividends can properly be paid without making good the previous loss; the nature of the business and the amount of the loss may be such that no honest and reasonable man of business would think of paying dividends without providing for it.'

In *Stapley* v. *Read Bros., Ltd* (1924) 40 T.L.R. 442, it was held that a company can pay a dividend out of current income where accumulated previous losses have been written off by the revaluation of goodwill. This rather follows the previous judgement given in the *Ammonia Soda* case above.

In *Rex* v. *Kylsant and Morland* (1932) 1 K.B. 442, the chairman of the Royal Mail Steam Packet Co., Ltd was found guilty of presenting false financial statements to shareholders with an intent to deceive them. In particular, this involved the manipulation of accounting data through undisclosed secret reserve movements, for example, by undervaluing an asset in one period and revaluing it in the next. The judge had this to say of secret reserve accounting: 'We have heard a great deal about the keeping of secret reserves, and we have heard a great deal about the commercial troubles which may flow from that practice. It may work very well in many cases; no doubt it does. It is a practice which is being followed, no doubt by many concerns, of the highest standing. On the other hand, it may be the subject of almost intolerable abuse. It is said to be a matter of domestic concern between the company and the shareholders, but if shareholders do not know and cannot know what the position is, how can they form any view about it at all?'

The answer to this question came very soon after the *Kylsant* case when, owing to the nature of its findings and judgements (the auditor was found guilty of aiding and abetting with regard to the false information), the practice of secret reserve movements began to disappear from the then generally accepted accounting practice.

Summarizing on the above cases, it is clear that the courts of law had a considerable influence on practices concerned with the measurement of income and asset values for reporting purposes.[29] The particular concern appears to have been with the determination of income figures with which to justify dividend payments, rather than with figures required for reporting purposes. However, as the reported income statement of these times appears to have been used to justify dividend payments, it is very clear that measurement practices for dividend purposes would also be used for reporting purposes. It should also be said that most of these judgements would not be regarded today as representative of best accounting practice; though they will have been mirroring that of the time in which they took place.

History and Development of Accounting Standards[30]

Ross has summarized the aim of accountants in relation to company financial reports as follows:

'Our essential service to the public thus boils down to assuring they have the benefit of the best financial statements we can devise; and this in turn boils down to producing the most useful accounting principles that we can and getting them generally accepted.'[31]

This almost self-evident statement also pinpoints one of the most important aspects of financial statements: the need for a generally acceptable body of practices with which to measure the required accounting information. In other words, if financial reports are to contain reliable data, they must be the subject of known and proven principles or standards (to use the contemporary term) of measurement and communication. These can be defined following the Littleton formula:

'A standard is an agreed upon criterion of what is proper practice in a given situation; a basis for comparison and judgement; a point of departure when variation is justifiable by the circumstances and reported as such. Standards are not designed to confine practice within rigid limits but rather to serve as guideposts to truth, honesty and fair dealing. They are not accidental but intentional in origin; they are expected to be expressive of the deliberately chosen policies of the highest types of businessmen and the most experienced accountants; they direct a high but attainable level of performance, without precluding justifiable departures and variations in the procedures employed.'[32]

The development of accounting standards has generally taken place within the context of professional development, particularly that of the professional accountancy bodies. Indeed, as the following paragraphs will reveal, government and the courts have tended to take second place to the accountancy bodies in this process. Nevertheless, although these bodies came into being in the mid to late nineteenth century, it was not until the mid 1920s that the debate about adequate accounting standards commenced. However, it has not receded since.

The reason for the lateness of the standards debate, in comparison to the much longer history of company financial reports, may probably be put down to the fact that the earlier professional accountants were concerned primarily with bankruptcies, liquidations and taxation, rather than with the accounting and auditing problems inherent in company financial reporting. In addition, the poor legislative requirements for disclosure of accounting information did not create the appropriate pressure to make the professional bodies look for a generally acceptable and coherent body of relevant practices. However, by the

1920s and 1930s they were becoming aware of deficiencies in the then accounting and reporting practices and were, on both sides of the Atlantic, beginning to look for ways to remedy the situation.

In the United States, the then American Institute of Accountants commenced discussions with the New York Stock Exchange concerning the most obvious of the problems in financial reporting which were being publicly commented on. From these discussions, the Institute formed the Committee on Accounting Procedure (1930) and the Committee on the Development of Accounting Principles (1933), the aim of which was to reduce the number of alternative accounting practices available for any one given business situation. This was done by codification and recommendation through published *Accounting Research Bulletins.*

A similar procedure took place in the United Kingdom, the Institute of Chartered Accountants in England and Wales being particularly active with its published *Recommendations on Accounting Principles.* This series of pronouncements, commencing in 1944, contained relatively simple statements of the main problem areas in accounting, together with recommended solutions. They were advisory by nature and, as with the American *Research Bulletins,* merely helped to add to the number of available practices in certain defined areas of accounting. This flexibility, coupled with the lack of a mechanism for the abandonment of bad or obsolete practices through time, created criticism of accounting and reporting practices, particularly when it was realized by the financial and investment communities that it was possible for a company to produce a number of alternative income statements and balance sheets, each based on the same transactions and so forth, but each different because of the various accounting practices applied.[33]

In the United States the criticism led to the formation, in 1959, of the Accounting Principles Board of the American Institute of Certified Public Accountants. This was supported by a Research Division, and several *Accounting Research Studies* were published concerning the fundamental truths and ideas in accounting. In other words, the initial approach was to pronounce on what should be rather than what is being accounted for. This produced such radically different forms of accounting that the Board was forced back to the previous system of *ad hoc* problem-solving. In addition, the recommended practices in *Accounting Principles Board Opinions* were eventually made mandatory on members of the American Institute. However, this created even more public criticism of accountants and their practices, and the Institute set up its Financial Accounting Standards Board[34] to replace the Accounting Principles Board in an attempt to produce accounting standards in a normative but acceptable fashion, backed by adequate research. So far there has been one major report on the objectives of financial statements.[35]

The British experience has been little different from the American one. Prior to 1969, the various accountancy bodies produced their individual research reports and recommendations, each of which failed to carry any mandatory provisions. Public criticism grew over the poor 'state of play' regarding accounting standards, and in 1969 the Institute of Chartered Accountants in England and Wales published its *Statement of Intent on Accounting Standards in the 1970s.*[36] Its main aim was to attempt to narrow the number of alternatives in accounting practice, and in light of this the Accounting Standards Steering Committee was formed with members from all the major accountancy bodies in the United Kingdom. Since then the Committee has initiated research in certain key areas, published *Exposure Drafts* of proposed accounting standards for public discussion and comment, and eventually issued certain *Statements of Standard Accounting Practice,* the contents of which are required to be implemented by members of the major professional accountancy bodies responsible for the production or auditing of company financial statements. If individual circumstances dictate that implementation of a particular standard is not appropriate, then the reasons for this must be fully explained to the shareholders in the relevant financial statements.

Conclusions

The present system of financial reporting by companies in Britain is primarily a legally based one, that base being the Companies Act 1948. In addition, it is being supported by a series of mandatory professional provisions which have the strength of the major professional accountancy bodies behind them (though they do not have the same legal status of the Act).

The Companies Act 1948 was amended significantly by the Companies Act 1967, particularly with regard to disclosure requirements, and it is to these specific present-day provisions that Chapter 3 will be directed.

Suggested Discussion or Essay Topics

1. A knowledge of the historical development of company financial reporting is necessary for an understanding of its present state and problems. Discuss.

2. The nineteenth-century development of the limited liability company created the need, first, for creditor protection, and, secondly, for shareholder protection. Comment on this statement, indicating the means by which protection was afforded.

3. Comment on the significance of railway accounting and reporting in relation to later developments in company financial reporting.

4. Early company income statements were no more than reconciliation statements to justify proposed dividend payments to shareholders. Discuss.

5. How important was the creditor or lender in the early legal and voluntary provisions for company financial reporting?

6. Up to the end of the nineteenth century there appears to have been a tendency, even in the minds of directors, to assume that outside shareholders needed to know little more than creditors. Discuss.

7. The balance sheet was the primary financial statement prior to the 1930s. Since then, the income statement has gradually gained in importance. What reasons can be given for this change in emphasis?

8. Undoubtedly, until the *Kylsant* case, company financial statements were subject to the abuses of secret reserve manipulations. Discuss the implications of these practices from the point of view of statement users.

9. What impact did court case decisions prior to the 1930s have on the development of company financial reports?

10. The Companies Act 1948 marked a major landmark in company financial reporting. Explain this, comparing the 1948 Act with earlier major enactments.

11. Discuss the significance of audit provisions contained in company legislation prior to the Companies Act 1948, with particular reference to the quality and credibility of company financial statements.

12. The accountancy profession has moved from a completely *laissez faire* system to one of compulsion with regard to accounting practices used to produce company financial reports. Discuss this, describing the relative advantages and disadvantages of each system.

Notes and References

1. R. H. Watzlaff, 'The Bubble Act of 1720', *Abacus,* June 1971, pp. 8-28.

2. A. C. Littleton and V. K. Zimmerman, *Accounting Theory: Continuity and Change,* Prentice-Hall, 1962, p. 81.

3. An excellent paper, from which much of the material in this section has been drawn, is H. Pollins, 'Aspects of Railway Accounting before 1868', in A. C. Littleton and B. S. Yamey, *Studies in the History of Accounting,* Sweet & Maxwell, 1956, pp. 332-55.

4. ibid., p. 336.

5. ibid., p. 338.

6. G. A. Lee, 'The Concept of Profit in British Accounting, 1760-1800', unpublished paper, University of Nottingham, 1974, p. 15.

7. P. Bird, *Accountability: Standards for Financial Reporting,* Accountancy Age Books, 1973, p. 2.

8. This is a problem which Pollins, see n. 3 above, studied in depth in connection with railway companies, and it is one at which a later section of this chapter looks.

9. The first professional accountancy body in the world, the Society of Accountants in Edinburgh, came into being in 1854. However, the primary work of these early accountants was bankruptcies and liquidations. It was not until the early 1900s that auditing became a major occupation for them.

10. Pollins, 'Aspects of Railway Accounting', loc. cit., p. 354.

11. ibid., p. 332.

12. Lee, 'The Concept of Profit in British Accounting', paper cit., p. 17.

13. ibid., p. 19.

14. H. C. Edey and P. Panitpakdi, 'British Company Accounting and the Law: 1844-1900', in Littleton and Yamey, *Studies in the History of Accounting,* pp. 356-7.

15. H. Rose, 'Disclosure in Company Accounts', *Eaton Paper 1,* 1965, p. 20.

16. Edey and Panitpakdi, 'British Company Accounting and the Law', loc. cit., p. 354.

17. Bird, *Accountability,* p. 27.

18. Edey and Panitpakdi, 'British Company Accounting and the Law', loc. cit., p. 361.

19. The complete provisions are reproduced in ibid., pp. 362-4.

20. ibid., p. 364.

21. A detailed account of this period is contained in ibid., pp. 368-71.

22. Lee, 'The Concept of Profit in British Accounting', paper cit., p. 26.

23. L. Hannah, 'Takeover Bids in Britain Before 1950: An Exercise in Business "Pre-History" ', *Business History,* January 1974, pp. 65-77.

24. ibid., p. 68.

25. ibid., p. 69.

26. Rose, 'Disclosure in Company Accounts', loc. cit., p. 22.

27. L. Hannah, 'Managerial Innovation and the Rise of the Large-Scale Company in Interwar Britain', *Economic History Review,* May 1974, pp. 252-70.

28. e.g. in *Flitcroft's Case* (1882), 21 Ch. D. 519.

29. Edey and Panitpakdi, 'British Company Accounting and the Law', loc. cit., p. 379.

30. Much of this comes from T. A. Lee, 'Accounting Standards and Effective Financial Reporting: a Review in Principle', *Accountant's Magazine,* January and February 1975, pp. 25-30 and 73-81.

31. H. I. Ross, 'The Current Crisis in Financial Reporting', *Journal of Accountancy,* August 1967, p. 66.

32. A. C. Littleton, *Structure of Accounting Theory,* American Accounting Association, 1953, p. 143.

33. See E. Stamp and C. Marley, *Accounting Principles and the City Code: the Case for Reform,* Butterworth, 1970, pp. 65-154.

34. *Establishing Financial Accounting Standards,* Report of the Study Group on Establishment of Accounting Principles, American Institute of Certified Public Accountants, March 1972.

35. *Objectives of Financial Statements,* Report of the Study Group on the Objectives of Financial Statements, American Institute of Certified Public Accountants, October 1973.

36. 'Statement of Intent on Accounting Standards in the 1970s', *Accountant's Magazine,* January 1970, pp. 11-12.

Selected Bibliography for Chapter 2

W. W. Bigg, *Practical Auditing,* HFL Publishers, 1965, pp. 314-48. Covers many of the relevant legal cases in some detail.

H. C. Edey and P. Panitpakdi, 'British Company Accounting and the Law: 1844-1900', in A. C. Littleton and B. S. Yamey, *Studies in the History of Accounting,* Sweet & Maxwell, 1956, pp. 356-79. A description of the legal development in the stated period.

R. W. Gibson, *Disclosure by Australian Companies,* Melbourne University Press, 1971. A detailed study of Australian practices from 1829 to 1969, these following the British example closely.

J. Kitchen, 'The Accounts of British Holding Company Groups: Development and Attitudes to Disclosure in the Early Years', *Accounting and Business Research,* Spring 1972, pp. 114-36. A detailed study of practices with regard to consolidated financial statements.

T. A. Lee, 'Company Financial Statements: An Essay in Business History 1830-1950', *Discussion Papers in Economics,* University of Liverpool, July 1974. An overall review of developments using the financial statements of a large public company.

A. C. Littleton and V. K. Zimmerman, *Accounting Theory: Continuity and Change,* Prentice-Hall, 1962, pp. 72-102. An overall review of the topic, including pre-company history.

H. Pollins, 'Aspects of Railway Accounting Before 1868', in Littleton and Yamey, *Studies in the History of Accounting,* pp. 332-55. A detailed study of the earliest practices.

3 Present-day Requirements for Company Financial Reporting

The Current Legal Requirements for Annual Reporting

Financial accounting and reporting by companies in Britain are governed by Sections 147 to 158 inclusive of the Companies Act 1948, and by Sections 3 to 12 inclusive of the amending Companies Act 1967. In addition, company auditing practices are legislated for in Sections 159 to 161 inclusive of the Companies Act 1948, and by Sections 13 and 14 of the Companies Act 1967. The following paragraphs give a brief description and summary of the main contents of these Sections.

Accounting records

Section 147, Companies Act 1948, stipulates that companies must keep adequate accounting records, particularly with regard to data essential for the production of financial statements of the type discussed in Chapter 1:

'(1)   Every company shall cause to keep proper books of account with respect to —
  (a)   all sums of money received and expended by the company and the matters in respect of which the receipt and expenditure takes place;
  (b)   all sales and purchases of goods by the company;
  (c)   the assets and liabilities of the company.
(2)   For the purposes of the foregoing sub-section, proper books of account shall not be deemed to be kept with respect to the matters aforesaid if there are not kept such books as are necessary to give a true and fair view of the state of the company's affairs and to explain its transactions.'

Thus, the adequacy of a company's accounting records is judged effectively in terms of their ability to provide data which have the qualities of truthfulness and fairness. Unfortunately, and this is a matter which will be discussed in detail later in the text, neither the Companies Act 1948 nor the Companies Act 1967 define the meaning of the phrase 'true and fair view' in relation to reported accounting information.

Financial statements

The requirement to provide shareholders annually with financial statements is contained in Section 148, Companies Act 1948:

'(1) The directors of every company shall at some date not later than eighteen months after the incorporation of the company and subsequently once at least in every calendar year lay before the company in general meeting a profit and loss account or, in the case of a company not trading for profit, an income and expenditure account for the period, in the case of the first account, since the incorporation of the company, and, in any other case, since the preceding account, made up to a date not earlier than the date of the meeting by more than nine months, or, in the case of a company carrying on business or having interests abroad, by more than twelve months.'

Shareholders are therefore legally entitled to receive an income statement and balance sheet annually. Section 149, Companies Act 1948, states the qualities to be attributed to such statements:

'(1) Every balance sheet of a company shall give a true and fair view of the state of the affairs of the company as at the end of its financial year, and every profit and loss account of a company shall give a true and fair view of the profit or loss of the company for the financial year.'

Once again, the phrase 'true and fair view' is used, without further definition, and the accountants responsible for producing the relevant financial statements are left to interpret it as best they can. However, the contents of these financial statements are governed by the 'minimum disclosure' requirements of Schedule 2, Companies Act 1967 (formerly Schedule 8, Companies Act 1948), which states the items of information which must be disclosed, where relevant, in the published income statement and balance sheet. The requirement to adhere to this Schedule is contained in Section 149(2), Companies Act 1948, as amended by Section 9, Companies Act 1967. Further additional information which must be disclosed where relevant, is provided for by Sections 3 to 8 inclusive of the Companies Act 1967. (Full details of all disclosure requirements which support the required 'true and fair view' in company financial statements are contained in the Appendix, page 226.)

Group statements

Reporting requirements for groups of companies are contained in Section 150, Companies Act 1948, which states *inter alia*:

'(1) Where at the end of its financial year a company has subsidiaries, accounts or statements (in this Act referred to as "group accounts") dealing as hereinafter mentioned with the state of affairs and profit or loss of the company and the subsidiaries shall . . . be laid before the company in general meeting when the company's own balance sheet and profit and loss account are so laid.'

Section 150(2) contains several exceptions to the above general provision for consolidated income statements and balance sheets, meaning that no such statements need be produced when, for example, the holding company is itself a wholly-owned British subsidiary, or when to produce group statements would be, in the opinion of the directors, immaterial, impractical, harmful, misleading, or would cause unnecessary delay in publishing the financial statements.

The form of the group financial statements is outlined in Section 151, Companies Act 1948:

'(1) . . . the group accounts laid before a holding company shall be consolidated accounts comprising —

(a) a consolidated balance sheet dealing with the state of affairs of the company and all the subsidiaries to be dealt with in group accounts;

(b) a consolidated profit and loss account dealing with the profit or loss of the company and those subsidiaries.'

If the holding company directors feel that this group financial information could be better presented, they can present more than one set of consolidated statements covering individual group companies or separate sub-groups within the group (Section 151(2), Companies Act 1948).

The quality of the information contained in the required financial statements of groups of companies is governed by Section 152, Companies Act 1948, and again contains the undefined 'true and fair view' phrase:

'(1) The group accounts laid before a company shall give a true and fair view of the state of affairs and profit or loss of the company and the subsidiaries dealt with thereby as a whole, so far as concerns members of the company.'

Section 152(3), as amended by Section 9, Companies Act 1967, also requires group financial statements to comply with the disclosure provisions of Schedule 2, Companies Act 1967. In addition, Section 153, Companies Act 1948, provides that, wherever possible, the financial years of the holding company and its subsidiaries should coincide for reporting purposes.

Thus, summarizing, each British company must present annually to its shareholders an income statement and a balance sheet; and, if it also happens to be a holding company which is not a wholly owned subsidiary, it should also present annually a consolidated income statement and balance sheet. These group statements are subject to the same 'true and fair view' and disclosure requirements as the holding company's own financial statements. However, certain subsidiary company data can be omitted from group statements if conditions warrant it. Lastly, group statements can be incorporated into the holding company's own statements if this is felt to be more convenient than producing separate consolidated information.

Company definitions

Section 154, Companies Act 1948, defines the terms *holding company* and *subsidiary company* to allow company directors to decide whether or not they have to comply with the group financial statement provisions.

'(1) For the purpose of this Act, a company shall ... be deemed to be a subsidiary of another if, but only if, —
(a) that other either —
(i) is a member of it, and controls the composition of its board of directors; or
(ii) holds more than half in nominal value of its equity share capital; or
(b) the first-mentioned company is a subsidiary of any company which is that other's subsidiary.'

Miscellaneous provisions

The Companies Act 1948 also contains several miscellaneous provisions relating to the provision of regular financial information for company shareholders. For example, Section 155 requires every company balance sheet to be signed by two directors (thereby acknowledging directorial responsibility for the production and quality of the financial statements); Section 156 states that the income statement, any group statements and the relevant audit report must be annexed to the signed balance sheet; Section 157 provides that a report of the directors must be attached to the balance sheet (which should include *inter alia* the recommended dividend figures, as well as information regarding changes in the nature of the business conducted by the company) (Sections 16 to 20 inclusive of the Companies Act 1967 added to these requirements, providing *inter alia* for the disclosure of significant fixed asset changes; reasons for movements in share capital; directors' interests in the shares and debentures of the company; turnover and profitability of each significant class of business conducted by the company, etc.); and Section 158 provides that:

'(1) A copy of every balance sheet, including every document required by law to be annexed thereto, which is to be laid before a company in general meeting, together with a copy of the auditors' report, shall, not less than twenty-one days before the date of the meeting, be sent to every member of the company (whether he is or is not entitled to receive notices of general meetings of the company), every holder of debentures of the company (whether he is or is not so entitled) and all persons other than members or holders of debentures of the company, being persons so entitled.'

The audit function

The above are therefore the main provisions dealing with the publication and presentation of annual financial statements to company shareholders, and, where relevant, to debenture holders. In each instance, the Companies Acts 1948 and 1967 provide for punishment by fine or imprisonment if directors fail to comply with them. Company financial reporting, however, is not simply a matter of legislating for the production of financial statements. In Britain, as in many other developed countries, such statements are also required to be audited by professionally qualified accountants. Provision for this is contained in both the Companies Act 1948 and the Companies Act 1967.

Section 159, Companies Act 1948, governs the appointment and remuneration of the auditor.

'(1) Every company shall at each annual general meeting appoint an auditor or auditors to hold office from the conclusion of that, until the conclusion of the next, annual general meeting.
'(2) The remuneration of the auditor of a company . . . shall be fixed by the company in general meeting or in such manner as the company in general meeting may determine.'

Moreover, subsections 2 to 6 inclusive provide for the appointment of an auditor by the directors prior to the first annual general meeting or when a casual vacancy occurs between meetings. The Department of Trade and Industry is also given legal powers to appoint an auditor when the company fails to do so.

The dismissal of company auditors is covered by Section 160, Companies Act 1948:

'(1) Special notice shall be required for a resolution at a company's annual general meeting appointing as auditor a person other than a retiring auditor or providing expressly that a retiring auditor shall not be reappointed.

'(2) On receipt of notice of such an intended resolution as aforesaid, the company shall forthwith send a copy thereof to the retiring auditor (if any).'

In addition, subsection 3 allows the auditor to make written representations to the shareholders on notice of his proposed dismissal. Thus, he is given the chance to state his case, if he so wishes.

Section 161, Companies Act 1948, as amended by Section 13, Companies Act 1967, deals with the qualifications required of a person whom it is proposed to appoint as company auditor. He must be a member of a recognized British professional accountancy body (that is, either a chartered or a certified accountant) or have been recognized by the Department of Trade and Industry as having adequate knowledge and experience to act as auditor. When the auditor is, in fact, a firm of accountants, these provisions apply to each member of the partnership concerned. Apart from this, subsection 2 of Section 161 specifically states:

'None of the following persons shall be qualified for appointment as auditor of a company —
  (a)   an officer or servant of the company;
  (b)   a person who is a partner of or in the employment of an officer or servant of the company;
  (c)   a body corporate.'

Thus, company directors and managers, and their partners and employees, are barred from holding the office of company auditor.

Originally contained in Section 162, Companies Act 1948, but now substituted by Section 14, Companies Act 1967, the duties of the auditor, once appointed, are as follows:

'(1) The auditors of a company shall make a report to the members on the accounts examined by them, and on every balance sheet, every profit and loss account and all group accounts laid before the company in general meeting during their tenure of office.

'(2) The auditor's report shall be read before the company in general meeting and shall be open to inspection by any member.

'(3) The report shall —
  (a)   . . . state whether in the auditor's opinion the company's balance sheet and profit and loss account and (if it is a holding company submitting group accounts) the group accounts have been properly prepared in accordance with the provisions of the principal Act and this Act and whether in their opinion a true and fair view is given . . . . '

Subsection 4 instructs auditors to carry out sufficient investigations to form such an opinion, and particularly to see that proper accounting records are kept and in agreement with the published financial statements. If this is not the case, then auditors must report to the shareholders accordingly. Subsection 5 gives every auditor the right of access to all evidence and information necessary to the audit, and subsection 7 states that all auditors are entitled to attend general meetings, receive notices regarding general meetings, and be heard at such meetings regarding business affecting their audit functions.

Thus, company financial statements are required to be examined and reported on by expert and qualified professional accountants, who are legally entitled to access to all matters necessary to the conduct of such an audit. Their report to the shareholders is expressed in terms of the truth and fairness criteria legally required of the financial statements.

The Current Legal Requirements for Prospectuses

Occasionally, companies require additional finance and make share or debenture issues to raise the necessary funds. If these securities are offered to the public, then the Companies Act 1948 requires the directors of the company concerned to publish a prospectus in which full details of the offer are contained. Sections 37 to 46 inclusive of the Act contain the relevant provisions regarding the dating, contents, registration, etc., of such a document. The Fourth Schedule of the Act contains details of all relevant matters which must be disclosed in it.

Part I of the Fourth Schedule states the 'matters to be specified' in the prospectus, and these include *inter alia* details of the directors; full particulars of the share or debenture issue being made; and particulars of any property being acquired from the proceeds of the issue. Part II specifies the reports which must be contained in the prospectus, including:

'(1)   A report by the auditors of the company with respect to —
   (a)   profit and losses and assets and liabilities . . . ; and
   (b)   the rates of the dividends, if any, paid by the company in respect of each class of share in the company in respect of each of the five financial years immediately preceding the issue of the prospectus . . . . '

So far as (a) is concerned, income figures should be given for the last five financial years (they should be those of the group if a group of companies is involved), and assets and liabilities should be stated as at the end of the last preceding financial year (again, being those of a group where relevant). In addition, if the proceeds of the share or debenture issue are to be used to acquire shares in another company, or another business, then an accountant's report containing data relating to the last five years' income of the company or business concerned (as well as its last reported assets and liabilities) must be contained in the prospectus. So far as the reporting accountant is concerned, Part III of the Fourth Schedule contains the following provision:

'Any report by accountants required by Part II of this Schedule shall be made by accountants qualified under this Act for appointment as auditors of a company . . . and shall not be made by any accountant who is an officer or servant, or a partner or in the employment of an officer or servant, of the company or of the company's subsidiary or holding company or of a subsidiary of the company's holding company; and for the purposes of this paragraph the expression "officer" shall include a proposed director but not an auditor.'

Therefore, when a company seeks funds from the public, it must also make public data relating to its last five years' income (where possible) and its latest reported asset and liability situation. This data must be reported on by expert professional accountants.

The Current Professional Requirements

Undoubtedly, the major influence on annual financial reporting by companies comes from the requirements of company legislation. Recently, however, an additional and powerful influence has appeared. This is connected with the programme of standardization currently being undertaken by the major professional accountancy bodies in Britain. Their *Statements of Standard Accounting Practice* are intended to notify reporting accountants of the prescribed practices which should be adopted in particular accounting situations. Thereby it is hoped to bring about a greater uniformity of practice, especially between companies with similar accounting problems. To date a number of *Statements* have been issued,[1] of which the second in the series[2] is most relevant to this particular part of the text.

Statement of Standard Accounting Practice 2 defines the general principles behind the process of standardization, and, in particular, states that:

'The accounting policies . . . followed for dealing with items which are judged material or critical in determining profit or loss for the year and in stating financial position should be disclosed by way of note to the accounts. The explanations should be clear, fair, and as brief as possible.'[3]

('Accounting policies' is the term adopted in these *Statements* for the particular accounting practices or methods adopted by the company when measuring its reportable accounting information.)

This requirement is supported by a complementary *Statement on Auditing,*[4] which effectively provides that company auditors must examine and report on the accounting policies adopted in producing the financial statements they are verifying. In particular:

'All significant departures from accounting standards made by the directors in preparing the accounts should be referred to in the auditors' report, whether or not they are disclosed in the notes to the accounts. The extent of the detailed description in the auditors' report will depend upon whether the departure is fully explained in the notes to the accounts. If it is, the auditors need make only a brief reference to the circumstances in their report, but if it is not, a more detailed reference will be necessary.'[5]

Thus, through these various standards and statements, professionally qualified accountants responsible for producing and auditing company financial statements are required to ensure that prescribed accounting practices have been followed and adequately disclosed to shareholders. The number of these prescribed practices is increasing over the years, owing to the work of the Accounting Standards Steering Committee, and the penalty for not adhering to them (or failing to disclose non-adherence) takes the form of disciplinary action against the offending accountant by his professional accountancy body. This could mean loss of his professional designation and status, and so the sanction is heavy, even if it lacks the full weight of law.

The Requirements of the Stock Exchange

The Council of the Stock Exchange has stated its role as follows:

'The Stock Exchange provides a market for the purchase and sale of securities. The efficient operation of such a market depends primarily upon adequacy of information, a quantity of securities whose distribution is sufficiently wide to provide marketability, and certainty of procedures for the settlement of business.

'Information is secured initially by the publication of a prospectus in a form approved by the Stock Exchange. . . . Thereafter the company is required . . . to maintain a regular supply of information to its shareholders and the investing public.'[6]

In other words, of particular concern to the Stock Exchange is the provision of reliable information from the point at which a company first seeks to market its shares, and thereafter throughout the subsequent period of its share quotation. The need for such information is seen in a much wider sense than is the case with the Companies Acts — existing and potential investors are obviously regarded as the primary users.

The information required to be disclosed in the prospectus seeking quotation is contained in Schedule II, Part A, of *Aamission of Securities to Listing,*[7] and includes *inter alia* particulars of share and loan capital; identification of directors, auditors, bankers, etc.; details of the nature of the company's business; a statement of the last five years' sales turnover on gross trading income, suitably analysed between activities; a statement of the financial and trading prospects of the company; where relevant, a trading income forecast together with a statement of the commercial assumptions on which it has been based; an audit report on the accounting adequacy of such a forecast; a statement by the directors on the adequacy of the company's working capital; a report by the auditors of the company covering *inter alia* its trading income during the last five completed financial years, and its balance sheet at the end of the last financial period; a similar audit report on the financial results of any other company which the reporting company has or is about to acquire since the end of its last financial period; particulars of any changes or issues of share capital of the company or its subsidiaries during the last two years; and details of directors' shareholdings, aggregate emoluments and material interests in company assets or contracts.

Details of the information which the Stock Exchange requires listed companies to provide to shareholders and potential investors is contained in its *Listing Agreement.*[8] This includes *inter alia* notification to the Quotations Department of the Stock Exchange of details of dividends in preliminary trading income announcements, changes in share capital, material acquisitions or realizations of assets, changes in the directorate, and any change in the general character of business. The quoted company must also prepare half-yearly income reports for shareholders, which must also be disclosed in the press. In addition, the directors' annual report to the shareholders must include *inter alia* the following data: a statement giving reasons for any departures from prescribed *Statements of Standard Accounting Practice;* a geographical analysis of sales turnover; details of shareholdings of more than 20 per cent in other companies; a statement giving detials of directors' shareholdings in the company; a similar statement of directors' interests in company contracts; and details of dividends waived by directors or shareholders. The latter details regarding directors' interests cover the period up to one month before the date of the relevant report.

Thus the Stock Exchange follows the fundamental reporting structure laid down in the Companies Acts and the mandatory provisions of the professional accountancy bodies. It also attempts to make these provisions more relevant to the investor by updating, where possible, to the date of reporting rather than to the date to which the financial statements, etc., are drawn up.

The Requirements of the Panel

As previously mentioned, the Panel on Takeovers and Mergers was set up at the request of the Bank of England to regulate takeover and merger transactions. The *City Code on Takeovers and Mergers* contains the various rules and regulations which companies must follow if involved in a takeover or merger. This in particular includes the provision[9] of certain information to all shareholders concerned in the transaction. Shareholders must be notified immediately by press notice of any firm offer to take over or merge that is made to their directors. In particular, and this applies to all statements given to the shareholders:

'Any document or advertisement addressed to the shareholders . . . must be treated with the same standards of care with regard to the statements made therein as if it were a prospectus within the meaning of the Companies Act 1948.'[10]

This is interpreted in terms of the relevant facts and opinions being 'fair' and 'accurate'. For example, the *Code* states:

'Shareholders must be put in possession of all the facts necessary for the formation of an informed judgement as to the merits and demerits of an offer. Such facts must be accurately and fairly presented and be available to shareholders early enough to enable them to make a decision in good time.'[11]

The *Code* particularly draws attention to the need to apply these standards to any trading income forecast which may be contained in the offer document.[12] The commercial assumptions upon which the forecasts are based must be stated, and the accounting practices utilized in their preparation must be reported on by the auditors or consultant accountants concerned. Any named financial advisor must report on the income forecast as a whole. Also, whether or not income forecasts are reported, the latest unaudited income figures, since the last date of formal reporting up to the date of the offer, must be disclosed. Thus the *Code* attempts to provide for the production of up-to-date financial data which are relevant to the decisions of the shareholders who are being faced with an offer to buy their shares. Income forecasts will relate to the offeror company, but may also relate to the offeree company if its shareholders feel that the offer should be rejected. Therefore shareholders of the offeror company may be presented with information relating to both companies involved in the possible takeover or merger. Whatever the situation, the documents received by the shareholders must contain details of the shareholdings of the offeror company in the offeree company, and, where relevant, holdings of the offeree in the offeror. In addition, directors' shareholdings in both companies must be disclosed. Finally, full details of the means by which the offer is to be satisfied must be given.

Concluding Remarks

The above paragraphs have attempted to give an outline of the main statutory and other provisions governing the supply of financial information to shareholders and others interested and involved in company affairs. They reveal that the major provision is for annually reported information of a general-purpose nature relating to profitability and financial position. Certainly the legal intention is that such information be part of the stewardship function to be exercised by company directors.

Other provisions for disclosure of information are, by contrast, concerned with providing specific-purpose information relevant to the making of investment decisions by existing or potential shareholders — that is, particularly concerning the publication of forecast income data. The remainder of this text, however, is mainly concerned with annually reported information, although reference will be made, where relevant, to other sources of reported data.

Interested readers will find a detailed analysis of all disclosure provisions affecting company financial reports in the Appendix at page 226.

Suggested Discussion or Essay Topics

1. What is meant by the legally required 'true and fair view' in company financial reporting?
2. Comment on the main features of the 'minimum disclosure' provisions of the Companies Act 1967. In what ways do they benefit shareholders and other users of financial statements?
3. In what circumstances do holding companies not require to publish consolidated financial statements which incorporate the financial results of all subsidiary companies?
4. The company auditor is a suitably qualified accountant who is given certain legal rights and privileges. Discuss.
5. Explain and discuss the role of the company prospectus in investment activities.
6. The professional accountancy bodies have a duty to seek improvements in accounting and reporting practices when legal provisions are inadequate. Discuss.
7. Comment on the provisions of the Stock Exchange and the City Panel in relation to financial reporting. How useful have their contributions been, particularly to the investor?

Notes and References

1. These include statements dealing *inter alia* with accounting for associated companies, earnings per share, extraordinary items and inflation.
2. 'Disclosure of Accounting Policies', *Statement of Standard Accounting Practice 2,* November 1971.
3. ibid., p. 3.
4. 'The Effect of Statements of Standard Accounting Practice on Auditors' Reports', *Statements on Auditing 1,* February 1971.
5. ibid., p. 1.
6. *Admission of Securities to Listing,* Stock Exchange, revised edition 1973, p. 1.
7. ibid., pp. 129-38.
8. ibid., pp. 14-46.
9. *The City Code on Takeovers and Mergers,* Issuing Houses Association, 1972, para 5.
10. ibid., para. 14.
11. ibid., para. 15.
12. ibid., para. 16.

Selected Bibliography for Chapter 3

The Companies Act 1948, HMSO, 1948. The basic accounting and auditing legal requirements.

The Companies Act 1967, HMSO, 1967. The amendments to the Companies Act 1948.

City Code on Takeovers and Mergers, Issuing Houses Association, 1972. Details of requirements regarding relevant accounting reports for takeovers and mergers.

Admission of Securities to Listing, Stock Exchange, revised edition 1973, pp. 14-70 and 168-9. Details of Stock Exchange requirements.

4 The Objectives, Uses and Users of Company Financial Reports

Introduction

What Chapters 1 to 3 have attempted to describe in some detail is the nature of company financial reports as they are constituted presently in Britain. From this analysis, the following points have emerged:

(a) A major part of the information relates to company profitability and financial position, with the main emphasis apparently on profitability.

(b) Most of the accounting measures are historic by nature, relating to past periods of company activity.

(c) By far the most significant source of information is contained in the annually and, where relevant, semi-annually published financial reports.

(d) The reported accounting information is measured in accordance with certain acceptable and prescribed accounting practices and conventions.

(e) Most of the reported accounting information is subject to an expert audit and report by independent and professionally qualified accountants so as to assess its credibility.

(f) The reported accounting information which is required to be published is usually specifically designated for company shareholders, although others may use it.

(g) The impetus for reporting on the financial results and affairs of companies comes mainly from company legislation, supported by professional and other regulatory provisions.

Thus, the apparent intention of corporate financial reporting in Britain is to provide shareholders with regular reports of past income and financial positions. In this way, shareholders can be identified as the primary users of such information, and the assumption is that the nature of the information is relevant to their particular needs. However, it is clear that shareholders are not the only potential users of company financial reports; and that very little is known of their specific information needs; or of the needs of other identifiable users, for that matter. As Staubus has succinctly put it:

'Accounting writers frequently mention owners, stockholders, creditors, or some other sub-classification of investors as readers of financial statements, but they seem to have made no special effort to show the relation between accounting and the problems facing investors. Rather, they have assumed that there is a relation without having bothered to analyse the problems of investors with a view to specifying just what information can be provided by accountants and also be useful to investors.'[1]

The purpose, therefore, of this chapter is to look in more detail at the potential users of reported company information so as to establish its broad objectives and the major uses to which it might be put. Because of the main emphasis of the book, the discussion will be within the context of regularly reported accounting information; particularly that which is contained in the annual financial statements.

The Concepts of Utility and Relevance

It almost goes without saying that company financial reports must be useful; otherwise there is little point in publishing them. The concept of utility is therefore fundamental to financial reporting, and has been specifically acknowledged as such by several writers.[2] However, it suffers from an obvious vagueness which requires the recognition of more explicit and understandable reporting concepts. In particular, the concept of relevance appears appropriate in this context. This has been advocated as vital to financial reporting for some time,[3] and has been defined typically as follows:

'Relevance is the primary standard and requires that the information must bear upon or be usefully associated with actions it is designed to facilitate or results desired to be produced. Known or assumed information needs of potential users are of paramount importance in applying this standard.'[4]

In other words, to be useful, and hence relevant, reported accounting information must be capable of influencing the behaviour of its potential user. If it does not do this, it cannot be said to be useful — particularly when he ignores it completely. But for such information to be a useful influence in this sense, its potential users must be identified and their information needs fully explored. Once user needs are established, information can be reported which is relevant to those needs. In this way, the role of accountants should be fulfilled, given the necessary distinction between the provision of information (which is part of the function of accounting) and the use of it (which is part of the 'investment' function in its broadest sense).

The General Purpose Approach

Despite the fact that company financial statements are intended legally for shareholders, it is clear that they can, and are, used for a number of different purposes. For example, May has recognized at least ten distinguishable uses:

'As a report of stewardship; as a basis for fiscal policy; as a criterion of the legality of dividends; as a guide to wise dividend action; as a basis for the granting of credit; as information for prospective investors in an enterprise; as a guide to the value of investments already made; as an aid to government supervision; as a basis for price or rate regulations; and as a basis for taxation.'[5]

Therefore the annual financial statements of a company can aid not only its management to regulate prices and follow a reasonable dividend policy, but can also help its external interests to be reasonably informed about its profitability and financial position; for example, existing and potential shareholders when evaluating the investment potential of the company's shares; creditors and lenders when assessing its creditworthiness and liquidity; and government departments in administering the system of taxing companies. It is arguable whether one set of financial statements of the type described in earlier chapters, can be of equal use and relevance to each of these groups of users. It may well be that some will find the information of more relevance than others, because of its emphasis on overall company profitability and general financial position; both being expressed in historic terms. Unfortunately, this is an as yet unresolved problem in accounting, but it will be returned to at a later stage.

The attempt to satisfy several different user groups with the same accounting information does indicate that they all may have something in common so far as their needs are concerned. Indeed, this is the case as all groups with a potential interest in companies are concerned with making decisions affecting their involvement or investment in such entities. These decisions are economic by nature (that is, they all involve assessments concerning the efficient allocation of scarce economic resources) and they all, by definition, must involve evaluations of the future. Thus, in the words of the Trueblood Study Group:

'The basic objective of financial statements is to provide information useful for making economic decisions.'[6]

In other words, reported accounting information must be capable of having a bearing on economic decisions if it is to be relevant to its users. Identifying the nature of these economic decisions is therefore essential to the proper reporting of information to them. This is the case whether the system is the present one of a general set of financial statements aimed at a heterogeneous group of users who are largely unidentified (with the possible exception of existing shareholders and the Inland Revenue) or an alternative one of providing specific information for each defined sub-group of users. It is not good enough simply to identify several groups as being possible users of company financial statements, and hope that the latter's general-purpose nature is sufficiently all-embracing to be of some relevance to them all. This was recognized by an American Accounting Association Committee[7] which *inter alia* suggested that research into financial reporting practices should concentrate on identifying users and their information needs; analyse the different ways in which information is used; determine the breadth of issues to be reported; and explain the effects which reported information has on share prices and the efficiency of the capital market.

Management and Company Financial Statements

The annual financial statements of companies are usually regarded as primarily for the use of persons and bodies not involved in the day-to-day management of corporate business activity. However, it would be unfair to imply that company management, and particularly boards of directors, have no use for such reports. It is true to say that the data they contain are relatively 'old news' to company managers, who should in any case be provided with a regular flow of relevant data throughout the financial year. Nevertheless, the income statement, balance sheet and funds statement can give managers and directors an overall review of a company's financial position and progress. This is in one sense the use of financial statements in a 'feedback' role; the data either confirming or rejecting managerial impressions and expectations of the company's performance throughout the year.

Accountability and Company Financial Statements

As indicated in Chapter 2 on the history of financial reporting, the early objective of financial statements was to satisfy management's stewardship functions with ownership. Company directors were, and still are, placed in a position of responsibility and trust by shareholders, and had, and have, an ethical and legal responsibility to account for their actions. The publication of annual financial statements is therefore intended as a major part of such an accounting. Rose has commented on this as follows:

'As an instrument of "accountability", rather than as a mere historical record, the business account has been the product of the joint rather than the one-man venture.

'In the past the paramount purpose of accountability, at least in the eyes of the law, has usually been identified with the prevention of fraudulent and other abuses of financial stewardship.

'. . . the trend in Britain over the years has been gradually to restrict the freedom of action of financial institutions in order to prevent insolvency or the exploitation of the public.'[8]

The disclosure of financial information has consequently been aimed at protecting shareholders from, originally, fraudulent practices, and nowadays from inefficient financial management. At the risk of curbing the freedom of company directors to manage as they see fit, the shareholder has been given a significant source of information with which to hold them accountable for their actions. Accountability must still be thought of as a major objective of financial reporting. Indeed, Carsberg *et al.* found in a recent pilot survey in Britain that professionally qualified accountants appear to favour the stewardship objective above all others.

'The higher ranking given to the stewardship objective was, perhaps, to be expected in view of the usual emphasis placed on stewardship in professional training programmes.'[9]

It has also received implicit support from a major professional accountancy body such as the Institute of Chartered Accountants in England and Wales[10] and from leading practitioners.[11] More explicit recognition has been given by Arthur Andersen & Co.:

'Communication of financial information not only serves economic decision-making processes, but ultimately also provides a means by which ethical and legal constraints are applied on those persons who manage or exercise power of one kind or another over the business enterprise and the resources entrusted to it. Thereby, managements are held accountable for achieving the goals of the enterprise.'[12]

This quotation also indicates, albeit indirectly, the direction in which the 'accountability' objective has been moving over the years — away from the original fraud-prevention aim into the area of managerial efficiency. Because of the growing public interest in companies, accountability must now be extended still further to encompass the broader social and economic responsibilities of the company. This can be evidenced in the recent disclosures in company financial reports in Britain of data relating to export sales and pollution costs. Such a trend has been well summed up by the Trueblood Study Group:

'Accountability extends beyond the element of stewardship involved in the safe keeping of assets entrusted to custody. It encompasses the use and conversion of those assets as well as decisions not to use them. Management is accountable for the values of assets as well as their costs. Enterprise managers are also accountable for actions taken to hedge against the economic impacts of inflation and deflation and technological and social changes.'[13]

This view is supported elsewhere[14] and obviously encompasses the interests of persons other than existing shareholders. In other words, because of its significant place in society, a company (through its directors) has a major responsibility to account in financial terms to its shareholders, creditors and lenders and employees, as well as to the public at large (including potential shareholders, etc.).

One of the major ways of judging the quality of financial management is to evaluate the profitability of the company — the greater the ability of the company to generate income, the greater is its ability to provide sufficient cash to maintain and expand its operations, pay lenders and creditors, and distribute reasonable dividends. The Trueblood Study Group acknowledges this accountability aim when it stated:

'An objective of financial statement is to supply information useful in judging management's ability to utilize enterprise resources effectively in achieving the primary enterprise goal.'[15]

(The primary enterprise goal is the maximizing of cash returns to shareholders for which income must be earned and available for distribution.)

However, recognizing that accountability, in its widest social sense, cannot be thought of solely in terms of reported income and maximization of dividends, the Study Group also stated that:

'An objective of financial statements is to report on those activities of the enterprise affecting society which can be determined and described or measured and which are important to the role of the enterprise in its social environment.'[16]

Summarizing so far, it seems fair to suggest that one of the major objectives of company financial statements has been, and continues to be, the provision of sufficient and relevant accounting information with which directors can inform shareholders and other interested users of the effectiveness of their managerial policies and actions. In this way, the statements not only inform but also protect the various interests of the shareholders and other users. Although this is an enlarging of the traditional stewardship function, it can also be regarded as decision-orientated in the sense that the information may cause its users to exercise their various legal rights against the directors if necessary. Such action inevitably involves decisions.

Investment Decisions and Company Financial Statements

By far the most significant general development in company financial reporting has been the use of accounting data by investors when making investment decisions.

Over the years, the gradual increase in the disclosure of accounting information by companies has undoubtedly provided investors with increased data with which to evaluate investment potential. This is obviously extending the provision of relevant information beyond the traditional limits of shareholder protection in the stewardship function discussed above. Indeed, Choi has suggested that by increasing accounting disclosure, and thereby reducing investor uncertainty about company activity and progress, investors would be attracted to above-average companies where investment uncertainty was relatively low owing to a higher-than-average disclosure of information.[17] If this is true, and it has yet to be empirically shown, then the need to increase shareholder protection, which is a matter of public policy, has aided the efficiency of the capital market by encouraging the available capital to go to the more profitable and efficient companies.

Information and prediction

As Staubus has argued,[18] the nature of an investor's decisions requires a consideration of the advantages and disadvantages of the alternative courses of action open to him: to invest or to refrain from investment; to continue to invest or to terminate the investment. These alternatives require appraisals of the dividend and realization cash flows that are to be expected from the shares concerned. In other words, the usefulness of reported accounting information is very much related to its predictive qualities.[19] Therefore, reported company accounting information may be said to be useful if it helps investors to predict future cash returns from investments:

'An objective of financial statements is to provide information useful to investors and creditors for predicting, comparing, and evaluating potential cash flows to them in terms of amounts, timing, and related uncertainty.'[20]

It should also be noted that beside being useful for predictive purposes, reported information must also be useful to the investor in a 'feedback' capacity by helping him to judge the soundness and accuracy of his earlier predictions and, possibly, causing him to amend his existing predictions in the light of published financial results.

The ability of reported accounting information to aid the investor in his role of predictor is, as yet, a little unclear, as empirical evidence has not been replicated sufficiently to draw any general conclusions. Raynor and Little[21] concluded that there is no evidence to suggest that above-average growth in reporting company incomes will continue at the same rate in the future; Singh and Whittington[22] found that above-average income levels can persist; and Whittington[23] concluded that average income levels tend to persist in the future but not to the same extent as in the past. Not surprisingly, Greenball[24] has gone so far as to suggest that reported accounting information was never intended to predict and cannot predict. This may be true in the sense that historic information relates to a past which may not repeat itself in the future. However, the past can be useful as a guide to the future, despite the inherent uncertainties; and if reported information is used for investment purposes, then it must inevitably be involved in predictions of future investment returns. Peasnell has supported this view, and stated that:

'The primary goal of financial reporting should be to "feedback" data about values of resources held by the firm as distinct from its shareholders.'[25]

This, of course, does not preclude the use of data for predictive purposes. It merely suggests the difficulties associated with such a use.

If the 'prediction' evidence is inconclusive, it is reasonably clear that investors do make use of company financial statements and their contents.[26] This has been shown in a number of studies, and despite the lack of generalized conclusions, published accounting information clearly has some degree of influence on investment decisions, and thus on share prices.

Most of the studies involve statistical analyses of the relationship between the reporting of accounting data and subsequent share-price movements (thus inferring that publication of data, and its subsequent use by investors, influences the movement in share prices by either confirming or rejecting prior expectations of share values, or helping to formulate new expectations of values). For example, when Ball and Brown[27] attempted to examine the usefulness of reported company income data to investors they concluded that 'the annual income number is useful in that if actual income differs from expected income, the market typically has reacted in the same direction'.[28] In other words, data are used by investors in a 'feedback' role, most of the information about annual company profitability being anticipated prior to the annual report mainly owing to interim company reporting of the income. Ball and Brown[29] commented that such anticipation is so accurate that there is little abnormal movement in share prices when annual income is reported, thus indicating that investors do take close cognisance of reported information when making their investment decisions, thereby causing share price movements. Indeed, one of the main comments made by Ball and Brown is most relevant to the assessment of the value of annual reported information to investors:

'Of all the information about an individual firm which becomes available during a year, one half or more is captured in that year's income number. Its content is therefore considerable. However, the annual income report does not rate highly as a timely medium since most of its content (about 85 to 90 per cent) is captured by more prompt media which perhaps include interim reports. Since the efficiency of the capital market is largely determined by the adequacy of its data sources, we do not find it disconcerting that the market has turned to other sources which can be acted upon more promptly than annual net income.'[30]

This suggests that annually reported accounting information from companies has a relatively smaller part to play in investment decision-making than might be supposed initially. This view is supported by Benston[31] who, when studying the relationship of annual and quarterly reported data and share price movements, stated:

'Thus, as measured in this study, the information contained in published accounting reports is a relatively small portion of the information used by investors.'[32]

In other words, investors are relatively insensitive to annual reports of profitability and financial position since prior information of these factors is gleaned from other sources. Beaver,[33] too, has produced evidence which supports that of Ball and Brown and Benston, but he does state[34] that there are indications that investors do look directly at reported income and do not look at other sources of information to the exclusion of company financial reports. This further supports the value of the 'feedback' role of accounting information, annual income statements in particular being used to confirm or reject prior expectations of profitability. It also suggests that there are other sources of information which may have a more significant effect on investment decisions and share prices — particularly information contained in interim financial reports from companies. The usefulness of interim reports of profitability is supported by several research findings. Brown and Kennelly[35] confirmed their hypothesis that investment strategies in which there was foreknowledge of company income because of interim reporting did better than strategies relying solely on the annual .reporting of income. Kiger[36] also produced evidence consistent with the hypothesis that interim reports are used by investors, particularly to predict annual income of the current period. May further confirmed this when stating:

'A conclusion that there is significant demand for quarterly accounting data to be used by investors in actual decisions seems to be justified by the first findings of the study, i.e. that price changes in the weeks of quarterly earnings are greater than average price changes. But the second finding of the study, that relative price change responses to quarterly earnings are not significantly less than responses to annual earnings, leads to the conclusion that investors may be unaware of, or unable to take account of, the difference in quality (reliability) of quarterly and annual accounting data.'[37]

In other words, interim reporting seems to be significant in investment decision-making, but investors seem unable to distinguish between the relatively lower level of credibility associated with interim reports (caused by the high degree of estimation required to produce them, as well as by the lack of auditing). This apparent lack of sophistication on the part of investors contrasts with the evidence produced by Ball[38] which suggests that they are able to distinguish between movements in levels of reported income arising from operational activity and corresponding movements arising from changes in the accounting methods adopted to measure reported income. In other words, changes in accounting method appear to have no significant effect on investment decisions and share prices. It should be noted, however, that these results contrast somewhat with evidence produced in earlier studies of the same problem.[39]

Thus, although the empirical evidence to date is not completely conclusive, and requires further replication to confirm it, it is not unfair to suggest that (a) published company financial statements (particularly, the income statement) have some significant impact on share prices, indicating that investors do use them for investment decisions; (b) interim income statements appear more likely to be of use to investors than annual statements when formulating predictions of company profitability, dividends and share values; (c) annual income statements appear to fulfil a 'feedback' role for investors, confirming or rejecting their prior expectations built up from earlier sources of information; and (d) investors may be using published accounting information more efficiently and effectively than is commonly supposed.

Degree of use of information

Apart from the fundamental question of whether or not investors make use of published company financial statements, there are the related issues of (a) whether investors are likely to make greater use of one type of information as compared with other available types (the assumption being that some types of accounting information are more relevant than others with reference to investment decisions); (b) whether the use of one type of information leads to more effective investment decisions than does the use of other types; and (c) whether increasing the degree of disclosure of accounting information necessarily leads to more beneficial investment decisions. Here, again, the empirical evidence is scarce, and consequently inconclusive. The major problem is obviously the fact that the need for reliable information[40] for investment decision-making depends on the investor involved[40] (that is, whether he is a private or an institutional investor; whether he is a large investor or a small investor; whether or not he has financial knowledge and expertise; and so on); and the nature of the investment (whether it is risky or riskless; whether it is income or growth orientated). For example, Falk and Ophir[41] found a positive relationship between the degree of use made of reported information and the risk of investment: the higher the risk connected with the type of investment being assessed, the greater the use of reported information. On the other hand, Falk[42] found that the use of financial statements positively correlated with the reading of financial journals by investors, and negatively correlated with a financial education, thus providing inconclusive evidence that the use of financial statements may be greater with investors who are well educated in financial and investment matters.

So far as the degree of disclosure of information is concerned, the following conclusion was arrived at by Singhvi and Desai in relation to empirical evidence of inadequate disclosure:

'. . . inadequate corporate disclosure is likely to widen fluctuations in the market price of a security since investment decisions, in the absence of adequate information, are based on less objective measures. These fluctuations . . . lead to inefficient allocation of capital resources in the economy.'[43]

In other words, inadequate information for investors does not help to reduce the inevitable uncertainty in investment decision-making. It may thereby help to maintain a level of excessive speculation and gambling in company shares, which can create wide fluctuations in share prices, but it does not help the investor to differentiate easily the weak companies from the strong, thus possibly reducing the efficiency of the capital market. Stallman[44] and Dascher and Copeland,[45] in complementary studies into investment behaviour, found evidence to suggest that the provision of additional information to investors did not lead them to place values on their investments any different from those who had not received such additional information. This may well indicate that, although increased disclosure of information can, in the first instance, help to reduce the uncertainty of its user vis-à-vis a company, it is always possible that certain additional disclosures may add nothing to the knowledge of the company to be gained from existing information. Also, apart from the obvious potential problem of disclosing so much information that the relevant issues become obscured, there is the attendant problem of whether the investor is capable of understanding the messages contained in the reported information. There is evidence to suggest that accounting information may be understood only by a very small audience of a high education level because of the technical language involved.[46] The warning of Fertakis is relevant here:

'A hypothesis might be stated with respect to present reporting practices that the greater the amount and diversity of accounting data to which the user is exposed, the greater is the potential for misunderstanding, confusion, and hindrance to rational investment action.'[47]

There have been many studies of the relative usefulness of different types of reportable accounting information to investors. The results cannot lead to generalized conclusions since doubts remain about the experimental design and lack of replication. In addition, there is the problem that alternatives to the present form of financial statements are unknown or unfamiliar to investors, and they may well at present have difficulty in responding to these alternatives. However, there are indications that the present system of reporting is regarded by investors and others as just as useful as alternative systems. For example, Brenner[48] found that income and other financial data, based on current replacement costs rather than on historic costs, was regarded by those surveyed as complementary to rather than an alternative to the existing historic cost data. Dyckman[49] came to the same conclusion with regard to data adjusted for the effects of inflation — participants in his study wishing for price-level adjusted statements as supplements to the traditional historic cost statements. Pankoff and Virgil[50] found that invest-ment analysts appeared to place a significant emphasis on information about the economy in general, and industries in particular, apart from the formally reported accounting information from individual companies.

Thus, it would appear to be wrong to think of useful and relevant information for investment decision-making solely in terms of the existing structure of state-ments of profitability and financial position, and based on the twin principles of historic cost and realization. Although such statements have been published and filed by companies for a great many years, and despite the apparent use of such statements by investors (Greenball[51] has suggested that investors might be better off if they used accounting data, regardless of its limitations, rather than ignored it altogether), there are other forms of information which appear to have greater relevance to the investor, and cases have been argued for them over the years. For example, within the general reporting framework of historic-income statements and balance sheets, the following suggestions or provisions have been made. (Note: it is not intended to discuss each fully at this stage, and further explanations will be given later in the text where relevant.)

(a) Provide a flow of funds statement as a supplement to the existing statements, disclosing sources and uses of new funds of the company concerned. This practice is now generally accepted in the United States[52] and is at the recom-mendation stage in Britain.[53]

(b) Account for the effects on reported data of inflation, particularly the fall in the purchasing power of the monetary measurement unit, which, if not accounted for, leads to accounting data being expressed in terms of a hetero-geneous mixture of money units, thus rendering comparisons difficult. So-called price-level restated supplementary statements have been recommended in the United States[54] and are now advocated for quoted public companies in Britain.[55] However, there is considerable doubt[56] with regard to the relevance and meaning of the adjusted figures to investors and other users, as well as with the stated aim of the requirement:

'It is important that managements and other users of financial accounts should be in a position to appreciate the effects of inflation on the busi-nesses with which they are concerned — for example, the effects on costs, profits, distribution policies, dividend cover, the exercise of borrowing powers, returns on funds and future cash needs.'[57]

(c) Account and report on income and financial position in terms either of current replacement costs for assets[58] or current realizable values.[59] The intention of these alternative proposals is to express company income and shareholders' equity in current valuation terms, thereby abandoning the historic cost/realization principles which severely restrict the reporting of current values of assets and, consequently, ignore income earned by the company but not yet realized at the date of reporting. It is felt by its proponents that this type of information provides much more relevant information to investors and others concerned with the current situation of companies and with income earned by them during the current period.

Beside these amendments to the existing structure of company financial reporting, other suggestions tend to advocate alternative structures. For example, Rayman[60] has advocated the separation of purely objective data from the more subjective value-based data so as to aid the investor when making decisions, the task of predicting being far more difficult when objective and subjective data are mixed, as in the present system of reporting.

Lee[61] and Lawson[62] have similarly advocated the minimization of subjectiveness in accounting measurements by the production of flow of funds statements based on cash movements alone. Such a system is said to concentrate on the one key factor in company activity which is of primary importance to all persons and groups involved or interested in companies — cash. Without cash, companies cannot hope to survive, and likewise, investors' expectations of dividends depend primarily on the availability of cash.

Sorter[63] has also suggested that the traditional form of financial statements has a somewhat limited usefulness and relevance for investors since it either tends to obscure data useful for predictive purposes, or it ignores relevant data because it cannot be measured easily in financial terms. He has therefore proposed that individually significant past events involving a company should be reported so as to provide relevant data for different prediction/decision situations.

The importance of human resources in business activity is obvious. Without an effective and efficient work force and management, no company can hope to survive in the long-term. However, accountants have traditionally avoided valuing and reporting on resources of a non-tangible nature, mainly because of the severe measurement problems involved. Nevertheless, there have been recent advocations[64] for accounting for human resources, particularly from the point of view of incorporating them as assets in the traditional balance sheet. One company, in fact, has produced separate statements for its shareholders which incorporates its human resources.[65] The objectives of such a system of reporting are, in essence, to provide more relevant information for decision-making than at present:

'Broadly the Human Resource Accounting Information System is designed to provide better answers to these kind of questions: What is the quality of profit performance? Are sufficient human capabilities being acquired to achieve the objectives of the enterprise? Are they being developed adequately? To what degree are they being properly maintained? Are these capabilities being properly utilized by the organization?'[66]

One further suggested amendment to the present system of financial reporting is the inclusion of forecast or budgeted statements, particularly relating to company profitability[67] or cash-flow data.[68] The reasoning behind the proposed reporting of predictive data is that, despite its acknowledged subjectiveness, it has significant relevance for investors and other interested persons who are concerned with making decisions vis-à-vis companies and, particularly, with attempting to assess the likely outcomes of the various investment alternatives confronting them. Unfortunately, as Elgers and Clark[69] point out, the debate so far on this issue has mainly concerned the problem of the inherent inaccuracy of forecasted data rather than the fundamental question of the need to supply relevant information to satisfy investors' needs.

Loan Decisions and Company Financial Statements

So far in this chapter, the objectives, uses and users of company financial statements have been discussed mainly within the context of the investor and his decision-making activities. However, there are other categories of potential users who should also be mentioned, although many of their apparent information requirements tend to be similar to those of the shareholder-investor. Indeed, the Trueblood Study Group specifically stated that the information needs of investors and creditors (this would include lenders) are essentially the same:

'Both groups are concerned with the enterprise's ability to generate cash flows to them and with their own ability to predict, compare, and evaluate the amount, timing, and related uncertainty of these future cash flows.'[70]

Thus lenders (and creditors) are assumed to be interested in reported data which will help them to evaluate a company's liability to repay the existing or proposed debt and any interest due thereon. No single factor about the company will aid the lender in this respect, although information relating to its liquidity and cash-flow position is of crucial importance. In addition, profitability and overall financial position data also appear to be of some considerable use to the lender when assessing its financial strengths and weaknesses. The importance of the role of financial statements for this purpose, however, may well be considerably less than the corresponding one for investors.[71]

Other Uses of Company Financial Statements

The other uses of the accounting information contained in the annual financial reports of companies are various. However, they mainly relate to the computation of corporate tax liabilities, government regulation of company activity, and the relatively infrequent but major investment decisions concerning takeovers or mergers of companies.

Taxation

The use of annual reported income data as a basis for computing tax due by companies to central government is well known.[72] In Britain, Section 46(1), Finance Act 1965, states that corporation tax shall be based on the income of companies, income in this context meaning annual reported trading income and other gains. Section 53(1) of the same Act further states that taxable income is to be computed in accordance with the principles of income tax law and practice. In other words, the annually reported income figure for a company is suitably adjusted in a way compatible with tax law so as to produce a further figure of taxable income with which to compute the tax due. The nature of these adjustments is, in many instances, complex,[73] but usually involves ensuring that all taxable revenues received are included in the taxable income figure; and similarly, that all deductible business expenses are deducted from it. However, such a process would be made far more difficult but for the prior measurement, admittedly for reporting purposes, of trading income.

Governmental regulation

Although companies operate within a so-called free-enterprise system, there is, and always has been, a certain amount of regulation and intervention by government in its workings to protect the public interest. This policing operation does, on occasion, involve annually reported accounting information, for the relevant financial statements contain data which are useful to government departments or quasi-governmental bodies concerned with such matters. First, Section 127, Companies Act 1948 (amended by Section 2, Companies Act 1967), requires all companies registered in Britain to file their annual financial statements with the Registrar of Companies. The files of the Registrar are open for inspection to any member of the public for payment of a small fee, and thus the annually reported accounting information of companies is available for public use. Secondly, company financial statements may be used in a more particular way by specific government departments or bodies monitoring company behaviour; for example, by the Monopolies Commission[74] when assessing possible monopoly practices by particular companies or industries; or by the Department of Trade and Industry when examining the case for government aid to vital companies or industries in need of financial support. More generally, governments will use financial statistics, compiled in part from reported accounting information, when determining economic and fiscal policies and strategies. Thirdly, although not specifically set up by government, the City Panel on Takeovers and Mergers,[75] constituted by the Bank of England and other leading financial institutions in Britain, does make use of annual financial statements when monitoring and investigating the propriety of company acquisitions and mergers.[76] In the United States, the Securities and Exchange Commission[77] is the government body which combines the activities of the Registrar of Companies, the Department of Trade and Industry and the City Panel in relation to company reporting.

Lastly in this section, it has already been mentioned that the City Panel is responsible for overseeing company acquisitions and mergers in Britain. It does this by applying the rules and regulations of the *City Code on Takeovers and Mergers,* which has been designed specifically to cause companies to comply with a recognized code of behaviour in such matters. One of the major provisions of the *Code* is the requirement that the acquiring or merging companies should provide an income forecast for their shareholders; that is, for what is usually a twelve-month period, but which may include part of the current accounting period.[78] In this respect, the following quote is significant:

'Any document or advertisement addressed to shareholders containing information, opinions or recommendations from the Board of an offeror or offeree company or its respective advisors shall be treated with the same standards of care as if it were a prospectus within the meaning of the Companies Act 1948. Especial care shall be taken over profit forecasts.'[79]

The forecasts require to be examined and reported on by the auditors or consultant accountants and financial advisors (if any). In this respect, although such forecasts obviously relate to managerial opinions and judgements regarding future business activity, cognisance must also be taken of past activity trends, and consequently reported accounting information (particularly that relating to profitability) must be of potential use. It is also only fair to suggest that decisions leading to potential takeover bids must at some stage or another involve a scrutiny of reported financial results.

The Quality of Company Financial Reports

The previous sections in this chapter have attempted to indicate the main uses to which company financial reports are, or could be, put. Hopefully, they have also indicated the main objectives of these reports. However, so far as reported accounting information is concerned, its overall usefulness, and therefore its potential to be used, depends on certain criteria being satisfied. Some are more obvious than others, and should require little elaboration. However, it will be noticeable that they can be divided into two main categories: those that predominantly relate to the measurement and reporting of the information concerned; and those that relate mainly to the use of it.

Measurement and communication criteria

Undoubtedly, one of the most basic qualities of reported accounting information is that it should be credible. The messages it contains should be capable of being believed by its users. If it is not credible, the probability is that it will not be used. Therefore, to maximize its credibility, the following further criteria are important to the reporting accountants:

(a) The information must be relevant;[80] that is, it must be capable not only of describing the factors it purports to describe as realistically as possible, but must also have the capability of influencing its potential user's behaviour by reducing his uncertainty and aiding him in his decision function.
(b) The information must be material;[81] that is, it must be significant enough in relation to the factors it describes to be classified as relevant to its potential user. In other words, it must not be concerned with trivia.
(c) The information must be fair;[82] that is, it must be measured and reported with as much objectivity and neutrality as possible. It must be based on firm, verifiable evidence (wherever possible), and it must not be such as to tend to benefit a particular user (or group of users) to the relative detriment of others.
(d) The information must be understandable;[83] that is, it must be capable of being understood by its potential users, even allowing for the fact that accounting is an extremely complex language.
(e) The information must be comparable;[84] that is, it must be prepared in such a way as to be capable of being compared realistically with previous or

similar information, remembering particularly that it is designed to aid users to make decisions which, by definition, involve comparisons of alternatives. In this respect, it is also necessary for the information to be prepared with some degree of consistency in methodology.

(f) The information must be timely;[85] that is, it must be prepared and communicated as quickly as possible to ensure that it is not so out of date as to be useless.

These are put forward as the main measurement criteria applicable to company financial reports. There are others, but these criteria appear to be the most significant. They are not given in any particular order of importance, for what *is* important in this respect is the balance achieved; the quality of reported information depends entirely on the circumstances of the company concerned and the nature of the information itself (whether it is, for example, historic or predictive). Relevance and materiality may have to be sacrificed in some measure to obtain a sufficient level of objectivity, or vice versa. Whatever balance is struck, however, will depend in general on the nature of the circumstances, and in particular on the information needs of the users:

'The qualitative characteristics of financial statements, like objectives, should be based largely upon the needs of users of the statements. Information is useless unless it is relevant and material to a user's decision. Information should be as free as possible from any biases of the preparer. In making decisions, users should not only understand the information presented, but also should be able to assess its reliability and compare it with information about alternative opportunities and previous experience. In all cases, information is more useful if it stresses economic substance rather than technical form.'[86]

User criteria

As previously mentioned, the reporting by companies of accounting information which describes aggregate measures of their financial progress and condition is primarily an attempt to aid investors and other potential users in their various decision activities. In this sense, it is a vitally important means of portraying the reality of company activity. It is therefore equally important that its users perceive that reality as accurately as possible if they are not to be misled or misinformed about the financial affairs of the company concerned. If company financial reports are to fulfil a meaningful role in society, they must not convey to their users messages of economic activity which do not reasonably conform to the reality of the situation. However, this is extremely difficult to guard against, for the process of perception is governed by a number of crucial factors:[87]

(a) What people perceive, or are willing to perceive, is determined in part by their needs and personal values. Thus, if company financial reports are not regarded as relevant and useful by a potential user, the probability of their not being used will be high. Perception of a company's financial affairs would therefore not be gained through this medium.

(b) The degree of perception of objects, qualities and relationships depends on a person's capacity to perceive — only so much data can be absorbed at one time, and this, in turn, depends on the skills and experience of the person concerned. This is important in financial reporting since perceptual capacity may vary from one user to the next. There is also the attendant problem of disclosing more and more data in financial reports until a point is reached when additional data may prove to be a positive disadvantage by obscuring the main messages being reported.[88]

(c) As mentioned in (b), perception is in part determined by the prior experience of the person concerned. In this respect, there are two main levels of perception: the level at which perception begins, and the more advanced level at which changes in the condition of the perceived objects, etc., are noted. This distinction has some importance in financial reporting because it must have some part to play in determining the materiality of data for reporting purposes. The problem for accountants, however, is one of trying to assess the ability of potential users to perceive what is material and what is relatively less material.

(d) There is a conditioning effect in perception. People can learn to perceive in a set way through familiarity — that is, as a process of learning. Thus, they can start to perceive what they expect or want to perceive rather than what they should perceive; this gives them security and avoids anxiety. If this happens, then it has implications for financial reporting: investors and others may become used to high levels of income or sound financial positions, and fail to notice changes quickly enough when they start to occur. (This last point is very much connected with that in (c) above.)

(e) Human attitudes, or the readiness to respond in a predetermined manner, underly most of the previous points. Attitudes[89] are formulated usually over long periods of time, and reflect personal values and biases. They create a rigidity of mind which, whilst not being enduring, can lead to preconception and can seriously affect judgements. This is important to any study of financial reporting practices because attitudes are inherent in both the processing and use of accounting information. They can obviously influence the quality and credibility of both processes. It is therefore important that the attitudes and consequential influences are as favourable and fair-minded as possible.

These have been given as some of the more obvious psychological factors affecting company financial reports. They involve several important problem areas for accountants which remain as yet unexplored. They also indicate that the process of producing and presenting financial reports is not merely an exercise in computing and aggregating financial figures.

General or Specific-Purpose Information?

Arguably, the most fundamental point to emerge from any description of the objectives, uses and users of company financial reports is that the information contained in them must be capable of satisfying the needs of its users. However, this relatively uncomplicated point raises one of the most burning issues in accounting today: is the present system of providing a set of reports of a standarized nature for all potential users likely to achieve the objective of satisfying all their information needs? Company legislation has consistently assumed over the years that so-called general-purpose information is likely to do just that. Income statements and balance sheets for a company or group of companies as a whole have been assumed to be sufficient to satisfy the needs of its shareholders, irrespective of their various individual differences (for example, as between private and institutional shareholders). In addition, the separate needs of other potential users have been largely ignored; the assumption presumably being that information for shareholders ought also to be of use to lenders, creditors, government departments, etc. Likewise, it has been assumed that income statements and balance sheets, based on the twin measurement principles of historic cost and realization, have a general relevance and usefulness to a variety of potential users.

The evidence to support the above assumptions is scant; but so, too, is the evidence to contradict them. *A priori* reasoning, however, suggests that the needs of individual users may be better served by presenting specific purpose information: information in a variety of forms suitable for use in a number of separately identifiable decision functions. This has recently been argued by a number of writers,[90] though there have been cases put forward for retaining the general-purpose structure in financial reporting.[91] Meanwhile the latter system continues, and its problems will be examined in greater depth in the following chapters.

Suggested Discussion or Essay Topics

1. If company financial reports are to be used to portray the efficiency as well as the integrity of management, then the traditional form of financial statements will become increasingly inadequate. Discuss.

2. The philosophy of financial reporting should regard the disclosure of accounting information as a matter of economic importance to society as a whole. Discuss.

3. It has been stated that the approach to accounting objectives that assumes a set of unknown users of financial reports has also assumed that information regarding the past profitability and financial position of a company is relevant for the many data needs of these users. Comment and discuss.

4. Share prices reflect investors' expectations of future profitability, and these expectations are determined, at least in part, by investors' perceptions of the future. Comment on the validity of this statement, with particular regard to the role of accounting information in investment decisions.

5. The importance of relating financial accounting information to the needs and requirements of its users (or potential users) is clearly evidenced in the general accounting objective of information utility and its related concept of relevance. Discuss with particular emphasis on the importance of the information user in contemporary accounting thought.

6. No matter how well it is measured, accounting information is, at best, useless and, at worst, positively misleading, unless it is adequately communicated and timeously reported. Discuss.

7. What is meant by the general-purpose approach to company financial reporting?

8. The periodic accounting by a steward to his master is a concept of relevance to fifteenth-century estate management, but not to twentieth-century company activity. Comment and discuss.

9. What are the generally accepted objectives of company management and how do they relate to the objectives of company financial reports?

10. The information contained in annual financial reports is of little use to company management. Discuss the validity of this statement.

11. What is meant by accountability in relation to company financial reports?

12. Economic decisions about companies are made principally by present or potential investors, by creditors, and by managers and employees who invest time and effort. What role has the company financial report to play with regard to these decisions?

13. There is evidence to suggest that reported accounting information influences movements in share prices. Discuss.

14. What sources of information, other than company financial reports, could be said to aid investors and others in their decision activities vis-à-vis companies?

15. Accounting information must be credible. Explain and comment.

16. How much could the degree of risk in investment decision-making affect the degree of use made of company financial reports?

17. Too much accounting information is as bad as too little. Discuss.

18. The past is irrelevant to a decision-maker. Comment on the validity of this statement with regard to the use made of company financial reports.

19. Company financial statements are produced because not to do so would be illegal. They have only a limited use and this concerns the computation of tax liabilities. Discuss.

20. The one basic accounting assumption underlying company financial reports may be stated as that of fairness — fairness to all segments of the business community, determined and measured in the light of the economic and political environment, and the modes of thought and customs of all segments. Discuss.

21. What people perceive is determined partly by their needs, values, skills and experience, and partly by the quality of their information sources. Comment and discuss in relation to company financial reports.

Notes and References

1. G. J. Staubus, *Accounting for Investors*, Scholars Book Co., 1971 reprint, p. 3.

2. e.g. Committee to Prepare a Statement of Basic Accounting Theory, *A Statement of Basic Accounting Theory*, American Accounting Association, 1966, p. 8; H. J. Snavely, 'Accounting Information Criteria', *Accounting Review*, April 1967, pp. 223-32; T. A. Lee, 'Utility and Relevance; the Search for Reliable Accounting Information', *Accounting and Business Research*, Summer 1971, pp. 242-9.

3. e.g. in addition to the references in n. 2 above, see R. J. Chambers, *Accounting Evaluation and Economic Behaviour*, Prentice-Hall, 1966, pp. 141-65; G. J. Staubus, 'Determinants of the Value of Accounting Procedures', *Abacus*, December 1970, pp. 105-19; and R. R. Sterling, *Theory of the Measurement of Enterprise Income*, University of Kansas Press, 1970, pp. 46-50.

4. Committee to Prepare a Statement of Basic Accounting Theory, op. cit., p. 7.

5. G. O. May, 'The Nature of the Financial Accounting Process', *Accounting Review*, July 1943, p. 190.

6. Accounting Objectives Study Group, *Objectives of Financial Statements*, American Institute of Certified Public Accountants, 1973, p. 13.

7. 'Report of the Committee on External Measurement and Reporting', Supplement to the *Accounting Review*, 1973, p. 244.

8. H. B. Rose, 'Disclosure in Company Accounts', *Eaton Paper 1*, 1965, p. 7.

9. B. Carsberg, A. Hope and R. W. Scapens, 'The Objectives of Published Accounting Reports', *Accounting and Business Research*, Summer 1974, p. 171.

10. 'Accountant's Liability to Third Parties', *Statement V8*, Institute of Chartered Accountants in England and Wales, 1965, esp. paragraph 8(b).

11. e.g. D. D. Rae-Smith, 'Protection for Shareholders', *Accountancy*, March 1968, pp. 159-67; and J. L. Kirkpatrick, 'Information for Proprietors and Others', *Accountant's Magazine*, November 1972, pp. 535-9.

12. Arthur Andersen & Co., *Objectives of Financial Statements for Business Enterprises*, Arthur Andersen & Co., 1972, pp. 2-3.

13. Accounting Objectives Study Group, op. cit., p. 25.

14. Rose, 'Disclosure in Company Accounts', loc. cit., pp. 8-13.

15. Accounting Objectives Study Group, op. cit., p. 26.

16. ibid., p. 55.

17. F. D. S. Choi, 'Financial Disclosure in Relation to a Firm's Capital Costs', *Accounting and Business Research,* Autumn 1973, p. 289.

18. Staubus, *Accounting for Investors,* p. 13.

19. ibid., p. 15.

20. Accounting Objectives Study Group, op. cit., p. 20.

21. A. C. Raynor and I. M. D. Little, *Higgledy Piggledy Growth Again,* Blackwell, 1966, pp. 76-81.

22. A. Singh and G. Whittington, *Growth, Profitability and Valuation,* Cambridge University Press, 1968, pp. 133-44.

23. G. Whittington, *The Prediction of Profitability and Other Studies of Company Behaviour,* Cambridge University Press, 1971, pp. 82-104.

24. M. N. Greenball, 'The Predictive-Ability Criterion: Its Relevance in Evaluating Accounting Data', *Abacus,* June 1971, pp. 1-7.

25. K. V. Peasnell, 'The Usefulness of Accounting Information to Investors', *ICRA Occasional Paper 1,* University of Lancaster, 1973, p. 20.

26. There are also indications of a general awareness by accountants of the importance of reported data in investment decision-making – see Carsberg, Hope and Scapens, 'The Objectives of Published Accounting Reports', loc. cit., p. 171.

27. R. Ball and P. Brown, 'An Empirical Evaluation of Accounting Income Numbers', *Journal of Accounting Research,* Autumn 1968, pp. 159-77.

28. ibid., pp. 169-70.

29. ibid., p. 170.

30. ibid., pp. 176-7.

31. G. J. Benston, 'Published Corporate Accounting Data and Stock Prices', *Empirical Research in Accounting: Selected Studies,* 1967, pp. 1-54.

32. ibid., p. 28.

33. W. H. Beaver, 'The Information Content of Annual Earnings Announcements', *Empirical Research in Accounting: Selected Studies,* 1968, pp. 67-92.

34. ibid., p. 84.

35. P. Brown and J. W. Kennelly, 'The Informational Content of Quarterly Earnings: An Extension and Some Further Evidence', *Journal of Business,* July 1972, pp. 403-15.

36. J. E. Kiger, 'An Empirical Investigation of NYSE Volume and Price Reactions to the Announcement of Quarterly Earnings', *Journal of Accounting Research,* Spring 1972, pp. 113-26.

37. R. G. May, 'The Influence of Quarterly Earnings Announcements on Investor Decisions as Reflected in Common Stock Price Changes', *Empirical Research in Accounting: Selected Studies,* 1971, pp. 150-51.

38. R. Ball, 'Changes in Accounting Techniques and Stock Prices', *Empirical Research in Accounting: Selected Studies,* 1972, pp. 1-38.

39. Ball and Brown, 'An Empirical Evaluation of Accounting Income Numbers', loc. cit.

40. See, for example, H. K. Baker and J. A. Haslem, 'Information Needs of Individual Investors', *Journal of Accountancy,* November, 1973, pp. 64-9, and H. Falk and Tsvi Ophir, 'The Effect of Risk on the Use of Financial Statements by Investment Decision-Makers: A Case Study', *Accounting Review,* April 1973, pp. 323-38.

41. ibid., p. 334

42. H. Falk, 'Financial Statements and Personal Characteristics in Investment Decision-Making', *Accounting and Business Research,* Summer 1972, pp. 209-22.

43. S. S. Singhvi and H. B. Desai, 'An Empirical Analysis of the Quality of Corporate Financial Disclosure', *Accounting Review,* January 1971, p. 137.

44. J. C. Stallman, 'Toward Experimental Criteria for Judging Disclosure Improvement', *Empirical Research in Accounting: Selected Studies,* 1969, pp. 29-43.

45. P. E. Dascher and R. M. Copeland, 'Some Further Evidence on "Criteria for Judging Disclosure Improvement" ', *Journal of Accounting Research*, Spring 1971, pp. 32-9.

46. J. E. Smith and N. P. Smith, 'Readability: A Measure of the Performance of the Communication Function of Financial Reporting', *Accounting Review*, July 1971, pp. 552-61; and F. J. Soper and R. D. Dolphin, 'Readability and Corporate Annual Reports', *Accounting Review*, April 1964, pp. 358-62.

47. J. F. Fertakis, 'On Communication, Understanding, and Relevance in Accounting Reporting', *Accounting Review*, October 1969, p. 689.

48. V. Brenner, 'Financial Statement Users' Views of the Desirability of Reporting Current Cost Information', *Journal of Accounting Research*, Autumn 1970, pp. 159-66.

49. T. Dyckman, 'Investment Analysis and General Price-Level Adjustments', *Studies in Accounting Research 1*, American Accounting Association, 1969.

50. L. D. Pankoff and R. L. Virgil, 'Some Preliminary Findings from a Laboratory Experiment on the Usefulness of Financial Accounting Information to Security Analysts', *Empirical Research in Accounting: Selected Studies*, 1970, pp. 1-48.

51. M. N. Greenball, 'Evaluation of the Usefulness to Investors of Different Accounting Estimates of Earnings: A Simulation Approach', *Empirical Research in Accounting: Selected Studies*, 1968, pp. 47-8.

52. As required in Article 11–A, *Regulation S*, Securities and Exchange Commission; and 'Reporting Changes in Financial Position', *Accounting Principles Board Opinion 19*, American Institute of Certified Public Accountants, 1971.

53. Exposure Draft 13, 'Statements of Source and Application of Funds', *Accountant's Magazine*, May 1974, pp. 169-71.

54. 'Reporting the Financial Effects of Price-Level Changes', *Accounting Research Study 6*, American Institute of Certified Public Accountants, 1963.

55. 'Accounting for Changes in the Purchasing Power of Money', *Provisional Statement of Standard Accounting Practice 7*, 1974.

56. e.g. R. S. Gynther, 'Why Use General Purchasing Power?', *Accounting and Business Research*, Spring 1974, pp. 141-57; and T. A. Lee, *Income and Value Measurement: Theory and Practice*, Nelson, 1974, pp. 125-30.

57. *Provisional Statement of Standard Accounting Practice 7*, p. 2.

58. See, e.g., E. O. Edwards and P. W. Bell, *The Theory and Measurement of Business Income*, University of California Press, 1961; and L. Resvine, *Replacement Cost Accounting*, Prentice-Hall, 1973.

59. e.g. see R. J. Chambers, *Accounting Evaluation and Economic Behaviour*, Prentice-Hall, 1966; and R. R. Sterling, *Theory of the Measurement of Enterprise Income*, University of Kansas Press, 1970.

60. R. A. Rayman, 'Is Conventional Accounting Obsolete?', *Accountancy*, June 1970, pp. 422-9.

61. T. A. Lee, 'A Case for Cash Flow Reporting', *Journal of Business Finance*, Summer 1972. pp. 27-36.

62. G. Lawson, 'Cash-flow Accounting', *Accountant*, 28 October 1971, pp. 386-9.

63. G. H. Sorter, 'An "Events" Approach to Basic Accounting Theory', *Accounting Review*, January 1969, pp. 12-19.

64. See, for example, R. L. Brummet, E. G. Flamholtz and W. C. Pyle, 'Human Resource Measurement – A Challenge for Accountants', *Accounting Review*, April 1968, pp. 217-28; and B. Lev and A. Schwartz, 'On the Use of the Concept of Human Capital in Financial Statements', *Accounting Review*, January 1971, pp. 103-12.

65. See the annual reports of the R. G. Barry Corporation, Columbus, Ohio.

66. Taken from the 1969 annual report of the R. G. Barry Corporation.

67. e.g. see W. W. Cooper, N. Dupuch and T. F. Keller, 'Budgetary Disclosures and Other Suggestions for Improving Accounting Reports', *Accounting Review*, October 1968, pp. 640-48; and C. R. Tomkins, 'The Development of Relevant Published Accounting Reports', *Accountancy*, November 1969, pp. 815-20.

68. Lee, 'A Case for Cash Flow Reporting', loc. cit.; and Lawson, 'Cash-flow Accounting', loc. cit.

69. P. Elgers and J. J. Clark, 'Inclusion of Budgets in Financial Reports: Investor Needs *v.* Management Disclosure', *Accounting and Business Research,* Winter 1972, pp. 53-61.

70. Accounting Objectives Study Group, op. cit., p. 20.

71. See Carsberg, Hope and Scapens, 'The Objectives of Published Accounting Reports', loc. cit., pp. 171-2.

72. Although this appears to be relatively less important than the previously mentioned objectives of financial reports, see ibid.

73. See, e.g. T. D. Lynch, *Direct Taxation in the United Kingdom,* Institute of Chartered Accountants of Scotland, 1965, pp. 54-72.

74. See, e.g., Alister Sutherland, *The Monopolies Commission in Action,* Cambridge University Press, 1969.

75. For an account of its establishment, see Edward Stamp and C. Marley, *Accounting Principles and the City Code: the Case for Reform,* Butterworth, 1970, pp. 3-62.

76. See I. J. Fraser, 'Accountancy and the Merger Movement', *Accountant's Magazine,* August 1971, pp. 405-10.

77. A. Barr, 'The United States Securities and Exchange Commission and the Accounting Profession', *Accountant's Magazine,* April 1969, pp. 209-15.

78. The City Code on Take-overs and Mergers, originally published 1968 (revised several times since); also in *Admission of Securities to Listing,* Stock Exchange, 1973, pp. 71-88.

79. City Code, op. cit., 'General Principles', para. 12.

80. See references in n. 3; and Accounting Objectives Study Group, op. cit., p. 57.

81. For a summary of this concept, see T. A. Lee, 'Materiality – The Elusive Concept', *Singapore Accountant,* 1971, pp. 19-25; see also Accounting Objectives Study Group, op. cit., p. 57.

82. See, e.g., L. Spacek, *A Search for Fairness in Financial Reporting to the Public,* Arthur Andersen & Co., 1969; and Andersen and Co., *The Objectives of Financial Statements* pp. 7-8.

83. Staubus, 'Determinants of the Value of Accounting Procedures', loc. cit., p. 118; see also Accounting Objectives Study Group, op. cit., p. 60.

84. See, e.g., T. A. Lee, 'Accounting Standards and Effective Financial Reporting: A Review in Principle', *Accountant's Magazine,* January and February 1975, pp. 25-30 and 73-81, passim; see also Accounting Objectives Study Group, op. cit., pp. 59-60.

85. See P. Grady, Inventory of Generally Accepted Accounting Principles for Business Enterprises', *Accounting Research Study 7,* American Institute of Certified Public Accountants, 1965, p. 41.

86. Accounting Objectives Study Group, op. cit., p. 60.

87. For a general introduction to this topic, see Report of the Committee on the Behavioural Science Content of the Accounting Curriculum, *Behavioural Science Content of the Accounting Curriculum,* American Accounting Association, 1971, pp. 249-52; E. R. Hilgard and R. C. Atkinson, *Introduction to Psychology,* Harcourt, Brace & World, 1967, pp. 187-268; and P. B. Warr and C. Knapper, *The Perception of People and Events,* Wiley, 1968, pp. 1-51.

88. See Fertakis, 'On Communication Understanding and Relevance in Accounting Reporting', loc. cit.

89. For a general introduction to this topic, see Report of the Committee on the Behavioural Science Content of the Accounting Curriculum, op. cit., pp. 257-60; Hilgard and Atkinson, *Introduction to Psychology,* p. 583-600; and M. Jahoda and N. Warren, *Attitudes,* Penguin Books, 1966, pp. 13-39.

90. e.g. R. S. Gynther, 'Accounting for Changing Prices', *Chartered Accountant in Australia,* December 1971, pp. 12-23; and E. Stamp, 'R. J. Chambers: Quo Vadis et Cui Bono?', *Chartered Accountant in Australia,* August 1972, pp. 10-12.

91. R. J. Chambers, 'Quo Vado?', *Chartered Accountant in Australia,* August 1972, pp. 13-15.

Selected Bibliography for Chapter 4

NOTE: It has been particularly difficult to select a representative list of suitable additional readings for this chapter. This is mainly because of the relatively undeveloped nature of this aspect of company financial reporting. However, the following are suggested as providing useful additional material; writings on more detailed points can be found in the references to the text.

Accounting Objectives Study Group, *Objectives of Financial Statements,* American Institute of Certified Public Accountants, 1973. Another very detailed study and review of the uses and users of company financial statements; also it looks at statements of non-profit making organizations.

Arthur Andersen and Co., *Objectives of Financial Statements for Business Enterprises,* Arthur Andersen and Co., 1972. A detailed study and discussion of company financial statements; their objectives and their users.

H. K. Baker and J. A. Haslem, 'Information Needs of Individual Investors', *Journal of Accountancy,* November 1973, pp. 64-9. A recent attempt to identify the information requirements of investors.

B. Carsberg, A. Hope and R. W. Scapens, 'The Objectives of Published Accounting Reports', *Accounting and Business Research,* Summer 1974, pp. 162-73. A report of surveys to establish opinions of accountants as to financial reporting objectives.

Committee to Prepare a Statement of Basic Accounting Theory, *A Statement of Basic Accounting Theory,* American Accounting Association, 1966, pp. 4-30. A description of the main criterion underlying the measurement and communication of accounting information, and the importance of the information user in theory and practice.

T. A. Lee, 'Utility and Relevance: the Search for Reliable Accounting Information', *Accounting and Business Research,* Summer, 1971, pp. 242-9. The importance of identifying the user of accounting information and producing financial statements relevant to his needs.

K. V. Peasnell, 'The Usefulness of Accounting Information to Investors', *ICRA Occasional Paper 1,* University of Lancaster, 1973. A detailed review of published accounting information with particular reference to its predictive ability.

H. B. Rose, 'Disclosure in Company Accounts', *Eaton Paper 1,* 1965, pp. 7-19. A general discussion of the main reasons for companies disclosing accounting information about their financial affairs.

G. J. Staubus, *Accounting for Investors,* Scholars Book Co., 1971 reprint, pp. 1-16. A study of the role of accounting information in investment decision-making.

D. E. Stone, 'The Objective of Financial Reporting in the Annual Report', *Accounting Review,* April 1967, pp. 331-7. A statement of the need to establish financial reporting objectives.

5 The Production of Company Financial Reports

Introduction

'The proper nature of accounting is a difficult question, and difficult questions do not admit easy answers — or perhaps any answers. It is for that reason wholly proper to go on asking them. All we can reasonably hope for is the clarification of minds. . . . It is perhaps the weakness of practical men and women . . . that they tend to shy away from abstract thought. . . . We can all recognize the pragmatist voice that seduces us, in the hurly-burly of everyday life, from taking the trouble of thinking things out.'[1]

These words of Morison spotlight a major feature of company financial reporting — that of identifying and recognizing that the production of reportable financial information is not a straightforward matter of observing and collating suitable data and presenting it in suitable statements for the potential user. Financial accounting is an extremely complex function and contains many significant problems. It is vital, therefore, for the producers and users of company financial reports to understand fully the nature of these problems (if only in general terms) so as to recognize that accounting information is not capable of being described in terms of accuracy and correctness.

The aggregate accounting data contained in financial statements can be regarded as no more than an expert impression or portrayal of aggregate company activity. As with any 'artistic' picture, its message depends on the techniques adopted to produce it; the perceptions, attitudes and skills of its producer; and the perceptions, attitudes and skills of its user. The aim of this chapter is to provide the reader with an outline of the process of producing company financial reports as they are presently constituted, thereby to give a necessary background to the criticisms and solutions which have been advocated in connection with them. The discussion, as previously mentioned, will centre on the information contained in the annual financial statements.

Producing Company Financial Reports

Before proceeding to the detail of the problems affecting the accounting function, it is useful to describe briefly the process undertaken to produce annual financial reports. The first point to make is that the primary responsibility for producing them lies, at least in Britain, with company management — that is, with the elected board of directors. This duty is laid down in Section 148, Companies Act 1948 (quoted on page 37). Directors are responsible for producing annually the required income statement and balance sheet with the supporting notes and explanations.

The auditors are not, as might be supposed, charged with this primary responsibility. Their job is to verify and report on the way in which the reported information has been measured and disclosed, and their role, as such, is a supporting one to that of the directors. Nevertheless, the auditor may be involved in preparing financial statements without having the primary responsibility for them. This occurs in situations, particularly with small private companies, where a company does not have employee accountants, and the auditor is given the job of both preparing and auditing the statements. The task of preparing the accounting information, however, is a totally separate function from that of auditing. In other words, the auditor in these cases has to wear two hats: one as producer and one as verifier. Whatever the circumstances, the directors of the company remain ultimately responsible to the shareholders for the financial statements.

The principal activity in producing the annual financial reports centres on the preparation and presentation of the income statement and balance sheet of the company. If it is a holding company, this will also involve similar tasks with regard to the relevant consolidated financial statements. In addition, the company may also publish an annual funds statement. The production of these statements is a complex affair, and much of the work takes place throughout the company's financial year on a day-to-day basis. What follows is therefore only a brief description of the various stages involved.[2] It assumes the traditional and existing system of annual financial reporting.

Data Processing

Every company is legally required in Britain to keep adequate and reliable accounting records from which annual financial statements can be prepared (Section 147, Companies Act 1948). These records, because of their nature and contents, are maintained on a day-to-day basis, and contain details of the daily transactions and activities of the company, most of which are expressed in monetary terms. This is the function of processing accounting data, and its objective is *inter alia* to gather together the data necessary to produce the required information on profitability and financial position.

The Nature of Data Processing

Data processing (or book-keeping as it is more normally termed) is the most objective and potentially accurate part of the entire process of producing company financial reports. It can, of course, contain errors, and there can be fraudulent manipulation of records to cover up theft or embezzlement. But, given a strong system of internal control,[3] with adequate checks and counter-checks and a proper division of employee duties and responsibilities, data processing is a relatively straightforward activity. Transactions and activities capable of being measured and accounted for are observed and made the subject of data processing. This will include the buying and selling of goods and services, the manufacture of goods (where relevant), the administration of the business, and so on. The processing can either be handled manually, by machine, or by computer, or, most probably, by a combination of these systems.

Data Collection

The observed transactions or activities are documented in a standard form (for example, as invoices, statements, orders, wages sheets, stock cards, etc.), and these documents are filed until periodically recorded in permanent records. These records may be books and ledgers, machine cards or computer printouts, depending on the system operated. The recording can be undertaken daily, weekly or monthly, and in all cases will be completed following the generally accepted rules of double-entry book-keeping.[4] Data necessary for producing the required financial statements are therefore collated and aggregated ready for the following process of putting it in a form in which information on company income and financial position can be reported. It should be noted at this point that the data concerned are being reduced to manageable proportions and are expressed in terms of the monetary values which occurred at the time of the transactions and activities — in other words, this is the basis for the familiar historic cost reporting system so widely practised throughout the history of companies.

Information Processing

Whereas data processing is a relatively factual and routine function of accounting, the next stage of information processing can be extremely complex and subjective.

Information processing and realization

The primary aim is to put the recorded accounting data into a series of informational propositions which articulate with one another to form the annual financial statements. The information is traditionally based on the original values of the recorded transactions — the so-called historic cost principle, in which past sales revenues are matched against their related historic costs to produce a net surplus termed accounting income — and the remaining unallocated historic costs are carried forward in the balance sheet to be offset eventually against appropriate sales revenues in the future.

The main measurement principle adopted in this process is that of realization,[5] now referred to in British practice as the concept of prudence:

'Revenue and profits are not anticipated, but are recognized by inclusion in the profit and loss account only when realized in the form either of cash or of other assets the ultimate cash realization of which can be assessed with reasonable certainty; provision is made for all known liabilities (expenses and losses) whether the amount of these is known with certainty or is a best estimate in the light of the information available.'[6]

In other words, traditional and existing accounting practice generally follows the pattern that asset value increases and therefore positive income elements are not to be accounted and reported on until such time as they have been realized by sale of the assets concerned. On the other hand, asset value decreases (negative income elements or losses) are required to be accounted and reported on as soon as they can be recognized, even if this is prior to realization.

The overall result of this practice in income measurement and asset valuation is that the information processing function is concerned mainly with reporting income which has been realized during the defined period, irrespective of when it accrued. Thus reported income of the period is a heterogeneous mixture of income elements accruing in previous periods and realized in the current one, together with elements earned and realized during the current period. Balance sheet asset values are, as a consequence, expressed largely in historic cost terms, with the possible exception of cash and debtors. The balance sheet does not therefore usually reflect all the current values of the company's reported assets. On the other hand, if an asset's value falls below its original cost, the prudence concept dictates that provision be made for the unrealized loss by reducing the cost to its current value. This is particularly followed in stock valuations with the traditional accounting rule of value at the lower of cost or market value.

The system of processing accounting information using the twin historic cost-realization principles is the generally accepted one in operation today. It is based on the convention of conservatism — that is, when measuring company profitability and valuing company assets, both for purposes of financial reporting, reasonable caution should be exercised by the accountant so as not to account for income which may not ultimately be realized.[7] In other words, it is a sophisticated version of the old adage of not counting chickens before they are hatched. However, the problem adhering to the prudence concept is not the only one associated with information processing.

It has to be recognized that, despite the business activity of a company being a continuous affair, financial reporting of that activity must be divided into defined periods. This is done to provide shareholders and other interested parties with regular financial statements describing the financial progress of the company during the periods concerned. As Moonitz has commented:

'If economic activity occurs during specifiable periods of time, then accounting must be continuously concerned with the recognition and allocation of events. The problem of recognition and allocation is made more difficult because the "events" often take longer to work themselves out than the reporting periods customarily in vogue. The results of operations for relatively short periods of time are tentative whenever allocations between past, present, and future periods are required.'[8]

In other words, during a defined financial period, certain of the transactions and activities completed during it will have commenced during previous periods, and certain of the transactions and activities commencing in it will be completed in following periods. The problem for the accountant is therefore one of allocating accounting data of each period in such a way that it properly relates to the events which took place during each period.

The allocation process

Examples of the process of allocation are numerous. For example, not all goods bought or manufactured during a period are also sold during it. Thus a company normally has a stock of finished goods and/or semi-processed goods and/or raw materials on hand at the end of each financial period, and this has to be physically counted or measured and its relevant historic cost to date carried forward as unsold stock in the balance sheet, and eliminated (in the income statement) from the computation of income realized during the period on goods sold. Similarly, a company may purchase a fixed asset such as a motor vehicle with a limited useful life. At the end of each financial period, the accountant must measure that proportion of its original cost which has expired during this period due to use and treat it as depreciation when calculating the period's income. Related allocation problems, caused by incomplete transactions, result at the end of each reporting period in computing figures for debtors (sales made during the period for which cash has not yet been received) and creditors (purchases made during the period for which payment has not yet been made).

The allocation problem involves decisions on whether expenditure of a defined period relates wholly to that period or whether it relates in part to following periods owing to any unexpired usefulness in the services it provides. For example, replacements of major parts of plant and machinery may be regarded as repairs, and consequently written off in total against income of the period in which they were incurred; or they may be regarded partly as capital expenditure and treated as a fixed asset to be depreciated over its useful life. The same can be said of expenditure incurred on research and development or advertising. The problem is whether its service potential has expired completely during the period in which it was incurred or whether its usefulness is more long-term, thereby justifying an allocation in a similar manner to the depreciation of fixed assets.

Subjective judgement

The above examples are typical of the allocation problems facing the accountant when he processes data for reporting purposes. A great many involve subjective (albeit expert) judgements from persons such as engineers, chemists and production managers: for example, judgements on what is the useful life of a fixed asset for depreciation purposes; how much is in stock when production is a continuous process and flowing through the factory at speed; and how long-term are the benefits from a development programme or an advertising campaign. These judgements have to be made to allocate the recorded accounting data in such a way that it properly reflects the profitability and financial position of the company for a defined period.

However, judgements can vary, and different judgements can produce different income and financial position figures derived from the same data and economic events. Potentially, therefore, the financial affairs and results of a company could be reported in a variety of ways, each depending on the particular allocation judgements arrived at.

The valuation problem

The potential flexibility in information processing is added to by the further crucial function of valuation. The basic accounting data recorded throughout the accounting period are, as previously mentioned, stated in terms of their original values — that is, the actual revenues and costs which were transacted. However, these historic values require either to be allocated to relevant reporting periods (for reasons already discussed) or amended in light of existing circumstances which make them unsuitable for reporting purposes.

The valuation problems associated with accounting allocation are most serious in relation to fixed assets and stock. With fixed assets, the problem is one of deciding how much of the undepreciated original cost has expired during the period owing to use, and how much represents unexpired service potential to be used in following periods. Much obviously depends on the initial estimate of each asset's useful life and the subsequent estimate of its relative usefulness in each period of that life. But a great deal also depends on the method of depreciation applied to the asset in accordance with that earlier judgement. There are several methods available,[9] each producing different periodic allocations of cost and therefore differing income statement and balance sheet figures. The company accountant has to decide which method appears most suitable in the circumstances. Other accountants, dealing with the same situation, could well decide to use other methods.

The valuation of stock and work in progress is yet another substantial problem area. Once stocks of raw materials and semi-processed and finished goods have been identified and physically counted at the end of the accounting period, there is the further process of placing a value on the total to represent its aggregate cost at that point. As with depreciation, this is a complex task which normally involves identifying past costs incurred in getting the stock to its existing state. However, there are many methods of computing such a cost,[10] each capable of producing a different aggregate value for reporting purposes. There is also the problem of placing possibly subjective valuations on items of stock whose current value is less than their historic cost (thereby implementing the realization or prudence concept). Although these values may be determined by managerial experts or valuators, there is obviously potential for variation in the estimates, given that no value is certain until it is fully realized in cash.

Debtors, too, present valuation problems involving subjective judgements owing to the inevitable necessity to reduce the recorded values of certain debts when it is evident or possible that the amounts due will not be fully recovered. Very often, estimates of the irrecoverable sums have to be made long before the position can be accurately determined.

Flexibility in accounting

The above paragraphs have attempted to give the reader some idea of the so-called flexibility problems in financial reporting. It is one which has given accountants increasing concern over the years.[11] Chambers, for example, when coming to the conservative conclusion that there are possibly more than one million different profit figures representative of the same economic events, summarized the issue:

> 'A million sets of mutually exclusive rules, each giving a true and fair view of a company's state of affairs and its profits! This is absurd. Where there are so many possible rules there are in effect no rules, and where there are no rules there can be no correspondence, no general comprehensibility, no language – a set of signs, maybe, but no language. It is as if there were a million people with different footrules, or a million motorists with different road rules. Reason and order are deposed and chaos is enthroned in their place.'[12]

If somewhat exaggerated, this statement highlights a major problem facing accountants faced with the task of producing annual financial statements – which accounting practices are the most suitable in the circumstances, and how can subjective judgements be minimized so as to produce reliable accounting information?

Although in the early days of financial reporting, little formal guidance existed to help accountants, the position nowadays is relatively better.[13] In Britain, the *Statements of Standard Accounting Practice* of the main professional accountancy bodies are intended to specify to practitioners the particular accounting methods which should be adopted in defined areas of accounting. These *Statements* are an attempt to narrow the areas of choice and difference in accounting, and thereby to create greater uniformity. A number of *Statements* have been produced to date, and several more are in the process of preparation. Generally speaking, they tend to cover problem areas common to most companies; to prescribe a particular treatment; and to allow a certain amount of freedom for companies where there are reasonable grounds for departing from the standard practice advocated. Accountants responsible for the production of the relevant accounting information must ensure, however, that prescribed standards are adhered to by their companies when reporting to shareholders. If there is a departure from such a standard, then this must be fully disclosed in the financial statement concerned. In addition:

'The accounting policies . . . followed for dealing with items which are judged material or critical in determining profit or loss for the year and in stating the financial position should be disclosed by way of note to the accounts. The explanations should be clear, fair, and as brief as possible.'[14]

The need for consistency

Therefore the information process involving the allocating of accounting data between defined periods, the amendment of original valuations and the application of certain prescribed accounting methods, is a function which also involves a great deal of expertise, subjective judgement and explanatory disclosure. It is also a process where the methodology adopted must be implemented consistently if it is to produce information comparable from one period to the next. Unless the methods adopted in producing the reporting information are the same from period to period, it is conceivable that figures reflecting company profitability and financial position could increase or decrease from one period to the next, apparently portraying changes in operational activities of the company, but, in fact, resulting from the use of different accounting methods. For example, by changing the depreciation policy or method of valuing stock, inter-period income and financial position figures would change when company activity had remained unchanged. As Moonitz has stated:

'The procedures used in accounting for a given entity should be appropriate for the measurement of its position and its activities and should be followed consistently from period to period.'[15]

However, as Stamp warns,[16] consistency is a tool and not an immutable principle. It is essential for a proper comparison of information between periods, but the information processor must change his methods of accounting when the circumstances of the company change materially enough to warrant it. In these cases, the change and its effect on the information concerned should be adequately disclosed.

Aggregation of information

Once the company accountant has processed the recorded data into a form suitable for preparing the annual financial statements, he may have two further problems. First, the company may have offices or branches overseas and therefore be receiving financial data relating to their operating activities. This data will require to be incorporated into that of the 'home' country, and this will probably involve the complex process of currency translation so as to present reportable information in the same currency terms.[17] Secondly, the company may also have associated and subsidiary companies, and their recorded data will need to be suitably consolidated with that of the holding company. In the case of associated companies (defined in Britain as a partner in a joint venture or an investment of not less than 20 per cent in voting equity capital), the investing company is required to incorporate into its income statement and balance sheet its share of the associated company's distributable income as well as its share of the associated company's retained income since the date of the investment.[18] With subsidiary companies, the situation is more complex, and the annual financial results of the holding company and its subsidiaries are usually required to be consolidated into one set of financial statements, after making suitable adjustments for minority interests, inter-company indebtedness, etc.[19] The incorporation of such data into the investing company's financial statements brings with it the problems of timing (that is, not only obtaining the data in time for inclusion, but also ensuring that it covers a financial period corresponding with that of the investing company) and judgement (particularly regarded decisions on the materiality and usefulness of including such data; with certain subsidiary or associated companies it may be immaterial or misleading to incorporate it, in which case it is permissible to omit it).

Therefore, once the company's data has been processed, and once the corresponding data from associated and subsidiary companies has been received, the final stage of producing the annual financial statements can be undertaken. This concerns the preparation and presentation of the published financial report.

Communicating the Processed Information

When looking at the purpose of accounting from the standpoint of communicating information, the following has been offered as a reasonable statement:

> 'The purpose of accounting is to communicate economic messages as the results of business decisions and events, in so far as they can be expressed in terms of quantifiable financial data, in such a way as to achieve maximum understanding by the user and correspondence of the message with economic reality.'[20]

The communication process in financial accounting is therefore concerned essentially with transmitting messages about the financial progress and position of a company to its external interests. The medium linking processor and user is, in general, the financial report, and, in particular, the financial statements. In this way, shareholders and other interested persons receive information about the company and thereby indirectly perceive its financial condition and investment potential. It is vital for these perceptions to correspond with the reality of the situation being reported. As Chambers has succinctly put it:

> 'The efficiency of communication is the capacity of the signals received to evoke in the receiver the same responses as would direct experience of the events which are the subject of the communication.'[21]

Thus, company management has a major problem on its hands once the reportable accounting data have been suitably processed and aggregated. The problem is one of presenting it in the form of a financial report in such a way that it adequately compensates for the inability of its users to perceive directly the economic activity and events of the company to which it relates. In the United Kingdom, the main channels of communication are legally prescribed as the income statement and balance sheet (for the company and its subsidiaries, if any), together with the reports of the directors and auditors. However, this is not simply a matter of preparing these reports in a mechanical and routine fashion. There are other factors to be considered.

Which data to be reported?

The financial accounting process produces, on a continuous basis, a great deal of data which are capable of being reported to shareholders and others. Consequently, because of its volume and range, management obviously has to select that which meets the needs of its users best. The needs of users, however, remain a somewhat indeterminate factor in financial reporting at the present time. There are indications that reported income figures are of use in investment decisions;[22] and, as mentioned in the previous chapter, there is evidence that income numbers do influence share price movement.[23] Further, it can be reasonably assumed and argued that certain data appear of considerable use to particular users: for example, liquidity data contain information of apparent use to lenders and creditors. Nevertheless, management is still very much left on its own with regard to the selection of useful and relevant reportable information, but with two important exceptions in Britain.

First, Schedule 2, Companies Act 1967, contains the current minimum disclosure requirements for annually reported financial statements (this specifies, in detail, items of financial information which must be disclosed, where appropriate, in the income statement, balance sheet and directors' report). Secondly, the *Statements of Standard Accounting Practice* of the major professional accountancy bodies provide for the disclosure of explanations of the main accounting practices adopted by companies when processing reportable information.

Despite these guidelines, there remain significant judgements to be made by management not only with regard to decisions concerning which accounting numbers to report, but also with regard to the nature and extent of any supporting explanations and comments on these figures. Accountants would generally follow the proposition of Moonitz that:

'Accounting reports should disclose that which is necessary to make them not misleading.'[24]

But few could with certainty specify exactly what should be disclosed to prevent misleading reports. As the complex nature of the accounting environment changes over time, so too do user needs. In fact, the problem of delineating the boundaries of accounting disclosure has been a vexed one for several years:[25] for example, the extent to which reported accounting numbers should be supported by explanations in footnotes; and the nature and extent of supplementary financial data which should be supplied with the legally required financial statements.[26] What company management has to take care over, therefore, is the identification of matters which can and should be reported to shareholders and other interested persons to allow them to make meaningful decisions. The rider to this general principle should not be ignored: that is, the disclosure of financial information should not be detrimental to the company concerned (certain disclosures may be harmful if they reveal data of use to a competitor in the field). The overall emphasis should nevertheless be to disclose sufficient information to satisfy the needs of its users.

Communicating accounting information is not just a matter of deciding which data to disclose in the relevant reports. There is the related problem of presenting it with a suitable wording. As Jordan has pointed out,[27] there can be no communication without understanding, and understanding depends on the information concerned both receiving the attention of its intended users and employing a language which is comprehensible and not subject to ambiguity, etc. In other words, the reported financial statements must be presented in such a way that the user will give his attention to them in a reasonable way; and their information content must be given in terms which are understandable.

Attention to financial reports can be gained by sensible presentation and layout of the information, particularly with regard to the positioning and summarizing of data. Material information must not be placed in such a position that it is hard to find in the report, nor must it be summarized to such an extent that it creates more questions than answers for its user. On the other hand, it must be remembered that there is a limit to how much data can be absorbed and used by the user, and that the advice of Hendriksen is appropriate in this respect:

'Because of the limitations of human spans of attention and comprehension, accounting data must be summarized to be meaningful and useful. The choice of how much information to present and the selection of what items to list separately are dependent on the objectives of the reports and on the materiality of the items. Brevity is a desirable goal in financial reports, but appropriate disclosure of detailed information should take precedence if it is necessary to make the reports significant for decision-making.'[28]

Understanding reported financial information is a matter of considerable concern to accountants, largely because accounting involves a highly complex and sophisticated technical language capable of not being understood by non-accountants — or worse, of being mistakenly understood. The problem, as stressed by Bedford,[29] is that the accounting terms used may not have a common meaning to the processor and user alike, and may, indeed, not have a stable meaning to accountants (terms can vary in meaning when used in different circumstances). For example, the term 'depreciation' may represent an allocation of fixed asset cost to an accountant but a fall in the value of a fixed asset to a non-accountant. Thus, company management must be extremely careful, when presenting accounting information in report form, to use terms which are likely to be generally understood. This, however, would appear to be an extremely difficult task, as when Smith and Smith concluded from an examination of the footnotes to certain annual financial statements that 'the readability level of the financial statement notes is restrictive'.[30] Their statement was arrived at from an analysis of the readability of the accounting and business terms used in explaining data in annual financial statements, paying particular attention to ease of comprehension. The need for clear communication only serves to reinforce the difficulties involved in the function of reporting accounting information once it has been formally processed. Yet it is the purpose of that function to communicate relevant information to potential users, and there can be no effective communication unless there is an understanding of the accounting messages received.

The adage of old news being no news is pertinent to the function of company financial reporting because, particularly with annual financial statements, the information is mainly historical. Therefore it is essential for it to be communicated as soon as possible after the end of the accounting period if its users are to obtain any benefit from it. Indeed, the need to report accounting information timeously has been acknowledged by one writer[31] as an essential part of accounting theory and practice.

Unfortunately, the processing of accounting data can be a time-consuming activity, even when there is an efficient system of data collection. For example, management may have to count certain assets physically to obtain relevant data for incorporation in financial statements (as with stock and work in progress, or stores of tools and expendable equipment). It also has to adjust and value certain items of data to put them in reportable form (as with debtors, creditors, depreciable fixed assets, and stock and work in progress). This takes time and often cannot be undertaken until the end of the accounting period concerned. In addition, annual financial reports are normally required to be audited, and this particular process is also time-consuming, though it may be alleviated somewhat by a considerable amount of the routine audit verification work being conducted throughout the accounting period.[32] The overall result, however, is that the annual financial report of a company is often inevitably delayed. Shareholders and other interested users therefore usually find that the information being communicated is becoming rapidly outdated not only because of its inherent nature, but also because of inevitable delays owing to its measurement and audit. This mainly affects annual reports, occurs to a lesser extent with interim reports, but should not apply to forecast data because these, by definition, should not be dated. The delay in annual reporting is evidenced in data produced by the Institute of Chartered Accountants in England and Wales[33] — during the last year or so, the average time between year-end and reporting date for 300 of the largest companies in the United Kingdom has been 120 days. Very few companies can report within 60 days but, on the other hand, equally few report more than 200 days after the year-end.

The Audit of Communicable Accounting Information[34]

Certainly in the United Kingdom, and also in many other developed countries, company management must ensure that a suitably qualified accountant or firm of accountants has verified and reported on the quality of the reported information. In Britain, this is legally required for annual financial reports to shareholders; and is also required for prospectus and takeover and merger accounting reports. It does not apply at present to interim financial reports. As this text is mainly concerned with annual reports, the audit will be explained in that context.

The purpose of the audit

In Britain, the board of directors of a company is legally responsible for producing the annual financial statements described in various parts of the text. As we have seen, the appointment of the auditor is intended to provide a measure of protection to company shareholders who are not normally in a position to verify the quality of the information personally.

The Companies Acts 1948 and 1967 require the auditor to give an opinion to the shareholders on the truth and fairness of the income statement and balance sheet. Although not defined by the Acts, this has been interpreted[35] as meaning an opinion on the correspondence of the information to the economic activity it purports to describe, and on the objectivity which has been exercised by management when processing it. In other words, the major objective is to ensure that shareholders are presented with credible information which they can use with a reasonable assurance that it has been prepared honestly and with due care. In this respect, it is essential to verify that the accounting process has complied with any legal and professional regulations concerning the measurement and disclosure of accounting information.

Company audits are at present legally intended only for shareholders. This is despite the fact that annual financial statements of companies are available for use by any member of the public who cares to inspect the files kept by the Registrar of Companies. To date, courts have refused to allow damages to injured persons other than shareholders.[36] (Injured, in this sense, means financial disadvantages caused through use of the reported information — for example, because of payment of dividends out of reported income which has been inadequately measured, thereby causing financial hardship or disaster to the company concerned.)[37] There has been considerable debate on this point,[38] but so far the legal decisions, and the attitude of the professional accountancy bodies, have been that annual financial statements are intended only for company shareholders; third parties who make use of them, and are misled by them because of inadequate information, are not regarded as entitled to sue the directors or the company for damages; and, indeed, shareholders can only sue for damages as a body, and only if injury has arisen out of inadequate stewardship on the part of the directors. It appears that injury to a single shareholder arising out of use of inadequate information for investment decision-making would not be acceptable for court action.[39] (The above comments are made in the light of existing case law and legal advice.)

The conduct of the audit

The first stage of the audit is one of familiarization: the auditor acquires the general background to the company which is essential for an efficient audit. This involves a study of the nature and location of the business of the company, as well as its internal regulations and systems (including the accounting function). It also requires a knowledge of the management and employees of the company. With this knowledge, the various audit processes can be commenced. However, it is relatively obvious that familiarization of this kind will be more extensive when the auditor is appointed in the first instance, and that subsequent familiarization will be concerned with updating his existing knowledge.

The first stage of the audit concerns the process of validating the company's data processing function to assess the accuracy and dependability of the data concerned. The auditor examines the system, judges its strength and weaknesses, and, by a sampling process, tests it by checking through it a number of transactions. This work is often conducted throughout the financial year, and once the auditor is satisfied with his tests, he can move on to the next stage of testing the information process. If he is not satisfied, he may conduct further tests or he may decide to report his findings to the shareholders if he believes these materially affect the truth and fairness of the financial statements.

The next stage in the audit concerns an examination of the process whereby the accounting data are put in a form which can be reported in the required financial statements. The auditor analyses and checks on the various accounting procedures used, paying particular attention to the application of relevant *Statements of Standard Accounting Practice* as well as to the crucial judgemental areas. He will also ensure the physical existence, ownership and condition of the company's assets described in the balance sheet. (A similar verification exercise takes place with its reported liabilities.) He will then verify that there has been adequate disclosure and presentation of the information in the financial statements, as required by law and best accounting practice. The auditor conducts these examinations on a test basis, the size of the samples depending on his confidence in the quality of the accounting system.

If he is satisfied with the results of these tests, he can then proceed to give his 'truth and fairness' report. If he is not satisfied, he will issue a report which will specify the nature and extent of his dissatisfaction. This can involve a qualified opinion (which states that the information is 'true and fair' with the exception of one or more datum); or an adverse opinion (which states that the information is not 'true and fair' as a whole); or a disclaimer of opinion (which states that no opinion is being given because of the extremely poor quality of the information). In all cases where the opinion is not the straightforward positive one required by law, the auditor is professionally bound to explain fully the nature of the problem(s) and the reasons for his dissatisfaction.

The audit opinion

From the above brief summary of the nature of the audit function, it should be reasonably clear that the auditor is an expert accountant (or group of accountants) employed to give a professional opinion on the quality of company financial statements. As such, his opinion cannot be conceived as anything other than an expert appraisal and judgement. It is not a statement guaranteeing the accuracy of the figures concerned: this would be impossible, given the nature of the information being audited. Nor is it a statement that the auditor is in some way responsible for the quality of the reported financial statements: this is the responsibility of the board of directors, and the auditor is only responsible for the quality of his audit and opinion. If his opinion is not a correct one, or is misleading, then the shareholders can sue him for damage if financial injury has resulted from reliance on that opinion.

In this respect, it should be noted that the existence of a qualified audit opinion does not necessarily mean that the reported information cannot be relied on, or is, in some way, sub-standard. Nor does it mean that the company directors and managers are in any way dishonest. Qualifications may arise because the audit report is an opinion, and obviously the auditor can differ from the directors in his judgement of some accounting matter. As there is considerable room for such differences to exist in accounting, it is not surprising that they lead to qualified audit reports. The nature of the qualification must be read carefully, and its effect on the overall quality of the information thereby assessed.

The management letter

Apart from his audit report, the auditor may produce a separate report to the board of directors which outlines any problem areas he has come across in the company and which, in his opinion, deserve managerial attention. This is called the management letter[40] and is produced on a purely voluntary basis with the aim of improving company systems of control, particularly as they affect the accounting function. These reports are not normally drawn to the attention of shareholders, except in so far as a particular problem area has also resulted in a qualification contained in the audit report.

The auditor

Lastly, a few comments on the auditor himself are appropriate. As already mentioned, 'he' is normally a firm of professionally qualified accountants employing a number of accountants (at varying stages in their training and experience) to conduct the audit. Auditors are therefore professional people (highly skilled and trained), and subject to the usual ethical rules governing professional conduct and work. In particular, those employed on the audit must act with reasonable care, integrity and independence. The latter quality[41] is particularly important as it is essential to the objectivity of the auditor's opinion. If it is not a balanced and unbiased opinion, then doubts may be created which effect the credibility of the audited financial statements. Auditor independence is therefore interpretable not only in terms of the auditor's attitude of mind but also in terms of his appearance of independence: he must not only be mentally independent but must also be seen to be independent. Thus, in Britain, the company auditor is not permitted to be an officer or servant of a client company nor a partner or employee of such an officer or servant (Section 161 (2), Companies Act 1948). At the present time, there is no legal requirement prohibiting an auditor from being a shareholder in a client company, although certain professional accountancy firms ban such holdings by their partners and staff members.

Summary

The preceding paragraphs have attempted to indicate to the reader the main stages involved in the preparation of financial reports, particularly from the point of view of those which appear annually for company shareholders. The process involves the collection of suitable accounting data; its subsequent processing, by allocation and valuation, into relevant informational messages; and the final stage of communicating these messages in a suitable report form. In addition, the external auditor is required to verify and report on the credibility of each of these stages, prior to the information being presented to the shareholders (at least, so far as annual reports are concerned).

However, these descriptions have also hinted at several of the major problems inherent in the present system of company financial reporting. The next task, therefore, is to discuss these at some length so that the reader may become more aware of the limitations of the system, and of some of the suggestions advocated to improve it. The context will be the annual financial report of a company in the first instance. The problems of other forms of company financial report will be explained separately.

Suggested Discussion or Essay Topics

1. Accounting accumulates and communicates information essential to an understanding of the activities of an enterprise. Discuss.

2. Comment on the suggestion that the measurement of financial accounting information of the type presently reported is as much based on subjective opinion as on objective evidence.

3. The choice of a time period of one year creates certain problems for the reporting accountant. Discuss.

4. Accountants and auditors adhere to the matching principle. What is meant by this term, and how significant is it in financial reporting?

5. Auditors do not certify or guarantee financial statmeents. Comment on the validity of this statement.

6. Financial accounting is concerned with obtaining a credible rather than an exact description of a company's financial affairs. Comment.

7. What is meant by the realization principle in accounting practice?

8. Accounting for periodic income is a relatively straightforward process of measuring revenues and costs and relating them to one another. Discuss this statement within the context of traditional income reporting.

9. The greater the lack of credibility in accounting information, the greater is the need to have such credibility established by the process of verification. Comment and discuss, particularly with a view to explaining the place of verification in contemporary accounting thought.

10. It should be emphasized that the financial statements of a company are prepared on the assumption that it will continue in business. Discuss the implications of this statement for financial reporting.

11. Discuss the importance of not delaying the reporting of financial information beyond certain tolerable limits.

12. The concept of audit care is based upon the prudent auditor — that is, the auditor who re-presents the average of his profession. What is meant by audit care, and how important is it to the quality of company financial statements?

13. The significance of independence in the work of the auditor is so well established that little justification is needed to justify its existence. Discuss.

14. The modern accountant lays claim to the role of 'information technologist'. Explain what you believe this to mean in relation to the production of financial accounting information.

Notes and References

1. A. M. C. Morison, 'The Role of the Reporting Accountant Today — 11', *Accountant's Magazine,* October 1970, p. 476.

2. Much of this description is taken from T. A. Lee, *Company Auditing: Concepts and Practices,* Gee & Co., revised edition, 1974, pp. 5-8 and 44-9.

3. For a review of this topic, see R. K. Mautz, 'Standards for the Review of Internal Control', *Journal of Accountancy,* July 1958, pp. 27-31.

4. Those readers not familiar with double-entry book-keeping should refer to a text such as H. C. Edey, *An Introduction to Accounting,* Hutchinson, 1973.

5. For a detailed review of this principle, see, e.g., S. Davidson, 'The Realization Concept', in M. Backer (ed.), *Modern Accounting Theory,* Prentice-Hall, 1966, pp. 99-115.

6. As stated in 'Disclosure of Accounting Policies', *Statements of Standard Accounting Practice 2,* November 1971, p. 3.

7. The fullest examination of conservatism is contained in R. R. Sterling, 'Conservatism: The Fundamental Principle of Valuation in Traditional Accounting', *Abacus,* December 1967, pp. 109-32.

8. M. Moonitz, 'The Basic Postulates of Accounting', *Accounting Research Study 1,* The American Institute of Certified Public Accountants, 1961, p. 33.

9. For a brief review of this subject, see, e.g., F. Bailey, *Current Practice in Company Accounts,* Accountancy Age Books, 1973, pp. 31-5. For a more detailed discussion, see P. N. McMonnies, 'Depreciation', *Accountant's Magazine,* February 1969, pp. 73-85.

10. For a review of this problem area in accounting, see 'Valuation of Stock and Work-in-Progress', *Research Report,* Institute of Chartered Accountants of Scotland, January 1968; and 'Accounting and Auditing Approaches to Inventories in the Three Nations', *Research Report,* Accountants International Study Group, January 1968.

11. See, e.g., E. Stamp, 'Reforming Accounting Principles', in E. Stamp and C. Marley, *Accounting Principles and the City Code: the Case for Reform,* Butterworth, 1970, pp. 65-154; H. I. Ross, 'The Current Crisis in Financial Reporting', *Journal of Accountancy,* August 1967, pp. 65-9; and L. Spacek, 'The Need for an Accounting Court', *Accounting Review,* July 1968, pp. 368-79.

12. R. J. Chambers, 'Financial Information and the Securities Market', *Abacus,* September 1965, p. 16.

13. For a review of the developments in this area of accounting practice, see T. A. Lee, 'Accounting Standards and Effective Financial Reporting: a Review in Principle', *Accountant's Magazine,* January and February 1975, pp. 25-30 and 73-81.

14. 'Disclosure of Accounting Policies', loc. cit., p. 3.

15. Moonitz, 'The Basic Postulates of Accounting', loc. cit., p. 53.

16. Stamp, 'Reforming Accounting Principles', loc. cit., pp. 133-5.

17. See, e.g., R. H. Parker, 'Principles and Practice in Translating Foreign Currencies', *Abacus,* December 1970, pp. 144-53; and 'The Treatment in Company Accounts of Changes in the Exchange Rates of International Currencies', *Accountant's Magazine,* September 1970, pp. 415-23.

18. 'Accounting for the Results of Associated Companies', *Statement of Standard Accounting Practice 1,* January 1971.

19. For an introduction to consolidation procedures, see H. S. Cilliers and S. Rossouw, *Consolidation of Financial Statements,* Butterworth, 1969.

20. J. R. Jordan, 'Financial Accounting and Communication', *The Price Waterhouse Review,* Spring 1969, reproduced in G. G. Mueller and C. H. Smith, *Accounting: A Book of Readings,* Holt, Rinehart & Winston, 1970, p. 139.

21. R. J. Chambers, *Accounting, Evaluation and Economic Behaviour,* Prentice-Hall, 1966, p. 184.

22. *The Professional Investor,* research report, Throgmorton Publications, 1969; and R. C. Copeman, 'Attitudes to Stockmarket Investment Decisions in the City of London', *Discussion Paper 24,* University of Birmingham, November 1970.

23. e.g., as in R. Ball and P. Brown, 'An Empirical Evaluation of Accounting Income Numbers', *Journal of Accounting Research,* Autumn 1968, pp. 159-77.

24. M. Moonitz, 'The Basic Postulates of Accounting', loc. cit., p. 50

25. See, e.g., J. G. Birnberg and N. Dopuch, 'A Conceptual Approach to a Framework for Disclosure', *Journal of Accountancy,* February 1973, pp. 59-63; and S. L. Buzby, 'The Nature of Adequate Disclosure', *Journal of Accountancy,* April 1974, pp. 38-47.

26. I. N. Gleim, 'Standards of Disclosure for Supplementary Data', *Journal of Accountancy,* April 1974, pp. 50-57.

27. Jordan, 'Financial Accounting and Communication', loc. cit., pp. 132-3.

28. E. S. Hendriksen, *Accounting Theory,* Irwin, revised edition 1970, p. 566.

29. N. M. Bedford, *Extensions in Accounting Disclosure,* Prentice-Hall, 1973, pp. 45-6.

30. J. E. Smith and N. P. Smith, 'Readability: A Measure of the Performance of the Communication Function of Financial Reporting', *Accounting Review,* July 1971, p. 560.

31. P. Grady, 'Inventory of Generally Accepted Accounting Principles for Business Enterprises', *Accounting Research Study 7,* The American Institute of Certified Public Accountants, 1965, pp. 41-2.

32. V. R. V. Cooper, *Student's Manual of Auditing,* Gee & Co., 1971, pp. 33-4.

33. *Survey of Published Accounts: 1972-73,* The Institute of Chartered Accountants in England and Wales, 1973, pp. 225-6.

34. Much of this section is derived from Lee, *Company Auditing,* esp. pp. 44-9.

35. ibid., pp. 30-32.

36. e.g., *Ultramares Corporation* v. *Touche* (1931) 255 N.Y. 170, 174 N.E. 441, 74 A.L.R. 1139, and *Candler* v. *Crane, Christmas and Co., C.A.* (1951) 2 K.B. 164; (1951) 1 All E.R. 426; (1951) I.T.L.R. 371.

37. See, e.g., *Verner* v. *General and Commercial Investment Trust Ltd* (1894) 2 Ch. 239; and *Wilmer* v. *McNamara and Co. Ltd* (1895) 2 Ch. 245.

38. e.g., R. F. Salmonson, 'CPA's Negligence, Third Parties and the Future', *Accounting Review,* January 1959, pp. 91-6.

39. 'Accountants' Liability to Third Parties – the *Hedley Byrne* Decision', *Accountancy,* September 1965, pp. 829-30.

40. See T. A. Lee, 'The Nature and Use of Management Letters', *Accountant's Magazine,* February 1973, pp. 79-85.

41. For a review of this concept, see J. L. Carey and W. O. Doherty, 'The Concept of Independence – Review and Restatement', *Journal of Accountancy,* January 1966, pp. 38-48.

Selected Bibliography for Chapter 5

N. M. Bedford, *Extensions in Accounting Disclosure*, Prentice-Hall, 1973, pp. 3-24. The nature of accounting disclosures.

H. Bierman, 'Measurement and Accounting', *Accounting Review,* July 1963, pp. 501-7. The nature and problems of measuring reportable financial accounting information.

R. J. Bull, *Accounting in Business,* Butterworth, 1972, pp. 65-85. A brief introduction to the recording of data for financial reporting purposes.

S. L. Buzby, 'The Nature of Adequate Disclosure', *Journal of Accountancy,* April 1974, pp. 38-47. Determining what is required to be disclosed in the light of user needs.

R. J. Chambers, *Accounting, Evaluation and Economic Behaviour,* Prentice-Hall, 1966. An explanation of the accounting system (pp. 124-40); the nature of accounting information and its processing (pp. 141-65); and the process of communicating accounting information (pp. 166-85).

J. R. Jordan, 'Financial Accounting and Communication', *The Price Waterhouse Review,* Spring 1969, reproduced in G. G. Mueller and C. H. Smith, *Accounting: a Book of Readings,* Holt, Rinehart & Winston, 1970, pp. 127-44. The communications aspects of the financial accounting process.

P. Kircher, 'Fundamentals of Measurement', *Advanced Management,* October 1955, pp. 5-8. An explanation of the key elements of the business measurement system.

G. A. Lee, *Modern Financial Accounting,* Nelson, 1973, pp. 307-56. A practical discussion of producing and presenting company financial reports.

T. A. Lee, *Company Auditing: Concepts and Practices,* Gee & Co., revised edition 1974. The financial accounting function (pp. 1-12); and the company audit function (pp. 12-50).

W. A. Paton and A. C. Littleton, *An Introduction to Corporate Accounting Standards,* American Accounting Association, 1940. Accounting in traditional terms for revenues, costs and income.

C. H. Smith, 'A Systems Approach to the Accounting Functions', in Mueller and Smith, *Accounting,* pp. 109-27. Accounting as an information system.

R. W. Wallis, *Accounting: A Modern Approach,* McGraw-Hill, 1970, pp. 56-87. An explanation of data processing and related accounting adjustments.

6 Issues and Problems in Company Financial Reporting

Introduction

The previous chapters have assumed the traditional system of company financial reporting which is presently used throughout the developed Western world: the system which focuses on the annual reporting of accounting data describing a company's past profitability and financial position. It is augmented, on occasion, by interim reports (again historical in description) and short-term forecasts of future income. Essentially, however, the major part of the total information flow to company shareholders is concerned with annual measures of past income, together with statements of the related financial positions at the end of each reporting period.

It is a system which has worked reasonably well. It is more than one hundred years old in Britain, and has remained virtually unchanged in principle during that time. In addition, there has not been any major outcry against it by shareholders. Nevertheless, this does not mean that it has no faults and does not need improving. It clearly does, and this and the following chapter are aimed at outlining its main problem areas as well as certain improvements which could be made to it. The reader should thus become aware of the system's obvious strengths and weaknesses, as well as its potential relevance and utility to its users.

The Valuation Issue

Present-day company financial reports disclose, in aggregate and summary form, measures of company profitability and financial position. The data concerned are representative of the financial results from past economic activity and are based on the original values attributable to the transactions and events involved. As previously mentioned, because historic cost is the valuation basis used, the relevant accounting numbers are effectively measured by the application of the realization principle, supported by the conservatism convention. It is this measurement process which has given rise to a great deal of criticism and debate in recent years.

The effects of the realization principle

The realization principle states that asset value increases should not normally be accounted for and reported on until such time as they have been realized, in terms of either cash or near-cash resources. Conversely, asset value decreases should be recognized and accounted for as soon as they arise, irrespective of when realization of the asset concerned will take place. The effects of this particular policy are twofold:

(a) Unless the current valuations of assets fall below their original costs, the balance sheet will 'value' unrealized assets at their original cost (minus any depreciation allocations in the case of fixed assets) and not at their current valuation. Thus, the traditional balance sheet is not a statement of the current value of the company, its assets, or its shares. It is rather a stewardship accounting of past transactions at their original transaction value.

(b) As a consequence of effect (a), the company income statement does not contain measures of income elements earned during the defined period. What it does contain is a heterogeneous mixture of income elements: gains earned and realized during the period, together with gains earned during previous periods but realized during the current one. However, it will also contain unrealized losses of the period, representing earned but unrealized asset value decreases.

The traditional income statement does not, therefore, contain measures of the current period's earned but unrealized asset value increases. Illustration 6 is a numerical example of these effects.

Illustration 6. *The realization principle.*

A company has two assets A and B. Asset A cost £1,000 at point t_0 and asset B cost £2,000 at the same time. During the period t_0-t_1, the company continued to hold both assets, and their realizable values at t_1 were £1,500 and £2,700 respectively. Asset A was sold during the period t_1-t_2 for £1,800, but asset B continued to be held at t_2, when its realizable value was £3,100. During the period t_2-t_3, asset B was sold for £3,500.

Following the realization principle, and assuming no other transactions, no taxation and an opening capital at t_0 of £3,000, the company's income statement and balance sheet figures would appear as follows:

Income statements	t_0-t_1	t_1-t_2	t_2-t_3	Total
Realized income for the period	£ —[a]	£ 800[b]	£1,500[c]	£2,300

Balance sheets	t_0	t_1	t_2	t_3
Asset A	£1,000	£1,000	£ —	£ —
Asset B	2,000	2,000	2,000	—
Cash	—	—	1,800[d]	5,300[e]
	£3,000	£3,000	£3,800	£5,300
Opening capital	£3,000	£3,000	£3,000	£3,000
Retained income	—	—	800[f]	2,300[g]
	£3,000	£3,000	£3,800	£5,300

(a) No asset was realized during the period, therefore no income was recognized; (b) gain on the sale of asset A, £1,800 − 1,000; (c) gain on the sale of asset B, £3,500 − 2,000; (d) sale receipt for asset A, £1,800; (e) sale receipts for assets A and B, £1,800 + 3,500; (f) gain on the sale of asset A, £800; (g) gains on the sale of assets A and B, £800 + 1,500.

Relaxing the realization principle

The example in Illustration 6 reveals how the realization principle, and the related adherence to the valuation base of historic cost, leads to the reporting of income and asset value increases only after realization has taken place. Illustration 7 uses the same figures, but relaxes the realization constraint on reporting.

Illustration 7. *Relaxation of the realization principle.*

Income statements	t_0-t_1	t_1-t_2	t_2-t_3	Total
Income earned during the period	£1,200[a]	£ 700[b]	£ 400[c]	£2,300

Balance sheets	t_0	t_1	t_2	t_3
Asset A	£1,000	£1,500	£ —	£ —
Asset B	2,000	2,700	3,100	—
Cash[d]	—	—	1,800	5,300
	£3,000	£4,200	£4,900	£5,300
Opening capital	£3,000	£3,000	£3,000	£3,000
Retained income	—	1,200[e]	1,900[f]	2,300[g]
	£3,000	£4,200	£4,900	£5,300

(a) Unrealized gains of the period on assets A and B (£1,500 − 1,000) + (£2,700−2,000); (b) realized gain of the period on asset A, £1,800 − 1,500 plus unrealized gain of the period on asset B, £3,100 − 2,700; (c) realized gain of the period on asset B, £3,500 − 3,100; (d) as per Illustration 6; (e) income of the period $t_0 - t_1$ £1,200; (f) income of the period $t_1 - t_2$, £700, plus retained income at t_1, £1,200; (g) income of the period t_2-t_3, £400, plus retained income at t_2, £1,900.

Thus, by taking the figures in Illustrations 6 and 7, the comparison emerges as in Illustration 8.

Illustration 8. *A comparative analysis of realization.*

Income statements	t_0-t_1	t_1-t_2	t_2-t_3	Total
With the realization principle	£ —	£ 800	£1,500	£2,300
Without the realization principle	1,200	700	400	2,300

Balance sheets: capital and retained income	t_0	t_1	t_2	t_3
With the realization principle	£3,000	£3,000	£3,800	£5,300
Without the realization principle	3,000	4,200	4,900	5,300

As these figures reveal, the realization principle in income and value measurement can considerably affect the reportable income and capital of the periods concerned. It delays the reporting of unrealized income until realized, it understates assets and capital, again until realization occurs. Users of traditionally measured accounting information cannot therefore be said to be informed about the earned income of a period or of the current values of assets held at its end. Yet the income statement purports to disclose the former, and the balance sheet gives the impression, particularly to the non-accountant, that it contains the latter. Historic cost-based information does not therefore give an up-to-date or full picture of a company's financial affairs, and as a result could be misleading.

By relaxing the restriction of the realization principle, the following reporting changes occur: (a) only income accruing during the period is reported, irrespective of when it is realized, thereby giving shareholders and other interested persons a measure of the earned rather than the realized income of the period; and (b) the balance sheet reflects up-to-date asset values rather than those occurring at the time of the original transactions. Financial report users are therefore in a better position to assess the recent financial progress of companies than if they used the existing historic cost-based system. The usefulness of the latter should nevertheless not be totally discounted, given its long history of use.

Arguments for and against historic cost

Financial reports which use historic costs have been defended on many occasions,[1] and, indeed, it is only in recent years that there has been a sustained voice of opinion against the traditional system. The major argument for it is that it has stood the test of time and that there are no signs that investors or other users are ignoring it in their decision-making activities. In fact, as already mentioned, the empirical evidence to date is that investors do take cognisance of reported income figures compiled on a historic cost basis.

Another major argument is that historic cost information is firmly based on known business transactions and events capable of being evidenced and verified. In other words, it has an apparent objectivity which is not as evident in alternative valuation systems. It has also been argued that, because of this objective and factual base, the traditional system is open to less disputation than other systems thus minimizing the cost of time and effort in producing the information.

The arguments against historic cost are well supported[2] and concentrate particularly on its lack of relevance to the investment decision-making function; it does not report on the income earned during a defined period nor does it indicate contemporary values for assets. In other words, the traditional system is an accounting for what happened during the defined period, mainly in terms of cost movements suitably adjusted when allocation of data is necessary between periods. It singularly fails to recognize, on a continuous basis, the changing values of assets before realization.

Alternatives to historic cost

The alternative to reporting in past value terms is to use current values, or values existing at the date of reporting rather than at the dates of the original transactions. By using current values, not only are assets reported in contemporary terms, but income will include unrealized and realized gain elements of the defined period, thereby ignoring the realization problem. This was seen in the example in Illustration 7. The problem, however, is one of deciding which current value to adopt for measurement purposes.

There are three possible interpretations attributable to current value: economic value, replacement cost and net realizable value. Each is a description of the current value of an asset, but each is different and therefore capable of producing a separate measure of periodic income. This indicates the somewhat elusive nature of income; its measurement depends on the particular values placed on the company's assets.

Economic value and periodic income

Following the traditional arguments of Fisher[3] and Hicks,[4] it can be argued that a conceptually correct value for a business asset is one which is based on the net revenues which, it is anticipated, will be received during its lifetime. In other words, the value to the company of an asset is determined by what it would pay for the economic benefits which could be received from it. This involves forecasting the net revenues which could be earned from the use of each asset, with a discounting of each forecast at a suitable rate of interest.[5] Once the economic value for each asset has been computed, the balance sheet position of the company can be evaluated at the beginning and end of the period concerned. Allowing for realized net revenues, dividends and share capital changes during the period, income is computed by measuring the periodic change in shareholders' equity based on these economic values.[6] Illustration 9 outlines such a computation.

Illustration 9. *Income and economic values.*

The aggregate economic value of the non-cash resources of a company at t_0 is estimated to be £25,000. At t_1 the corresponding figure is £37,000. During the period $t_0 - t_1$ cash resources increased from £5,000 to £12,000, of which £4,000 was received from shareholders subscribing to a new issue of shares. Income for the period $t_0 - t_1$ would then be (£37,000 − 25,000) + (£12,000 − 5,000) − £4,000 = £15,000, ignoring taxation.

Although theoretically valid, the use of economic value in the practice of income measurement is fraught with problems,[7] not the least of them being the forecasting of future economic benefits to be derived from a company's assets. Apart from the extreme subjectivity of the exercise, there is the related problem of identifying particular revenues, and so on, with individual assets. There is also the question of which discount rate to use in the computations. An alternative approach would be to compute the economic value for the company as a whole rather than for its individual assets. However, this would involve the forecasting of total net revenues over the lifetime of the company. The impossibility of this task is relatively obvious. Therefore economic value is generally regarded as theoretically attractive but impracticable as an alternative to historic cost.

Replacement cost and periodic income

Advocated by Edwards and Bell[8] and many others,[9] the measurement of periodic income and asset values using current replacement costs is now a well-known potential alternative to historic cost. It has been suggested that, failing the use of economic values, the obvious choice is a current market value, and replacement cost seems appropriate, first, because it reflects the continuity and indefinite life of the business; and secondly, because it represents (in most situations) the maximum loss a company would suffer if deprived of the assets concerned.[10] Edwards and Bell[11] have also demonstrated that, by using replacement costs for financial reporting purposes, it is possible to segregate income elements earned by selling assets from income elements earned by holding them. Both for managerial and investment decision-making purposes, it is argued that such a segregation is useful when predicting future income elements: it helps distinguish income earned by deliberate managerial policy from income earned by luck and chance. Illustration 10 gives a brief example of this distinction.

Illustration 10. *Income and replacement costs.*

At t_0 a non-manufacturing company held the following items of stock, with the appended values:

	Original cost	Replacement cost
Item A	£200	£210
Item B	300	380
Item C	400	430

During the period t_0-t_1, item A was sold for £270 (replacement cost at time of sale, £230), and item B was sold for £450 (replacement cost at time of sale, £430). Item C continued to be held at t_1 at a replacement cost of £460. In addition, a further item, D, had been bought during the period for £500 (replacement cost at t_1 was £530). Ignore taxation.

Operating income, period t_0-t_1

Item A	(£270 − 230)	£40
Item B	(£450 − 430)	20
		£60

Holding income, period t_0-t_1

Item A	(£230 − 210)	£20
Item B	(£430 − 380)	50
Item C	(£460 − 430)	30
Item D	(£530 − 500)	30
		£130

Total income, period t_0-t_1 — £190

The figures in the illustration reveal that, of the total income of £190 earned during the period, only £60 represented income from trading (sales revenue minus current replacement cost), the remainder being the result of rising replacement costs during the various holding periods. By way of contrast, traditional accounting practice would have measured income for the period as: item A (£270 − 200) + item B (£450 − 300) = £220, being the total realized income of the period.

The replacement cost alternative, however, has its problems. For example, what replacement cost should be used for each asset? With certain assets, there may not be a readily available replacement cost (for example, as with intangible assets such as goodwill). With other assets, the problem is whether the replacement cost should be that for an identical asset or for one giving equivalent services to the existing one. Technological changes can cause existing assets to be non-replaceable in identical form, and the problem is finding a suitable replacement cost for an equivalent asset. There is also the problem that not all assets will be replaced; the use of replacement costs assumes that this will occur in all cases. Similarly, replacement costs assume that the company will continue in business indefinitely, and, with the exception of cash and near-cash resources, do not necessarily reflect the realizable value of its assets. The conclusion to be drawn from this may well be one suggested by Macdonald that,[12] whereas the replacement cost alternative to historic cost may produce a realistic measure of periodic income, it does not necessarily produce a balance sheet any more relevant to the decision-maker than the traditional one.

Realizable value and periodic income

The third alternative current value is net realizable value:[13] what the company could realize for an asset if it were sold in an orderly liquidation. Based on the well-known economic concept of opportunity cost (the sacrifice the company is making by not having its assets in the next best alternative form of funds), it expresses the alternatives open to the company should its resources be liquidated. Obviously this is of particular concern to shareholders, given that one of the decisions facing them is whether or not the company should continue in its present form. Therefore, although periodic income measures can be derived from this valuation base (by comparing opening and closing balance sheet positions, and allowing for dividends and share capital changes), the main emphasis is on producing relevant balance-sheet data for the investor. An example is given in Illustration 11.

Illustration 11. *Income and realizable values.*

At t_0 a company has the following assets, all measures using net realizable values: fixed assets, £10,000; current assets, £35,000. Its current liabilities at the same date amount to £15,000. At t_1, the corresponding realizable figures are: fixed assets, £12,000; current assets, £47,000. Its current liabilities are £17,000. During the period $t_0 - t_1$, the company paid a dividend for the period of £3,000 and received £5,000 from its shareholders for a new issue of shares.

Realizable income, period $t_0 - t_1$

	t_0	t_1
Fixed assets	£10,000	£12,000
Current assets	35,000	47,000
	£45,000	£59,000
Less: current liabilities	15,000	17,000
	£30,000	£42,000
Less: financial position at t_0		30,000
Increase in realizable resources		£12,000
Add: dividend paid for the period		3,000
		£15,000
Less: share capital increase		5,000
Realizable income for the period		£10,000

During the stated period, and ignoring the question of taxation, the income of the company in realizable value terms is, in the illustration, £10,000, though its total realizable resources have increased by £12,000. This gives shareholders and other interested persons a reasonable indication of the company's capacity to adapt, which would not be possible with a historic cost or replacement cost balance sheet.

The balance sheet-orientated realizable value alternative to historic cost is nevertheless subject to the criticism that it concentrates too much on asset value changes, and not enough on the operational effectiveness of the company as de-picted by its income measures. Apart from this, it can be argued that the use of realizable values implies that the assets of the company are to be liquidated (which may not be the case, at least in the short-term), or that the company has a definite life (which is extremely difficult to predict with any degree of certainty).

The alternatives compared

The periodic income of a company, together with its related balance-sheet position, can be described in a number of ways, each depending on the particular valuation concept used. Historic cost produces a measure of income, based on the original values attributable to the underlying transactions, which aims to maintain intact the monetary value of shareholders' capital. In other words, allowing for new capital and capital repayment, as well as dividends, historic cost income is the difference between the opening and closing shareholders' equities in the traditional balance sheet. It cannot exist unless the opening equity figure has been maintained intact. However, in most instances it ignores unrealized income.

Replacement cost income, on the other hand, recognizes unrealized gains and aims to measure income after achieving a maintenance of the productive capacity of the company's resources by valuing them in replacement cost terms at the beginning and end of the period concerned. Similarly, realizable value income contains unrealized gain elements, but income exists only after the maintenance of the company's capacity to adapt as represented by the aggregate realizable value of its net assets.[14]

Traditional historic cost income therefore has the income and value omissions brought about by the implementation of the realization principle. However, the two feasible current value alternatives, while abandoning realization, do not necessarily produce income statements and balance sheets of complete relevance to their users. Replacement cost income seems more relevant than realizable income, but realizable balance sheets seem more relevant than their replacement cost equivalent. This leads to a possible conclusion advocated by Macdonald[15] that too much reliance may be placed on producing income statements and balance sheets which articulate with each other because of the use of the same valuation basis in each. It may well be more suitable to use replacement cost for income reporting and realizable value for balance sheet reporting. This, however, has yet to be tested and proven.

The Monetary Unit Problem

The discussion of the valuation problem in financial reporting has so far been undertaken with the implied assumption that the monetary measurement unit (in this text, the pound sterling) has a stable value in terms of its generalized purchasing power. In other words, that there has been no inflation or deflation, and that value changes in company financial reports are entirely the result of specific price movements reflecting real rather than inflationary (or deflationary) changes in the values attributable to company resources. For example, if the reported value of stock and work in progress has increased from £100,000 to £150,000 over the period concerned, the assumption has been that the £50,000 increase is the result either of a 50 per cent increase in the quantity of stock held (assuming the specific prices of items have remained stable), or of a 50 per cent increase in the specific prices of items (assuming quantities had remained stable), or a combination of both. The question of whether all or part of the value change has been because stock has become more expensive owing to the diminishing purchasing power of money has not been considered, and it is the purpose of this section to look at this question. The discussion will assume the more usual contemporary economic condition of inflation.

Accounting implications

Inflation is the term used by economists to denote the general movement upwards in prices of goods and services in an economy over a stated period. In other words, it is an economic factor resulting from all price movements, and as such represents the diminution in the generalized purchasing power of money rather than an increase in the value of goods and services. The effect of inflation is that the monetary unit loses value rather than the alternative of goods and services becoming more valuable. Thus, if a good's value increases during a period of inflation, then part, all or even something in excess of the increase may be owing to the fall in the purchasing power of money; the remainder of the change being the result of other economic factors, such as demand and supply.

The fall in the value of money during a period of inflation has serious implications for financial accounting and reporting. Unless cognisance is taken of it, the reported data will be based upon monetary units with differing purchasing powers, each depending on the value of money at the date of each relevant transaction. By aggregating, allocating and matching data measured in differing purchasing power terms, the consequence would be to fail to report on the real profitability of companies since there will be a failure to exclude inflationary gains and losses which neither reflect real changes in values nor real changes in the physical resources, and so forth, underlying these values. Income would therefore be measured by a maintenance of capital in monetary rather than purchasing power terms.

For example, assuming no capital issues or repayments, or dividends, income for the period $t_o - t_1$ (unadjusted for inflation) was £10,000; being the difference between capital at t_o of £25,000 and capital at t_1 of £35,000.

Here opening and closing capitals have been measured in purely monetary terms to derive income for the period. However, if the concept of monetary purchasing power is introduced, it means that opening and closing capital (and therefore the underlying assets and liabilities) should be re-expressed in monetary units of the same purchasing power. This involves translating all asset and liability items at both t_o and t_1 into current purchasing power terms. Thus, assuming these transactions had been made, and opening and closing capitals were adjusted to £31,000 and £38,000 respectively, the inflation-adjusted income would be £38,000 − 31,000 = £7,000.

Data unadjusted for the effects of inflation can therefore be somewhat misleading to its users. Despite this, the traditional practice of accountants has been to assume that the monetary units with which they measure accounting information have a stable purchasing power. As a result, beside the problems created by the use of historic costs and the proliferation of accounting practices, the measurement of income and financial position is affected by the monetary unit problem. The combination of all three factors obviously makes the traditional process of accounting measurement a questionable process, particularly from the point of view of users who require relevant and credible data for their decision and other activities.

Many writers[16] have in the past argued against the monetary stability assumption in practice. These arguments have been mainly in the area of historic cost-based financial statements, the claim being that not to adjust them for the effects of inflation produces misleading information about past profitability and financial position. However, the same argument applies equally to alternative valuation bases, such as replacement cost and net realizable value. Reporting in current value terms does not remove the additional necessity to account for the effects of inflation — that is, by removing the inflationary elements from income measured on the basis of current values. In other words, the nature of so-called inflation accounting is not, like the function of historic cost or current value accounting, a valuation process. Rather its purpose is to segregate the inflationary elements of the periodic capital value increase, leaving income to be reported in real terms.

The inflationary effect

Several professional accountancy bodies[17] have acknowledged the need to introduce inflation accounting, at least so far as historic cost data are concerned. However, until recently none have felt the rate of inflation to be serious enough to warrant any changes in accounting practice. This attitude has changed in Britain in recent years, and the professional accountancy bodies have produced a *Statement of Standard Accounting Practice*[18] which requires quoted companies to produce, in addition to their historic cost-based financial statements, inflation-adjusted income statements and balance sheets.

The process whereby historic cost statements are translated into terms of a monetary unit with a single purchasing power is relatively complex, and consequently difficult to explain fully within the context of this book. The reader who needs to research further is therefore referred to the notes and selected bibliography at the end of the chapter. In the meantime, the following notes and illustration will help to give an introductory understanding of the process. The comments and figures are explained solely within the context of the traditional system of historic cost reporting.

First, inflation accounting is akin to a translation process: the unadjusted historic cost data, expressed in monetary units of differing purchasing power, is translated into units expressed in terms of monetary purchasing power at the relevant period end. The general effect of these adjustments is to inflate the reported data by the inflation factor, in both the income statement and the balance sheet, with the exception of those items which may already be reported in current purchasing power terms (if the relevant transactions have taken place near the period end) or else cannot be translated for legal reasons (i.e. cash and contracted liabilities).

Secondly, the translation process which is applied to historic cost data depends on the use of a relevant inflation factor for the period — that is, a suitable indicator of inflation for the period. In the United Kingdom, the recommendation is that the most suitable indicator presently available is the monthly retail price index which is published as a government document and based upon a statistical averaging of monthly (and, eventually, annual) price movements for certain consumer goods and services. The use of such an index as a guide to the annual rate of inflation in other areas of economic management is one of the main reasons for its use in inflation accounting. The other main reasons include its ready availability and its universality.

Illustration 12 attempts to explain certain of the main adjustments for inflation which are necessary for the translation of the annual income figure. While these are not the only adjustments that need to be made to the annual financial statements, the information is intended to give an adequate picture within the limits of the present text.

Illustration 12. *Inflationary effects in financial reports.*

A company bought goods costing £90,000 at t_0 It sold them at t_1 for £160,000. At t_0 it had cash in the bank of £23,000 and a debenture loan of £100,000. At t , cash at the bank was £30,000 (the additional £7,000 accumulating evenly throughout the period, and the debenture loan remaining at £100,000). In addition, the company had plant which cost £100,000 at t_0 and was being depreciated periodically at 10 per cent on a straight-line basis with an estimated nil scrap value. Assume that retail prices increased in general by 15 per cent during the period, and ignore taxation.

Sale of goods $t_0 - t_1$

Traditional historic cost accounting practice would measure income on these transactions at £160,000 − 90,000 = £70,000. However, assuming a 15 per cent rate of inflation, the adjusted cost of the goods sold at t_1 would be £90,000 + 3/20 x 90,000 = £103,500; and the adjusted historic cost income on the transactions would be £160,000 − 103,500 = £56,000. In other words, by measuring the transactions in terms of monetary purchasing power at t_1, the traditional income figure is composed of an inflationary element of £70,000 − 56,500 = £13,500 (not representing any real increase in resources available to the company), and £56,500 representing the 'real' historic cost gain.

Depreciation $t_0 - t_1$

Historic cost depreciation for the period would be 10 per cent of £100,000 = £10,000. However, to adjust it for inflation, the historic cost of the plant would need to be translated into t_1 purchasing power terms: that is, £100,000 + 3/20 x 100,000 = £115,000. Inflation-adjusted depreciation of the period would then be 10 per cent of £115,000 = £11,500. Thus both the original cost of the plant and its related periodic depreciation would be re-expressed in current purchasing power terms.

Holding cash $t_0 - t_1$

Cash of £23,000 was held throughout the period, when its generalized purchasing power declined by 15 per cent. Thus, to maintain its purchasing power in terms of money at t_1, the company would require to have had cash resources of £23,000 + 3/20 x 23,000 = £26,450. Likewise, the £7,000 accumulated throughout the period has diminished in purchasing power by t_1 by an average rate for the period of 7½ per cent. By t_1 an equivalent sum of £7,000 + 3/40 x 7,000 = £7,525 would be required to maintain the purchasing power of t_1 cash resources at a level enjoyed by resources at t_0. Thus, although the company held £30,000 at t_1, it should have held £26,450 + 7,525 = £33,975 to maintain its purchasing power during a period of 15 per cent inflation. It has therefore 'lost' £33,975 − 30,000 = £3,975 of purchasing power by holding cash during a period of inflation, and this effect is not accounted for by traditional accounting practice.

Long-term liability $t_0 - t_1$

A similar but opposite effect to holding cash occurs with long-term liabilities. During the period $t_0 - t_1$, the debenture loan remained at £100,000. But with inflation at 15 per cent, the purchasing power of the money to be repaid fell by such a percentage. Thus the company 'gained' by 15 per cent of £100,000 = £15,000 by 'holding' such a liability during $t_0 - t_1$. Again, traditional accounting practice ignores this inflationary effect.

Summary of effects $t_0 - t_1$

The traditional approach to accounting would measure income for the period $t_0 - t_1$ at £70,000 − 10,000 = £60,000 (the trading income after deduction of depreciation). By way of contrast, and following the recommended practice in the United Kingdom at the present time, inflation-adjusted income would be as follows:

Adjusted trading income		£56,500
Less: adjusted depreciation on plant		11,500
		£45,000
Add: net gain on monetary items:		
Gain on long-term liability	£15,000	
Less: loss on holding cash	3,975	11,025
		£56,025

In other words, whereas unadjusted income in the illustration is, after depreciation, £60,000, the adjusted figure is £45,000, which is augmented by a further
net gain on monetary items of £11,025, this not being recognized in traditional
practice. There can therefore be considerable differences between adjusted and
unadjusted income data, indicating the serious effect which inflation can have
on historic cost-based information.

Doubts about inflation accounting

The full extent of inflation accounting adjustments may be explored in detail
in other sources.[19] Nevertheless, the example contained in Illustration 12 indicates
the seriousness of the problem, as is now recognized in Britain.[20] The result of
translating historic cost financial statements in this way has been examined by
Cutler and Westwick,[21] who have estimated that translation would cause the
reported income figures of most companies to be reduced from their unadjusted
levels (particularly in the case of fixed asset-intensive companies with large
depreciation provisions for fixed assets which have been held for some time).
However, they also demonstrated that, in the case of companies with significant
long-term liabilities and/or considerable bank borrowings, the effect would be
considerably to increase reported income because of the inflationary gain on
holding monetary items of this kind. Nevertheless, the adjustments have created
doubts and criticisms about the usefulness of the process.

Accounting and reporting on the effects of inflation is obviously a serious
attempt to resolve a serious problem. Inflation effects all companies to some
extent, and it is proper to try to reflect this in published financial reports.
Nevertheless the task is not a straightforward one, and it can create as many
problems as it attempts to solve.

Adjusting historic costs

Inflation adjustments are normally advocated and applied to historic cost data.
The aim is to recognize periodic income only when the purchasing power of
shareholders' equity has been maintained. However, the adjusted figures in the
income statement and balance sheet are somewhat difficult to interpret: they
represent neither the original values of the transactions concerned nor any
revaluations in so-called current value terms. They are simply a translation
from one monetary unit to another, and, as such, the basic principles of historic
cost and realization remain undisturbed. The major problem is that users may
believe the adjusted figures to be current values and assume that the advantages
of current value accounting have been obtained in the form of up-to-date balance
sheet values and incorporation of unrealized gains. Therefore adjusting historic
cost statements for the effects of inflation could be potentially misleading.

Making the adjustments

Inflation accounting proposals and requirements have until now seemed to rely on two assumptions. First, there is the assumption that inflation affects all companies in the same way and at the same rate. This is evidenced in the proposals and provisions for the use of one general index by all companies which are required to account for the effects of inflation. Second, there is the assumption that consumption-orientated indices are meaningful indicators of the fall in the purchasing power of the monetary unit. The use of the Index of Retail Prices is a British example of this point.

Inflation affects different people and different companies in different ways. Much depends on what is being purchased by the individual company or person. Thus the rate of inflation will vary according to individual circumstances. However, inflation accounting seems to ignore this, and the result may well be that the use of a generalized measure of inflation fails to account properly for the individual effect on an individual company. This, of course, runs entirely contrary to the stated aim of such adjustments.

Companies purchase different goods and services in order to stay in business. Very often these products are highly complex and specialized. The question is then raised as to whether an index comprising prices from a domestic 'shopping basket' are relevant to companies involved mainly in non-domestic expenditure. In any case, the available indices are only statistical averages and cannot therefore reflect changes in all prices. Consequently, the use of consumer and retail indices is open to question when considering the relevance and utility of the inflation adjustments.

The place of inflation accounting

Accounting and reporting on the effects of inflation has been debated over many years. It now has a limited application in practice in Britain with the adjustment of historic cost data and the presentation of statements as supplements to the legally required income statement and balance sheet. As such, it can be seen as, essentially, a translation exercise to ensure that all reported data are expressed in terms of a monetary unit with a fixed purchasing power; that is, fixed at the end of each reporting period.

By making these translations, inflationary gain and loss elements are segregated from other elements which represent a real increase in the physical resources of the company concerned. Hence they are not exclusive to historic cost data. They can be applied to economic values, replacement costs and realizable values so as to isolate the effects of inflation from trading and financial results. Their major disadvantage is that they may be believed to be valuation rather than monetary translation exercises; and another disadvantage is that it is potentially misleading to assume a universal rate of inflation. These doubts and criticisms are obviously serious points to consider when assessing the overall usefulness and relevance of the reported information.

The Flexibility Problem[22]

The most vexed issue in financial reporting for many years has arguably been the growing number of possible accounting practices available to accountants when preparing financial reports. The problem concerns the flexibility of accounting practice in which a given set of financial circumstances, events and transactions can be measured in a number of possible different ways, thereby producing substantially different measures of income and financial position. However, in no way can it be regarded as a new problem. It has confronted accountants throughout the decades during which company financial reporting has progressed and developed. The question is therefore why it has become such an important and, indeed, public issue in recent times.

The answer would appear to be related to the increasing expertise of the main users of accounting information (including the financial press) and the increasing complexity of company activity, which demands a greater communication and use of accounting information. The first point is a relatively easy one to explain: as users become more knowledgable about the nature and problems associated with accounting information, the problems inevitably become more public. The second is rather more difficult to explain, but seems to revolve around the merger and acquisition activity of the 1960s.

During the late 1960s, the corporate sector of private enterprise developed to a considerable extent by means of merger or acquisition: companies have either combined to form larger entities created for the purpose (for example, British Motor Holdings Ltd and the Leyland Motor Corporation Ltd combining in 1967 to form British Leyland Motor Corporation Ltd); or one company has been taken over by another (for example, Schweppes Ltd acquired Cadbury Ltd in 1969). These activities create significant accounting and reporting problems, all of which have had (and still have) a bearing on the flexibility problem.

First, with an acquisition or merger, the companies concerned can produce both historic and forecast data relating to profitability and financial position to help their shareholders decide whether or not to agree to the acquisition or merger. Because of the flexibility of accounting practice, particularly before the 1970s, one participant company could be using certain practices while the other could be using different practices. However, once the merger or acquisition is accomplished, a uniformity of practice may be established for both companies, which can render the comparison of pre and post-merger or acquisition financial results extremely difficult. In addition, forecast data may be produced on the basis of one set of practices, but actual data prepared using a differing post-merger or acquisition approach; again, comparisons will be difficult. This situation is best demonstrated in the case of Associated Electrical Industries Ltd in 1967-8 where, because of a takeover bid from General Electric Co. Ltd, an income forecast of £10 million was issued to its shareholders. The actual achievement, however, was a loss of £4.5 million. Of the difference of £14.5 million, £9.5 million was largely the result of differences in pre and post-takeover accounting treatment.

Secondly, once a merger or acquisition has been completed, there arises a further accounting and reporting problem which is, again, caused by the inherent flexibility in accounting practice. At the present time, at least in the United Kingdom, there are two distinct methods of incorporating the net assets of acquired or merged companies for financial reporting purposes, each of which reflects an entirely different balance-sheet position. The first is to account for the combination at so-called 'fair value'; thus, the net assets of the acquired or merged companies are incorporated into the financial statements of the combined entity at their current valuation (including a valuation of any goodwill which has been acquired at the time). The second is much less sophisticated, and is usually referred to as 'pooling of interests' or 'merger' accounting; the net assets of the acquired or merged companies are incorporated into the financial statements of the combined entity at their reported 'values' at the time of acquisition or merger. This means that, unlike 'fair value' accounting, shareholders are given little indication of the value of the net assets taken over, nor will goodwill be accounted for unless it happens to appear in the pre-takeover balance sheet of the acquired or merged company.

The above problem, reflecting flexibility in accounting practice and potentially serious differences for financial reporting purposes, despite similar circumstances, can be evidenced in recent company combinations in the United Kingdom. In 1968 the British Leyland merger took place on a pooling basis, as did the Cadbury Schweppes combination in 1969. Yet, in 1969, when General Electric combined with English Electric, fair value accounting was used, resulting in a disclosure of acquired goodwill amounting to £167.13 million. These were both very large combinations, taking place at about the same time, with all four companies profitable. Yet, in the former case, no account was taken for financial reporting purposes of the current valuation of combined net assets; nor was the existence of goodwill acknowledged. In the latter case, this was done, revealing a massive undervaluation of net assets in the companies concerned, as well as considerable goodwill.

The merger and acquisition situation may well prompt criticism of the inherent flexibility of accounting practice, and may well demonstrate examples. However, it is not the only area in which the problem can arise, and Illustration 13 and the following sections attempt to outline and evidence the extent of the problem.

Illustration 13. *Flexibility of accounting practice.*

Assume a company commences business at t_0 with capital subscribed in cash of £1,000. During the period t_0-t_4, stock was bought on three occasions: at t_0, 100 units at £50 each; at t_1, 200 units at £60 each; and at t_3, 50 units at £70 each. During the same period, the following sales were made: at t_2, 150 units at £80 each; and at t_4, 100 units at £85 each. All transactions were in cash, and the question of taxation should be ignored.

The following possible income and financial position figures could be measured. The first set assumes unsold stock is valued at the latest possible cost; the second set assumes it is valued at the earliest possible cost; and the third set assumes it is valued at an average cost.

Income and financial position t_0-t_4 (possibility 1)

Sales t_0-t_4 (150 x £80) + (100 x £85)	£20,500
Less: cost of sales t_0-t_4 (100 x £50) + (150 x £60)*	14,000
Income t_0-t_4	£ 6,500
Stock at t_4 (50 x £60) + (50 x £70)†	£ 6,500
Cash at t_4 (£1,000 + 20,500) − (£5,000 + 12,000 + 3,500)	1,000
Capital at t_4 (£1,000 + 6,500)	£ 7,500

* Earliest possible costs; first-in, first-out basis.
† Latest possible costs; first-in, first-out basis.

Income and financial position t_0-t_4 (possibility 2)

Sales t_0-t_4	£20,500

Less: cost of sales (150 x £60) + (50 x £70) + (50 x £60)*	15,500
Income $t_0 - t_4$	£ 5,000
Stock at t_4 (100 x £50)[†]	£ 5,000
Cash at t_4	1,000
Capital at t_4 (£1,000 + 5,000)	£ 6,000

*Latest possible costs; last-in, first-out basis.
†Earliest possible costs; last-in, first-out basis.

Income and financial position $t_0 - t_4$ (possibility 3)

Sales $t_0 - t_4$	'£20,500
Less: cost of sales (150 x £56.67) + (100 x £60)*	14,500
Income $t_0 - t_4$	£ 6,000
Stock at t_4 (100 x £60)[†]	£ 6,000
Cash at t_4	1,000
Capital at t_4 (£1,000 + 6,000)	£ 7,000

*Weighted average cost at point of sale.
† Weighted average cost at period end.

This illustration, though simplified, reveals that, by using three entirely permissible methods of stock valuation within the historic cost system of valuation, it is possible to produce three different income figures and three different capital figures. Yet the financial circumstances are identical on each case. It is obviously a situation ripe for confusion, for what is to be regarded as the 'right' or 'correct' figure: is income, for instance, to be measured as £5,000, £6,000 or £6,500? Given that this flexibility is to be found in other areas of accounting practice affecting the production of company financial statements (for example, with depreciation of fixed assets; and accounting for research and development expenditure, deferred taxation, goodwill and mergers and acquisitions), it is not surprising that Chambers[23] concluded that a conservative estimate of the possible number of ways of measuring and reporting the same financial circumstances could be well over one million.

The empirical evidence

Obviously, the messages of doom spelt out by Chambers and others[24] may be somewhat exaggerated since they are writing of the potential scope for flexibility. In fact, there does tend to be a general acceptance of specific practices in particular areas of accounting, and this imposes a degree of uniformity in financial reporting. This can be shown from empirical data gathered from various studies of practices adopted by companies in their financial statements. The following are given as brief examples.

Valuation of stock and work in progress

The Institute of Chartered Accountants in England and Wales, in its annual surveys of 300 of the largest UK companies, reveals the data relating to stock valuations which are given in Table 1.[25]

Table 1. *Stock and work-in-progress valuation.*

Valuation basis*	Number of companies			
	1969-70	*1970-71*	*1971-72*	*1972-73*
Cost	35	32	32	14
Cost or under	14	9	15	19
Lower of cost or net realizable value	236	235	240	263
Lower of cost or replacement price	22	18	21	15
Lowest of cost, net realizable value and replacement price	15	15	15	7
'Base stock' at historical cost of original stocks, or as subsequently revised	6	6	5	5
'On bases and by methods of computation considered appropriate in the circumstances of the business, consistently applied'	15	12	8	3
Miscellaneous bases	22	20	22	8
	365	347	358	334

*These are abbreviated definitions of the terms used:

Cost: this includes all expenditure directly incurred in purchase or manufacture, plus, if appropriate, a proportion of works and general overhead expenses attributable to bringing the stock to its existing condition and location.

Net realizable value: the amount considered likely to be realized from disposal of the stock in the normal course of business.

Replacement price: the amount which would currently have to be expended to acquire or manufacture the stock.

NOTE: Several companies used more than one basis.

The figures appear to indicate a uniformity of practice in this area: in each year approximately 60-65 per cent of the companies concerned used the 'lower cost or net realizable value' basis. However, this statistic does not reveal the full story, for the 'cost' definition requires to be analysed to find out how it is accounted for in practice. Owing to a lack of adequate disclosure of information on this point by the companies concerned, the English Institute surveys are unable to supply the required data. Nevertheless, a more detailed study of such practices was made in 1967 by the Institute of Chartered Accountants of Scotland,[26] and it revealed the data[27] summarized in Table 2.

Table 2. *Defining cost in stock valuations.* *

	Number of companies
Raw materials stock	
Unit cost	71
Standard cost	63
Average cost	66
First in, first out	67
Last in, first out	3
	270
Work in progress	
Unit cost	65
Standard cost	94
Average cost	44
First in, first out	43
Last in, first out	—
	246

Finished goods	
Unit cost	58
Standard cost	90
Average cost	45
First in, first out	41
Last in, first out	2
	236

Work in progress	
Cost, including a proportion of works expenditure	142
Cost, including a proportion of general administration expenses	66
	208

Finished goods	
Cost, including a proportion of works expenditure	139
Cost, including a proportion of general administration expenses	63
	202

*The following are abbreviated definitions of the terms used:

Unit cost: stock valued at the aggregate of the costs of each individual unit.
Standard cost: stock valued at a budgeted or predetermined cost.
Average cost: stock valued at the average cost of goods received during the period concerned.
First in, first out: stock valued at the cost of the goods most recently received.
Last in, first out: stock valued at the cost of the earliest possible purchases.
Base stock: the original cost of the minimum quantity of goods operationally required to be in stock.

Allowing for the possible unrepresentativeness and age of the figures in the table, it could be said that there does appear to be a lack of uniformity in the accounting treatment of stock and work in progress valuations among the companies concerned owing to an inherent flexibility in the definition of cost applied. Nevertheless, practice does appear to fall into a relatively few main categories, suggesting that it is not unreasonably flexible in this area.

Depreciation of fixed assets

Once again, our figures are extracted from surveys of the Institute of Chartered Accountants in England and Wales,[28] and these are summarized in Table 3.

Table 3. *Depreciation of fixed assets.*

Basis adopted*	Number of companies				
	1968-69	*1969-70*	*1970-71*	*1971-72*	*1972-73*
Straight-line	65	81	96	131	204
Reducing-balance	3	4	1	4	5
Mixture of methods	16	13	17	17	20
Basis not disclosed	216	202	186	148	71
	300·	300	300	300	300

*The following are abbreviated definitions of the terms used:
Straight-line: depreciation calculated as a fixed proportion of original cost.
Reducing-balance: depreciation calculated as a fixed percentage of the declining amount of unallocated original cost.

From this rather limited data, it is clear that there is in practice a good deal of uniformity in the methods of depreciation used by those companies disclosing information on the subject. This is confirmed by a relatively recent questionnaire survey of eighty-nine companies conducted by the Institute of Chartered Accountants of Scotland. A summary of the results available is given in Table 4.[29]

Table 4. *Depreciation of buildings and plant.*

	Number of companies* Depreciation of	
	Buildings	Plant
Annual depreciation based on:		
Historic cost	65	84
Revaluations	14	8
Replacement cost	2	1
Other bases	2	—
	83	93*

	Number of companies*
Estimated lifetime of fixed assets based on:	
Time	79
Usage	30
Obsolescence	23
Other factors	7

	Number of companies* Depreciation of	
	Buildings	Plant
Depreciation method adopted:		
Straight-line	58	57
Reducing-balance	17	37
Sum-of-the-years'-digits†	—	1
Other	3	1
	78	96*

*Certain companies adopted more than one basis.
†A variation of reducing balance.

Therefore, as we can see from the tables, companies do now appear to prefer the straight-line basis for computing annual depreciation charges, thereby possibly introducing an actual substantial element of uniformity. However, as the Scottish Institute figures suggest, a material degree of flexibility can be introduced when implementing the 'standardized' method adopted, that is, in relation to estimating the life of the fixed asset for depreciation purposes.

Treatment of goodwill

Goodwill can be a substantial element of a company's financial position, representing, as it so often does, intangible resources which may be extremely valuable. Generally speaking, goodwill is only accounted for in traditional accounting practice when it is acquired by the company concerned, either for cash or for some other consideration (such as shares or loan stock).[30] Thus, when a company acquires or merges with another company or business, the assets acquired or merged can include those intangibles termed 'goodwill'. However, as a recent survey reveals,[31] the methods of accounting for this item can vary significantly in practice. Table 5 summarizes the data collected in this study.

Table 5. *Accounting for goodwill.*

	1962	1963	1964	1965	1966	1967	1968	1969	1970	1971
Number of companies with dis-disclosure of goodwill	45	43	45	46	52	58	60	66	66	66
Percentage* of companies disclosing goodwill as: (a) a fixed asset	31	30	27	24	19	26	20	15	14	14
(b) neither a fixed nor a current asset	24	21	22	28	25	26	28	29	27	32
(c) a separate deduction from reserves	18	19	22	22	21	16	12	9	9	9
(d) a reserve	13	12	11	9	8	10	10	11	9	8
(e) a write-off to income re-tained or reserves	49	44	40	50	42	57	55	62	62	58

*Certain companies adopted more than one basis of accounting for goodwill.

These figures, derived from an analysis of the financial statements of a hundred of the largest industrial companies in the United Kingdom, show an apparent trend of uniformity from treating goodwill as a reportable asset towards accounting for it as a write-off to past and present income. Despite this movement, however, it is evident that there remains a great deal of flexibility in practice, and that this has been the case among the companies concerned for a number of years.

Accounting for acquisitions and mergers

There are two main methods of accounting for acquired or merged companies.[32] They can be consolidated into the financial statements of the acquiring company either at their existing book value, based on original costs (in which case, no account is taken of their current valuation at the time of acquisition or merger); or at their current valuation (in which case, assets and liabilities, including any goodwill, are revalued and accounted for at the relevant figures). As a recent study shows,[33] it is extremely difficult, if not impossible, to ascertain which method companies have adopted, since they do not adequately disclose details of their acquisitions and mergers. Table 6 summarizes this, and reveals an apparently significant flexibility in this area of accounting practice.[34]

Table 6. *Accounting for acquisitions and mergers.*

	1962	1963	1964	1965	1966	1967	1968	1969	1970	1971
Number of companies with definite disclosure of acquisitions and mergers	24	30	35	33	43	42	45	53	53	58
Percentage of companies directly disclosing details of values for acquisitions, etc.	17	26	23	27	23	36	47	28	26	31
Percentage of companies where values can be calculated for acquisitions, etc., despite lack of direct disclosure	33	7	9	6	9	10	31	30	24	22
Percentage of companies where values are unknown for acquisitions, etc., being neither directly disclosed nor calculable	50	67	68	67	68	54	22	42	50	47
Percentage of companies giving details of exchange for acquisitions, etc.	55	63	60	57	54	52	27	32	26	43

Although the figures reflect a reasonable uniformity of practice, it is obvious that there is no clear-cut standard practice, even with a relatively simple issue such as disclosure of information.

Accounting for funds flow

The previous sections have mainly concentrated on the lack of uniformity in the measurement of accounting information, but with that immediately preceding looking at flexibility in disclosure practices. This latter issue has been examined more closely in a recent study of funds statement practices.[35] It was found that there is a considerable flexibility in the accounting treatment of particular funds' items.[36] There are in the United Kingdom, however, indications of a growing concensus on the nature of the funds being accounted for, the most popular definition seeming to be that which reconciles the various funds' flows to the periodic change in cash or near-cash resources of a company. This can be more clearly demonstrated by the information contained in Table 7.[37]

Table 7. *Definition of funds movements.*

	1968	1969	1970	1971	1972
Number of companies publishing funds statements	10	15	22	28	35
Percentage companies accounting for funds as changes in:					
Working capital	—	—	—	—	—
Cash or near-cash resources	50	47	64	64	63
All financial resources	50	53	36	36	37

Admittedly, these figures are small, though the companies concerned represent the largest UK industrial concerns of the present time. But they do reveal an increasing uniformity, conducted on a purely voluntary basis and free of any professional regulations,[38] thereby supporting the contention that, in many accounting matters, flexibility in practice is nowhere near the level of the theoretically possible range.

The need for accounting standards

Littleton[39] has defined an accounting standard as an agreed-upon criterion of what is regarded as best practice in a given set of circumstances, thus allowing adequate comparisons and judgements to be made of periodic data.

Thus, accounting standards are accepted as practical measures to improve the quality of reported financial information. They have evolved out of the concern and criticism which the flexibility in accounting practice has created. Standards exist to help the accounting practitioner to apply those accounting practices regarded as the most suitable for the circumstances concerned, and, as such, they formalize the previously unwritten but generally acceptable practices. In addition, they place individual companies and their managements in the position of having to justify whatever practices they adopt when producing their financial statements. Management should not be allowed to adopt any form of accounting it likes, for this type of anarchy could lead to significant doubts about the quality of reported accounting information, and thereby reduce its credibility and potential usefulness.

Without question, the main aim of accounting standards is to protect users of company financial statements by providing them with information in which they can have confidence. In so doing, this also helps to minimize the inherent flexibility in accounting practice by imposing a necessary but realistic uniformity on accounting practice. Thus, the individual information user can attempt adequate comparisons between companies and between periods for the same company through the use of reported financial statements. Standardization is not therefore intended to put accounting in a straight-jacket. Rather is it an attempt to limit the theorically possible flexibility and to give practitioners realistic working guidelines. If the individual circumstances of a particular company are such that an existing standard is not suitable, then alternative practices, regarded as more suitable, can be adopted. Thus, as pointed out by Stamp,[40] it is possible to achieve both uniformity and flexibility in accounting practice. These two apparent opposites are not incompatible.

The accounting standards process

The need to formalize accounting practice by producing acceptable accounting standards has long been recognized in many countries. In both the United Kingdom and the United States the search for standards has been in progress since the 1930s, but only recently has any significant advance been made. Up to the mid-1930s, accounting practices developed in a relatively aimless manner, individual companies accounting usually as they thought fit. Any general acceptance in the process was derived through custom and habit. However, the proliferation of practices which tended to increase flexibility was eventually recognized by professional accountancy bodies, and from the 1930s to the early 1960s in the United States, and by the late 1960s in the United Kingdom, accounting standards were formulated in particular problem areas and recommended for implementation by accountants and company management.[41]

This period of standardization by recommendation did give practitioners some guidance, but due to a lack of any mechanism to remove obsolete practices, as well as a lack of mandatory sanctions, the inherent flexibility in financial reporting continued (as did the consequential criticism). In the United States,[42] the recommended practices became mandatory on most qualified accountants from 1963 onwards, and a similar position was reached in 1970 in the United Kingdom with the commencement of a programme to produce the now familiar *Statements of Standard Accounting Practice.*

Of particular concern to United Kingdom readers are these latter statements. They are produced mainly by a committee, and following a period of exposure and comment on the proposed practices, are mandatory for all relevantly qualified accountants[43] involved in producing financial statements. They must ensure that stated standards are implemented by the companies by whom they are employed, unless circumstances dictate that there should be a departure; in which case, this has to be fully disclosed in the published financial statements.[44] Company auditors are also required to verify that companies have been following standard accounting practice, and report on the acceptability of any departures made.[45] Despite these impositions on accountants, however, it must be said that the *Statements of Standard Accounting Practice* are not mandatory on the persons ultimately responsible for the production and quality of financial statements (company directors), unless they also happen to be accountants to which the *Statements* apply. Thus, it is quite conceivable that company managements can deviate from the stated accounting standards, irrespective of the circumstances, though this will require to be reported on by their auditors. In other words, professional statements of this kind do not have the same force as those contained in statutory instruments such as the Companies Acts. The onus for implementation is largely with individual accountants.

Accounting standards problems

The process of trying to introduce a reasonable degree of uniformity into financial reporting practices is fraught with problems, many of which have not been fully recognized. This section attempts to outline certain of these problems, albeit briefly.

Uniformity and comparability

Accounting standards are designed specifically to reduce existing and potential flexibility in financial reporting practice. Hopefully, this is done to allow information users to make better use of the reporting data, and particularly to improve inter and intra-company comparisons (especially for assessing alternatives in decision-making activities). However, no two companies are alike, despite apparent similarities in business activity. Therefore the danger is that standardization may impose a uniformity which creates a false comparability. In particular, it may obscure a company's 'personality' which can be assessed, in part, by the way in which its reported accounting information is measured.[46] There is a behavioural argument which suggests that the attitudes of company management can be partially evaluated from an analysis of the accounting practices it adopts (that is, dynamic and risk-taking or conservative and risk-avoiding). For example, a company writing off its research and development expenditure immediately against income could be said to be more conservative than another company which prefers to amortize it over its expected useful life. It may be suggested that this type of analysis is impossible to make if a standard accounting practice was adopted which mandatorily required every company to write off such expenditure immediately.

The short-term and the long-term

The existing system of financial reporting by companies is based upon historic cost values and the realization principle. The process of standardization attempts to reduce the flexibility of such a system. As such, it seeks to improve the quality of historic cost measures of income and financial position. But standardization does not, itself, provide answers to the long-term problems of accounting. In particular it provides no direct answer to the question of what is the most relevant information to be reported to the potential users of company financial reports. It merely 'tidies up' one of the available alternative systems. The danger, therefore, is that the efforts put into the short-term aims of the standardization process may very well divert attention away from the more long-term need to search for the best possible blend of accounting information for reporting purposes. Indeed, it could well be that the seeming improvements in the existing historic cost system might be taken as long-term answers in themselves. If this were so, it would be disastrous to the future of the company financial reporting system and the accountancy profession, for the latter has a primary responsibility to seek improvements in the former.

The need to reappraise

One of the major lessons to be learnt from a study of the history of financial reporting practices is that they have evolved largely in response to changes in the economic, social and technological environment of accounting. Thus, the Industrial Revolution introduced the problems of accounting for fixed assets; the development of stock markets created the need for greater disclosure of accounting information; and the social responsibilities of companies are now receiving attention in much of what is presently disclosed in financial reports. It can be reasonably assumed that changes will continue to occur and influence corresponding changes in the nature and quantity of information reported by companies. This means that the process of accounting standardization must always be regarded as a continuous one, with individual standards being the subject of continual reappraisal to assess their validity in light of changing circumstances. One of the faults of the previous 'recommendation' stage in accounting was that it did not contain a mechanism to remove invalid or obsolete recommendations, thereby helping to 'inflate' accounting flexibility. The danger with mandatory standards is that the same fault may be perpetuated.

Responsibility for standards

The question of who should be responsible for formulating and monitoring accounting standards is one of the biggest problems in the quest to minimize accounting flexibility. Accountants, and their professional bodies, have traditionally accepted this responsibility, with general support from statutory instruments such as the Companies Acts, and particular guidance from decisions upheld in courts of law. However, the existing system of mandatory standards has brought its attendant problems of responsibility.

First, company management, in the form of boards of directors, has overall responsibility for the quality of published financial reports, but the mandatory accounting standards do not cover those directors who are not members of the professional accountancy bodies concerned. Therefore, although individual accountants may have a duty to ensure that prescribed standards are implemented, the mandatory scope of the standards is not sufficient to give them the same status as a statutory instrument. It could be argued that standards should become part of company law so as to make company management fully responsible for their implementation. However, as already said, accounting standards will be required to change over time, and this is much more difficult to accomplish once they are enshrined in, for instance, a Companies Act.

Secondly, there can be instances of particular accounting standards being of such consequence that their formulation cannot be regarded as the sole responsibility of the accountancy profession, and so government or other interested groups may step in to take a rightful share of responsibility. In such cases, the accountancy profession must allow these other interests to assume certain of the responsibility to avoid conflict and confusion which may prove detrimental to the credibility of company financial reports. A recent example of this type of co-operation in the United Kingdom is the accounting standard produced to measure the effects of inflation on the purchasing power of money in company financial statements.[47] Because of the public interest in this matter, central government set up a committee to examine the problem in the widest possible way. Meantime, the UK accountancy bodies have produced a provisional *Statement of Standard Accounting Practice.*[48]

Extent of standardization

Business activity is rapidly becoming an extremely complex multinational affair, with a continuous movement towards bigger units and companies. The process of accounting standardization cannot, therefore, be thought of simply as a 'local' issue, affecting all companies in the locality concerned. In each such locality there will exist small and large companies; some will trade nationally, and some will trade internationally; some will have large bodies of shareholders, and others will have a small number. These developments, which have existed for many years, raise important questions on the extent of standarization to be employed.

First, should mandatory accounting standards formulated by the professional bodies (and, where necessary, other interested groups) be applicable to all companies, irrespective of size, nature of business, shareholder population, etc.? So far, in the United Kingdom and most other relevant countries, little or no attention has been paid to these corporate differences, mandatory standards applying to all companies. Exceptions to this policy can be seen in Continental Europe, where several countries distinguish in their legislative requirements between different sizes of company (this being mainly determined by the size of subscribed share capital). However, in the United Kingdom, legal and professional standards affecting financial reporting make no such distinctions, and so many existing or proposed accounting standards do not seem to have universal application; for example, those dealing with accounting for the financial results of associated companies,[49] acquisitions and mergers,[50] earnings per share,[51] research and development expenditure[52] and goodwill.[52] There would therefore seem to be a strong case for standardization according to size and type of company, so as to impose a uniformity in accounting practice where this is desirable and necessary.

Secondly, as individual countries develop their own accounting standards to deal with 'local' problems in financial practice, it is apparent that these problems are not as localized as they may seem, and, indeed, many of them are common to most developed countries with an established investment market and company reporting system. It therefore seems sensible to bring about some degree of harmonization of accounting standards between countries so as to prevent significant differences arising which could cause confusion, particularly from the point of view of investors investing in companies in different countries, and of companies which trade in several countries. Once common international standards are adopted, investors have the assurance that reported information from different countries has been measured on a generally accepted basis. Companies, too, would not have to cope with conflicting standards of varying quality when consolidating accounting data from various countries for reporting purposes. With these points in mind, it is interesting to see the formation taking place of international bodies of accountants to deal with cross-frontier harmonization of accounting standards: for example, the various Study Groups of the European Economic Community, the Accountants International Study Group, and the International Accounting Standards Committee. But this proliferation of accounting standards bodies brings with it an attendant danger: the problem of various bodies producing different standards to deal with the same accounting problem. So far those matters which have been standardized have not produced this potential divergence, but it could happen in the future, and what are companies to do when it does? Which standard should they adhere to? Should it be a national one, or an international one? Presumably national considerations should prevail, but this could mean a violation of an international standard, as in the case of a UK company following a *Statement of Standard Accounting Practice* which differed materially from an equivalent European Economic Community *Directive*.

Summary on flexibility

Hopefully, the previous sections have given the reader some idea of the issues and problems associated with the inherent flexibility of financial accounting practice, many of which remain unresolved. It must in particular be made clear that, short of instituting legal provisions requiring all companies to measure and report accounting information according to a completely inflexible code of rules, it is impossible to envisage absolute uniformity in accounting practice, even with mandatory standards. The individual circumstances of each company, coupled with the degree of subjective judgement which is so necessary in accounting measurement, make it virtually impossible to envisage statements of accounting standards which can impose rigid uniformity. In other words, flexibility in accounting practice should never be eliminated completely; to do so is undesirable and liable adversely to affect the quality of financial reports.

The Communications Problem

Anatole France wrote in *Revolt of the Angels* that: 'It is better to understand little than to misunderstand a lot.' This is most apt when looking at company financial reports, which are intended to be the major means by which company management communicates the results of its efforts on behalf of shareholders. However, the messages they contain are couched in the highly technical language of accounting, which may not always be clearly understood by the report user who lacks accounting training or experience. Thus, irrespective of the relevance of the data contained in financial reports, there is an obvious danger of their utility being seriously eroded because of the way in which the data are communicated. As Bedford has stated:

'Accounting disclosures rely heavily on symbols, which represent things and actions in the socioeconomic world, and whose use is based on the assumption that the message sender (accountant) and the message receiver (decision-maker) have a common understanding of the meaning of the symbols.'[53]

It is this assumption which demands continuous scrutiny, for accounting messages have become more complex in recent years owing to the inevitable expansion in legal, governmental and professional requirements for disclosure. The remaining sections of this chapter attempt to highlight several of the more important points in this problem area.

A common understanding

As already implied, the idea behind the disclosure of accounting information is that its producer and user will have interpreted the meaning of the messages contained in it in the same way, and that no confusion will arise owing to there being no difference in such an interpretation. However, this is extremely difficult to achieve in accounting because of the flexibility in its practice. For example, the terms 'income' and 'profitability' mean different things to different people in differing circumstances: to present-day accountants, reported income is usually realized income of the period concerned (because of the generally accepted use of the historic cost and realization principles). However, if these principles are relaxed, and replacement costs or net realizable values are used instead, then income becomes that which is earned during the period (whether realized or not). The danger is that users may believe reported income to be that which is earned rather than that which is realized. This could lead to confusing and misplaced interpretations of company profitability.

A similar problem could also arise in the area of accounting for the changing purchasing power of money when it is applied to the existing system of historic cost accounting. As suggested in the recent UK standard practice,[54] this process involves translating historic cost figures into contemporary purchasing power terms. To someone not fully versed in the rationale underlying such adjustments, this may well give the impression of revaluation rather than translation of company assets. Thus, the translated balance sheet particularly could be mistaken for a current valuation statement of company net resources.

As Bedford[55] has pointed out, there are other similar areas of potential confusion. It is therefore vital for the users of company financial reports to be adequately informed of the precise meaning of the figures supplied to them. This is perhaps more easily said than done, although company managements and their accountants are becoming increasingly conscious of the need to give explanations of data reported in their published statements. Indeed, this is now required of accountants in the United Kingdom who are responsible for producing these statements.[56]

Differences in perception

Possible variations in the way in which different financial report users perceive the same economic activity through the use of the same financial report is one of the least explored areas of accounting, and it has distinct implications for the effectiveness of accounting communications. It is a well-known pyschological concept of human behaviour[57] that, despite the reality of a situation, different people will manage to perceive it differently — whether the perceptions are direct (that is, via direct observation or contact with the object or person being perceived) or indirect (that is, via some means by which the object or person is indirectly observed or contacted; as with newspaper accounts of politicians).

These perceptual differences can arise for a variety of reasons. For one thing, personal experience limits the ability to perceive reality (a person who has never observed or experienced the use of a chair is hardly likely to perceive its particular use on first observing or coming into contact with one). In other words, the more experienced or used to the perceived object or person the perceiver is, the more likely he is to arrive at a reasonably accurate perception.

On the other hand, irrespective of past experience, the perceiver can distort what he observes by his attitudes. His prejudices and biases can therefore lead him to see things which he wants to see, or to ignore things which he does not want to see, irrespective of what is actually there to see. Finally it is possible for the reality of the objects or persons being perceived to be distorted in such a way that the perceiver fails to observe accurately (for example, as with a very rusty motor car that has been resprayed to cover up structural defects when it is being offered for sale).

All the above points have some relevance to the communication of reportable accounting data, and therefore present problems in the financial reporting function. Company financial reports form a significant means by which shareholders and other interested parties can perceive the activities and affairs of companies. The nature and quality of these perceptions depend to a large extent on the experiences and attitudes of the users concerned. It also depends on how the data are communicated. In other words, the accuracy of user perception will increase the more the user is experienced in reading and analysing accounting information; the more open-minded he is when using the information (for example, his expectations of company performance should not be so inflexible that he perceives what he believes company performance ought to be); and the more objective is the process of producing and packaging the information in report form. The major problem is thus one of ensuring objectivity and integrity in the communication process, so far as both the producer and user of information are concerned. This is something which obviously cannot be legislated for, or regulated; it has to be worked at by all concerned. If this is not done, then a situation exists in which the report user could perceive company activity and performance inaccurately, with consequential disbenefits to himself from misguided decisions.

Different user information needs

As seen in previous chapters, there are several distinct groups of company financial report users, each with its own particular informational requirements. However, the present system of financial reporting concentrates on one set of financial statements (income statements, balance sheets, etc.) which, though legally intended for shareholders, adopts a general-purpose nature because of its use by various interested groups. Thus company management communicates with those groups using one main medium. The assumption must then be made that a general-purpose financial report is capable of enabling all interested persons to perceive accurately the various aspects of company activity in which they are particularly interested.

There is little or no evidence to validate the above assumption at the present time, but reasoning suggests that general-purpose reports may not, because of their general nature, fully satisfy each group. This, coupled with the perceptual problems discussed above (which affect each interested user) further suggests that the present system of reporting may result in inadequate communication of data to interested users.

Quantity of information

One of the most significant features of company financial reporting in recent years has been the increase in the quantity of information disclosed in reports. Successive Companies Acts in the United Kingdom, together with the various requirements of the professional accountancy bodies, have increased disclosure to such an extent that the financial reports of quoted companies in particular have become highly complex technical documents. The problem then becomes one of attempting to pinpoint the essential messages when reading these reports. This may be possible for highly qualified expert users (such as stockbrokers, investment analysts and professional accountants), but it may not be possible for the less qualified. In addition, as pointed out by Shwayder,[58] there is a limit to the amount of information which an individual can observe and absorb at any one time. Therefore, irrespective of the technical competence of the user, there is always the problem that the disclosure of too much information may paradoxically result in a lack of communication. Companies and their accountants must be extremely careful not only in deciding what information to report but also how much of it to report. This is a difficult task because of the statutory and mandatory provisions for disclosure which now exist in practice.

Presentation of information

One further communication problem is worth mentioning and concerns the presentation of accounting information in financial reports. Because these reports are complex and highly technical, and because their users cannot absorb every message contained in them at the one time, it is possible that users will tend to concentrate on selected items of information rather than on the total available. In this way, by a process of selection, the user attempts to identify what he regards as the most relevant items of information to him, and avoids the problems of complexity in reporting by focusing his attention on these.

However, this selection process also has its problems for it is perfectly possible for the producer of reported information to highlight data he wishes the user to observe, and to attempt to remove from the user's immediate attention those data he does not wish to be observed. This can be done by a careful positioning of data in the final report, as well as by layout and print size. The most obvious area where this could happen is in the presentation of annual financial statements in general, and footnotes to main statement figures in particular. The experienced and expert user of financial reports should be able to guard against this: but, unless the 'non-expert' user becomes involved in analysing the detail of financial statements, it is doubtful if he will be able to minimize its effects.

Accounting terminology

One of the biggest problems in communicating accounting information is accounting terminology, simply because it can be extremely complex and lacks, on occasion, definitions which are generally acceptable. If this is the case, and existing evidence tends to suggest that it is, then financial reports may not as yet be adequately fulfilling their function of communicating. Soper and Dolphin,[59] when applying specific readability formulae to certain annual financial reports, found that comprehension was likely to be difficult, and that this was the case when the reports were assessed by persons both trained and untrained in financial matters. Smith and Smith[60] conducted a similar exercise to footnotes in annual financial statements and found the level of comprehension such as to make the use of these reports significantly restricted. Still[61] produced a British study of the readability of the chairman's report in the annual financial report from the point of view of company employees, and concluded that '. . . it appears that most reports to shareholders made by chairmen of British companies are likely to be found difficult or impossible to comprehend by a majority of employees'.[62]

As shareholders and other groups are composed of persons both trained and untrained in accountancy and financial matters, it is likely that all such groups would find difficulty with the chairman's report, and also, presumably, with other more technical statements such as the income statement and balance sheet. If this is the case, then the required and needed communication is not being achieved.

Suggested Essay or Discussion Topics

1. Arguably the most fundamental problem in company financial reporting is valuation because different valuation measures produce different income measures. Discuss.

2. The realization principle in historic cost accounting has been criticized on numerous occasions over the years, yet it has continued to survive. Why?

3. The economist and the accountant are poles apart in their thinking on the concept of income. Discuss the validity of this statement, and suggest ways in which these differences (if any) could be reconciled.

4. It has been suggested that because there are so many ways of measuring periodic income of a company for reporting purposes, this gives the impression of lies being reported. In other words, income is an absolute rather than a relative concept, and hence there should be only one way of describing it. Discuss.

5. The function of adjusting accounting data for changes in the purchasing power of the monetary measurement unit is a process of translation rather than valuation. Discuss.

6. The validity of general price-level adjusted accounting data hinges on the reliability of the index used. Comment on this statement in relation to existing suggestions in the United Kingdom and United States.

7. Explain the problems associated with the treatment for reporting purposes of current value holding gains, and monetary gains and losses, as elements of income.

8. 'Uniformity of accounting is said to be bad – that it stifles incentive and creative thinking, that it would bar experimentation in accounting. The uniformity bugaboo is a red herring that turns away and discourages searching inquiry into the problems. Seeking to improve or define accounting principles has been labelled as an attempt to establish uniformity, as seeking a straitjacket for accounting. Yet in simple truth, uniform accounting principles as applied to specific transactions foster reliability, quality performance and honesty, and require more original thinking than any of the so-called experimental practices we are now following.' Comment and discuss this statement on the problem of standardization of accounting practice.

9. There is a grave danger that increasing uncertainty as to the credibility and reliability of published financial statements will lead to potential users ignoring these sources of information and seeking others which they believe to be more reliable and relevant. Comment.

10. Why is it necessary to standardize accounting practices? What evidence exists to suggest that flexibility in such practice is a bad thing?

11. The type and amount of disclosure of accounting information in company financial statements depends, at least in part, on how expert the reader can be expected to be in interpreting accounting data. Comment on this statement in relation to the potential users of these statements.

12. Describe the relationship between the concepts of relevance, materiality and adequate disclosure in company financial reporting.

13. The trouble with financial reports is that they disclose too much data rather than too little. Everything is distilled and aggregated into figures which obscure vital messages concerning the financial performance and condition of companies. What is wanted is a reduction in disclosure, thus reversing the previous trend. Discuss.

Notes and References

1. e.g., A. C. Littleton, 'The Significance of Invested Cost', *Accounting Review,* April 1952, pp. 167-73; E. K. Kohler, 'Why Not Retain Historical Cost?', *Journal of Accountancy,* October 1963, pp. 35-41; and Y. Ijiri, 'A Defence of Historical Cost Accounting', in R. R. Sterling (ed.), *Asset Valuation and Income Determination,* Scholars Book Co., 1971, pp. 1-14.

2. e.g., American Accounting Association, *A Statement of Basic Accounting Theory,* 1966; Arthur Andersen & Co., *Objectives of Financial Statements for Business Enterprises,* Arthur Andersen & Co., 1972; K. MacNeal, *Truth in Accounting,* Scholars Book Co., 1970 reprint; and H. Ross, *Financial Statements – A Crusade for Current Values,* Pitman, 1969.

3. As in, e.g., I. Fisher, *The Theory of Interest,* Macmillan, 1930, pp. 3-35 (reprinted as 'Income and Capital', in R. H. Parker and G. C. Harcourt (eds.), *Readings in the Concept and Measurement of Income,* Cambridge University Press, 1969, pp. 33-35).

4. J. R. Hicks, *Value and Capital,* Clarendon Press, 1946, pp. 171-81 (reprinted as 'Income' in Parker and Harcourt (eds.), *Readings in the Concept and Measurement of Income,* pp. 74-82).

5. For details of discounting procedures, see C. J. Hawkins and D. W. Pearce, *Capital Investment Appraisal,* Macmillan, 1971.

6. For fuller coverage of these concepts, see T. A. Lee, *Income and Value Measurement,* Nelson, 1974, pp. 25-43.

7. ibid., pp. 39-41.

8. E. O. Edwards and P. W. Bell, *The Theory and Measurement of Business Income,* University of California Press, 1961.

9. American Accounting Association, op. cit.; R. T. Sprouse and M. Moonitz, 'A Tentative Set of Broad Accounting Principles for Business Enterprises', *Accounting Research Study 3,* American Institute of Certified Public Accountants, 1962; P. J. Dickerson, *Business Income*

    – *A Critical Analysis,* Institute of Business and Economic Research, University of California, 1965; and L. Revsine, *Replacement Cost Accounting,* Prentice-Hall, 1973.

10. A concept adapted from J. C. Bonbright, *The Valuation of Property,* McGraw-Hill, 1937.

11. Edwards and Bell, *Theory and Measurement of Business Income;* see Lee, *Income and Value Measurement,* pp. 72-87, for a detailed description of the computations involved.

12. G. Macdonald, *Profit Measurement: Alternatives to Historical Cost,* Accountancy Age Books, 1974, p. 93.

13. Advocated, e.g., in R. J. Chambers, *Accounting, Evaluation and Economic Behaviour,* Prentice-Hall, 1966; MacNeal, *Truth in Accounting;* and R. R. Sterling, *Theory of the Measurement of Enterprise Income,* University of Kansas Press, 1970. Computations and problems are covered in detail in Lee, *Income and Value Measurement,* pp. 88-99.

14. See ibid., pp. 91-4.

15. Macdonald, *Profit Measurement,* pp. 127-30.

16. e.g., American Institute of Certified Public Accountants, 'Reporting the Financial Effects of Price-Level Changes', *Accounting Research Study 6,* 1963; R. S. Gynther, 'Accounting for Price Level Changes – One General Index or Several Specific Indices?', *Accountancy,* July 1962, pp. 560-64; R. L. Mathews, 'Income, Price Changes and the Valuation Controversy in Accounting', *Accounting Review,* July 1968, pp. 509-16; W. E. Parker, 'Changes in the Purchasing Power of Money', *Accountancy,* January 1963, pp. 8-14, and February 1963, pp. 121-6; and L. S. Rosen, *Current Value Accounting and Price-Level Restatements,* Canadian Institute of Chartered Accountants, 1972.

17. e.g., American Institute of Certified Public Accountants, op. cit.; and Institute of Chartered Accountants in England and Wales, 'Accounting in Relation to Changes in the Purchasing Power of Money', *Recommendation on Accounting Principles N15,* May 1952.

18. 'Accounting for Changes in the Purchasing Power of Money', *Provisional Statement of Standard Accounting Practice 7,* May 1974.

19. See fuller descriptions in Lee, *Income and Value Measurement,* pp. 106-30.

20. *Provisional Statement,* op. cit.

21. R. S. Cutler and C. A. Westwick, 'The Impact of Inflation Accounting on the Stock Market', *Accountancy,* March 1973, pp. 15-24.

22. Much of this section has been developed from T. A. Lee, 'Accounting Standards and Effective Financial Reporting: A Review in Principle', *Accountant's Magazine,* January and February 1975, pp. 25-30 and 73-81.

23. R. J. Chambers, 'Financial Information and the Securities Market', *Abacus,* September 1965, pp. 3-30.

24. e.g., L. Spacek, *A Search for Fairness in Financial Reporting to the Public,* Arthur Andersen & Co., 1969; and E. Stamp and C. Marley, *Accounting Principles and the City Code: the Case for Reform,* Butterworth, 1970, Part II.

25. Taken from various editions of *Survey of Published Accounts,* General Educational Trust, Institute of Chartered Accountants in England and Wales.

26. 'Valuation of Stock and Work-in-Progress', *Research Report,* Institute of Chartered Accountants of Scotland, 1968.

27. ibid., p. 26.

28. Taken from various editions of *Survey of Published Accounts,* op. cit.

29. P. N. McMonnies, 'Depreciation: Its Meaning, Purpose and Accounting Treatment', *Accountant's Magazine,* February 1969, pp. 73-85.

30. For the detail of this problem area, see T. A. Lee, 'Goodwill – an Example of Will-o'-the-Wisp Accounting', *Accounting and Business Research,* Autumn 1971, pp. 318-28; and T. A. Lee, 'Accounting for Goodwill – an Empirical Study of Company Practices in the United Kingdom: 1962 to 1971', *Accounting and Business Research,* Summer 1973, pp. 175-96.

31. Lee, 'Accounting for Goodwill', loc. cit.

32. For fuller details, see A. T. McLean, 'Accounting for Business Combinations and Goodwill', *Research Series 1,* Institute of Chartered Accountants of Scotland, 1972.

33. T. A. Lee, 'Accounting for and Disclosure of Business Combinations', *Journal of Business Finance and Accounting,* Spring 1974, pp. 1-33.

34. ibid., p. 25.

35. T. A. Lee, 'The Funds Statement', *Research Series 5,* Institute of Chartered Accountants of Scotland, 1974.

36. ibid., pp. 36-48.

37. ibid., p. 69.

38. The figures were produced before the publication of an exposure draft in the United Kingdom, Accounting Standards Steering Committee, 'Source and Applications of Funds Statement', *Exposure Draft 13,* 1974.

39. A. C. Littleton, *Structure of Accounting Theory,* American Accounting Association, 1953, p. 143.

40. E. Stamp and C. Marley, *Accounting Principles and the City Code: the Case for Reform,* Butterworth, 1970, p. 140.

41. For a fuller description of this development in several countries, see S. A. Zeff, *Forging Accounting Principles in Five Countries: a History and Analysis of Trends,* Stipes, 1972.

42. ibid., pp. 110-268.

43. i.e. those members of the professional accountancy bodies concerned.

44. See 'Disclosure of Accounting Policies', *Statement of Standard Accounting Practice 2,* November 1971.

45. See 'The Effect of Statements of Standard Accounting Practice on Auditors' Reports', *Statement on Auditing 1,* February 1971.

46. See, e.g., G. H. Sorter and S. W. Becker, 'Corporate Personality as Reflected in Accounting Decisions: Some Preliminary Findings', *Journal of Accounting Research,* Autumn 1964, pp. 183-96.

47. 'Accounting for Changes in the Purchasing Power of Money', *Provisional Statement of Standard Accounting Practice 7,* May 1974.

48. ibid.

49. 'Accounting for the Results of Associated Companies', *Statement of Standard Accounting Practice 1,* January 1971.

50. Accounting Standards Steering Committee, 'Accounting for Acquisitions and Mergers', *Accountant's Magazine,* February 1971, pp. 60-63.

51. 'Earnings per Share', *Statement of Standard Accounting Practice 3,* March 1972.

52. Both part of the on-going research of the Accounting Standards Steering Committee at the time of writing.

53. N. M. Bedford, *Extensions in Accounting Disclosure,* Prentice-Hall, 1973, p. 45.

54. 'Accounting for Changes in the Purchasing Power of Money', op. cit.

55. Bedford, *Extensions in Accounting Disclosure,* pp. 44-7.

56. 'Disclosure of Accounting Policies', op. cit.

57. For a detailed study of indirect and direct perception of people, events and objects, see P. B. Warr and C. Knapper, *The Perception of People and Events,* John Wiley & Sons, 1968, esp. pp. 1-49.

58. K. Shwayder, 'Relevance', *Journal of Accounting Research,* Spring 1968, pp. 86-97.

59. F. J. Soper and R. Dolphin, 'Readability and Corporate Annual Reports', *Accounting Review,* April 1964, pp. 358-62.

60. J. E. Smith and N. P. Smith, 'Readability: A Measure of the Performance of the Communication Function of Financial Reporting', *Accounting Review,* July 1971, pp. 552-61.

61. M. D. Still, 'The Readability of Chairmen's Statements', *Accounting and Business Research,* Winter 1972, pp. 36-9.

62. ibid., p. 38.

Selected Bibliography for Chapter 6

American Institute of Certified Public Accountants, 'Reporting the Financial Effects of Price-Level Changes', *Accounting Research Study 6*, 1963. An American analysis of the nature of general price-level adjustments to historic cost data.

N. M. Bedford, *Extensions in Accounting Disclosure*, Prentice-Hall, 1973. A detailed analysis of the problems associated with disclosure of accounting information.

S. L. Buzby, 'The Nature of Adequate Disclosure', *Journal of Accountancy*, April 1974, pp. 38-47. A comprehensive coverage of the main problems associated with disclosure of accounting information.

R. C. Dockweiler, 'The Practicability of Developing Multiple Financial Statements: A Case Study', *Accounting Review*, October 1969, pp. 729-42. A practical attempt to test the feasibility of reporting price-level adjusted and replacement cost data in addition to conventional historic cost data.

E. S. Hendriksen, 'Disclosure in Financial Reporting', *Accounting Theory*, Irwin, revised edition 1970, pp. 559-81. The theory and practice of financial statement communication.

Institute of Chartered Accountants in England and Wales, *Accounting for Stewardship in a Period of Inflation*, 1968. The UK approach to general price-level adjustments of historic cost data.

T. A. Lee, *Income and Value Measurement*, Nelson, 1974. A review and discussion of the various alternative income, value and capital maintenance models available for financial reporting purposes.

T. A. Lee, 'Accounting Standards and Effective Financial Reporting: A Review in Principle', *Accountant's Magazine*, January and February 1965, pp. 25-30 and 73-81. A review of the accounting standards process; its nature, problems and objectives.

G. A. Macdonald, *Profit Measurement: Alternatives to Historical Cost*, Accountancy Age Books, 1974. An alternative analysis of the problems of income measurement.

L. Revsine and J. J. Weygandt, 'Accounting for Inflation: the Controversy', *Journal of Accountancy*, October 1974, pp. 72-8. The argument for and against general and specific price-level adjustments.

L. Spacek, *A Search for Fairness*, Arthur Andersen & Co., 1969. A book of readings by Spacek on the uniformity/flexibility issue in financial reporting.

E. Stamp and C. Marley, *Accounting Principles and the City Code: the Case for Reform*, Butterworth, 1970, pp. 129-40. An argument for uniformity and flexibility in accounting practice.

7

Further Issues and Problems in Company Financial Reporting

The Problem of Satisfying User Needs

On a slightly more complicated level, but nevertheless of vital importance to the practice of financial reporting, is the question of establishing a blend and quality of accounting information likely to meet the needs and requirements of potential users of financial reports from companies, including shareholders, lenders, creditors, employees, government agencies and financial analysts. As we have seen, if financial reports do not satisfy their users, then the accounting function is not being fulfilled. It is therefore essential that accountants should continuously re-appraise their financial reports (annual, interim and occasional) to ensure that, as best as can be determined, the consumer is satisfied.

The present-day system of company financial reporting is centred on annual statements of income and financial position, measured in accordance with the historic cost and realization principles. These annual statements are now supplemented, in certain cases, by funds statements, interim income statements and inflation-adjusted statements.[1] However, all present-day financial information which is reported on a regular basis is historical in outlook, concentrating on past profitability and financial position. Only rarely do companies report forward-looking data in the form of income forecasts when making a new issue of shares for public subscription, or when acquiring or merging with other companies. On the whole, the major part of the total information flow is contained in general-purpose reports of a historical nature, intended primarily for existing shareholders so as to satisfy stewardship requirements, but, in practice, used by a number of differing groups of individuals with different needs. In particular, these needs appear to relate to the making of decisions, and therefore to an assessment of future prospects vis-à-vis the companies concerned.

Users, decisions and the future

If users of financial reports are mainly concerned with making decisions and assessing the future, then it would seem appropriate to question the relevance of historically based financial statements to these activities. In particular, it seems necessary to question the validity of historic cost-based information. Is information relating to past company activity and performance necessarily useful to persons interested in future activity and performance? And, even if it is, should it concentrate on income and capital measurements based on historic costs?

Certainly it is debatable whether historic cost-based information on income and capital is relevant to a variety of users concerned with the future. As previously discussed, this does not give an adequate impression of current values for company assets, nor does it give a reasonable portrayal of income earned by a company during a specified past period (concentrating, as it does, on income realized during the period). Thus report users are deprived of realistic information about asset values and income performance which, even if related to the past, could be of relevance to their assessments and ultimate decisions through extrapolation. Still within historical terms, it is possible to produce income and capital measures using current values (either based on replacement costs or realizable values), thus giving up-to-date data on asset values and earned income. It is also possible, within terms of each of these three historical models of income and capital, to adjust for the effects of the changing purchasing power of money, thereby segregating real from inflationary gains.

In other words, if it is accepted that financial reports of past profitability and financial position are relevant to users, there are six main reporting models available: historic cost, historic cost adjusted for inflation, replacement cost, replacement cost adjusted for inflation, realizable value and realizable value adjusted for inflation. Which of these is best for particular users is problematic. The present system of historic cost is well tried, but the others are largely or completely untried in practice.[2] All that can be said at the present time is that (a) the alternatives to historic cost (adjusted or unadjusted) appear to alleviate its major measurement deficiencies and, presumably, give the interested user more relevant data; (b) replacement costs (adjusted or unadjusted) give a useful split between operational gains (the difference between sales revenue and the current replacement cost of goods or services sold) and holding gains (changes in the replacement cost of goods held prior to sale), thus providing users with a clearer picture of the composition of company income when assessing its future levels; and (c) realizable values (adjusted or unadjusted) provide useful data relating to the financial position of a company, particularly what might be realized by it on an orderly liquidation of its assets, thus giving users some idea of the asset cover available to back its shares, loans and other obligations. More research is needed to assess the relative merits and demerits of each, but the case for multiple financial statements, incorporating the various alternative valuation bases, seems to have support.[3] In other words, to benefit from the advantages of each basis, it may be necessary to report income and capital under each basis, and thereby provide users with a choice from a range of alternatives. The users could then use the data most suited to their particular needs. However, this solution to user needs has its problems and objections,[4] the most fundamental being the questions of whether historical measures of income and capital are relevant to users, and, if not, what should be reported in their place.

Past or future?

By definition, a decision-maker looks to the future. In financial reporting, the present emphasis is on past performance and position. Therefore can the future be adequately assessed through the use of historical data, given the rapidly changing circumstances of modern industry and society? Do past figures form an adequate basis for predictions? Answers to these questions are difficult; it is not easy to dismiss the past in any assessment of the future since it may contain vital clues for prediction. On the other hand, the past need not repeat itself and trends may not continue. The answer is possibly a compromise: that the past is of some use, but that some data relating to the future could be extremely beneficial.

With this last point in mind, the company financial reporting function has had some experience of the formal communication of forecast or budgeted data in relation to share issues and takeovers and mergers in the United Kingdom. However, these limited and infrequent exercises have given rise to suggestions that companies should provide regular information of a predictive nature as supplements to historical data.[5] These have mainly concerned the forecasting of company income for up to one year ahead. From a study of the relevant literature, there seems to be little general resistance to the idea in principle: predictive data relating to income does appear to have relevance in providing report users with information likely to satisfy their needs. For example, in a recent survey of accountants, company managers and financial analysts, Asebrook and Carmichael[6] concluded that accountants and analysts agreed that publication of forecasts for the general investing public should be encouraged, although managers tended to disagree. There also appeared, however, to be general agreement that publication of forecasts should not be made mandatory, since a 'general concern exists that the average investor may misinterpret the significance of a published forecast'.[7]

In other words, report users may believe forecasts to be more accurate and objective than they are or can be. Indications of the potential range of differences between forecasts and actual data were found in a recent study by Dev and Webb[8] of income forecasts in company prospectuses. In particular, it was found (perhaps not surprisingly) that forecasting inaccuracies appeared to be greater in industries and businesses in which there was an inherent trading uncertainty. From this it was concluded:

'It is possible that, if profit forecasts were published annually, comparison of the forecast with reported results would prove to be a better indicator of the uncertainties faced than observation of the yearly variation in reported profits.'[9]

Hence forecast data could give report users clearer insights into the risks and uncertainties associated with companies, and thereby improve the quality of accounting communications. However, the following associated problems must be recognized.

Managerial opposition

It is clear that, at a very practical level, there is opposition from company management to the idea of publishing forecast data. Skousen *et al.*[10] came to this conclusion when seeking various opinions on the disclosure of budgetary data, the main reason for opposition seeming to be the danger of injuring the competitive advantage of companies by disclosing their future plans, particularly those affecting international markets.

Managerial manipulation

Because published forecasts of income, sales turnover and so forth could be used by report users to measure managerial effectiveness (by comparing them with actual results), it could be suggested that management would deliberately manipulate budgeted data so as to appear to meet their goals successfully.[11] This, of course, would provide misleading data and comparisons for the report user.

It could also be envisaged that manipulation might take place to influence share prices in the short-term by causing investors' expectations to change;[12] for example, falsely inflated income predictions could cause investors to believe shares to be undervalued and, through consequent purchasing, to inflate prices over the short-term, though obviously not over the long-term. It has already been mentioned that historical data, when published, have an influence on share prices;[13] it is not unreasonable to assume that forecast data will have a similar effect. However, forecast data is far more subjective than traditional information, and consequently the opportunities for managerial manipulation are much greater. Forecasting could therefore introduce the problem of undue managerial influence on the financial reporting function, to the potential detriment of the report users.

These problems, however, could be offset,[14] first, by the separation in financial reports of the effects of poor prediction from those of trading when comparing forecast and actual data; secondly, by the reporting of a statement of the trading and commercial assumptions underlying forecast data; and thirdly, by an expert verification and audit report on the quality of forecasts and their assumptions.

Forecasting inaccuracies

Financial reports of a predictive nature are, by definition, subjective and capable of including material inaccuracies from forecasting errors. The future is not known, and uncertainty is bound to be a major factor in predictive data. If forecasts are published on a widespread and regular basis, it must be remembered that these inaccuracies will occur, and report users must be fully aware of this when using the data. Carmichael had this to say about the problem when commenting on UK opinions given in his survey:

'In the UK investors and others have had a fair amount of experience in using profit forecasts in financial decision making. Nevertheless, many UK accountants felt that the general understanding of the inherent inaccuracies of profit forecasts was inadequate. Presenting forecasts in ranges rather than as point estimates is one way of communicating the probabilistic nature of forecasts. While UK accountants were quite sympathetic to this objective, they did not believe range presentation was an adequate means of communicating the inherent inaccuracy of a forecast. If publication of forecasts is permitted, some sort of publicity campaign on the nature of forecasts would seem essential.'[15]

Verification of forecasts

The subjectiveness and scope for managerial manipulation which forecast reports contain make it essential for their credibility to be tested and reported on if they are to be issued to shareholders and others. This is at the moment done in the United Kingdom when income forecasts are included in financial reports published in the process of an acquisition or merger, and a guidance statement for accountants reviewing income forecasts has been issued by the Institute of Chartered Accountants in England and Wales.[16] In particular, the following statement is pertinent:

'In consequence profit forecasts are not capable of confirmation and verification by reporting accountants in the same way as financial statements which present actual results, and there is no question of their being "audited" in any sense, even though the reporting accountants may also be the company's auditors. It is important that the reporting accountants should make this clear when they accept instructions to review profit forecasts, and in their report they should take care to avoid giving any impression that they are in any way confirming, underwriting, guaranteeing or otherwise accepting responsibility for the ultimate accuracy and realization of forecasts. Moreover, bearing in mind their special status and authority, reporting accountants should do or say nothing to encourage directors, third parties or the public to place mistaken reliance on statements as to future profits, the achievement of which must always be subject to uncertainty.'[17]

An expert and independent assessment of forecast data is therefore possible. But the main emphasis is not on the overall accuracy of the figures. Rather, it is concerned with the reasonableness of the underlying trading and other assumptions made, as well as the appropriateness and consistency of the accounting standards adopted. In this sense, reporting accountants are not auditors and do not themselves have any responsibility for the forecasts. Their liability is limited to reviewing and reporting on the means by which the data have been computed. In addition, because of the inherent subjectiveness of forecasts, the English Institute has recommended as follows:

'Because profit forecasts are subject to increasing uncertainty the further forward they reach in time, reporting accountants should not normally undertake to review and report to directors on profit forecasts for more than the current accounting year, and, provided a sufficiently significant part of the current year has elapsed, the next following accounting year.'[18]

Feasibility of reporting forecast data

The commentary in the previous sections has looked at some of the main problems associated with reporting forecast data, particularly from the point of view of reporting it on a regular basis to meet the predictive needs of investors and others. These problems have already been experienced in the United Kingdom in relation to occasional acquisition and merger forecasts of income. This experience raises the question of the feasibility of reporting predictive data; that is, whether its relevance to report users exceeds its inherent subjectiveness and inaccuracy. If forecasting inaccuracies were too large, then they would fail to give their users anything worthwhile upon which to base their assessments and decisions. On the other hand, inaccuracies can be permissible if kept within certain tolerable limits and the users appreciate that this is the case.

Daily,[19] in a recent empirical study of internal forecasts of certain US companies in different industries, came *inter alia* to the following conclusions:

'The experience of the firms studied indicates that a reasonable doubt should exist regarding the ability of firms to forecast operating results with the degree of accuracy and precision necessary to satisfy the requirements of the investor.'[20]

He went on to suggest that a criterion for accuracy was necessary, possibly based on the concept of materiality, and that, on the basis of his investigations, inaccuracies of between 10 per cent and 15 per cent might be permissible. Daily also found that forecasting sale revenues seemed to be more accurate than forecasting profitability, and that forecasting inaccuracies varied according to the uncertainty factor in particular industries. His results have been confirmed by those of Dev and Webb,[21] who concluded from a study of prospectus forecasts that, from their figures, the degree of error in forecasting sales turnover could be large enough to equate with the total figure for reported income, thus causing some concern. Unless there were similar inaccuracies in expenditure, the error in the sales forecast could create an enormous percentage error in the income forecast.

All in all, therefore, while forecast data for reporting purposes may appear attractive so far as information relevance is concerned, because of inaccuracies it may not be as practically suitable at least until such time as forecasting techniques improve.[22]

In 1961, Solomons remarked:

'Each of us sees the future differently, no doubt. But my own guess is that, so far as the history of accounting is concerned, the next twenty-five years may subsequently be seen to have been the twilight of income measurement.'[23]

His warning was that income, which is central to financial reporting, is not an effective tool for financial planning and control, and that other factors, such as funds flow, may prove more beneficial. This argument has been examined closely recently,[24] and much of what follows is derived from this source.

The faults and problems of income measurement

No one would deny the importance of measures of income in company financial reporting, particularly over the last thirty to forty years. It has become central to most assessments of company performance over time. However, there are several problems associated with its measurement which raise doubts about its relative high position of importance in accounting thought. Whether these doubts are serious enough to cause income to lose its prestigious position, as forecast by Solomons, has yet to be proved conclusively. That doubts do exist, however, is grounds enough to examine them to assess their seriousness. It is also important to look at other reporting concepts which may have been ignored or neglected over the years simply because attention has been directed mainly at developments and improvements in the income concept. In other words, the quest for information to satisfy the varying needs of investors and others may have been too concerned with solutions in terms of measures of periodic income rather than with a range of alternative concepts.

The elusive concept of income

Arguably the most serious fault of the income concept is its elusive nature. What it attempts to do is to encompass, in aggregate form, all of the activity of a company over a period of time which is capable of being described in monetary terms. Essentially, therefore, it is a distillation of a myriad of transactions, events and activities. Yet, despite the reality of a given company situation, numerous measures of income, each one different from the next, can be produced to describe it. Different valuation bases (for example, historic cost, replacement cost or realizable value) will produce different income measures. These can be further varied by introducing inflation adjustments to account for the change in the purchasing power of money. In addition, further variation in income can be seen because of the inherent flexibility in accounting practice: even with the advent of professional statements on accounting standards, it is unlikely that flexibility will cease to exist because of the subjective personal judgements which enter into the accounting process and which cannot be standardized. On top of all this, it is clear that income is a less than perfect measure of company performance since it is, more often than not, produced omitting significant company resources from the relevant accounting data: accounting capital does not usually include important and valuable intangible resources (normally classified as goodwill) nor does it include human resources. Instead, it concentrates mainly on tangible resources, and consequently the resultant measures of income take no cognisance of movements in the value of the omitted resources.

The meaning of income

Since income measures tend to be complex aggregations of company activity over defined periods of time, they encompass much of what goes on within a company: the good and bad, the successes and failures, the desirable and undesirable, and so on. The problem is therefore one of deciding what income measures really represent vis-à-vis the company and its management. In other words, what does the report user look for when income measures are communicated to him? Does he regard income as simply a quantified measure of the increase in company capital (this depending on the valuation basis adopted); or is it an indicator of company or managerial success or failure; or is it merely a basis for determining shareholders' dividends; or is it the figure from which the company's taxation liabilities can be derived?

Income can certainly be interpreted as the periodic movement in valued capital. However, care must be exercised when looking at it in this way. Capital value may have changed, but this depends on the valuation adopted, the accounting standards used and the subjective judgements employed, as well as on the resources accounted or not accounted for. In other words, income, as a measure of the change in company capital, seems to be subject to too much potential and actual variation to be of much use in assessing aggregate value movements. This is particularly so when historic costs are the basis for measurement.

Income can also be regarded as a means of determining dividends and taxation. Certainly case law reveals that income has played a substantial part in the determination of gains available for distribution. However, given the inherent, if reducing, flexibility in accounting practice, it is hard to regard reportable income as an accurate indicator of dividend levels. In addition, so long as original subscribed share capital is not being repaid by payment of excessive dividends, it is difficult to justify the retention of income reporting specifically for this purpose. Dividends are, after all, dependent on the availability of cash as much as income, although recent examples of companies satisfying dividends by issuing further shares instead of paying by cash make this argument less strong than it once was. Taxation, too, need not depend entirely on income measures. At present, the usual basis is annual income, but this need not be so since it is not the only basis available: taxes could be levied on sales turnover or dividends distributed.

In summary, therefore, what the above paragraphs have briefly tried to indicate is that income is used frequently in a variety of capacities to indicate some financial or economic factor, whether taxable capacity, dividend proposals or managerial success. But income measures are subject to a great deal of flexibility which renders them somewhat less than precise indicators. And, in any case, they are not entirely essential to assessments of the factors concerned. Therefore the question raised is whether income justifies the high importance rating it has been given in company financial reporting over many years.

The alternatives to income

The previous section has outlined doubts about the general and particular usefulness of income. It has been used extensively for a variety of purposes, and subject to a lack of evidence to the contrary, appears to have established itself as a significant financial indicator. Much attention has therefore been given to ways of improving the quality of income measurements over the years, culminating in the United Kingdom and other countries in various programmes for the standardization of accounting practices. Most of the work in this direction has concentrated on improvements in the historic cost-based concept in income, and only recently has much attention been paid to alternative valuation bases for income purposes. Little or no effort has therefore been given to the task of exploring alternatives to income, the implicit assumption being that it is the most relevant reporting concept on which to concentrate.

Despite the apparent reticence of the accountancy profession to look at alternatives to income reporting, there are signs of proposals being put forward by individual writers, and it is appropriate at this stage to examine the main ones briefly. The following paragraphs attempt to do so.

Funds and cash flow reporting

One definite indication of a de-emphasizing of income reporting is the gradual increase in the publication of funds statements by companies (already commented on in this book). Thus the requirement to report on all financial flows over a period of time is satisfied by this additional statement in a way which the traditional income statement and balance sheet cannot do. The income statement reflects the periodic income inflow and dividend outflow, but does not indicate other financial flows. The balance sheet is, by definition, static, and therefore cannot of itself reveal flows. The funds statement, which is basically a derivation of the latter two statements, can do so.

However, funds flows are subject to certain problems already discussed. They incorporate the periodic measure of income, and rely, in most cases, on the flexible accounting practice necessary to the measurement of income. They also depend considerably on the particular valuation basis adopted as they incorporate data derived from the traditional balance sheet. In other words, funds statements are an extension of traditional income and financial position reporting, and therefore contain and involve most of the valuation and flexibility problems associated with the production of income statements and balance sheets. They provide additional information about companies for interested readers, and have without doubt helped to improve the quality and relevance of company financial reports. Nevertheless, they cannot break away from the problems of income reporting and do not, as such, provide a distinct alternative to the existing system of reporting.

Rayman,[25] recognizing the valuation and flexibility problems in accounting, has suggested that the apparent relevance of funds flow reporting should continue to be identified, but that these problems should be segregated from flow measurements to produce a funds statement which gives a factual account of the company's financial transactions with the outside world. In other words, it would describe the company's cash and credit transactions without the subjectiveness and flexibility of stock valuations, depreciation and other cost allocations, as well as other asset valuation problems. Income and balance sheet reporting need not necessarily be excluded from this system; the segregated funds statement simply attempts to present factual data separate from the somewhat more subjective data of the traditional type. It has, however, been criticized[26] for its implied diminution in the status of income and financial position reports, as well as for its apparent reluctance to grapple with the fundamental problems of value-based accounting.

The importance of accounting for financial flows has also been recognized recently in an alternative form. Lawson,[27] for much the same reasons as Rayman (that is, the inherent measurement problems in accounting), has advocated the complete abandonment of income and financial position reporting, and suggested in its place a system on cash flow reporting expressed in pure cash terms and not, therefore, including credit transactions. Lawson regarded the simplicity of cash flow, its lack of involvement in measurement problems, and its relevance to investors and others concerned with assessing future cash benefits to be derived from investment, as significant reasons for concentrating on this aspect of a company's financial affairs.

The idea of cash flow reporting on a regular basis has recently been developed as an additional reporting concept.[28] It was argued that, despite its inherent problems, the financial report should continue to contain statements of income and financial position since these reveal data of apparently great significance to report users.

However, it was also argued that:

'. . . there is one economic factor which is crucial to a proper assessment of the dividend potential, etc., of the enterprise and that is its capacity to survive as an enterprise — indeed, it could be argued that survival should be the primary enterprise objective. If the enterprise does not survive over the long-term, there will be no flow of dividends, no payments of interest, and no repayment of loans and other amounts due. Therefore, it can be argued that investors and other interested parties require information which enables them to assess and predict the development and progress of the individual business enterprise over time; its capacity to survive over time; and its capacity to pay its dividend, interest, and repayment commitments over time.

'Ideally, the information required should be expressed as a flow of funds in order to reflect these factors. In particular, it should also be measuring the one resource which indicates progress, survival and the ability to provide returns on investments — that is, cash. A business cannot survive, progress, repay loans and other debts, or pay dividends without cash.'[29]

The system of cash flow reporting advocated[30] includes the publication of actual cash inflows and outflows over a number of years; forecast cash flows for possibly one or two years ahead; statements of the assumptions upon which these forecasts have been based; explanations of the differences between actual and forecast data; and an independent audit report on the credibility of the published data. Thus the main emphasis is on supplying report users with relevant data which are alternatives to the present income-orientated system, and which attempt to avoid the flexibility and subjectiveness of such a system without abandoning it.

Cash flow accounting proposals are subject to some criticisms. Among them is the comment that they tend to ignore the problems of income measurement by presenting an over-simple portrayal of a company's financial affairs (this need not be the case if cash reports are published as well as the other traditional reports). Then there is the criticism that cash flow forecasts are subject to all the problems and difficulties mentioned above in the forecasting section (this is undeniable, but the balance of relevance and feasibility has yet to be decided with regard to any form of forecast; at least cash forecasts avoid certain of the subjective judgements contained in income forecasts because of the avoidance of problems such as the forecasting of certain valuations and cost allocations).

Human resource accounting

It has been mentioned several times throughout this text that the traditional system of company financial reporting tends to concentrate on accounting for tangible resources for which transactions have taken place. Little or no account is usually taken of intangible resources, which can include the skills and experience of the company's labour force, including its management. Presumably because human beings in industry and commerce are 'rented' or 'leased' for their services rather than purchased outright (as in slavery), they have not been treated for reporting purposes as measurable assets.

Nevertheless, in recent years, a significant body of literature has been built up advocating the incorporation of human resource values into the traditional reporting system.[31] The concept involves the identification of historic costs incurred on expenditure relating to human resources employed by the company, which, it is estimated, will have an expected value stretching beyond the period in which the outlay took place. This would include costs incurred on recruiting, training and developing the skills of employees, and would be treated for accounting purposes in much the same way as a fixed asset, with a gradual amortization of the 'capitalized' aggregate cost over its estimated useful life (as with depreciation of fixed assets).

As such, this does not seem to represent an alternative to the present system of reporting. However, in a conceptual sense it is a positive attempt to break away from accounting for physical resources of the company, and thus approaches the economist's concept of entity value, which is to value it as a whole, including all its resources: tangible and intangible, human and non-human.[32] It should be stated, however, that the system presently advocated, now used in practice by one American company, is subject to the major criticisms that (a) it utilizes a rather crude cost allocation process to determine human asset values; (b) it also involves a great deal of subjective judgement in the subsequent amortization process; and (c) it is presently conceived within terms of the traditional historic cost-based system of reporting, and therefore does little to alleviate the latter's inherent faults and problems.

Events accounting

Arguably the most extreme proposal as an alternative to income reporting is that originally conceived by Sorter[33] and supported by Johnson.[34] This is the so-called 'events' accounting process, which Johnson has summarized as follows:

> 'In order for interested persons (stockholders, employees, managers, suppliers, customers, government agencies, and charitable institutions) to better forecast the future of social organizations (households, businesses, governments, and philanthropies) the most relevant attributes (characteristics) of the crucial events (internal, environmental, and transactional) which affect the organization are aggregated (temporally and sectionally) for periodic publication free of inferential bias.'[35]

Thus the 'events' theorists recognize the need in financial reporting to provide users with information relevant for predictions and decisions. Their major argument is that the present system is essentially concerned with valuation (to produce income statements, balance sheets and funds statements), and that this approach contains several faults detrimental to users concerned with predicting: (a) a loss of information occurs in value accounting owing to aggregation (because of the process of distilling data into a relatively few figures, such as periodic income, crucial information about events affecting the future of the company are hidden from the user); (b) not all relevant events affecting the future of the company are reported in the value-based system because they are not capable of being valued conventionally (for example, resources which are leased rather than purchased, as well as the problem mentioned earlier of human resources); (c) the factual and verifiable nature of events accounted for is obscured by the accountant's valuation procedures which allocate and match accounting data, based on his predictions of the company's rather than the user's future.

In other words, the events approach is mainly directed against the interference by accountants in the reporting process in such a way as to obscure matters crucial to predicting the company's future by accountants' subjective judgements of that future. The report users are thus at a disadvantage in attempting to make their own personal judgements. The events approach would therefore ignore valuation and, consequently, income; it would favour historical reporting and reject forecasting in reports; and it would, as a result, give far more detailed information about the basic events affecting the financial life of the company. This would include data which need not necessarily be capable of measurement in financial terms. It would be fair to say, however, that events accounting is at present very much at the theory stage.

Problems for the Auditor

As mentioned several times throughout this text, it has been a traditional requirement for reported company accounting information to be audited by a suitably qualified and independent accountant. In the United Kingdom, this is the case with annually reported financial statements of profitability and financial position (both for single companies and groups of companies) as well as with occasional prospectus or acquisition and merger reports. With historic data, the auditor's main task is to examine and verify reported information so as to report on its quality in terms of the familiar 'true and fair view' opinion, thereby establishing its credibility for shareholders and other interested report users. In the case of predictive data, mainly because of its inherent total subjectiveness, the audit emphasis is on establishing and reporting on the credibility of the accounting practices used rather than the underlying trading assumptions (this latter aspect of auditing is usually conducted by non-accountants acting as financial or banking advisors to the company concerned with making the forecast). Interim financial reports, even though of a historical nature, are not at present required to be audited prior to publication.

This section seeks to outline the main problem areas facing the auditor when verifying the quality of reported information. Hopefully, it will give the reader an understanding of problems in company financial reporting other than the measurement and communication ones which are usually commented on.

Maintaining independence

One of the most crucial factors in an audit of published financial statements is that the auditor should be independent, meaning totally unbiased in his judgement and opinion. If he is not, or if he does not appear to be, then there exists a very real danger that the credibility of the financial statements may be negated by a lack of auditor credibility in the minds of the statement users.[36] In the United Kingdom, company legislation[37] has attempted to give the auditor an appearance of independence by (a) not allowing him to be an officer or servant of the company; (b) leaving the matters of appointing, remunerating and dismissing him in the hands of shareholders rather than company management; and (c) giving him the right of access to all information and explanations he deems necessary for his audit. In other words, he cannot be a company manager, nor should he be restricted or constrained by the actions of company management. However, although auditors in the United States are provided with independence guidelines as part of a written code of ethics published by the American Institute of Certified Public Accountants,[38] UK auditors are required to maintain their independence without such help. The main areas of conflict are as follows.

Auditors as shareholders

There is nothing in present UK company legislation or regulations of the professional accountancy bodies to prevent an auditor, or his relatives or business associates, being a shareholder in a client company. Nor is there any requirement that he should disclose such an interest should he have one. Similarly, he could lend or trade with a client company. By way of contrast, if an American auditor (who is a member of the American Institute of Certified Public Accountants) is not independent, because of such financial or other interests, he must state this in his audit report and must not give an opinion on the financial statements concerned. As has been stated:

> 'Financial interests of this type conflict with the appearance of independence which the shareholders and other users of the company's financial statements are entitled to expect. In addition, such interests may create the possibility of the auditor being mentally influenced by them during his audit — for example, when he has to judge and give an opinion on accounting information, the result of which may materially affect the value of the shares he holds in the company.'[39]

A similar situation can arise where the auditor is related to individual members of a client company's management. Although prevented from being a manager, or associated with one in a business sense, there is nothing to prevent him being related to one. It therefore appears sensible for auditors to attempt to avoid financial or personal relationships which could damage the appearance of independence and the credibility of the audit opinion. Several professional accountancy firms in the United Kingdom are known to prohibit staff financial interests in client companies for this reason.

Management services[40]

Auditors are often asked by a client company to undertake management services in addition to their audit commitment. These could include handling the company's tax affairs, preparing its accounting records and/or financial statements, financial and investment consultancy, and information and control systems consultancy. In certain of these situations, therefore, it may well be that the auditor is giving his audit opinion on work he has also been responsible for. This, again, gives the appearance of a lack of independence, as, for example, when he prepares and audits annual financial statements.

A number of writers[41] have argued that auditors should not be involved in these services; others[42] argue that it is perfectly defensible so long as the service is advisory and not decision-taking (that is, the auditor is not involved in implementing his advice); and still others[43] argue that there is no danger to independence at all. Certain professional accountancy firms have attempted to minimize the problem by setting up separate associate firms to provide management services. Nevertheless, the danger of a loss of appearance of independence is always present despite such arrangements. The separation of audit and consultancy firms seems the best solution in an imperfect world.

Third parties and independence

The company audit, as presently constituted, is intended for shareholders. However, there are other interests in the company which benefit from the audit and the auditor's opinion. At present, however, the shareholders' interests are legally intended as the primary (indeed, sole) concern of the auditor. This arrangement works well until a situation arises where other financial interests (such as those of lenders, creditors and employees) are being prejudiced despite a 'true and fair view' opinion being given vis-à-vis the reported information and the shareholders' interest in it.

A recent Australian situation[44] revealed that although there may be a 'true and fair view' so far as shareholders are concerned, there can also be an 'untrue and unfair view' so far as debenture holders are concerned. If the auditor fails to report this (and this is perfectly within his present legal rights), then his apparent and actual independence is called into question. He is seen to be acting for the benefit of one group, but not for others who are being prejudiced. The answer to this problem would be to widen the accepted responsibility of auditors to cover third parties, but so far this has been rejected by the courts of law,[45] despite a non-accounting case to the contrary.[46] Meantime, auditors would appear to be morally bound to guard against not giving an opinion which unrealistically reflects the quality of reported information vis-à-vis all obviously interested groups.

Improving independence

There have been several suggestions over the years of ways in which the auditor's appearance of independence could be improved. These have included appointment by government or a government agency; disclosure of financial interests and personal relationships in much the same way as is presently required for company directors in the annual directors' report; legal prohibition of such interests and relationships; rotation of auditor appointments every few years; and the use of an audit court, compromising eminent practitioner judges to which difficult audit problems could be taken for assessment.[47] None of these measures, however, can compensate for the reality of independence: the need for the auditor to exercise mental independence when reviewing, examining, testing and giving an opinion on reportable accounting information.

Auditor responsibility

It is a fundamental postulate of auditing financial statements that:

> 'The auditor can be held accountable for the quality of his work and the nature of his opinion on the accounting information in the company's financial statements.'[48]

In other words, the auditor has a duty of care to those to whom he is responsible. If he is negligent in his work, he must be capable of being held accountable. If this were not the case, then no one could rely upon his verification work and audit report, and his services would not be sought. This topic is a complex one, and is covered in depth elsewhere.[49] However, it does deserve some comment in the context of this chapter, and the following are given as indicators of the main problem areas of responsibility facing the auditor today.

To whom is the auditor responsible?

From previous sections and chapters it can be seen that the auditor of company financial statements in the United Kingdom (and many other countries) is legally responsible to the shareholders of a client company. This means that if he is negligent, and is found to have damaged the shareholders because of such negligence, he can be sued by them, collectively, for damages. This is supported in the judgement in such cases as *London and General Bank (No. 2)* (1895) 2 Ch. 673, *The London Oil Storage Co. Ltd* v. *Seear, Hasluck and Co.* (1904) 31 Acct, L.R.I., and *Candler* v. *Crane, Christmas and Co.,* C.A. (1951) 2 K.B. 164; (1951) 1 All E.R. 426; (1951) 1 T.L.R. 371. The last-mentioned case went one stage further and decided that, even if the auditor were negligent and damaged persons other than the shareholders, he would not be legally responsible to those third parties.

It is this last point which is of so much concern to company auditors, for, as other parts of this text have made clear, company financial statements are of potential interest and use to many groups of persons and bodies other than shareholders. It is therefore quite conceivable that the auditor could, if negligent, harm third parties. Therefore is the auditor legally responsible or not to these other persons and bodies? The answer so far has been in the negative, despite a recent non-accounting case, *Hedley, Byrne and Co. Ltd* v. *Heller and Partners Ltd* (1963) 2 All E.R. 575; (1963) 3 W.L.R. 101; (1964) A.C. 465, in which the judgement suggested that third-party responsibility for practitioners such as accountants did exist. However, Counsel's advice at the time was that:

'. . . third parties entitled to recover damages under the *Hedley Byrne* principle will be limited to those who by reason of accountants' negligence in preparing reports, accounts or financial statements on which the third parties place reliance suffer financial loss in circumstances where the accountants knew or ought to have known that the reports, accounts or financial statements in question were being prepared for the specific purpose or transaction which gave rise to the loss and that they would be shown to and relied on by third parties in that particular connection. There is no general principle that accountants may be liable for damages if a report or statement which proves to have been prepared negligently by them is shown casually or in the course of business to third parties who suffer loss through reliance on the report or statement.'[50]

This statement was taken at the time to mean the exclusion of third parties from the legal responsibility of auditors. But nowadays, with a greater awareness of the various potential uses to which audited financial statements can be put, auditors must realize that shareholders are not the only persons who could be damaged through use of negligently audited information. Therefore, although no specific third-party responsibility has been outlined in a legal sense, the auditor must have at least a moral responsibility to all potential users of company financial reports, and take this into account when conducting his verification procedures and formulating his audit opinion.

For what is the auditor responsible?

In the United Kingdom, the Companies Acts 1948 and 1967 charge company directors with the responsibility for producing the required financial reports and statements. They are therefore collectively responsible for the nature and quality of accounting information contained in these documents. The auditor, on the other hand, is responsible for the nature and quality of his expert opinion on the information which is required to be audited. He is not responsible, in his capacity as auditor, for the quality of the information he audits. The main problem facing the auditor in this connection is one of what exactly he is responsible for in his audit work and opinion.

First, it is clear on the basis of decisions in past court cases that the auditor cannot be held responsible for searching out and reporting on fraud or errors which have been committed within a client company. Such may have been the purpose of auditing at the turn of the century,[51] but nowadays the emphasis is very much on establishing the credibility of reported information. The cases of *Irish Woollen Co. Ltd* v. *Tyson and Others* (1900) 26 Acct. L.R. 13, *Henry Squire (Cash Chemist) Ltd* v. *Ball, Baker & Co.* (1911) 44 Acct. L.R. 25, and *S. P. Catterson & Sons Ltd* (1937) 81 Acct. L.R. 62 have conclusively shown that the auditor's responsibilities for searching out fraud and error are limited to those occasions when his suspicions about such matters are sufficiently aroused in the course of his audit to cause him to ensure that company management is aware of the situation and doing something about it. Besides this, however, should his audit techniques be inadequate and fail to arouse his suspicions regarding fraud and error, he could be held to be negligent (as in the case of *Thomas Gerrard & Son Ltd.* (1968) Ch. 455; (1967) 2 All E.R. 525). Therefore the auditor has a limited responsibility for searching out fraud and error. But the size of companies and the volume of their transactions would make such a task an impossibly time-consuming and costly operation. If undertaken, it would considerably delay the publication of company financial reports to the detriment of shareholders and other report users. The words of Lord Justice Lopes in the case of *Kingston Cotton Mill Co. (No. 2)* (1896) 2 Ch. 279 are pertinent:

> 'Auditors must not be made liable for not tracking out ingenious and carefully laid schemes of fraud where there is nothing to arouse their suspicion, and when those frauds are perpetrated by tried servants of the company and are undetected for years by the directors. So to hold would make the position of an auditor intolerable.'

Secondly, one of the most fiercely debated issues in auditing in recent years[52] concerns the auditor's responsibility for giving an opinion on accounting information which has been partly audited by other auditors. This occurs with group financial statements where the holding company auditor is responsible for the overall audit opinion but has to rely on other audit opinions on financial statements of subsidiary companies incorporated into the group statements. The problem is whether he should accept these opinions without checking on the quality of the audit work undertaken. It is clear from two recent cases, *Atlantic Acceptance Corporation* in Canada[53] and *Pacific Acceptance Corporation* in Australia,[54] that the auditor is now expected to inquire in some detail into the quality of audits of subsidiaries not audited by himself. In fact, as a result of these cases, Canadian and Australian legislation has been amended to give holding company auditors the right of access to all accounting records, and so forth, of subsidiaries not being directly audited by them. In addition, in Australia, the holding company auditors' report is expected to state that such subsidiaries' financial statements are adequate for consolidation purposes. The situation in the United Kingdom is, as yet, unclear, though a recent Institute of Chartered Accountants of Scotland paper[55] does detail steps which the holding company auditor should undertake so as to satisfy himself of the quality of subsidiary company financial statements and their audit. Thus, to summarize, it should now be clear that although the auditor's opinion may cover the quality of the financial statements of a group of companies, it does not mean that he has been responsible for all the auditing concerned. However, he must be responsible for seeing that all auditing is of such a quality that makes his overall opinion valid vis-à-vis the group statements. In any case, he must state in his report that he has relied on the work of other auditors in coming to his opinion.

Thirdly, arising out of several recent American cases (*Escott et al.* v. *Barchris Construction Corporation et al.* (1968) 283 F. Supp. 643, 703; S.D.N.Y.; and *United States* v. *Simon* (1968) United States District Court, S.D.N.Y.), it is clear that auditors are being expected to adhere to higher standards than ever before. In fact, it appears that courts are setting standards before they gain general acceptance within the accountancy profession. In the *Barchris* case[56] it was decided that the auditor has a duty continuously to reappraise past audits of financial statements to ensure that subsequent circumstances have not invalidated their original audit opinions. This occurs mainly with accounting information contained in annual reports which are subsequently used for prospectus purposes. In the other case, usually referred to as *Continental Vending*,[57] the decision concerned how far an auditor must go to establish the reliability of reported accounting information. The implication of the decision was such that the court expected auditors to seek audit evidence much more widely than is presently the case. Thus, auditors are faced with the problem not only of meeting generally accepted standards of the day but also of possibly attaining standards beyond those presently appearing to receive general acceptance.

Lastly, auditors in many countries are now faced with verifying the implementation of mandatory accounting standards by companies; in the United Kingdom, for example, these are contained in *Statements of Standard Accounting Practice*. This could well present auditors with serious problems. These are not impossible to face when a client company departs from a published standard, and the auditor has a duty[58] to report this in his audit report to shareholders, also stating whether or not he agrees with the departure. However, there may be cases where an auditor disagrees with the prescribed standard, irrespective of whether the client company implements it or not. Does he then state this in his report and give his reasons for doing so? Or does he accept that the mandatory standard is regarded as generally acceptable and hide his personal views in the matter? The problem has not been resolved and reflects the relatively unstable state of the art of accounting at the present time. However, the advice of Rosenfield and Lorenson[59] seems sound in this respect when they say that for auditors publicly to state their disagreement with prescribed practice would undermine the credibility of that practice as well as financial statements. In other words, by working through their professional bodies, auditors should seek to improve accounting standards rather than to undermine public confidence in published financial statements.

Verification problems

The practice of auditing financial statements is not a straightforward matter of checking figures and documents. There are several major problems facing the auditor in this area, and this brief section can do no more than outline the main ones.[60]

The first problem has already been discussed: verification that the financial statements concerned have been produced in accordance with recognized accounting practice. In the United Kingdom this refers specifically to the implementation of mandatory *Statements of Standard Accounting Practice.* The main issue facing the auditor in this context is the decision on whether or not a company's departure from a recommended standard is valid. His duty is to report on such a departure and to comment on its validity. He must therefore be extremely careful in coming to his decision so as not to create doubts and suspicions in the minds of report users vis-à-vis the credibility of the information. In particular, he must ensure that he has objectively reviewed the circumstances of the company, the nature of the relevant prescribed standard and management's reasons for departure.

Secondly, the auditor will inevitably be faced with giving an expert opinion on a mass of data which have to be aggregated and reported in financial statement form. Given the constraints of time and cost, it is relatively obvious that he cannot personally examine every figure, transaction or document. This would be an impossible task to undertake, especially in large companies or groups of companies. Therefore he must verify data on a test basis, having first established the various strengths and weaknesses in the accounting system. The more confident he is of the reliability of the system, the smaller will be his tests and checks. The opposite is true for a weak system. Statistical sampling techniques should be used in this connection. The auditor's problem is assessing the strength of the system and the size and nature of his samples so as to provide sufficient evidence of the quality of the data on which he has to report.

Thirdly, as previously explained in various parts of this text, the process of producing reportable accounting information inevitably involves a great deal of managerial opinion, particularly relating to the allocation and evaluation of accounting data. This presents an enormous problem for the auditor since he has to examine the credibility of these subjective judgements to determine his own personal opinion on the credibility of the aggregate information. It is extremely difficult for an accountant to judge the quality of a judgement made by an engineer, chemist, lawyer, surveyer or whatever. In most instances, unless he can seek an independent assessment from a suitably qualified expert, he must rely on the integrity of the managers concerned. This explains why auditors of predictive data such as income forecasts confine their attention to the accounting practices used rather than the underlying trading and commercial assumptions.

In conclusion, therefore, it should be clear from the above paragraphs that the auditor, when he reports on company financial statements, is not guaranteeing their accuracy or credibility. He is giving an expert opinion on the basis of tests he has conducted. Given the flexibility of accounting, reported information cannot be regarded as accurate. There can be no such thing in financial accounting, given the many different ways of reporting the same economic and financial circumstances. This is true whether the basic data is historical or periodical; and obviously more so with the latter than with the former.

Suggested Discussion or Essay Topics

1. The amazing thing about published accounting information is that it is predominantly concerned with the past. Yet its readers use it as if it was describing the future. Comment on this apparent inconsistency.

2. The future is not known, and therefore there can be no reliable information produced to describe it. Predicted data is not information; it is guesswork, no matter how expertly guessed. Discuss this statement in the context of producing forecast data for financial reporting purposes.

3. What reasons can be given to justify the predominant position in company financial reports of measures of periodic income?

4. Income is the end-result of an aggregation and collation process which attempts to squeeze the entire economic activity of a company into one figure. Comment on the validity of this criticism.

5. Funds flow accounting is simply an extension of income accounting. It has often been confused with cash flow accounting. Explain.

6. What is the case for multiple financial reporting and the end of the traditional general approach?

7. Human resources are an essential and extremely valuable contribution to economic activity. Yet they are ignored by companies when producing their financial statements. Comment on the validity of this statement.

8. In economic decision-making, it is better to be able to predict events than to know the financial consequences of past events. What relevance has this statement got for company financial reporting?

9. What effect would there be in investor behaviour with regard to company financial statements if the independent audit function was withdrawn and data were published in unaudited form?

10. It has been suggested that the accountancy profession is evolving in the direction of regarding the public as the primary client of the auditor. Might such a development resolve a good deal of the confusion that now surrounds the matter of legal liability, and what would the auditor's standard of liability become under such circumstances?

11. Unless the company auditor satisfies himself as to the existence of fraud or error in the accounting function, he cannot give an opinion on the quality of the reported financial statements. Discuss.

Notes and References

1. Funds statements are not, at present, mandatorily required under a Statement of Standard Accounting Practice; interim statements are issued by Stock Exchange quoted companies; and quoted companies are asked to follow the provisions of 'Accounting for Changes in the Purchasing Power of Money', *Provisional Statement of Standard Accounting Practice 7*, May 1974.

2. The exception to this general statement is the Netherlands, where replacement cost accounting has been used in practice to a limited extent over a number of years; see, e.g., J. Vos, 'Replacement Value Accounting', *Abacus*, December 1970, pp. 132-43; and R. Burget, 'Reservations about "Replacement Value" Accounting in the Netherlands', *Abacus*, December 1972, pp. 111-26.

3. See, e.g., R. S. Gynther, 'Accounting for Changing Prices', *Chartered Accountant in Australia*, December 1971, pp. 12-23; and E. Stamp, 'R. J. Chambers: Quo Vadis et Cui Bono?', *Chartered Accountant in Australia*, August 1972, pp. 10-12.

4. R. J. Chambers, 'Quo Vado?', *Chartered Accountant in Australia*, August 1972, pp. 13-15.

5. e.g., R. Schattke, 'Expected Income – A Reporting Challenge', *Accounting Review*, October 1962, pp. 670–76; W. W. Cooper, N. Dopuch and T. F. Keller, 'Budgeting Disclosure and Other Suggestions for Improving Accounting Reports', *Accounting Review*, October 1968, pp. 640-47; and C. R. Tomkins, 'The Development of Relevant Published Accounting Reports', *Accountancy*, November 1969, pp. 815-20.

6. R. J. Asebrook and D. R. Carmichael, 'Reporting on Forecasts: a Survey of Attitudes', *Journal of Accountancy,* August 1973, pp. 38-48.

7. ibid., p. 46.

8. S. Dev and M. Webb, 'The Accuracy of Company Profit Forecasts', *Journal of Business Finance,* Autumn 1972, pp. 26-39.

9. ibid., pp. 36-7.

10. K. F. Skousen, R. A. Sharp and R. K. Tolman, 'Corporate Disclosure of Budgetary Data', *Journal of Accountancy,* May 1972, pp. 50-57.

11. ibid., p. 57.

12. ibid.

13. R. Ball and P. Brown, 'An Empirical Evaluation of Accounting Income Numbers', *Journal of Accounting Research,* Autumn 1968, pp. 159-77.

14. As suggested by P. Elgers and J. J. Clark, 'Inclusion of Budgets in Financial Reports: Investor Needs *v.* Management Disclosure', *Accounting and Business Research,* Winter 1972, pp. 53-60, at p. 60.

15. D. R. Carmichael, 'Reporting on Forecasts: a UK Perspective', *Journal of Accountancy,* January 1973, p. 44.

16. 'Accountants' Reports on Profit Forecasts', Institute of Chartered Accountants in England and Wales, August 1968.

17. ibid., p. 1.

18. ibid.

19. R. A. Daily, 'The Feasibility of Reporting Forecasted Information', *Accounting Review,* October 1971, pp. 686-92.

20. ibid., p. 692.

21. Dev and Webb, 'The Accuracy of Company Profit Forecasts', loc. cit., p. 28.

22. J. C. Chambers, S. K. Mullick and D. D. Smith, 'How to Choose the Right Forecasting Technique', *Harvard Business Review,* July-August 1971, pp. 45-74.

23. D. Solomons, 'Economics and Accounting Concepts of Income', *Accounting Review,* July 1961, p. 383.

24. T. A. Lee, 'Enterprise Income: Survival or Decline and Fall?', *Accounting and Business Research,* Summer 1974, pp. 178-92.

25. R. A. Rayman, 'An Extension of the System of Accounts: The Segregation of Funds and Value', *Journal of Accounting Research,* Spring 1969, pp. 53-89; 'Is Conventional Accounting Obsolete?', *Accountancy,* June 1970, pp. 422-9; 'Accounting Reform: Standardization, Stabilization, or Segregation?', *Accounting and Business Research,* Autumn 1971, pp. 300-8.

26. T. K. Cowan and B. Popoff, 'Funds Statements: The "Way Out" for Accountants?', *Accountancy,* June 1971, pp. 302-5.

27. G. Lawson, 'Cash-Flow Accounting', *Accountant,* 28 October 1971, pp. 386-9.

28. T. A. Lee, 'A Case for Cash Flow Reporting', *Journal of Business Finance,* Summer 1972, pp. 27-36.

29. Lee, 'Enterprise Income', loc. cit., p. 190.

30. This is detailed in Lee, 'A Case for Cash Flow Reporting', loc cit.

31. e.g., see R. L. Brummet, E. G. Flamholtz and W. C. Pyle, 'Human Resource Measurement – A Challenge for Accountants', *Accounting Review,* April 1968, pp. 217-28; B. Lev and A. Schwartz, 'On the Use of the Economic Concept of Human Capital in Financial Statements', *Accounting Review,* January 1971, pp. 103-12; and E. Flamholtz, 'Towards a Theory of Human Resource Value in Formal Organizations', *Accounting Review,* October 1972, pp. 666-78.

32. See Lev and Schwartz, 'On the Use of the Economic Concept. . .', loc. cit.

33. G. H. Sorter, 'An "Events" Approach to Basic Accounting Theory', *Accounting Review,* January 1969, pp. 12-19.

34. O. Johnson, 'Towards an "Events" Theory of Accounting', *Accounting Review*, October 1970, pp. 641-53.

35. ibid., p. 650.

36. See T. A. Lee, *Company Auditing: Concepts and Practices*, Gee & Co., revised edition 1974, pp. 67-85.

37. See T. A. Lee, 'The Impact of Company Legislation on Auditor Independence', *Accountant's Magazine*, July 1968, pp. 363-7.

38. *Code of Professional Ethics*, American Institute of Certified Public Accountants, Rule 1.01.

39. Lee, *Company Auditing*, p. 77.

40. See, e.g., R. S. Gynther, 'Management Services and the Independence of Auditors', *Accountancy*, October 1967, pp. 647-50.

41. R. K. Mautz and H. A. Sharaf, *The Philosophy of Auditing*, American Accounting Association, 1961, p. 228.

42. K. S. Axelson, 'Are Consulting and Auditing Compatible?', *Journal of Accountancy*, April 1963, pp. 54-8.

43. As commented on in R. W. Schattke and A. Smith, 'Management Services and Auditing – Ethical Problems', *Accountancy*, August 1966, p. 550.

44. E. Stamp, 'Independence – an Australian Case', *Accountancy*, August 1964, pp. 685-90.

45. See, e.g., R. F. Salmonson, 'CPA's Negligence, Third Parties and the Future', *Accounting Review*, January 1959, pp. 91-6.

46. See 'Accountant's Liability to Third Parties – the *Hedley Byrne* Decision', *Accountancy*, September 1965, pp. 829-30.

47. E. Stamp and C. Marley, *Accounting Principles and the City Code: the Case for Reform*, Butterworth, 1970, pp. 119-28 and 168-87.

48. Lee, *Company Auditing*, p. 59.

49. ibid., pp. 86-111.

50. 'Accountants' Liability', loc. cit., p. 829.

51. Lee, *Company Auditing*, pp. 22-7.

52. See, e.g., D. Flint, 'Audit of Group Accounts (Reliance on Other Auditors)', *Accountant's Magazine*, August 1967, pp. 366-78.

53. E. Stamp, 'The Atlantic Acceptance Report: Some Lessons', *Accountant's Magazine*, July 1970, pp. 303-9.

54. 'The Auditor's Duty', *Accountant's Magazine*, August 1971, pp. 410-13.

55. 'Parent and Subsidiary Company Auditor Relationships', *Accountant's Magazine*, October 1972, pp. 483-92.

56. J. M. Renshall, 'Barchris and Continental Vending – 1968's Legacy for American Auditors', *Accountancy*, January 1969, pp. 7-10.

57. 'Continental Vending Decision Affirmed', *Journal of Accountancy*, February 1970, pp. 61-9.

58. 'The Effect of Statements of Standard Accounting Practice on Auditors' Reports', *Statements on Auditing 1*, 1971.

59. P. Rosenfield and L. Lorenson, 'Auditors' Responsibilities and the Audit Report', *Journal of Accountancy*, September 1974, p. 82.

60. See Lee, *Company Auditing*, pp. 112-39, for further details.

Selected Bibliography for Chapter 7

D. R. Carmichael, 'Reporting on Forecasts: a UK Perspective', *Journal of Accountancy*, January 1973, pp. 36-47. A useful description of the problem of reporting forecast data.

D. Flint, 'The Role of the Auditor in Modern Society: An Exploratory Essay', *Accounting and Business Research*, Autumn 1971, pp. 287-93. An analysis of the widening responsibilities and duties of the auditor.

T. A. Lee, 'A Case for Cash Flow Reporting', *Journal of Business Finance,* Summer 1972, pp. 27-36. A reasoned argument for cash flow reporting and a description of such a system.

T. A. Lee, *Company Auditing: Concepts and Practices,* Gee & Co., revised edition 1974. A coverage of the main conceptual and practical issues and problems facing the auditor of company financial statements.

T. A. Lee, 'Enterprise Income: Survival or Decline and Fall?', *Accounting and Business Research,* Summer 1974, pp. 178-92. A detailed criticism of the concept of income for company financial reporting purposes.

R. K. Mautz and H. A. Sharaf, *The Philosophy of Auditing,* American Accounting Association, 1961. The most comprehensive conceptual analysis of company auditing to date.

R. A. Rayman, 'Is Conventional Accounting Obsolete?', *Accountancy,* June 1970, pp. 422-9. A critique of traditional financial reporting concepts and an advocation of funds flow accounting.

C. R. Tomkins, 'The Development of Relevant Published Accounting Reports', *Accountancy,* November 1969, pp. 815-20. The case for disclosure of budgeted data.

8 The Context for Using Company Financial Reports

Introduction

The previous chapters have attempted to provide the reader with a broad understanding of the nature and problems associated with producing company financial reports. In particular, the main emphasis has been on the measurement and communication of relevant accounting information, with the intention of familiarizing the reader with financial reporting practice while remaining relatively uninvolved in the mechanics of the exercise. These latter aspects of accounting are more than adequately covered in other sources.[1]

However, financial reporting is not just a complex process of producing relevant accounting figures. It is also concerned with the use made of accounting data in economic activities of various forms. Thus, the aim of this and the following chapter is to attempt to describe the function of using the accounting information which has been reported. As such, the text will concentrate on the use made of financial reports by persons and bodies external to companies rather than by company managements.

Report Analysis and Decisions

In a perfect world, in which everyone has perfect knowledge, the need for a formal financial reporting system would not exist. The future would be known with absolute certainty, and decisions and actions could be taken in the security of such a certain future. However, the real world is an uncertain one in which knowledge is limited and information is a scarce commodity. Decisions and actions have to be taken in the face of a good deal of uncertainty, despite the existence of factual data relating to past activity. The company financial reporting system is intended specifically to provide such factual data on a regular basis, albeit occasionally supplemented by management's forecasts of future activity. As such, its fundamental purpose is to provide its potential users with a knowledge of company activity which they did not have previously. Hopefully, this knowledge will be useful to them when assessing and formulating alternative courses of action in their various decision functions. As Sorter *et al*. have stated:

'An economic decision-maker must explicitly or implicitly estimate the amount, timing, and related uncertainty of benefits and sacrifices affected by decisions. Since part or all of the benefits or sacrifices lies in the future, these variables cannot be known with certainty. . . .

'Past results are all that is known with certainty. Since all economic decisions concern the future, conjecture about what may happen is necessarily based in part on information concerning what has happened. That is, knowledge about past events is not sufficient for predicting the future. Also required is an evaluation of past events in terms of the variables relevant for decisions under review. Thus, to facilitate the estimation, comparison, and control of future sacrifice-benefit relationships, information in financial statements should help decision-makers evaluate past sacrifice-benefit relationships.'[2]

The above are clear statements of the importance of reported accounting infor- mation (even of a mainly historical nature) in relation to the making of decisions. By definition, these decisions involve assessing what has to be given up so as to obtain some future benefit, and, as such, reported information is an important input into the decision model concerned. What is equally clear, however, is that general-purpose information must be subjected to some form of analysis prior to incorporation into such a model; that is, it must be translated into specific purpose data if it is to be capable of influencing the behaviour of the decision-maker. In this way, decision-making in a world of uncertainty is made more efficient and effective than it might be otherwise. The major problem is determining the analysed information relevant to a particular decision, and thus of determining the nature of the particular decisions to which the analysis must be directed.

The Nature of Decisions

People make decisions as part of the process of achieving certain defined objec- tives. In economic terms this involves the optimal use of scarce resources, and, as already indicated, the need for reliable information in this exercise is relatively self-evident. It is therefore pertinent, when assessing the usefulness of different types and items of information, to look more closely than hitherto at the nature and characteristics of the decisions (and underlying objectives) to which the reported data may be applied. When this is done, the reasons and aims of report analysis become more apparent than may be the case by casual observation.

First, it is evident that decisions, no matter what their individual nature, concern assessments of the future. They must also concern assessments of alternative courses of action. Therefore, if reported information is to be of use in decision-making, it needs analysing to produce data capable of providing insights into the potential benefits and costs of alternative courses of action. The alternatives must likewise be identified to select relevant data for analysis. Once this is done, the relevance of the analysed information can be judged in terms of what is usually described as its predictive ability: its usefulness in enabling its users to forecast the future benefits and disbenefits associated with identifiable alternatives.[3]

In other words, alternative courses of action will always involve potential benefits and sacrifices, for, when pursuing a certain course of action, benefits can only be derived by making certain sacrifices. For example, to obtain a future stream of income from his investment, an investor must be prepared not only to forgo a sum of money equivalent to the cost of that investment, but also to forgo the in- come streams obtainable from alternative investment sources to which the money could have been put. It is therefore important for analysed data to have a bearing on identifying and assessing the various benefits and sacrifices associated with a particular decision and its related alternative courses of action; and predicting their future monetary value.

Secondly, decision-making is normally conducted with a certain strategy and objective(s) in mind, and it is reasonable to assume that once a decision has been made, and a particular course of action followed, the decision-maker will monitor events to ensure that his objectives are being achieved. In this way, he can further decide either to continue with the existing course of action, switch to an alternative course of action, or amend his existing strategy and objectives. Whatever he does, he will require relevant data to aid him in this control function, and report analysis has a significant part to play identifying data useful in the monitoring of decisions. In this respect, it is particularly important for the analysis to contain data relating to both actual and expected performance so that adequate comparisons can be made for control purposes. It is equally important that comparative data, if it is to be useful to the decision-maker, should be measured and analysed on the same bases. If this is not the case, then comparisons become at best difficult and at worst meaningless, the user never being quite sure whether differences are the result of economic factors and financial factors or of differences in the methods used to measure these factors.

Report Analysis Objectives

It should be reasonably clear so far that the main purpose of report analysis is to provide financial statement users with data relevant to the predicting and controlling functions which constitute the decision process. In this sense, the aim of analysis is to refine and translate the reported data: to convert it from its general-purpose state to a specific-purpose form. The user can then make use of the analysed data to construct a profile of the company (its management, financial condition, income, dividends, liquidity, and so on). This provides part of the relevant background to the decision-maker's eventual decisions, remembering, of course, that company financial reports are not the only source of information about companies available to him. The required profile cannot be obtained from a casual observation of published financial reports, for this could only give a superficial impression of the important financial features of the company at one particular point in time. Analysis, on the other hand, particularly when conducted on a regular basis, provides a detailed description of these features over time as well as at particular points of time. However, it must be noted that no matter how good the techniques of analysing financial reports, the quality and reliability of the analysed data are only as good as the financial reports themselves. If the latter are inadequately measured or ineffectively presented, these basic faults will not be remedied by detailed analysis. On the other hand, it is true to say that expert analysis can offset presentation faults, in the sense that once particular data have been chosen for analysis, the original presentation of financial reports becomes less important. Nevertheless, the effect of measurement faults will be carried through to the analysed data, and presentation faults can impede the selection of relevant data for analysis purposes. It is for this reason that the previous chapters have concentrated on providing a general understanding of the main problems associated with the production of company financial reports. Unless the production process is of the highest possible quality, providing information of relevance to potential users, the stated objective of report analysis – the provision of relevant data for prediction and control in decision-making – cannot be achieved. As has recently been stated:

'Information contained in financial statements to satisfy users' needs should possess the qualitative characteristics of relevance and materiality, reliability, freedom from bias, comparability, consistency, understandability, and the recognition of substance over form. Information is not useful unless it is relevant and material to the users' decision. In making decisions, users should be able not only to understand the information presented, but to assess differences in its reliability, to rely on its fairness, to compare it with information about alternative opportunities, and to assess its consistency with previous presentations.'[4]

Types of Decision

Having established that the main aim of analysing company financial reports is to provide a needed input into decisions to be made by their potential users, it is necessary to identify the main types of decision to which analyses are directed in practice. As mentioned on page 49, there are a number of uses to which company financial reports can be put, and as a start, it is useful to requote those advocated by May:

'As a report of stewardship; as a basis for fiscal policy; as a criterion of the legality of dividends; as a guide to wise dividend action; as a basis for granting credit; as information for prospective investors in an enterprise; as a guide to the value of investment already made; as an aid to government supervision; as a basis for price rate regulation; and as a basis for taxation.'[5]

If the use of financial reports by employees and their unions is added to the above list, it provides an adequate description of the main uses of financial reports. The right of employees and their representatives to receive information about the companies in which they are employed has been increasingly recognized in recent years. In Britain, this can be evidenced at present in industrial legislation being proposed which suggests that employees and their representatives should be given the right of access to internal management information as well as the traditional financial reports. The need for information of this kind is relatively obvious. Employees are concerned with the financial performance and progress of companies, not only from the point of view of decisions affecting wage negotiation, but also with regard to operational tasks delegated to them, job employment prospects, and so on.

Internal management uses

This particular grouping includes uses related to the legality of dividends and the prudence of dividend action, as well as to employee wage-bargaining procedures. In other words, data relating to company profitability (for example, the availability of income for dividend purposes) and financial position (for example, the liquidity position) will aid management in certain aspects of its financial policy and decision-making. Wage negotiators will also find it useful when discussing the merits and feasibility of wage claims, etc.[6] However, these are uses with which this text is not primarily concerned, and are therefore excluded from further examination, though readers should note that they do suggest the practical usefulness of published accounting information, even to internal managements who have a continuous and detailed knowledge of company matters.

External uses

The remaining uses relate to persons and organizations outwith the company who tend to rely on its formal financial reports as a major source of information about it. To quote the Trueblood Study Group:

> 'An objective of financial statements is to serve primarily those users who have limited authority, ability, or resources to obtain information and who rely on financial statements as their principal source of information about an enterprise's economic activities.'[7]

In other words, the following sections are mainly directed at those potential users of company financial reports who, because of the structure of the company, are unavoidably prevented from gaining an intimate knowledge of its activities through regular and close contact with its operations and management.

They can be divided into two groups:

(a) *Governmental uses:* The government is a major user of company financial reports, the uses including those concerned with fiscal policy, government supervision, price regulation and taxation. In the case of the latter function, the required information is contained in the annual financial report, and the analysis work involved with it is a relatively simple identification of individual items of revenue and expenditure which may or may not be incorporated in the measurement of the figure for annual income to be taxed. In this sense, the analysis is not an exercise conducted to refine the basic information and highlight specific characteristics of the company for purposes of decision-making; it is simply concerned with adjusting reported figures to conform with existing tax law.

Likewise, the remaining governmental uses relate to the collection of reported information for statistical purposes to provide governmental policy and decision-makers with aggregate data of use in their industrial, regional and national intervention and regulation activities. As such, the analysis is not concerned with the characteristics of individual companies, except in occasional circumstances where government aid is being sought by a company, or when an individual company's trading activities are under examination. In these cases, however, the use of information is akin to the 'investing' category described next.

(b) *Investment uses:* What is now left of May's original list of financial report usage can be classified as primarily concerned with investment: the provision of short, medium and long-term finance to the company with the expectation of eventual repayment and a suitable financial return. 'Stewardship', for example, relates to the reporting of information which attempts to describe the effectiveness with which company management has employed the sources of finance invested in the company. Such information should therefore be potentially useful to shareholders, lenders and creditors of the company, particularly in the sense of 'feedback' data which can be used in the controlling or monitoring aspect of investment decision-making. However, to fulfil this role, the information contained in financial report form (particularly that contained in financial statements) must be subjected to detailed analysis if it is to identify the essential indicators of stewardship as well as decision-making.

The Use of Financial Information by Investors

Investment in companies can be conveniently divided into two main categories: (a) short and medium-term investment by creditors and lenders, and (b) more long-term and permanent investment by shareholders. This section attempts to make this distinction while concentrating on the more familiar information use by shareholders.

Use by creditors and lenders

The function of granting credit can be interpreted as relating to decisions concerning the provision of existing or potential finance by bankers and creditors, usually on a short or medium-term basis. Therefore the accounting information contained in company financial statements can, once suitably analysed, be used as an input into the types of decision made by such providers of finance. In particular, bankers and creditors are concerned with assessing a company's ability to repay its debts in accordance with the terms of the contracts and agreements concerned, particularly the repayment of capital and interest when due. The purpose of report analysis in this context is therefore the identification of financial factors relevant to assessments which are essentially concerned with expectations of cash receipts from the company to the providers of finance. Indicators of liquidity are obviously important, but an overall profile of the company is equally helpful. The same comments could be applied to lenders who provide more long-term finance to companies – for example, debenture holders and mortgage holders.

Use by shareholders

Existing and potential shareholders constitute the remaining group of investment users of company financial reports. As suggested by May in his list of uses, they are primarily concerned with the value of company shares and the future flow of benefits to be derived from such investments. Buying of shares involves the sacrifice of a sum of money (equivalent to their cost of purchase) in expectation of future dividends and realization proceeds whose aggregate present value is reckoned to be more than the purchasing value.[8] Likewise, the holding of shares involves the sacrifice of a sum of money equivalent to their current realizable value, again in the expectation of future receipts with an aggregate present value in excess of the realizable value. Existing and potential investors are therefore constantly weighing up the alternatives of having cash to consume presently or investing to receive cash for consumption at various future points of time. This gives rise to the familiar investment valuation identity of:

$$V_o = \sum_{t=1}^{n} \frac{d_t}{(1+i)^t} + \frac{r_n}{(1+i)^n} \; ;$$

where V_o is the present value of the investment at point t_o; d_t are the anticipated dividends receivable at points t; r_n are the anticipated sale proceeds of the investment if realized at point n; and i is the investor's personal rate of time preference, assumed to be constant throughout the period of investment t_o to t_n.

This valuation model formally represents the value of shares to the individual shareholder (existing or potential), value being based on a discounting of the cash returns he anticipates during the period of investment. The discount rate is taken as the rate of return which the investor estimates he would be satisfied with as compensation for sacrificing present for future consumption. It is also usually taken to represent the degree of risk the investor associates with the shares concerned; the higher the anticipated risk, the higher the rate of discount necessary. The present value so calculated (albeit very informally in many cases in practice) is then available as a standard for comparison with the current market values of the shares. In other words, the potential investor's decision model is a comparison of his estimate of the shares' present value with their current purchase value; so long as there is a positive net present value, he will benefit from investment. For the existing shareholder, the comparison is between the shares' present value and current realizable value; and again, so long as a positive net present value exists, the shareholder will benefit from continuing with his investment.

The above is necessarily a simplification of the investment decision,[9] but it should reveal enough to explain the main features of the information needs of existing and potential shareholders which should be recognized in the process of report analysis. First, assuming that current market values are available to the individual shareholder (these are more readily available in a quoted company than in any other), his major information requirement would seem to be data of use in predicting future dividend receipts. Secondly, the investor may also require data to help him to evaluate the anticipated period of investment, the eventual realization proceeds, and the appropriate rate of discount (and, thus, the degree of risk associated with the investment). These requirements suggest that the process of report analysis should be concerned largely with producing data with a maximum predictive capability. In particular, as in credit and loan decisions, it should be capable of enabling the decision-maker to discriminate between shares giving higher returns than others, thereby helping him to maximize his expected consumption over time. It should also be capable of reducing the uncertainties facing the decision-maker; if it does not do so, it cannot be said to be relevant information. However, given the predominantly historical nature of reported accounting information, it is difficult to envisage how relevant are such analysed data when predicting future dividend flows, realizable share values and the degree of risk attached to alternative investments.[10] It is also difficult to prove the validity of the underlying assumption that decision-makers (of any kind) will act rationally by identifying the available alternative courses of action; evaluating the financial consequences of each (by making use of available accounting and other information); and selecting the alternatives which meet their preconceived strategies. There is little or no evidence of how decisions are reached, or by how much reported accounting information influences them. Report analysis assumes, therefore, that decision-makers will not only make use of the analysed data, but will also find it relevant.

As explained in Chapter 4 (particularly pages 53-5), the evidence to date of the predictive capability of reported accounting information is scant. Raynor and Little,[11] Singh and Whittington[12] and Whittington[13] have produced evidence to suggest that past income levels and income growth rates can be expected to recur in the future, but not to the same extent as before, particularly if past figures tended to be above average. In other words, prediction of future incomes, etc., cannot be done on the basis of a straightforward extrapolation of past trends. Likewise, studies by Brown and Niederhoffer[14] and Green and Segall,[15] among others, have revealed somewhat inconclusive evidence that interim reports of income are of use in predicting annual income figures. Brown and Kennelly,[16] on the other hand, have produced more positive evidence of investors using interim reports to predict annual income figures, and thereby producing better investment strategies than investors who rely solely on annual reports. O'Connor[17] has also concluded that financial ratios (that is, significant accounting data relationships), when used on their own, have a doubtful usefulness to shareholders interested in predicting and ranking rates of return to be expected from alternative investments – in other words, who attempt to distinguish between shares yielding a high return and shares yielding a lower return. Beaver,[18] on the other hand, has found that financial ratios have a positive if limited usefulness in predicting the eventual financial failure of companies. Certain ratios prove better predictors than others, and are more helpful for predicting potentially successful companies than for predicting potentially unsuccessful ones. Beaver,[19] in a later study, has also shown that whereas financial ratios can predict business failure several years before it occurs, and whereas movements in share prices prior to failure indicate that investors are consciously allowing for a deteriorating situation in their investment decisions, there is inconclusive evidence on the degree to which analysed accounting data has a part to play in these predictions and resultant price movements.

Criteria for Analysed Data

Summarizing and expanding on the discussion in the preceding section, it is now possible to stipulate certain criteria which are useful guidelines in the analysis of accounting information contained in financial reports.

First, the analysed data must be relevant to the various decisions which information users are likely to make. This means that the decisions must be identifiable and the related information needs determinable. To date, however, accountants have paid relatively little attention to this aspect of report analysis; the assumption presumably being that the basic information and the analysed data are relevant to potential but largely unidentified users. As previous chapters have attempted to indicate, this is a largely untested assumption which is made even weaker by the several major faults contained in the traditional system of financial reporting. Thus, report analysis cannot be divorced from the problems of financial reporting: it is simply an extension of the latter function. In particular, it is clear that the general-purpose nature of financial statements must be countered when they are being analysed, the analysed data being prepared with the specific needs of the user in mind. It is therefore important for the analyst to be capable of identifying the accounting relationships specifically relevant to the individual user.

Secondly, examination of the decisions of potential users of company financial reports indicates that, irrespective of their individual identities, all are concerned with prediction and consequential monitoring of prior decisions. Thus, analysed data has a dual role to play: that of providing relevant information for forecasting company activities and financial results, as well as providing information of use when assessing the success or failure of prior decisions. However, it cannot be emphasized too often that the existing system of reporting accounting information is a mainly historical one (at least so far as regular periodic reporting is concerned), and even the suggestions for improving such a system (including improvements in the measurement process) are also conceived mainly within it. Therefore, within these constraints, financial report users are attempting to analyse their content to produce indicators of past performance which may provide guidelines to future performance. The following conditions are essential in these circumstances.

First, that the analysed data used for predictive purposes are sufficient to provide their users with a reasonable basis for forecasting. In particular, this means the preparation of several years' data (where possible) to identify trends and fluctuations which may recur in the future. Such data must be measured, however, on the same accounting basis from one period to the next if it is to be comparable; and it must be free of any exceptional or non-recurrent items which, because of their nature, should not affect future financial results.

Secondly, that analysed data from financial reports are not regarded as the sole source of information for predictive and control purposes. Company financial reports are a major source of information, but they are not the only one, and because of their mainly aggregate composition, they tend to obscure details of company operations and activities which may prove to be important influences on decisions. Companies operate within a very complex and ever-changing environment often causing their future to be somewhat different from their past. Aggregate figures for past profitability and financial position, even when supported by relatively detailed notes, are not necessarily suitable for assessing these vital decision-making factors. Certainly, as studies by Brearley[20] and Whittington[21] have shown, it is a somewhat dubious exercise simply to project past income trends into the future. Not even the largest companies have that sort of stability, as Whittington[22] has demonstrated in a recent paper describing the changing fortunes of companies over relatively short periods of time: the composition of the top 100 company classification has changed considerably over two decades; certain companies have grown faster than others; and other companies have appeared or disappeared through acquisition and merger activity.

And thirdly, that the availability of reported accounting and other information, and the relevance of analysed data, cannot eradicate the essential subjectiveness of decision-making. In other words, report analysis can only be regarded as a means of diminishing some of the uncertainty in decisions. Because the future cannot normally be forecast with accuracy, analysed data must be treated with a great deal of care and expertise in its application to decisions. This is particularly true of data relating to past activity: the decision-maker must exercise a considerably subjective judgement when translating measures of past performance into predictions of future activity.

The Investment Example

The analysis of company financial reports, and its relative importance, can best be put in context by looking more closely at the investment decision and the overall function of investment analysis (of which financial report analysis is only one part).

Investment analysis is the process of analysing alternative investments so as to make certain decisions regarding buying or selling. The overall objective is to compute present values for shares which are being considered for sale or purchase — that is, for sale if they are already held, and for purchase if they are not already held. These intrinsic and highly subjective values are prepared for comparison with existing market values for the shares concerned to determine whether sale or purchase is desirable as well as which shares should be bought or sold. As previously explained, present values are computed on the basis of forecast dividends and realization proceeds discounted at the investor's time preference rate. Illustration

14 provides a simple example of this process, the problems of taxation and inflation being ignored for the sake of simplicity.

Illustration 14. *A simplified investment decision.*

Assume an investor has £1,000 available for investment in quoted ordinary shares, and he is considering shares in two companies, A and B. Shares in A are currently quoted at £10 a share, and the last dividend per share was £1. Shares in B are currently quoted at £8 a share, and the last dividend per share was 90p. The investor anticipates that A's dividends will increase annually by 10 per cent (the first being due in approximately twelve months' time); he anticipates that B's dividend will increase annually by 11 per cent (the first being due in approximately twelve months' time). He plans to sell his investment shortly after receiving his second dividend when he forecasts A and B's shares will have a market value of £15 and and £13 respectively. He requires a yield of 6 per cent from an investment in A, and 7 per cent from B; in his opinion A being less risky than B.

(1) *Present value of an investment in A: 100 shares*

Time	Estimated cash receipts £	Discount factor (6 per cent)*	Present value £
End of year 1	110(a)	0·943	104
End of year 2	121(b)	0·890	108
Shortly after end of year 2	1,500(c)	0·890	1,335
Present value			1,547
Total purchase price: beginning of year 1(d)			−1,000
Net present value			547

(2) *Present value of an investment in B: 125 shares*

Time	Estimated cash receipts £	Discount factor (7 per cent)*	Present value £
End of year 1	124(e)	0·935	116
End of year 2	136(f)	0·873	119
Shortly after end of year 2	1,625(g)	0·873	1,418
Present value			1,653
Total purchase price: beginning of year 1(h)			− 1,000
Net present value			653

Therefore an investment in A produces a subjective net present value gain of £547 compared with a corresponding figure of £653 for B. Therefore, assuming these were the only alternatives open to the investor, he would invest in B, which would give him the highest return despite being the riskier investment.

(a) 100 x £1 + 10% x £100; (b) £110 + 10% x £110; (c) 100 x £15; (d) 100 x £10; (e) 125 x £0.90 + 10% x £112; (f) £124 + 10% x £124; (g) 125 x £13; (h) 125 x £8.

It should be noted in the illustration, however, that the problem of risk in investment is one which cannot be dismissed completely in the simplicity of this example. Indeed, risk is an extremely complex factor which seriously affects the computation of financial values. For example, the latter are affected by risks related to the type of businesses being evaluated and the level of interest rates and inflation, as well as the risk associated with the marketability of the investments concerned. Generally speaking, the more risky the businesses, the higher the interest rates and inflation, and the less marketable the investments, the greater will be the risk associated with investment. In addition, the risk factor is complicated by the natural aversion from risk by investors. They may well tend to opt for investments with smaller present values and returns because they are less risky than those with high values and returns. In the above example, investment A may be chosen because it is less risky than investment B, despite a higher net present value. (Readers interested in studying this problem in greater detail should refer to Carsberg in the selected bibliography at the end of this chapter on page 173).

The figures used in Illustration 14 follow the traditional approach to investment values and decisions: the forecasting of dividends and realization proceeds, the assessment of risk and the application of the discounting technique. It is this approach which lends itself to what is normally described as fundamental analysis: the economic and statistical researching necessary to produce and identify factors which could provide guidelines to the future performance of a company and the present value of its shares.

Fundamental Analysis

Before proceeding to a detailed account of the fundamentalist approach to investment evaluation, it will be useful to compare briefly the different approaches to the latter function, of which fundamental analysis is only one. In fact, there are three main approaches. First, there is the process of fundamental analysis which relies on the detailed use of all available information about the companies being evaluated. This is done to build up individual company financial profiles which can be used as foundations for investment decision-making. Secondly, investment decisions are often made on the basis of technical analysis — that is, by the examination of past share price movements to predict future movements. As such, this process does not depend on a detailed use of available information about individual companies as is the case in the fundamentalist approach. Lastly, there is a further school of thought, based on the so-called random walk theory, that suggests that quoted share prices move randomly around their true value and so, as a result, no individual investor can put himself at an advantage to other investors by using available information about companies because this is publicly available. This philosophy seems to reject both the fundamentalist and technical approaches to investment evaluation. Each, however, will be discussed separately in the following sections.

The fundamental philosophy

Because it is attempting to locate and isolate significant factors concerning the future of a company, fundamental analysis relies on an adequate information system from which indications of these factors can be drawn. A substantial part of the required information comes from analyses of company financial reports, but there are other sources of information available to the analyst, including aggregate national and international economic statistics and specific industry data as well as individual company information. From these various sources, the analyst attempts to construct detailed profiles of individual companies from which he can forecast future dividend and share realization flows. This provides him with a basis for computing present values for alternative shares, which can then be introduced to his investment decisions. Thus the emphasis is on forecasting future returns so as to compute intrinsic values for decision-making, i.e. present share values. The fundamentalist approach is not, therefore, concerned primarily with forecasting share price movements.

This traditional approach to investment decision-making is open to some criticism. The main one is that, despite the detailed analysis of available information, the decisions subsequently made can be no more successful than those made on the basis of 'a technical study of the past pattern of share price movements (that is, the process of technical analysis in which past share prices are analysed to predict future prices) or of present prices (that is, the random walk theory which states *inter alia* that the current market values of shares approximate to their intrinsic values, and that it is unnecessary to undertake detailed analysis to compute these latter values). The latter two approaches to investment analysis will be discussed in much more detail later in this chapter, but meantime, in answer to the critics of fundamental analysis, the conclusion of Briston is worth noting:

'At the present time such analysis is being subjected to considerable criticism, primarily based upon the inaccuracy of its past predictions. However, the faults lie not in the theory itself but in the lack of information made available to investors and in the extreme difficulties encountered in making predictions in an uncertain world.'[23]

In other words, the information used in the process of fundamental analysis is mainly historical, and it is extremely difficult to predict the future of companies on the basis of their past activity and performance. Nevertheless, information is available for analysis, no matter how imperfect it may be, and rational decisions would appear to dictate the use of such information so long as its imperfections are fully understood and great care is exercised in the analysis.

Sources of information for fundamental analysis

These are three main categories of information which can be analysed for purposes of forecasting dividends, etc., and computing present values of shares: (a) company information; (b) industry information; and (c) general economic information.

Company information

When building up a profile of a company for decision-making purposes, the investor is obviously primarily interested in specific data about the company itself. Much of this emanates from the company, and has already been described in some detail in earlier chapters: the annual financial reports, including statements of past profitability and financial position; the interim financial statements (for quoted companies); and the occasional prospectus and merger or acquisition reports, which include short-term forecast data. These reports will come direct to individual shareholders, but, particularly in the case of quoted companies, can be obtained by potential shareholders by application to the company. In addition, every company in the United Kingdom must deposit copies of its annual financial reports and prospectuses with the Registrar of Companies, and these are open to public inspection for a small fee. The Registrar is also required to receive from each company a copy of its Memorandum and Articles of Association (giving details of its internal regulations); details of any legal charges secured over any of its assets; and its annual return giving details *inter alia* of its capital, directors, loans and changes in ownership during the year covered (the annual financial report is also attached to this return). The company is also legally required to keep registers of shareholders, debenture holders, directors and directors' shareholdings at its registered office, again for public inspection, which can be made for a small fee.

Most of these information sources about a company can be assessed personally for analysis by the existing or potential investor. However, much of the data can also be obtained indirectly by him from organizations or entities which specialize in information analysis services for the investor. For instance, the Exchange Telegraph Co. Ltd provides a daily statistical service for quoted companies, and this, on a card system, gives, *inter alia*, a detailed analysis of key accounting information over the last ten years, as well as brief comments on the history and background of the companies, with summarized financial statements for the last three years. It also gives details of their share price records over the last ten years. Moodies Services Ltd operates a similar service, but can also provide analyses and forecasts of leading industry and commodity performances. Moodies also produces a quarterly investment handbook and an annual investment digest, both of which analyse, in a great deal of detail, the significant financial accounting figures and indicators for a large population of leading companies. In this sense, therefore, subscriptions to these services by investors avoids much of the detailed analysis work necessary to condense and refine all the available information for investment decision-making into manageable proportions.

Investors may also be able to obtain similar services from their stockbrokers, many of whom produce detailed analyses of accounting information derived from the published financial reports of individual companies. Of particular concern in these analyses are indicators of managerial performance and financial structure as well as income and dividend potential. A similar but far less detailed and extensive coverage of company performance is available in the serious financial press, including *The Investor's Chronicle, The Financial Times* and *The Times Business News Section.* In other words, investors should never be short of analysed information about individual companies if they are unable to analyse it personally. It must be said, however, that the available analysed information is subject to two criticisms: first, there are very considerable doubts as to its relevance and usefulness (mainly because it is based largely on published accounting information which is subject to the doubts and problems discussed at length in the previous chapters); and secondly, it is often of a highly complex and technical nature, thereby raising doubts as to its usefulness to the private investor with little or no skill and experience with such material (this is particularly true of the services offered by such organizations as Exchange Telegraph and Moodies, which are mainly directed at the professional investor with the skills required to interpret it).

Industry and economy information

Although investors are primarily concerned with assessments of individual companies, they are also interested in the context in which these separate entities operate. For this reason, investors following the philosophy of fundamental analysis should be interested not only in the industries of which companies form a part, but also in the economy in general. In other words, the future of a company cannot be assessed adequately without considering the present and future state of the particular industry and the economy.

The nature and state of the industry in which a company operates seems to be of fundamental importance to the analyst, not only in an absolute sense but also as a point of comparison of the company itself. The size and history of the industry; its past and potential growth; its profitability trend; the nature and size of its markets; the quality of its management and labour force; its industrial relations — these are all factors which provide an essential background for the analyst assessing individual companies. He should provide himself with industry criteria (for example, sales, production, profitability and capital expenditure) with which to compare individual companies so as to assess whether their performance is above or below the industry average.

Sources of information about particular industries are varied, but can be divided into two main categories: (a) industrial and (b) governmental. Many industries and trade associations produce aggregate statistics which, when available, can provide interesting insights into industry trends. There are also occasional reports from the various industrial sub-committees of the National Economic and Development Council, which give similar data on trends and prospects. Governmentally, industry information can be obtained in a number of ways. For example, the annual publication, *National Income and Expenditure*, contains tabulations of data concerning domestic consumption of goods and services, capital expenditure in various industries, as well as aggregate industrial income. On a more regular basis, publications such as *Trade and Industry* contain data relating to orders, deliveries, production and stock in individual industries. The five-yearly *Census of Production* also gives aggregations of regional and industry production and capital expenditure.

Governmental publications also provide useful background data for analysis and decision purposes. The state of the economy, and its future prospects, seem to be relevant features of any assessment of individual companies. The trend and prospects for national and international trade, unemployment, production, credit and banking facilities, interest rates, retail prices, monetary exchange rates, etc., are all matters which must impinge eventually on individual companies. It would, for example, be impossible to assess the future profitability and dividend prospects of a manufacturing company which was heavily involved in export sales without considering the state of international trade, the relative value of the pound in relation to other currencies, the availability of bank and other credit facilities, the availability of skilled workers in the industry, and so on. The above-mentioned government publications all contain aggregate data of use in this context, but other publications are also available, including the *Monthly Digest of Statistics* and *Economic Trends*. In addition, the *Bank of England Quarterly Bulletin* provides useful summaries of many of these factors. Thus the fundamental analyst who wishes to incorporate aggregate industrial and economy data into his computations appears well provided with sources of available information.

The process of fundamental analysis

Essentially, the investment decision, when use is made of the process of fundamental analysis, is concerned with assessing the future prospects of individual companies, and particularly with their future profitability, dividend potential and share price. Given the mainly historical nature of the available information about an individual company, it is relatively obvious that past data trends will form a major part of the exercise of formulating these predictions. However, the latter can in no way be regarded as accurate because of the inherent uncertainty about the future. Nor is it possible to extrapolate a past trend of data and hope that such an analysis will provide reliable predictions. Although such trends may contain elements which remain relatively stable over the long-term, there are other factors which are much more variable; for example, cyclical elements cause long-term fluctuations in trends and are relatively difficult to predict; random factors, because of their 'once-and-for-all' nature, tend to be unpredictable.

It is for this reason that a thorough analysis of available information from all relevant sources should be undertaken so as, first, to establish past trends of significant data such as income and dividends which could be used as bases for estimating future data; secondly, to identify and segregate factors which are of a stable, cyclical or random nature so far as the company is concerned, and which are necessary ingredients in the process of adapting past trends to formulate future ones; and thirdly, to aid the analyst to assess the degree of risk and uncertainty associated with investment in a particular company. In all these matters it is relatively clear that general industry and economy data should be relevant to the exercise of using specific company information to project future data of use in the investment decision. In addition, it should be remembered that not all of the information used in the processes of analysis and prediction will be of a quantitative nature. For example, chairmen's reports and reviews of prospects are more often than not couched in purely qualitative terms but contain significant insights to the future of companies.

The major problem in fundamental analysis, therefore, is the translation of historical data into meaningful predictions of future company performance. The problem is accentuated the more the analyst is required to move into the future and the more uncertain are the company, industry and general economic factors and conditions to be considered. For instance, an investor contemplating a twelve-month investment in shares of a relatively stable trading company in equally stable industrial and economic conditions would find the process of predicting for investment decision-making purposes much easier than if he were contemplating a five-year investment in a volatile company in times of great industrial and economic uncertainty and fluctuation.

In addition, in fundamental analysis, the investor making the analysis (or the person or organization making it on his behalf) is faced with predicting share prices as well as such factors as income and dividends; this being needed for his computation of the intrinsic values of the shares being assessed. In this respect, the analyst must not only make use of his predictions of income and dividends and related data on the financial position and condition of the companies concerned, but must also attempt to predict the predictions of other investors. No wonder Briston has concluded:

> 'As a result an investor must not only analyse all available information but must also endeavour to assess the likely reaction of the stock market to that information. . . . Much of the work involved in predicting security prices is thus a matter of guesswork, with investors guessing at the reaction of other investors to the events which they have predicted.'[24]

Although it would be wrong not to admit that guesswork is the major ingredient to the investment decision, it must be stated that such guesswork should be of an expert kind. Fundamental analysis attempts to inject this expertise, and, as with the prediction of future income and dividends, the prediction of share prices should be made on the basis of a careful analysis of all available information, but particularly on industry and economy information. As Coen, Gomme and Kendall[25] have demonstrated, there appear to be significant lagged correlations between share price levels (as described, for example, in the *Financial Times Index*) and levels in other economic variable (such as, for example, UK car production, commodity prices, bank rate and sterling liability). In other words, levels in these economic variables appear to be reasonable indicators of future levels in share prices. However, this assumes rational behaviour on the part of investors, which is not always the case. As Briston has further commented in relation to this aspect of market psychology:

'For instance, an investor may feel that a particular company is extremely risky. However, if he guesses that the market irrationally regards the company as very safe and that it will continue to over-value its shares, he may choose to invest in the company even though he personally regards the company as inferior. Conversely, he may refuse to invest in a company which he regards as extremely safe because he suspects that other investors will not share his view.'[26]

This process of attempting to 'out-do' other investors appears to be contrary to the philosophy of fundamental analysis associated with rational assessments of intrinsic share values. That it does exist, there is no doubt. Therefore, it should not be assumed that all investors adopt the fundamental approach.

Prediction and trend analysis[27]

Fundamental analysis is primarily concerned with processing data so as to make relevant predictions for share valuation purposes. Because of the historical nature of the data being processed, it is consequently concerned with analysing past trends of variables relevant to share valuation. Once these trends have been established, it is then possible to attempt to predict values for these variables so as to incorporate them into the share valuation model. The analyst uses trends as starting-points for his projections, which must, necessarily, incorporate factors which he believes will affect the absolute values of the variables in the future. In particular, he will require to identify the various components of trends to predict future movements properly in the variables being considered.

Trends can be composed of a number of factors, though not all of them may be apparent in particular time series of data. These components are, first, the secular component (T) caused by factors whose influence tends to be in the same direction over the long-term; secondly, the seasonal component (S), which causes movements in the trends owing to seasonal variations; thirdly, the cyclical component (C), which causes movements owing to long-term cyclical fluctuations; and fourthly, the residual component (R), which causes movements owing to random factors of an ad hoc nature which are unpredictable. The effect of these various components on actual data (A) can either be identified as their sum $(A = T + S + C + R)$ or as their product $(A = T \times S \times C \times R)$. The first identity assumes that the effects on data are additive (which may be true over short periods), whereas the second identity assumes they are proportionate (which is more likely to be the case, particularly over longer periods of time). Although the secular and residual components will appear in every trend, the other components may not be applicable. Where relevant, however, the purpose of trend analysis is to isolate these various components to enable reasonable predictions to be made.

The first stage in the decomposition of data is to estimate the secular component of the series. This can be done in a number of ways: for example, by graphically plotting the trend data and, by estimation, fitting a line which approximates to the trend; by calculation of moving averages; or by the least-squares method to derive a linear trend. It is not the purpose of this text to explain statistical techniques in detail, but Illustration 15 attempts to describe briefly each of the aforementioned techniques.

Illustration 15. *The analysis of a trend of income.*

Assume a company with a time series of income as follows: period t_0-t_1, £2,000; period t_1-t_2, £6,000; period t_2-t_3, £8,000; period t_3-t_4, £5,000; period t_4-t_5, £7,000; period t_5-t_6, £6,000; and t_6-t_7, £9,000.

(a) *Fitting a trend line*

By this method, income would be plotted against time, and a treehand trend line drawn.

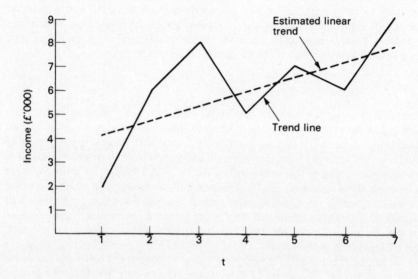

This method is very approximate indeed, and is subject to considerable judgement and estimation. It can only serve as a first estimate and indication of trend.

(b) *Calculating a simple moving average*

Assuming a three-period average, the following tabulation can be prepared:

Period	Actual income	Sum of three periods	Three-period average
t_0-t_1	£2,000		
t_1-t_2	6,000		£5,333
t_2-t_3	8,000	£16,000	6,333
t_3-t_4	5,000	19,000	6,667
t_4-t_5	7,000	20,000	6,000
t_5-t_6	6,000	18,000	7,333
t_6-t_7	9,000	22,000	

This methodology is a useful way of analysing the past, but it tends to have drawbacks regarding prediction, particularly its omission of average data at the beginning and end of the time series (the effects of these omissions are greater when the moving average is extended to cover larger series, e.g. five or seven periods).

(c) *The least-squares approach*[28]

This method attempts to establish the trend line using the straight-line identity:

$$Y_{t_n - t_{n+1}} = a + bx_{t_n - t_{n+1}};$$

where Y is the dependent variable being analysed over time t (in this case, income); a is the linear constant equal to Y when $x = 0$ (the numerical difference between the origin and the point of intersection of the straight line and the y-axis); b is the linear constant equivalent to the value of the tangent to the angle formed between the straight line and the horizontal; and x is the independent variable being analysed (in this case, time).

Period	Actual income	Periods from beginning	Periods around median period			Trend line*
	y		x	x^2	xy	$y = a + bx$
$t_0 - t_1$	£ 2,000	0	−3	9	£ −6,000	£4,001
$t_1 - t_2$	6,000	1	−2	4	−12,000	4,715
$t_2 - t_3$	8,000	2	−1	1	−8,000	5,429
$t_3 - t_4$	5,000	3	0	0	0	6,143
$t_4 - t_5$	7,000	4	1	1	7,000	6,857
$t_5 - t_6$	6,000	5	2	4	12,000	7,571
$t_6 - t_7$	9,000	6	3	9	27,000	8,285
	£43,000		0	28	£ 20,000	

*By placing the origin in the median period $t_3 - t_4$ so that $x = 0$, the normal least-squares equations reduce to: $\Sigma y = na$ (where n = the number of observations of y) and $\Sigma xy = b \Sigma x^2$. Therefore:

$$a = \frac{\Sigma y}{n} \quad ; \text{ and } b = \frac{\Sigma xy}{\Sigma x^2}$$

With values for x, y, xy and n, a and b can then be computed:

$$a = \frac{£43,000}{7} = £6,143; \text{ and } b = \frac{£20,000}{28} = £714$$

Therefore: $y = £6,143 + 714 x$. And, e.g. for period $t_0 - t_1$: $y = £6,143 + 714 (−3) = £4,001$.

These figures thus provide trend values for the complete series, and allow for easier projections to be made than is possible under the moving average approach (though the values derived under both systems are relatively similar). They can be depicted and compared graphically with the moving average and estimated linear figures, as follows:

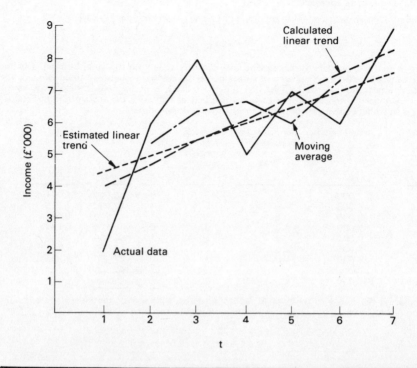

It can be seen from the graphs in the illustration that the estimated and moving average lines give little clear indication of the underlying trend of past figures, and it is for this reason that the mathematical least-squares approach is to be favoured.

The next stage in trend analysis is to use the moving average or linear trend values to estimate the remaining trend components, remembering that these trend values represent only the secular component. The other seasonal, cyclical and residual components also have to be identified for forecasting purposes, using the previously defined identities of $A = T + S + C + R$ (if additivity is assumed) or $A = T \times S \times C \times R$ (if proportionality is assumed); that is, $A - T = S + C + R$ or $\frac{A}{T} = S \times C \times R$. However, for purposes of investment analysis, and further assuming that investment forecasting is not so short-term as to require seasonal analysis and not so long-term to require cyclical analysis, then the data for trend analysis will require to conform to modified trend models; that is, either $A - T = R$ or $\frac{A}{T} = R$. In other words, annual time series will have no seasonal component and may well contain no cyclical component. Therefore, as R is, by definition, unpredictable, the main emphasis in investment analysis should be to determine T. Once this has been done, the analyst can then use the trend line as a basis for prediction, adjusting the underlying secular trend projections for factors which he believes will affect income, dividends and share value prices in particular periods in the future. These adjusting factors will necessarily include values which will comprise residual components of future trends, and could, as previously mentioned, include seasonal and cyclical items, depending on the time series being predicted.

Trend analysis and fundamental analysis

The advantage of trend analysis, particularly if it is conducted on a mathematical basis, is that it makes use of past data in the forecasting of future data. Much of this data will be derived from company financial reports in general, and financial statements in particular. It is, for this reason, especially important that the accounting information used in this exercise be (a) measured on a consistent basis from one period to the next; and (b) free of any faults and biases in measurement which could make it unreliable for analysis purposes. The data used to establish a trend must not be affected by errors or changes in measurement practices which are likely to distort it. The analyst must therefore be fully conversant with the quality of the measured data he is using, and therefore with the methods of measurement used. For example, if there has been a significant change in the measurement practices adopted in a time series, he must be able to make some attempt at adjusting it so that it conforms to the same measurement practices throughout the periods concerned. In other words, before trend analysis is undertaken, the time series must be examined and, if necessary, suitably adjusted to conform with the principle of consistency.

So far as investment analysis is concerned, the fundamentalist approach would use trend analysis techniques with such data as income, dividends and share prices. Dividends are an essential ingredient of intrinsic valuation and are traditionally regarded as proportionally related to available income. In other words, forecasting future income from an analysis of a past income-time series should provide valuable data for forecasting future dividends so long as there is some positive correlation between available income for dividend purposes and actual dividends distributed. This could be done by taking the current level of dividend and adjusting it appropriately for forecast changes in available income. Illustration 16 attempts to show some of the major considerations in this matter.

Illustration 16. *Forecasting dividends for share valuation purposes.*

Assume the same situation and figures as in Illustration 15 (see page 158), excepting that the actual time series is reduced to more comparable proportions by describing income as 'earnings per share', i.e. the proportion of available income to each available ordinary share. Similarly, the equivalent past time series of dividends is expressed as 'dividends per share'. Both these measures will be explained in greater detail in Chapter 10. The available series is as follows (assuming 20,000 share units throughout):

Period	Earnings per share	Dividend per share
$t_0 - t_1$	10p	5p.
$t_1 - t_2$	30p	12½p.
$t_2 - t_3$	40p	17½p.
$t_3 - t_4$	25p.	12½p.
$t_4 - t_5$	35p.	17½p.
$t_5 - t_6$	30p.	17½p.
$t_6 - t_7$	45p.	20p.

(A) *Coefficient of correlation: earnings to dividends*

The first step would be to establish whether there is any significant relationship between dividends and earnings in this case. Using the Pearsonian coefficient of correlation:[29]

$$r = \frac{n \Sigma xy - \Sigma x \Sigma y}{\sqrt{[(n\Sigma x^2 - (\Sigma x)^2)(n \Sigma y^2 - (\Sigma y)^2)]}}$$

the following tabulation emerges (assuming x = earnings per share and y = dividend per share):

x	y	x^2	y^2	xy
10	5.0	100	25.00	50.0
30	12.5	900	156.25	375.0
40	17.5	1,600	306.25	700.0
25	12.5	625	156.25	312.5
35	17.5	1,225	306.25	612.5
30	17.5	900	306.25	525.0
45	20.0	2,025	400.00	900.0
215	102.5	7,375	1,656.25	3,475.0

$$r = \frac{(7)(3,475) - (215)(102.5)}{\sqrt{[(7)(7,375) - (215)^2][(7)(1,656.25) - (102.5)^2]}}$$

$$= \frac{2,287.5}{\sqrt{5,875,200}} = \frac{2,287.5}{2,433.9} = +0.94$$

In other words, in this situation dividends and earnings are positively and significantly correlated.

(B) *Estimating future dividends*

The trend line, y = a + bx, in Illustration 15, revealed the following secular trend values for income, the origin of the series being taken as $t_3 - t_4$:

Period	Trend line	Trend line as earnings per share
$t_0 - t_1$	£4,001	20.00p
$t_1 - t_2$	4,715	23.57p
$t_2 - t_3$	5,429	27.14p
$t_3 - t_4$	6,143	30.71p
$t_4 - t_5$	6,857	34.28p
$t_5 - t_6$	7,571	37.85p
$t_6 - t_7$	8,285	41.43p

Taking y = £6,143 + 714 x, and with $t_3 - t_4$ as the origin, it can be estimated that the trend of income and earnings per share for the next three periods will continue as follows:

$t_7 - t_8$	£8,999	45.00p
$t_8 - t_9$	9,713	48.56p
$t_9 - t_{10}$	10,427	52.13p

This establishes the secular trend forecast values, and these now need to be amended because of specific factors (seasonal, cyclical or random) which the analyst believes should be incorporated into his earnings forecasts. It is this aspect of fundamental analysis to which information analysis relates; i.e. by analysing available data (including that contained in published financial reports), the analyst can provide himself with indicators of these special factors. Therefore it can be assumed that, forecasting such residual component adjustments, the forecasts of income and earnings per share in the next three periods are:

$t_7 - t_8$	£9,500	47.5p
$t_8 - t_9$	12,000	60.0p
$t_9 - t_{10}$	11,500	57.5p

The problem is then to forecast the dividends which it is anticipated will be distributed out of these predicted income figures. It has already been demonstrated that, in this case, income and dividends are significantly and positively correlated, and the analyst must therefore now estimate what dividends per share will be in each of the three periods, knowing that his dividend forecasts can reasonably follow his income forecasts. The following table reveals the percentage of dividends per share to earnings per share during the previous seven periods.

Period	Earnings per share	Dividend per share	Percentage of dividends to earnings
$t_0 - t_1$	10p	5.0p	50
$t_1 - t_2$	30p	12.5p	42
$t_2 - t_3$	40p	17.5p	44
$t_3 - t_4$	25p	12.5p	50
$t_4 - t_5$	35p	17.5p	50
$t_5 - t_6$	30p	17.5p	58
$t_6 - t_7$	45p	20.0p	44
	215p		

The weighted average percentage dividend/earnings ratio is approximately:

$$\frac{10,240}{215} = 48 \text{ per cent}$$

and therefore, applying this to the forecast earnings per share figures, produces the following anticipated dividends which could be incorporated into the share valuation model based on a discounting of future dividends.

Period	Anticipated earnings per share	Anticipated dividends per share
$t_7 - t_8$	47.5p	22.8p
$t_8 - t_9$	60.0p	28.8p
$t_9 - t_{10}$	57.5p	27.6p

Having been through the calculations shown in Illustration 16, the analyst will be in a position to incorporate his estimation of the eventual realization of the shares concerned into the valuation model. This is an extremely subjective aspect of fundamental analysis, for the analyst is assessing not only the future prospects of the individual company, but also the attitude of other investors to its shares in the future. A mathematically derived linear trend analysis of past share prices may be of some assistance in this respect, but the bulk of the analysis work will be concerned with examining all available information relating to the company, the stock market and the economy. The significance of forecasting the eventual realization price will vary, however. If the investment is to be short term (say, less than a year), then the forecasting of such a price will assume primary importance as future dividends will not figure to any considerable extent in the present value calculation. On the other hand, if the investment is to be long-term (say, more than ten years), then the realization price for the shares is far less significant than the forecast flow of dividends, and any inaccuracies in it will be considerably minimized by the discounting process.

Technical Analysis

In relative opposition to the philosophy of fundamental analysis is the process of technical analysis, which, instead of aiming to produce forecasts of dividends for share valuation purposes, analyses trends of past share prices actually achieved so as to forecast future prices. It therefore assumes that fundamental analysis is, at best, a technique to be used to confirm forecasts of share price movements, and, at worst, a useless technique which cannot add any further information to that already taken into account in deriving past and present share prices. Technical analysis therefore uses the previously mentioned technique of trend analysis, being concerned with long-term trends in prices (say, of more than one year) as well as short-term trends within the long-term fluctuations. Illustration 17 gives a brief example of a long-term trend analysis of share prices for an individual company using the mathematically based linear approach.

Illustration 17. *Linear trend of share prices.*

Time	Share price (y)	Time points	Points around median (x)	x^2	xy	$y = a + bx$*
t_0	£1	0	−5	25	£ −5	£2.05
t_1	2	1	−4	16	−8	2.42
t_2	4	2	−3	9	−12	2.79
t_3	3	3	−2	4	−6	3.16
t_4	2	4	−1	1	−2	3.53
t_5	5	5	0	0	0	3.90
t_6	6	6	1	1	6	4.27
t_7	7	7	2	4	14	4.64
t_8	4	8	3	9	12	5.01
t_9	3	9	4	16	12	5.38
t_{10}	6	10	5	25	30	5.75
	£43		0	110	41	

$$* \quad a = \frac{\Sigma y}{\cdot n} = \frac{43}{11} = 3.9; \text{ and } b = \frac{\Sigma xy}{\Sigma x^2} = \frac{41}{110} = 0.37$$

Having established the secular trend line for this particular share, the technical analyst is in a position to decompose the data further so as to segregate any cyclical and residual trends. Ignoring the residual factors, which are, by definition, unpredictable, the analyst can take the secular and cyclical trend lines and use these as his basis for predicting future share prices. However, the major weapon in the technical analyst's armoury is the chart of graphical presentation of share price movements and trends. From an analysis of these charts, the analyst attempts to discern particular patterns of price changes. To eliminate the graphical distortions of absolute changes using an arithmetic scale, the usual procedure is to use logarithmic scales: by plotting the logarithms of the actual values, proportionate price changes are graphed, thereby giving the analyst a sounder portrayal of price trends. Illustration 18 outlines this approach to technical analysis.

Illustration 18. *Arithmetic and logarithmic charts of share prices.*

Assume that the price of a particular share has moved as follows:

t_0	£2.00	Log	0.3010
t_1	3.00		0.4771
t_2	4.50		0.6532
t_3	6.75		0.8293
t_4	10.12		1.0051

Plotting the absolute changes on an arithmetic scale, the graphical trend would appear in the following form:

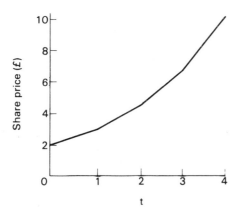

This gives the analyst little indication of the proportionate changes in the share's price, which, assuming an investor has a given sum to invest, is of much greater relevance than absolute changes. The following graph plots these proportionate changes, using a logarithmic scale.

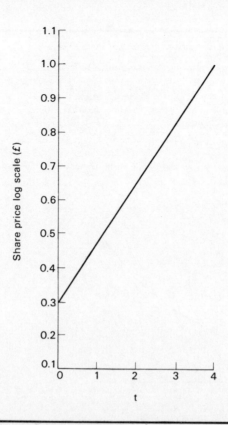

Therefore, by using logs, the straight-line proportionate trend can be readily discerned. This sort of technique can be adopted on a daily, weekly, monthly or yearly basis, depending on the particular trend regarded as important, daily and weekly trends being part of monthly trends, which, in turn, are part of yearly trends.

In addition to graphical representation of share price movements and trends, the analyst is also concerned with the trend of the volume of shares traded, although this data is not always available. When it is, it can be incorporated into the share price chart in the form of a bar chart. The trend of prices indicates what investors think about the future value of the shares concerned; the trend of volume of trading indicates the degree of buying being undertaken by investors, and this, again, indicates what they think about the future of the shares.

The main problem in technical analysis is therefore the identification of trends and the taking of appropriate investment action quickly enough to benefit from the predicted direction of the trend – that is, buying when the predicted trend is upwards, and selling when the predicted trend is downwards. Obviously, the analysis and interpretation of short-term trends in this context is extremely subjective since fluctuations in price can be numerous and substantial, and consequently difficult to predict. The technical analyst is therefore looking for particular patterns to which he can apply specific investment decision rules, these rules having been devised for this type of analysis.

The most typical patterns to be found in charts of share price movements are 'head and shoulders' and 'triangles'. In the former, the share price rises until it meets some resistance (usually the volume of buying dropping off); the price then levels off until there is another surge upwards; there is then a reversal in trend with the price coming down, levelling off and then finally dropping to a low point which marks the beginning of another upward trend (again, the volume of trading usually follows this pattern). Illustration 19 gives an outline example of such a graphical pattern.

Illustration 19. *Head and shoulders trend pattern.*

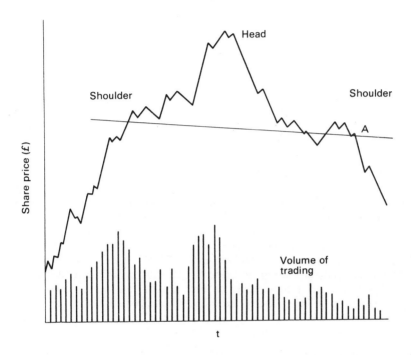

The graph in Illustration 19 depicts the point at which the pattern is said to be complete (that is, A), and the prediction would then be a downward trend in share price, assumed to be equal to the upward movement above the 'neckline'. The technical analyst therefore looks for the completion of this pattern to justify the selling of shares (they would not be held beyond point A), and to predict the end of the downward trend and the beginning of the next upward trend. The volume of trading is of help when analysing this pattern, since it indicates when buying is on the increase or decrease in the share concerned. The 'head and shoulders' pattern can also appear in reverse (that is, Illustration 19 would appear inverted) and would be used to support the prediction of upward trends and the buying of shares.

The other familiar graphical pattern is the triangle which is created when share prices have been fluctuating up and down for some time. In many instances, when these fluctuations settle down to a discernible trend, the triangle is complete and the point of investment decision reached; this depending on the direction of the trend.

The context for using company financial reports   167

Illustration 20. *Triangle trend pattern.*

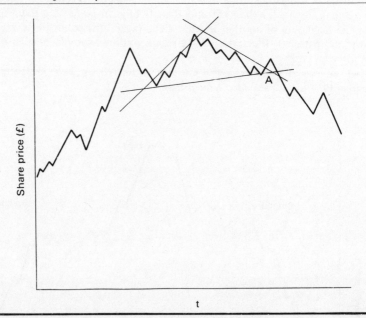

Illustration 20 shows this pattern. In this case, once the triangle is complete at point A, the technical analyst will suggest that the shares be sold at that price.

The chartist approach to investment analysis, described here very briefly, has been the subject of a number of criticisms over the years, mainly because of its lack of fundamental analysis prior to investment decisions; its inherent subjectiveness in predicting future price movements on the basis of past trends established as a result of numerous variables; and its assumption that future prices can be predicted from past prices, thereby indicating some degree of dependence. However, the conclusions of Roberts and Beckman are not to be disregarded:

'A chart then is not akin to a crystal ball. It is nothing more than a visual orderly arrangement of recorded data. . . . Above all though it does show what investors are actually doing, not what others feel that they ought to be doing. . . . Looked at another way, a chart merely formalizes what is at the back of every investor's mind when gauging the prospects of a share. The year's high/low, recent trend, yesterday's price, etc., are factors considered important by most before making a sale or purchase. Market feel, flair, and other compliments to individual judgement are often only a reflection of the mind's ability to draw conclusions from price behaviour. Why not then assist the mind in its interpretation by setting out as accurately as data will permit, the history of price performance?'[30]

In other words, despite its apparent or potential disregard for information contained in such sources as company financial reports, technical analysis depends on the use of relevant data; in this case, share price movements and share trading volumes, both related to time. However, compared with the techniques of fundamental analysis, the use of available information to support investment decisions is relatively small. Technical analysis is far more concerned with the aggregate behaviour and attitudes of investors in the market than in the characteristics and qualities of the individual company and its management. Certainly, the analysis of company financial reports appears to have little part to play in the process of technical analysis, unless it is used in a support role to confirm findings from chart computation and interpretation. On the other hand, there appears to be a very strong argument in favour of regarding technical analysis not just as a separate investment analysis approach but more as an extension of the process of fundamental analysis; past share price trends being important information ingredients to the investment decision.

The Random Walk Theory

It would be wrong to conclude this section on investment analysis without mentioning a conceptual argument which, when tested empirically, suggests that both fundamental and technical analysis are of limited use in making investment decisions. The argument is contained in the random walk theory, and it states, in the words of Williamson:

> 'First, the theory says that new information about a company, its industry, or anything that effects the prospects of the company is disseminated very quickly, once it becomes public. Second, the price of a stock at any particular time represents the judgement of all investors, based upon all the information that is public. And third, new information about a company is disseminated randomly over time.'[31]

In other words, share prices at any time will reflect the interpretations and expectations of investors from all available information, and because such information is deemed to be publicly available, no investor can put himself at an absolute advantage to others by attempting to analyse and refine past information. Such information is already reflected in existing share prices, which change in the future as a consequence of new information becoming public and investors amending their judgements of share prices. As this new information becomes publicly available on a random basis, fluctuations in share prices will appear randomly as investors absorb and interpret it. Similarly, as share prices are determined in an uncertain world, and investors will interpret new information differently, the actual price of shares will tend to move randomly around their intrinsic values.

These propositions about the randomness of absolute share price changes, and the use of available information, raise serious questions of fundamental and technical analysis.

First, if existing share prices reflect all available information to date, and change randomly in the future owing to the release of new information, then future prices do not depend on the trend of past prices. In other words, the random walk theory appears to run contrary to the major assumption of technical analysis that past price trends can be used to predict future trends. However, heed must be taken of the warning of Granger,[32] who pointed out that the random walk theory is concerned primarily with absolute price changes while technical analysis is concerned with the trend of relative price changes. Nevertheless, the random walk theory does suggest that the past should not be relied upon absolutely when predicting the future. The apparent validity of this is to be seen in the findings of researchers such as Brearley.[33] He found from various correlation tests that share prices were not related from day to day or from period to period, and that movements in share prices, when they did persist in one direction, did so only in the very short-term.

Secondly, if all the available and public information has already been taken into account by investors in determining existing share prices, then there seems little benefit in conducting fundamental analyses of companies and their shares. This would produce no new information likely to be of advantage to the investor, and would, in turn, appear to render meaningless the analysis of company financial reports and other sources of information. Investors would simply wait until new information became publicly available, and then, by making suitable assessments of its significance in relation to existing share prices, would cause these to move further randomly around their intrinsic values. Evidence of the stock markets' quick absorption of new information and the consequential movement in share prices is seen in various studies already mentioned in relation to the degree of influence which accounting information has on share price movements. For example, Ball and Brown[34] found evidence to suggest that share prices do not move abnormally when annual income figures are reported, thereby indicating that investors have already made use of other sources of information (such as interim reports) and that the data aggregated into the annual income figure have already been used to establish existing share prices. This early use of available new information is also to be evidenced in the studies of the effects of interim financial reporting by Brown and Kennelly,[35] Kiger[36] and May.[37]

There are, however, arguments against the random walk hypothesis which suggest that fundamental and technical analyses are not as irrelevant as might appear at first glance. First, the theory of the random walk is concerned with absolute share price movements and not with relative share price movements. Technical analysis is largely concerned with the latter, and the suggestion that it is not useful for predicting absolute share values in the future can be seen as not particularly constructive when it is understood that the technical analyst is concerned with predicting the future trend of share prices. Secondly, the random walk theory is based on the assumption that the stock market is efficient; that is, that investors will make use of all available information; that information is available to all investors at the same time; that all investors are skilled and experienced enough to make use of the information; that investment decisions will be made rationally; and so on. However, it can equally be argued that the market is not efficient; that is, that the available information is not available to every investor; that it is not always completely reliable or relevant; and that different investors place on it differing interpretations. Thus, fundamental analysis, far from being irrelevant, is entirely necessary to a rational evaluation of shares and current and future values. In other words, contrary to the random walk hypothesis, the market values of shares may vary considerably from their intrinsic values owing to market imperfections and inefficiencies, and fundamental analysis is a meaningful way of attempting to assess these intrinsic values.

Conclusions

Much of this chapter has been concerned with discussing the part that information has to play in aiding a variety of interested persons and organizations to assess the past and predict the future financial performance of companies. In particular, it has concentrated on one particular use to which available information can be applied: the investment decision. This example of potential information usage reveals that, despite arguments to the contrary owing to the assumed random nature of share behaviour, there is a significant part to be played by analysed information in the making of investment decisions. Logically it can therefore be postulated that the same can be said of other decisions such as those relating to loans and credit. Of particular importance in the context of this book, therefore, is the role of analysed accounting information in the making and monitoring of decisions. Chapters 9 and 10 will look specifically at this matter and will discuss not only the process and mechanics of analysing available accounting information, but also the significance of the analysed data when assessing the financial performance of companies.

Suggested Discussion or Essay Topics

1. Almost by definition, economic activity means the making and taking of decisions. It has been suggested that to undertake these functions without the use of available information would be foolhardly. Why should this be so?

2. What is meant by the analysis of available information in relation to economic decisions? Why is it necessary to analyse data for this purpose?

3. Many writers have pointed out the numerous faults and problems inherent in the measurement and communication of accounting information. Knowledge of them will therefore be of crucial importance to the analyst of company financial reports. Discuss.

4. By far the most significant use to be made of company financial reports is in relation to the investment decision. Describe what is meant by the term 'investment decision' and comment on the validity of the statement.

5. If future dividends are the most significant aspect of investment decision-making, then historical financial reports of company profitability and financial position are largely irrelevant to this exercise. Discuss.

6. It has been suggested that one way of finding out whether or not published accounting data are useful to investors is to examine share price movements in relation to publication of data. Describe, in general terms, this approach to assessing information utility, and comment on any doubts you may have with regard to such an association.

7. Rarely does the publication of financial statements have any important or lasting effect on share prices. Discuss.

8. Interim financial reporting appears to be more relevant to investors than annual financial reporting. Explain why this should be the case, giving brief details of available evidence to support the statement.

9. What is meant by the intrinsic value of a share? Have company financial reports any part to play in its determination?

10. It has been stated that there is a need for financial data to be factual and objective if it is to be used by investors as a guide to the future. Discuss.

11. The process of fundamental analysis utilizes data from a variety of sources. Define what is meant by fundamental analysis, and explain the relative importance of the major sources of information to the analyst.

12. Describe what is meant by trend analysis. How reliable is it as an investment technique?

13. Forecasts of company income, dividends and share prices have little value. The uncertainties of the company's world combined with those of the investment world produce substantial margins of error, and these margins increase with the length of the forecast. Comment.

14. Investment appears to be more a matter of flair, intuition and individual judgement than a precise science. The investor should therefore be more concerned with attempting to 'outguess' the decisions and judgements of other investors than in trying to evaluate the true worth of shares. Discuss.

15. Explain and comment on the debate and apparent conflict between the fundamental and technical analysts.

16. Can the random walk theory be proved or disproved?

17. If the propositions in the random walk theory are valid, what implications do they have for the reporting, analysis and use of accounting information?

Notes and References

1. Readers are particularly directed to G. A. Lee, *Modern Financial Accounting,* Nelson, 1973.

2. G. H. Sorter, M. S. Gans, P. Rosenfield, R. M. Shannon and R. G. Streit, 'Economic Decision-Making and the Role of Accounting Information', in *Objectives of Financial Statements: Selected Papers,* American Institute of Certified Public Accountants, 1974, pp. 68 and 69.

3. For studies of the predictive ability of accounting information, see, e.g., K. V. Peasnell, 'The Usefulness of Accounting Information to Investors', *ICRA Occasional Paper 1,* 1973; W. H. Beaver, J. W. Kennelly and W. M. Voss, 'Predictive Ability as a Criterion for the Evaluation of Accounting Data', *Accounting Review,* October 1968, pp. 675-83; and M. N. Greenball, 'The Predictive Ability Criterion: Its Relevance in Evaluating Accounting Data', *Abacus,* June 1971, pp. 1-7.

4. *Objectives of Financial Statements,* Report of the Study Group on the Objectives of Financial Statements, American Institute of Certified Public Accountants, 1973, p. 66.

5. G. O. May, 'The Nature of the Financial Accounting Process', *Accounting Review,* July 1943, p. 190.

6. See, e.g., K. T. Maunders and B. J. Foley, 'Accounting Information, Employees and Collective Bargaining', *Journal of Business Finance and Accounting,* Spring 1974, pp. 109-27.

7. *Objectives of Financial Statements,* report cit., p. 62.

8. For more detailed explanations of the investment decision, see J. Freear, *Financing Decisions in Business,* Accountancy Age Books, 1973; and B. Carsberg, *Analysis for Investment Decisions,* Accountancy Age Books, 1974.

9. See references in n. 8.

10. For a discussion of risk and uncertainty, see J. Small, 'Risk and Uncertainty', *Accountant's Magazine,* January 1969, pp. 8-23.

11. A. C. Raynor and I. M. D. Little, *Higgledy Piggledy Growth Again,* Basil Blackwell, 1966, pp. 76-81.

12. A. Singh and G. Whittington, *Growth, Profitability and Valuation,* Cambridge University Press, 1968, pp. 133-44.

13. G. Whittington, *The Prediction of Profitability and Other Studies of Company Behaviour,* Cambridge University Press, 1971, pp. 82-104.

14. P. Brown and V. Neiderhoffer, 'The Predictive Content of Quarterly Earnings', *Journal of Business,* October 1968, pp. 488-97.

15. D. Green and J. Segall, 'The Predictive Power of First-Quarter Earnings Reports', *Journal of Business,* January 1967, pp. 44-55.

16. P. Brown and J. W. Kennelly, 'The Informational Content of Quarterly Earnings: An Extension and Some Further Evidence', *Journal of Business,* July 1972, pp. 403-15.

17. M. C. O'Connor, 'On the Usefulness of Financial Ratios to Investors in Common Stock', *Accounting Review,* April 1973, pp. 339-52.

18. W. H. Beaver, 'Financial Ratios as Predictors of Failure', *Empirical Research in Accounting: Selected Studies,* 1966, pp. 71-111.

19. W. H. Beaver, 'Market Prices, Financial Ratios, and the Prediction of Failure', *Journal of Accounting Research,* Autumn 1968, pp. 179-92.

20. R. A. Brearley, *An Introduction to Risk and Return from Common Stocks,* M. I. T. Press, 1969.

21. Whittington, *The Prediction of Profitability.*

22. G. Whittington, 'Changes in the Top 100 Quoted Manufacturing Companies in the United Kingdom: 1948 to 1968', *Journal of Industrial Economics,* November 1972, pp. 17-34.

23. R. J. Briston, *The Stock Exchange and Investment Analysis,* Allen & Unwin, revised edition, 1974, p. 213.

24. ibid., p. 238.

25. P. J. Coen, E. D. Gomme and M. G. Kendall, 'Lagged Relationships in Economic Forecasting', in B. Taylor (ed.), *Investment Analysis and Portfolio Management,* St Martin's Press, 1970, pp. 162-81.

26. Briston, *The Stock Exchange and Investment Analysis,* p. 239

27. It is not the purpose of this text to explain in detail the principles of trend analysis. However, the reader should refer to K. A. Yeomans, *Statistics for the Social Scientist: 1,* Penguin Books, 1968, pp. 208-44, for an introductory explanation of this topic. Much of what is explained in this section of Yeomans is used for the purpose of explaining trend analysis in relation to the investment decision.

28. For further details of this statistical technique, see ibid., pp. 170-81.

29. For further details of this statistical technique, see ibid., pp. 186-92.

30. C. Roberts and R. Beckman, 'The Charisma of Charts and All That', *Accountancy,* July 1973, p. 71.

31. J. P. Williamson, *Investments: New Analytical Techniques,* Longmans, Green, 1971, pp. 182-3.

32. C. W. J. Granger, 'What the Random Walk Does *Not* Say', in Taylor (ed.), *Investment Analysis and Portfolio Management,* pp. 185-7.

33. Brearley, *An Introduction to Risk and Return.*

34. R. Ball and P. Brown, 'An Empirical Evaluation of Accounting Numbers', *Journal of Accounting Research,* Autumn 1968, pp. 159-77.

35. Brown and Kennelly, 'The Informational Content of Quarterly Earnings', loc. cit.

36. J. E. Kiger, 'An Empirical Investigation of NYSE Volume and Price Reactions to the Announcement of Quarterly Earnings', *Journal of Accounting Research,* Spring 1972, pp. 113-26.

37. R. G. May, 'The Influence of Quarterly Earnings Announcements on Investor Decisions as Reflected in Common Stock Price Changes', *Empirical Research in Accounting: Selected Studies,* 1971, pp. 119-63.

Selected Bibliography for Chapter 8

'Objectives of Financial Statements', *Report of the Study Group on the Objectives of Financial Statements,* American Institute of Certified Public Accountants, 1973. A comprehensive coverage of the uses to which reported accounting information is, and should be put.

R. J. Briston, *The Stock Exchange and Investment Analysis,* Allen & Unwin, revised edition 1974. An introduction to investment analysis (pp. 211-44); descriptions of sources of information available to the investors (pp. 245-68); an introduction to technical analysis (pp. 371-83); and an introduction to the random walk theory (pp. 395-401).

B. V. Carsberg, *Analysis for Investment Decisions,* Accountancy Age Books, 1974. A thorough and recent coverage of the investment decision.

E. F. Fama, 'Random Walk in Stock Market Prices', *Financial Analysts' Journal,* September-October 1965, pp. 55-9. An expert and very readable commentary on the random walk theory.

P. Freeman, 'Some Aspects of Technical Analysis', *Investment Analyst,* October 1967, pp. 9-19. A useful description of the theory and practice of technical analysis.

K. V. Peasnell, 'The Usefulness of Accounting Information to Investors', *ICRA Occasional Paper 1,* 1973. An analysis of the predictive ability of accounting information compared with its use as feedback data.

G. H. Sorter, M. S. Gans, P. Rosenfield, R. M. Shannon and R. G. Streit, 'Economic Decision-Making and the Role of Accounting Information', in *Objectives of Financial Statements: Selected Papers,* American Institute of Certified Public Accountants, 1974, pp. 66-79. An analysis of decisions and their relationship to published accounting information. And J. Ronen, 'A User-Orientated Development of Accounting Information Requirements', in ibid., pp. 80-103. An analysis of information criteria from the point of view of using accounting information.

D. Weaver, *Investment Analysis,* Longmans, Green, 1971. A description of technical analysis (pp. 108-21) and the forecasting of company income (pp. 122-41).

9 The Nature of Financial Ratios

Introduction

From the preceding chapter, the reader should now be aware that decisions dominate the use of company financial reports; that is, the information contained in them, coupled with other available sources of data, provides means by which various decision-makers can assess their alternative courses of action. The two main areas of activity to which financial reports can be brought to bear are prediction and control, the decision-maker typically having to adapt mainly historical data to formulate the predictions underlying his decisions, then using the same data to compare actual financial results with his previously formulated expectations.

It has also been suggested that because of the predominantly historical nature of available information (including financial reports), it is important for the decision-maker to conduct a rigorous and a detailed analysis of data akin to the process of fundamental analysis in investment decision-making. This should provide him with a necessary background with which to evaluate the company concerned and predict future benefits to be derived either from his existing or his potential involvement in it. In this sense, financial report analysis is concerned with the construction of a financial profile of the company (preferably over a period of time) which will allow the decision-maker to assess its past, present and possible future strengths and weaknesses. Of particular concern to him in this respect are the related problems of what future benefits he can expect from the company, and, possibly most importantly, whether or not the company will survive in the future and thereby remain in a position to provide those expected benefits.

The accounting information contained in company financial reports can be used to build up this profile by providing the basis for prediction and consequent control through the process of ratio analysis, or the computation and interpretation of significant indicators of company progress and performance. These indicators take the form of ratios describing relevant relationships between individual data usually contained in published financial statements. The analyst therefore must be skilled and experienced enough to identify the relevant accounting data and to match them in such a way that meaningful indicators are made available for decision-making purposes. He must also be capable of interpreting the meaning of computed ratios and understanding the implications of material changes in them over time.

This suggests that ratio construction and analysis, as with the function of fundamental analysis of which it is a part, should be conducted by skilled professionals. Indeed, in practice, this tends to be the case, particularly in the decision-making of institutional investors (such as investment companies, unit trusts, insurance companies, pension funds and merchant banks) which employ teams of analysts to construct company profiles using such techniques as ratio analysis. However, it should also be said that ratio analysis and construction are not the sole prerogative of the employed analyst. So long as the user of published financial statements is fully aware of their nature and meaning, as well as their relative strengths and weaknesses, and so long as he is also aware of the nature and construction of the key relationships which can be derived from them, then he is in a position to use them in a way which facilitates his decisions. Nevertheless, as Welsch and Anthony rightly emphasize, many decision-makers do not or cannot put themselves in this position of advantage:

> 'Some decisions are made intuitively and without much supporting data. In these cases there is no systematic attempt to collect measurable data such as those provided in financial reports. The decision-maker does not attempt to array, measure, and evaluate the advantages and disadvantages of each alternative. There are numerous reasons for intuitive decisions of this sort. Time and cost may prevent a careful analysis. Frequently, the decision-maker is unsophisticated; he does not understand the systematic approach to decision-making. Unsophisticated decision-makers tend to oversimplify the decision-making process and quite frequently overlook the financial impacts.'[1]

This and the following chapter, as with the rest of the text, therefore assume the sophisticated user of company financial statements, and the remaining sections will attempt to describe and explain the process whereby published accounting information, together with other available data, is used to construct financial ratios useful for decision-making. As before, the emphasis will be on understanding rather than computation as the latter is adequately covered by other writers.[2] It should also be noted at the outset that the process of financial ratio analysis is concerned mainly with the use of reported accounting information. There are other ratios which can be computed using other sources of information (such as industry data), but these are regarded as largely outwith the scope of a text mainly concerned with the use of company financial reports. On the other hand, certain financial ratios do make use of data derived from the Stock Exchange (for example, share prices), and these will be fully explained at appropriate stages in Chapter 10.

Objectives of Financial Ratios

The process of producing financial ratios is essentially concerned with the identification of significant accounting data relationships which give the decision-maker insights into the company being assessed. In particular, the aim of financial ratios is to provide indicators of a company's past performance (in terms of its operational activity and profitability) and near-present financial condition (for example, relating to its liquidity and financial structure), so as to give the decision-maker a basis for predicting future performance and financial condition. Provision of key ratios over a period of time can enable him to construct a pattern of company behaviour and condition which he can then incorporate into his decision model by formulating predictions of future dividends and so forth which make use of such a pattern.

For the purpose of this text, which is primarily concerned with external decision-makers to the company, the main financial ratio users appear to be existing and potential shareholders, lenders and creditors. The informational needs of each of these groups are largely unspecified and consequently assumed. For example, shareholders can be divided into different groupings: preferred, ordinary and deferred, they can be institutional or private individuals; they can be investing for income, capital value appreciation or a combination of both; they can be willing to accept differing degrees of investment risk; and they can be investing for short-term gain or long-term benefit. As yet, little is known of their precise informational needs except what is postulated in the accountancy literature.[3] The same remarks can be applied to lenders or creditors except that their assumed groupings appear to be less complex than those of investors. Lenders and creditors 'invest' for different periods of time with expectations of repayment on dates which are usually contractually agreed. It is therefore difficult to be precise as to what financial ratios are particularly relevant to each such group. However, the following very general indications can be given.

Financial ratios and investors

Chapter 8 described how investors are mainly concerned with the flow of future dividends which they predict will be attributable to their existing or potential investment. They are also interested in the ultimate realization proceeds for the particular investment being considered. From this it can reasonably be assumed that investors are concerned with financial ratios which aid them in the prediction of dividends and share realization values. Therefore relevant ratios would appear to include those depicting company profitability (income being an essential ingredient in the computation of dividends, the latter usually being some proportion of available income); liquidity (dividends are usually paid in cash form if there are sufficient liquid resources to allow distributions to be paid; and the long-term survival of the company as a going concern depends on the adequacy of its liquid resources); and capital structure (for example, the way in which the company is financed will have a significant part to play in determining investment risk; the more it relies on loans and credit, the more risk there is of falls in income levels and cash resources constraining the distribution of dividends).

Financial ratios and lenders and creditors

Because of their concern in the eventual repayment of monies due to them, together with any related interest payments, lenders and creditors would appear to be liable to use similar ratios to those of the investor. For example, interest payments will depend on the availability of income and liquid resources; and the latter are also essential to repayment of capital sums. Similarly, data on the capital structure of the company not only helps the investor to assess his investment, but will also help the lender or creditor to assess the risk he is taking when investing in the company.

Criteria for Financial Ratios

To be useful to the decision-maker, financial ratios should satisfy certain criteria. These may appear to be relatively self-evident, but should not be forgotten when preparing ratios. If they are neglected, then, no matter how arithmetically correct the computed relationships, there is a very real danger that subsequent interpretations could be either misleading or erroneous. The following are the most obvious of these criteria.

Comparability

By definition, decisions are concerned with the assessment of alternative courses of action. This has certain implications for the use of information in the prediction and control phases of decision-making. First, prediction of future benefits for a number of alternatives requires the information used to be comparable; that is, that the information related to one alternative course of action be capable of being meaningfully compared with information related to another alternative. Secondly, when analysing information over time for predicting benefits related to a particular course of action, it is equally necessary to ensure that the data of one period can be compared with that of other periods. Thirdly, when monitoring the results of previous decisions, it is essential that the information pertaining to actual performance can be not only compared with predicted data, but can also be used for inter-period comparisons of actual performance.

Comparability is, in this sense, largely concerned with the measurement of the information used in financial ratio computation as well as in the measurement of the ratios themselves. Unless the information and the resultant ratios are measured on the same basis for purposes of comparisons at one point of time or over time, it is exceedingly difficult to deduce whether significant differences in comparisons are the result of differences in the underlying financial performance and condition or of differences in the measurement techniques employed. Thus there is an obvious need for consistency in the accounting treatment of reported data which are going to be used for financial ratio purposes, not only between periods for the same company but also between companies within the same trade or industry.

The need for consistency in accounting is widely recognized by the accountancy profession. For example, Moonitz has clearly stated that:

'The procedures used in accounting for a given entity should be appropriate for the measurement of its position and its activities and should be followed consistently from period to period.'[4]

However, he went on to counsel against extending this proposition too far:

'The proposition refers to accounting "for a given entity", not for a given industry or entire economic system. Whether, for example, all steel companies should follow the same procedures is neither affirmed or denied by this proposition. We take it, however, that no accounting entity following an appropriate set of procedures should change to a less appropriate set merely for the purpose of making its reports consistent with those of others in the same industry, nor should it refrain from adopting an improved practice on the grounds that to do so would destroy comparability.'[5]

In other words, whereas comparability may well be achieved for the one company over time, it is a much more difficult task to achieve it between apparently similar companies. The major problem in this respect is that companies tend not to be identical even when they may appear, on the surface, to have similar features. Apparently similar companies tend to behave in different ways; the mix of their operations may vary; their managerial philosophy and practice may differ; their operational environment may be dissimilar. The problem has become even more acute in recent years, the process of takeover and merger having created companies with widely diversified interests and operations which make them difficult subjects for industrial classification.[6] Nevertheless, the counter-argument of Stamp should be noted as inter-company comparisons seem to be important aspects of ratio analysis and consequential decision-making:

'Many accountants have argued that such a goal is unattainable in accounting since no two accounting situations are ever exactly alike. To argue this way is a counsel of despair, and ignores achievements in other fields where the intellectual difficulties of correlation and rationalization are at least as difficult as they are in accounting. . . . The next, and much more important, step is to classify and organize and arrange . . . in such a way that similarities are identified and stressed; this almost invariably involves the intellectual process of abstraction, and it is only by following such a process that the human mind is able to make sense out of its environment.'[7]

The need for consistency in accounting practice to achieve comparability has been recognized in the programmes of accounting standardization which are now in operation in the United Kingdom and elsewhere. This is having the effect of improving the uniformity of accounting measurements for reporting purposes, and consequently the computation and use of financial ratios are being made more relevant to decision-making than before, owing to the gradual elimination of differences caused by accounting method rather than economic activity. However, it must be clearly stated that measurement differences still remain. For example, no two companies are absolutely identical and measurement differences may be entirely appropriate to reflect fairly the characteristics of each. Similarly, the circumstances and characteristics of individual companies tend to change over time, and this will cause changes in methodology from one period to the next. Finally, the programmes of standardization are continuous, long-term processes which attempt to minimize accounting flexibility. They cannot 'legislate' for every possible area of flexibility, particularly in those areas where subjective judgements by qualified experts are the bases for measuring accounting information. In other words, uniformity and consistency of practice are desirable properties of accounting information which is to be translated into ratio form for comparative purposes. However, the financial ratio user must be aware of the impossibility of achieving absolute uniformity, and thus of achieving absolute comparability.

Data limitations

Ratios describing an individual company's financial progress and position are very much a derivation of its published accounting information. As such, they are subject to the measurement limitations of the underlying information, the main features of which have been described in some detail in Chapters 6 and 7. The problems of valuation from the traditional use of the principles of realization and historic cost, together with the convention of conservatism, an unstable monetary unit (owing to its diminishing or increasing purchasing power) and of significant resource omissions (accountants traditionally measuring on the basis of verifiable past transactions), as well as of the flexibility issue, all affect the reliability and relevance of financial ratios. That is why it is so important for the decision-maker who makes use of financial ratios to be fully aware of the problems affecting the underlying accounting information. He must understand, for example, the limitations of ratios which rely on measures of accounting income based on the realization principle. They reflect realized rather than earned income of the period. Similarly, ratios utilizing asset valuations from a traditional balance sheet (for example, fixed asset or stock and work in progress values) should not be interpreted as indicating current values, or not, at least, in the normal case. Ratios are only as reliable and relevant as the accounting information upon which they are based.

Proliferation of ratios

As previously mentioned, and as will be shown in detail in Chapter 10, financial ratios are usually an expression of the relationship between one accounting measure and another: for example, earnings per share describes the proportion of distributable periodic income attributable to each ordinary share unit of the company concerned. Within the typical set of financial statements (particularly annual statements), there is a very large number of measures available for ratio computation. However, the relevance of the latter process depends on recognizing pertinent relationships. It is perfectly feasible to relate all available reported data, and thereby to produce an extremely large number of ratios. But it is equally feasible to suggest that most of these ratios will be meaningless to the user, either because he has no use for them in his particular decision model or, more important, because the computed relationships are themselves meaningless as they do not convey or indicate important characteristics of the company's financial performance or condition. As Benishay has commented:

'In the financial analyst's trade, ratios are frequently used tools which must be employed with diagnostic skill, empirical sense, and good judgement. Yet these tools are often blunted or rendered useless by the corrosive powers of redundant ratio computations, ignorance of empirical facts and lack of interpretive sophistication. There exists a persistent tendency to compute too many ratios and to present them as if they were, truly and logically, independent units of evidence.'[8]

In other words, there is a basic set of financial ratios which can be derived from financial statements, which give all the data necessary to compute others if need be. This set contains the independent ratios from which other dependent ratios can be computed. The advantage of this approach is that it provides a set of relevant ratios which can be extended by the experienced analyst to include other ratios, but using the data in the original set to do so. This therefore tends to cause the analyst to think of the relevance and usefulness of ratios before he computes them, and thereby tends to minimize the potential proliferation of unnecessary ratios.

The effect of extraordinary items

If, as has been explained throughout this text, the use of accounting information in decision-making is largely concerned with historical data from which predictions of future benefits are derived, it is extremely important to ensure that analysed past data are devoid of factors not likely to recur in the future. In accounting terms, this refers particularly to so-called extraordinary gains and losses affecting the measurement of periodic income.

It is inevitable that a company will benefit or suffer financially from certain events or transactions which are of a non-recurrent nature: for example, gains or losses arising from the closing down of part of its trading operations; the sale of long-term investments; the confiscation of properties in a foreign country; and the major devaluation or revaluation of foreign currencies. The accounting treatment of these items for income reporting purposes has concerned accountants for many years, the alternative treatments being their separate disclosure, either in the balance sheet as movements in the company's reserves or in the income statement as adjustments to normal operating income. The latter has recently received professional approval in the United Kingdom,[9] its main aim being the separation of recurring and non-recurring income elements to aid the report user in his assessment of company performance over time. Therefore the production of financial ratios using reported income data can be undertaken more easily, the non-recurrent items being ignored in the computation of comparable ratios for prediction purposes.

However, although ignoring extraordinary gains and losses in ratio computation and analysis seems entirely appropriate to the establishment of comparable data for decision-making, it does raise two related questions: first, what is an extraordinary item of a non-recurring nature, and secondly, assuming that these items can be identified, does their exclusion from computed ratios improve their predictive capability? The problem of what is a non-recurrent gain or loss has long vexed accountants, and despite the existence of professional standards,[10] the situation remains largely unresolved. As Hendriksen[11] has questioned, what item of gain or loss can ever be regarded as absolutely non-recurrent? In other words, it may be more reasonable to regard these items as infrequent rather than non-recurrent. But this raises the question of how infrequent they have to be to be treated as non-recurrent: is it to be recurring every two, ten or fifty years? In addition, it is relatively self-evident that gains and losses may well be non-recurring for one company but not for another, the degree of recurrence depending on the nature of business. Therefore it is extremely difficult to standardize matters in this respect since there is a danger in so doing of imposing a uniformity in accounting practice which ignores the diversity of company activities and thereby produces meaningless comparisons. As yet there are no clear answers to these questions, and it is doubtful whether any are forthcoming.

So far as concerns improving the predictive capability of financial ratios by the exclusion of extraordinary items from income measures, logic appears to suggest that such exclusions will produce accounting relationships which provide more relevant comparisons of data both over time and between companies. However, as Nichols[12] has demonstrated from a study of data from seventy-eight companies, using trend analysis techniques, there is evidence to suggest that, at least so far as predicting future company income is concerned, inclusion and exclusion of extraordinary gains and losses provides equally good predictions. It would be wrong to generalize from this isolated study, but it does provide encouragement for accountants attempting to resolve the problem of extraordinary items in the reporting and use of accounting information. It may well be that their segregation is not as vital as might first appear. Meanwhile, the problem does exist, and the computation of financial ratios would seem to benefit by the exclusion of extraordinary items. Therefore the analyst must be capable of identifying potentially non-recurring items according to the circumstances of the individual companies concerned. This does not appear to be an area in which he can be guided in any detailed sense because of the differing circumstances of companies.

Materiality

Unquestionably, one of the most significant aspects of financial ratio computation and analysis is the materiality of the data being used. This has been defined in the following way by Dohr:

> 'A statement, fact or item is material, if, giving full consideration to the surrounding circumstances, as they exist at the time, it is of such a nature that its disclosure, or the method of treating it, would be likely to influence or to "make a difference" in the judgement and conduct of a reasonable person. The same tests apply to such words as significant, consequential, or important.'[13]

This is one of the most crucial aspects of accounting, and, as such, it affects not only decisions regarding data to be measured and communicated in financial reports, but also data to be analysed. The producer of accounting information must ensure that he measures and discloses material data (in other words, that trivia should not be reported), while its users must equally ensure that the reported data selected for analysis purposes are material enough to be capable of influencing their decisions. However, this poses a problem because there are no generally accepted guidelines to aid the analyst with regard to data materiality. The latter is very much a matter of personal judgement which has to be made in light of the surrounding circumstances at the time of judgement. It concerns not only the nature of the data being used, but also the size of the quantification, either in relative or absolute terms. For example, if the financial report contains information that the managing director has defrauded the company of a relatively small monetary sum, then, irrespective of the insignificance of the sum involved, the nature of the item is important enough to have an influence on the behaviour of shareholders and others. On the other hand, if the analyst has computed the company's earnings per share and found the figure to be 0.5 per cent below what was generally expected for the period concerned, then, irrespective of the relevance of the computation, the absolute size of the difference may well be regarded as immaterial when formulating subsequent decisions. The problem for the analyst in these circumstances is judging when an absolute or relative datum ceases to be immaterial and becomes relevant to the decisions under consideration. It is well summed up in a publication of the Institute of Chartered Accountants in England and Wales, which, although written in the context of producing and auditing financial statements, is equally pertinent to their analysis and interpretation:

> 'The interpretation of what is "material" is a matter for the exercise of professional judgement based on experience and the requirement to give a true and fair view.
>
> 'Materiality can only be considered in relative terms. In a small business £100 may be material, whereas £1 million may not be material in classifying the expenditure of a very large undertaking, especially as elaboration could obscure the true and fair view. Those responsible for preparing and auditing accounts have to decide which, out of the many facts available to them, are the ones that have a real bearing on the true and fair view which the accounts must give.'[14]

Suggested Discussion or Essay Topics

The contents of this and the following chapter are part and parcel of the same topic: financial ratios. The essay and discussion topics relating to both chapters will accordingly be found at the end of Chapter 10 on pages 217-20.

Notes and References

1. G. A. Welsch and R. N. Anthony, *Fundamentals of Financial Accounting,* Irwin, 1974, pp. 580-1.

2. See, e.g., R. A. Foulke, *Practical Financial Statement Analysis,* McGraw-Hill, 1971; or R. T. Sprouse and R. J. Swieringa, *Essentials of Financial Statement Analysis,* Addison-Wesley, 1972.

3. e.g. *Objectives of Financial Statements.* Report of the Study Group on the Objectives of Financial Statements, American Institute of Certified Public Accountants, 1973.

4. M. Moonitz, 'The Basic Postulates of Accounting', *Accounting Research Study 1,* American Institute of Certified Public Accountants, 1961, p. 50.

5. ibid., p. 43.

6. See, e.g., R. A. Fawthrop, 'The "Equivalent Risk Class" Concept, Industrial Classifications, and the Cost of Capital', *AUTA News Review,* Autumn 1972, pp. 3-40.

7. E. Stamp and C. Marley, *Accounting Principles and the City Code: the Case for Reform,* Butterworth, 1970, p. 136.

8. H. Benishay, 'Economic Information in Financial Ratio Analysis: A Note', *Accounting and Business Research,* Spring 1971, p. 174.

9. 'Extraordinary Items and Prior Year Adjustments', *Statement of Standard Accounting Practice 6,* April 1974.

10. ibid.

11. E. S. Hendriksen, *Accounting Theory,* revised edition, 1974, p. 192.

12. D. R. Nichols, 'The Effect of Extraordinary Items on Predictions of Earnings', *Abacus,* June 1973, pp. 81-92.

13. J. L. Dohr, 'Materiality – What Does It Mean in Accounting?', *Journal of Accountancy,* July 1950, p. 56.

14. 'The Interpretation of "Material" in Relation to Accounts', *Statement S10,* Institute of Chartered Accountants in England and Wales, 1968, p. 2.

Selected Bibliography for Chapter 9

See combined bibliography for Chapters 9 and 10 on page 221.

10 The Computation and Use of Financial Ratios

Introduction

It is now appropriate to describe in some detail the main financial relationships which can be expressed in ratio form prior to use in a number of decision situations. The emphasis will be on meaning and interpretation, although necessary computations will be explained fully. For tuition in the mechanics of the exercise, readers should refer to a text such as Sprouse and Swieringa.[1]

The ratios with which the remainder of this section will be concerned can be divided into three main groups: (a) 'internal' financial ratios (ratios comprising relationships of data derived entirely from published financial statements); (b) 'external' financial ratios (ratios comprising relationships of data from published financial statements and data from external sources such as Stock Exchange quotations of share prices); and (c) industrial financial ratios (ratios comprising aggregate relationships of data comprising the financial results of industries as a whole). The first two categories make extensive use of published financial statements, which, particularly for quoted companies, are readily available. The last category is not so accessible, though official government publications such as *Company Finance* do contain ratios useful for comparative purposes.

Ideally, the use of computed financial ratios would be concerned with comparing those in the first two categories (both over time and between companies) with those in the third category. However, the comparability problem must be faced in this context. It is difficult enough to ensure consistency of accounting treatment over time for the one company (for example, when comparing 'internal' and 'external' financial ratios in a time series). But it is more difficult to ensure consistency of accounting between companies (that is, when comparing 'internal' and 'external' ratios of comparable companies). The difficulties in the latter situation are multiplied when it is realized that, because of the complexity and diversity of industrial and commercial activity conducted within a single company or group of companies, it is virtually impossible to ensure absolute comparability. This latter problem is accentuated when either 'internal' or 'external' ratios are compared with their industrial equivalents. The complexity and diversity of activity within individual companies makes it extremely difficult to classify them industrially, therefore it is problematic whether the ratios of an individual company and its assumed industry classification are indeed comparable. For this reason, the undernoted ratio descriptions will concentrate on 'internal' and 'external' financial ratios, although the reader should note that industrial ratios are available, on occasion, for comparison should the analyst believe this to be relevant to the construction of his company profiles.

The ratios which will now be examined will be concerned with the following aspects of a company's financial profile: profitability, liquidity, and financial structure (including its market performance). These factors are believed to be the main ones which the analyst should be interested in when using published accounting information for assessing companies prior to making decisions. This proposition would appear to remain valid, no matter what the nature of the decision. Profitability factors, in terms of measured income, dividend and retention levels, not only allow the analyst to assess potential dividends, but also to examine company financial success or failure (assuming it is accepted that income is a reasonable indicator of these matters). Liquidity factors are crucial to the future payment of dividends and interest, credit and capital repayments, as well as the long-term survival of the company. Assessments of a company's financial structure give important insights into the nature and quality of its financial management, and to the degree of risk associated with the various sources by which it has been financed. Finally, indicators of market performance relate the performance of a company, as expressed in its published accounting information, to market assessments of that performance. They can be regarded as a separate category of ratios, but, for purposes of this text, are discussed within the context of assessing the financial structure of a company.

The basic and summarized data in Illustration 21 are assumed throughout the remainder of the chapter, the accounting basis being the traditional historic cost-realization approach. It is also assumed that the measurement practices utilized are consistent in the periods covered.

Illustration 21. *Basic data for financial ratios.*

(A) *Comparative income statements*

		Periods	
		t_0-t_1	t_1-t_2
		£	£
Sales		300,000	350,000
less:	cost of sales (including depreciation)	240,000	270,000
		60,000	80,000
less:	debenture interest paid	8,000	8,000
		52,000	72,000
less:	corporation tax	30,000	33,000
		22,000	39,000
less:	dividends on ordinary shares	16,000	20,000
Income retained		6,000	19,000

(B) *Comparative balance sheets*

	Time	
	t_1	t_2
	£	£
Land and buildings at cost	200,000	200,000
Plant and machinery:		
Cost	300,000	390,000
less: aggregate depreciation	250,000	310,000
	50,000	80,000
	250,000	280,000
Stock and work in progress	63,000	71,000
Debtors	25,000	31,000
Bank and cash balances	6,000	—
	94,000	102,000
	344,000	382,000
less: creditors	39,000	46,000
bank overdraft	—	5,000
taxation	30,000	33,000
dividends	16,000	20,000
	85,000	104,000
	259,000	278,000
less: 8% debenture loan	100,000	100,000
	159,000	178,000
Share capital : ordinary £1 shares, fully paid	100,000	100,000
Retained income : previous year	53,000	59,000
current year	6,000	19,000
	159,000	178,000

(C) *Market price of ordinary shares and debentures*

	Time	
	t_1	t_2
	£	£
Ordinary shares: price per £1 unit	1.75	2.00
Debentures: price per £1 unit	0.90	0.95

A Note on Company Taxation

The UK company tax system, which has been assumed for purposes of the illustration data, is the so-called *imputation system*. It is not the purpose of this text to discuss at length the details of company taxation and financial reporting since this is a complex and technical matter which, if introduced at earlier stages, would have tended to obscure the crucial principles and problems of reporting. In addition, the system of assessing company taxation liabilities tends to vary considerably over time. In the United Kingdom, prior to 1965, companies were subject to income tax and profits tax (both being based on company reported income), with dividends being paid to shareholders net of income tax, distributable profits having already borne income tax. Between 1965 and 1973, this system was replaced by corporation tax based on reported income: dividends being remitted to shareholders net of income tax, which companies then had to remit to the Inland Revenue in addition to their corporation tax liabilities. Since 1973, the imputation system has replaced the so-called classical system of corporation tax, and changes such as these make it extremely difficult to produce a textbook which will not date relatively rapidly. However, for purposes of computing meaningful financial ratios, the tax system must be explained, albeit briefly. Readers who wish to know more about the treatment of taxation in financial statements should refer to more detailed sources.[2]

The main features of the imputation system are reasonably clear. A company is charged with corporation tax at a single rate (assumed for purposes of this text at 50 per cent, the rate tending to vary from year to year). The basis for corporation tax is the company's reported income prior to taxation and distribution of dividends. However, if the company distributes part of its available income in the form of dividends, it is required to make a payment to the Inland Revenue equivalent to a proportion of the gross dividend distributed (the rate assumed for purposes of this text being taken as 30 per cent since this also tends to vary from one year to the next). This remitted tax is termed *advance corporation tax*, and is normally set against the company's total corporation tax liability (termed *mainstream corporation tax*) when assessing the payment to be made to the Inland Revenue for corporation tax. In other words, in the normal case, the company will suffer to the extent of its total corporation tax liability. However, if dividends are paid, it has to remit a proportion of this at the time of the distribution. The remainder is remitted some time after the end of the financial year concerned.

For purposes of financial statement presentation, the mainstream and advance corporation tax liabilities are aggregated and the total then deducted from the figure for income before tax. Dividends, paid net of advance corporation tax, are deducted from available income at the net figure. For example, taking the illustrated figures and assuming the tax rates mentioned above, the notes given in Illustration 21a support the given figures for corporation tax and dividends in the two income statement sets.

Illustration 21a.

(A) *Corporation tax*

	Periods	
	$t_0 - t_1$	$t_1 - t_2$
	£	£
Corporation tax at assumed 50% rate*	30,000	33,000
Composed of:		
Advance corporation tax on gross dividends at an assumed 30% rate[†]	6,857	8,571
Mainstream corporation tax	23,143	24,429
	30,000	33,000

*It should be remembered that, although corporation tax is based on reported income, taxable income may differ considerably owing to the application of existing tax rules in its computation; for example, in period $t_0 - t_1$ reported income is £52,000 but taxable income is £60,000, assuming a 50 per cent tax rate; the figures for period $t_1 - t_2$ are £72,000 and £66,000 respectively.

†The advance corporation tax, which is set against the total corporation tax liability to compute the mainstream corporation tax payment, is limited to a proportion of the company's taxable income (30 per cent thereof if a 50 per cent corporation tax rate is assumed). No such restriction is required in either of the periods in this example.

(B) *Dividends*

	Periods	
	$t_0 - t_1$	$t_1 - t_2$
	£	£
Gross dividends declared of approximately 23%/28.5% of ordinary share capital	22,857	28,571
less: advance corporation tax at assumed 30% rate	6,857	8,571
Net dividends as per income statements	16,000	20,000

There are additional complications in the imputation system because of such matters as investment income and foreign income received by the company, but these are ignored for purposes of this text.

Financial Ratios Reflecting Profitability

The aim of this group of ratios is to assess how successful the company has been in terms of income; that is, particularly in relation to the financial return achieved from the use of its resources. In other words, the achievement of periodic income is not of itself sufficient to assess operating and financial success or failure. Instead, it must be related to other relevant factors to indicate financial performance.

Return on investment

Often referred to as the income yield, this profitability indicator relates reported income to capital employed in the company. Because of problems in defining income and capital for this purpose, there cannot be said to be any one particular way of computing the yield or return, which, in general terms, is as follows:

$$\frac{\text{Defined periodic income}}{\text{Defined capital employed}} \times 100$$

The traditional way of computing the yield (using the figures on pages 185–6) would be either:

$$\frac{\text{Reported income before corporation tax but after deduction of interest for the period}}{\text{Reported share capital + retained income at the end of the period}} \times 100$$

$$= \frac{52,000}{159,000} \times 100 = 32.7 \% \text{ (for period } t_o - t_1); \text{ and}$$

$$= \frac{72,000}{178.000} \times 100 = 40.4\% \text{ (for period } t_1 - t_2);$$

or

$$\frac{\text{Reported income before corporation tax and interest for the period}}{\text{Total assets at the end of the period}} \times 100$$

$$= \frac{60,000}{344,000} \times 100 = 17.4\% \text{ (for period } t_o - t_1); \text{ and}$$

$$= \frac{80,000}{382,000} \times 100 = 21.0\% \text{ (for period } t_1 - t_2).$$

The first set of ratios (32.7 per cent and 40.4 per cent) indicates the financial return before tax on the recorded book value of the investment provided by shareholders. Investors looking at these figures can use them in an attempt to assess how well or badly the equity 'investment' in the company has been or could be used. This will require comparison with some predetermined standard, either with expected returns for the company or returns made by other similar companies. Comparability is improved by dealing with 'income before tax' data, thus avoiding the distortions which corporation tax deductions can cause (the computation of corporation tax depending on the tax law of the day and the individual circumstances of the company, both of which can vary over time).

The second set of ratios (17.4 per cent and 21.0 per cent) concentrates on the financial return on the recorded book value of the total investment provided by shareholders, lenders and creditors, thus giving a wider and more general view of company profitability. In this case, to ensure that the numerator and denominator are related properly, it is necessary to use income data before deduction of debenture interest; the latter being the debenture holders' financial return. Therefore, whether it is the shareholders' investment or the total investment which is being used, the earnings yield gives a better insight into profitability than does a simple comparison of reported income levels. For example, reported income after deduction of interest, but before deduction of tax, has increased from £52,000 (in period $t_o - t_1$) to £72,000 (in period $t_1 - t_2$); that is, by 38.5 per cent. But the income yield on shareholder investments has increased from 33.7 per cent to 40.4 per cent; an increase of 23.5 per cent. It would be wrong to draw any further inferences from these limited data, but it is clear that the function of information analysis benefits from the use of relative rather than absolute data.

It should be noted, however, that the denominator can also be taken as 'net total assets'; that is, total assets net of current liabilities. Some would argue that the latter gives a more stable figure than the 'gross total assets' used for purposes of this example. Much depends on the business concerned, and whether it is subject to the volatility of seasonal and cyclical factors which could cause current asset data at each period end to be either below or above the normal level for the period concerned. Netting with current liabilities in these cases would tend to minimize the effect of these distortions. Therefore, if business is volatile, the net figure would probably be more appropriate. It has been assumed for purposes of this example that such factors do not exist.

Alternative returns on investment

Before proceeding to examine other financial ratios of profitability, it is only proper to explain certain other variations of the return on investment, each of which is caused by a different interpretation of income and/or capital.

First, it could be argued that, because the numerator of the return refers to periodic income derived from the use of funds invested during the period, it would be more appropriate to use an average denominator of either shareholders' investment or total investment. For example, taking period t_1-t_2, and assuming the computation of the return on the shareholders' average investment, the relevant ratio would appear as:

$$\frac{72,000}{\dfrac{159,000 + 178,000}{2}} \times 100 = 42.7\%$$

This compares with the previous year-end based figure of 40.4 per cent and appears to reflect more fairly the financial return on the capital employed throughout the period rather than that existing at the end of it.

Secondly, as a result of the imputation system of company taxation, it has been recommended by a leading body of investment analysts[3] that the income numerator in the return on investment ratio should be that which is the maximum available for distribution to shareholders. This is found by grossing up the figure for income after deduction of corporation tax by adding an amount equivalent to the advance corporation tax which would be payable if that income was distributed. For example, if income after deduction of tax was £500, then the maximum gross dividend the company could pay to its shareholders would be £714 (£500 + 3/7 × £500), assuming advance corporation tax at 30 per cent; that is, it could pay out a net dividend of £500.

Taking the figures on page 185, this approach would result in return on shareholders' investment figures as shown in Illustration 21b, grossing up the relevant net income data.

Illustration 21b.

	Periods	
	$t_0 - t_1$	$t_1 - t_2$
	£	£
Income after corporation tax	22,000	39,000
Add: advance corporation tax assumed thereon: 3/7	9,429	16,714
Maximum dividends distributable	31,429	55,714

These figures can now be used as the numerators of the ratio computations, with year-end equity data as the denominators:

$$\text{Return on investment } (t_0 - t_1) = \frac{31,429}{159,000} \times 100 = 19.8\%$$

$$\text{Return on investment } (t_1 - t_2) = \frac{55,714}{178,000} \times 100 = 31.3\%$$

These ratios compare with those of 32.7 per cent and 40.4 per cent respectively, using the traditional method. The advantage of the imputation-adjusted ratios, however, is that they attempt to reflect the distributable returns on investment, after allowing for corporation tax, but prior to any distribution of dividends. The traditional approach avoids the problem of taxation, and thus gives the analyst little indication of the maximum distributable return. It follows, too, that the imputation-adjusted return could be computed using an average capital employed figure as suggested previously.

. Whichever approach to the computation of return on investment is used, it must remain a relatively imprecise reflection of company profitability for decision-making purposes if it is assumed to be derived from accounting data measured on the historic cost-realization basis. It is subject to all the measurement problems previously mentioned in this text. The flexibility of accounting practice (despite mandatory provisions from the professional accountancy bodies) affects both the numerator and denominator of the ratio. The instability of the monetary measurement unit similarly affects it, although, at least in the United Kingdom, inflation-adjusted financial statements are becoming available for use in ratios of quoted companies (though doubts as to the relevance of such adjustments must raise doubts as to the relevance of ratios derived from adjusted data).

The valuation problem in financial reporting must also affect the return on investment (different valuation bases producing different income and capital data for ratios). As yet, because there is little experience in reporting systems using replacement costs or net realizable values, it is difficult to assess the usefulness of return on investment ratios based on these values.[4] However, the apparent advantages of these bases over historic costs would warrant the suggestion that ratios based on them may well be more relevant than historic cost ratios to investors and others.

Earnings per share

A test of profitability for the ordinary shareholders of a company can be found by measuring the reported income attributable to each ordinary share unit; that is, by measuring earnings per share. This particular ratio is normally taken as:

> Reported income after taxation and preference dividends, but before inclusion of extraordinary items
> _____
> Number of ordinary share units issued by the company

In the case of income attributable to a group of companies, the numerator would also be after deduction of that proportion of net income attributable to minority interests; leaving earnings attributable to the shareholders of the holding company to be used in the computation. Assuming there are no complications with foreign income or unrelieved advance corporation tax owing to the latter exceeding the statutory limit under the imputation system, earnings per share would be as in Illustration 21c, using the figures supplied on page 185.

Illustration 21c.

	Periods	
	$t_0 - t_1$	$t_1 - t_2$
Reported income after tax	£22,000	£39,000
Number of £1 share units	100,000	100,000
= earnings per share	22p	39p

These figures are not on their own particularly useful. However, when taken as part of a trend analysis, or when compared with similar data for other comparable companies, they give some insight into future prospects for ordinary shareholders. If it is accepted that dividends are related to available income after deduction of tax (and this seems a reasonable assumption), then earnings per share data can help the investor to assess prospects for further dividends per ordinary share unit. In this respect, studies of earnings per share data are somewhat more meaningful than studies of the absolute 'income after tax' figures. The latter are less reliable for assessments of future dividends, for they take no account of changes in share capital, and this can result, despite increased earnings levels, in less earnings and dividends per ordinary share unit. For example, assume, in the figures used, that ordinary share units in period $t_1 - t_2$ had increased from 100,000 to 200,000 because of an issue of new shares on the market to help with company development and expansion. The earnings-per-share figures would then be as in Illustration 21d.

Illustration 21d.

	Periods	
	$t_0 - t_1$	$t_1 - t_2$
Reported income after tax	£22,000	£39,000
Number of £1 share units	100,000	200,000
= earnings per share	22p	19.5p

Thus, although reported 'income after tax' had increased by 77.3 per cent, earnings per share had fallen by 11.4 per cent and considerably reduced prospects for increased dividends per share, despite increased earnings. This reveals the importance of using relevant financial indicators when analysing available data. It also indicates the dangers which can arise unless the data are comparable. For example, the above figures indicate a significant fall in earnings per share from one point to the next. However, this resulted from the assumption of an increase in share units owing to a new issue for cash. If, in fact, the issue had been a bonus issue out of reserves to existing shareholders, then the change is simply a restatement of share capital and involves no new shareholders or resources. To achieve proper comparability in earnings per share, it would be necessary to adjust and translate the share units of period t_0-t_1 into share units of period t_1-t_2 (see Illustration 21e).

Illustration 21e.

	Periods	
	t_0-t_1	t_1-t_2
Period income after tax	£22,000	£39,000
Number of £1 share units	200,000	200,000
= earnings per share	11p	19.5p

This restores the comparability of the data owing to an internal transfer which has not altered the dividend prospects of existing shareholders.

Earnings per share calculations are subject to problems similar to those already discussed in relation to the return on investment. That is, the imputation system of taxation; valuation; monetary instability; and flexibility in accounting practice each affect the problems of computing earnings per share. Specifically, each influences the calculation of the earnings numerator in much the same way as for the return on investment. For example, taking the imputation system issue, it could be argued that a more reasonable measure of earnings per share (as an indicator of dividend potential) would be one in which earnings were computed on the basis of a maximum distribution. As previously explained, this would mean grossing up the income after corporation tax data at the advance corporation tax rate (assumed for purposes of this chapter to be 30 per cent). This would give the earnings per share data for the two periods as in Illustration 21f.

	Periods	
	$t_0 - t_1$	$t_1 - t_2$
	£	£
Reported income after tax	22,000	39,000
Add: advance corporation tax assumed thereon:		
3/7 of the net income	9,429	16,714
Maximum distributable earnings	31,429	55,714
Number of £1 share units	100,000	100,000
Earnings per share	31.4p	55.7p

As with the return on investment calculation which uses maximum distributable earnings, the answer seems to give the most reasonable expression of this particular aspect of company profitability when expressed in traditional accounting terms. However, because of problems which arise from the possible existence of tax on foreign income under the imputation system, it has not received general acceptance in practice, and the net earnings approach has been recommended.[5]

Income margins

One further aspect of company profitability which the analyst can examine as part of his construction of a company's financial profile is the income earned by the company as a proportion of its sales. This gives the analyst a fundamental indicator of managerial performance by looking at management's attempts to maximize sales revenues while also attempting to minimize related costs. However, it should be stated as well that any assessment of managerial performance which relies entirely on a study of income margins is incomplete and could be misleading. In particular, it ignores the question of the investment in resources to achieve the stated sales and income. For example, a significantly high level of income may have been earned on sales, but only after investment of such a level of resources that the return on investment was significantly small. In other words, ratios of income margins should be studied in conjunction with the related return on investment ratios as well as with earnings per share data.

Income margin ratios normally take the following form:

$$\frac{\text{Income before deduction of tax and interest}}{\text{Total sales revenues for the same period}} \times 100$$

This definition of income is usually used to assess managerial performance without any distortions caused by the taxation system and the financial structure of the company. It corresponds with the return on investment ratio of:

$$\frac{\text{Income before deduction of tax and interest}}{\text{Total assets at the end of the period}} \times 100,$$

and could therefore be used in conjunction with it. However, income may also be defined in terms of income after deduction of tax and interest, or income after tax and interest but grossed up at the advance corporation tax rate (as explained in relation to the return on investment). Whichever approach is used, it should be on a consistent basis when relating it to return on investment data. For purposes of illustration, the definition of income before deduction of tax and interest is used, and the data in Illustration 21g emerge, applying the figures given on page 185.

Illustration 21g.

	Periods	
	$t_0 - t_1$	$t_1 - t_2$
	£	£
Income before deduction of tax and interest	60,000	80,000
Total sales revenue for the period	300,000	350,000
= income margins (x 100)	20%	22.8%

From these figures, it is apparent that the margin on sales has increased by 14 per cent between the two periods. These statistics could be used in any trend analysis, as well as in any comparative study either with data for other similar companies and industries or with return on investment data.

For example, taking the previously computed returns on total investment (page 189), and the above income margins, the comparison in Illustration 21h can be made (all figures are stated as percentages, and income is before deduction of tax and interest).

Illustration 21h.

Periods	Return on total investment	Income margin
$t_0 - t_1$	17.4	20.0
$t_1 - t_2$	21.0	22.8
Percentage change	20.7	14.0

These figures reveal that, whereas income margins have improved by 14 per cent, the improvement in income as a return on total capital employed has been greater at 20.7 per cent, indicating more effective use of total company resources in period $t_1 - t_2$ than in period $t_0 - t_1$. This particular message would not have been available if the analyst had merely examined income margins.

It should be noted that income margins, as well as being affected by problems imposed on the definition of income by the imputation system of tax, valuation, monetary instability and accounting flexibility, can also be examined in a more specific sense from the point of view of the ordinary shareholder (instead of the company as a whole, as above). Thus, the income margin can be defined as:

$$\frac{\text{Income after deduction of tax and interest}}{\text{Total sales revenue for the period}} \times 100$$

Using the available figures on page 185, the relevant income margins would be as in 21i.

page 185

Illustration 21i.

	Periods	
	$t_0 - t_1$	$t_1 - t_2$
	£	£
Income after deducting tax and interest	22,000	39,000
Total sales revenue for the period	300,000	350,000
= income margins (x 100)	7.3%	11.2%

These statistics are now in a form to be used in conjunction with related return on investment and earnings per share data as shown in 21j (if income is after deduction of tax and interest and investment is that of the shareholders only).

Illustration 21j.

Period	Income margin	Return on investment*	Earnings per share
$t_0 - t_1$	7.3%	13.8%	22p
$t_1 - t_2$	11.2%	21.9%	39p
Percentage change	53.4%	58.7%	77.3%

*This particular set of data, using net income figures, has not been computed previously, as returns are normally described in income-before-tax terms. The computations are 22,000/159,000 and 39,000/178,000 for the two periods respectively (using shareholders' equity data at each period end).

This tabulation, using data produced on a comparable basis, begins to give the analyst an overall profile of company profitability over the two periods, in this case from the point of view of ordinary shareholders. Income margins on sales have improved considerably, and the more effective use of company resources provided by shareholders has produced an even better improvement in their net of tax returns. A stability in share units has, in turn, led to an even higher improvement in earnings per share. The analyst could then compare these figures with those produced for earlier periods if he wished to use trend analysis techniques. He could also compare them with other companies or industry averages. However, it must be stated that, to achieve this sort of analysis, it has been necessary to ignore the effects of the imputation tax system and to allow tax and interest deductions partially to distort the income measures used.

It should also be noted in this context that there is a significant relationship between the income margin and return on investment ratios which provides the analyst with data to help to explain essential differences between businesses. The relationship is as follows:

$$\frac{\text{Income (as defined)}}{\text{Total sales revenue}} \times \frac{\text{Total sales revenue}}{\text{Capital employed (as defined)}} = \frac{\text{Income (as defined)}}{\text{Capital employed (as defined)}}$$

This identity reveals two major influencing factors in the determination of the return on investment: the income margin on sales and the number of times capital has been 'turned over' during a period to achieve that sales revenue. For example, to achieve a reasonably high return on investment, a company could afford to have a relatively low income margin, but only if it also has a rapid turnover of capital employed. Alternatively, a low capital turnover rate will require a high income margin.

In the example used in this chapter, and defining income as before deduction of tax and interest, and capital employed as gross total assets, the ratios given in 21k have been computed for the two periods.

Illustration 21k.

	Periods	
	$t_0 - t_1$	$t_1 - t_2$
Income margin (1)	20.0%	22.8%
Return on investment (2)	17.4%	21.0%
$\therefore$ Capital turnover $= \dfrac{(2)}{(1)}$	0.87	0.92

In other words, in period $t_0 - t_1$, the return on investment (as defined above) of 17.4 per cent was achieved by a combination of a relatively high income margin with a relatively low turnover of capital. Similarly, in period $t_1 - t_2$, the improvement in the return on investment to 21 per cent has been achieved by even higher income margins at 22.8 per cent and a speedier turnover of capital at 0.92.

Much of the above data is obviously of direct concern to existing and potential investors in the company, in the sense that they are primarily interested in its profitability from the point of view of future dividend distribution. They are also concerned with the quality of managerial performance. Certainly, over the long-term, the success of share investment in companies depends to a large extent on these matters. However, lenders and creditors must also be interested in these factors, for the ability of the company to meet its obligations is determined in part by how profitable it is and how well it is managed. If it is not profitable or well managed, then insufficient cash resources will be generated to meet their claims.

Financial Ratios Reflecting Liquidity

The next group of financial ratios is used by the analyst who is concerned with assessing a company's ability to meet its financial obligations. It is vital that companies should be able to pay their way by repaying liabilities as and when they become due. In other words, a company must be profitable and liquid if it is to be successful over the long-term. It can be highly profitable yet unable to meet its obligations, and if this is the case, its chances of remaining in existence in the long-term are fairly remote, unless its liquidity position can be improved.

Generally speaking, measures of liquidity involve comparisons of a company's relatively immediate liabilities with those assets available (or potentially available) to meet them. The following are offered as the most frequently used of these measures.

Working capital

The most general of the available liquidity ratios is working capital. This statistic is based on the relationship of total current assets to current liabilities.

$$\frac{\text{Current assets}}{\text{Current liabilities}}$$

This ratio is measured to assess the cover available to meet the existing current liabilities, these being assumed to require repayment in the relatively near future. In other words, current liabilities contain obligations which are due almost immediately, but also contain other items due at various times over a period of a year or more. Likewise, current assets contain resources already in cash or near-cash forms, as well as items which, at varying times over a period of a year or more, will be converted into cash resources (for example, stock and work-in-progress, and debtors). Therefore, given the time lags in both the numerator and denominator of the ratio, it can be argued that working capital is a reasonable measure of a company's ability to meet its obligations. In addition, however, it can be argued that the ratio should reflect a surplus of current assets over liabilities, indicating a margin of safety to allow for the differing rates of maturing current assets and current liabilities, as well as meeting unexpected obligations. In other words, the analyst should be looking for a working capital ratio in excess of 1.

Using the figures given in the illustration on page 186, the working capital data emerge as in 211.

Illustration 211.

	Time	
	t_1	t_2
	£	£
Current assets	94,000	102,000
Current liabilities	85,000	104,000
= working capital ratio	1.11	0.98

Thus, from a position with a marginal surplus of current assets at t_1, the company has developed a marginal deficit by t_2, indicating a worsening liquidity position. From a study of the detailed figures in the illustration, much of this results from the decrease of £11,000 in cash resources; that is, from a balance of £6,000 at t_1 to an overdraft of £5,000 at t_2. Therefore, although the previous section has indicated that the company was increasingly profitable over the two periods, its overall ability to meet its financial obligations has deteriorated; although not disastrously. Its liquidity position obviously needs to be improved, particularly so far as cash resources are concerned. This information is of considerable interest to existing and potential creditors and lenders whose immediate concern is the availability of cash to meet their claims. It is also of interest to investors who wish to see the company continue to prosper and develop, pay dividends and obtain further funds from lenders and creditors to finance its future operations.

The computation and use of the working capital ratio is subject to three major problem areas, each of which makes it a somewhat imperfect indicator of company liquidity. First, its credibility depends to a large extent on the classification of asset and liability items as current assets and current liabilities. For example, with current assets there can be classification problems with investments in other companies, etc., as well as with plant and machinery. If an investment is being held on a temporary basis (to make profitable use of cash which is surplus to current operational requirements), there are good grounds for treating it as a current asset. If, however, it is being held on a more permanent basis (for example, as an investment in a subsidiary or associated company), then treatment either as a fixed asset or under a separate asset category could be justified. The classification problem lies mainly with temporary investments: how temporary have they got to be to be classified as current assets? Obviously the working capital ratio can be materially inflated or deflated by a wrong investment classification.

A similar problem can arise with small items of plant and loose tools held by a company: should they be treated as fixed assets or be included in company stocks under current assets? Again, depending on the materiality of the figures involved, a wrong classification can affect the overall working capital position.

This problem can also be extended to current liability classifications: for example, when does a financial obligation (such as a loan) cease to be a long-term liability and consequently become a current liability? Inadequate care in these situations will obviously affect the level of current liabilities used in the working capital calculations, and may therefore lead to significant under or over-statements of company liquidity.

Secondly, the flexibility, valuation and monetary instability problems in accounting affect the working capital computation, and thus any assessment of company liquidity derived from it. One of the major components of working capital (stock and work in progress) is affected to a considerable extent by all three measurement issues. As commented on in Chapter 6 (pages 102–4) in greater detail, there is a variety of methods available for stock valuation, particularly with regard to its composition; that is, the various elements of cost (raw materials, labour and overheads) which can be incorporated in the aggregate valuation for financial reporting purposes. Therefore the eventual figures for current assets and the working capital ratio can be influenced significantly by the stock valuation methods adopted, different methods producing different working capital ratios.

Furthermore, it would be wrong to think of such ratios solely in terms of the historic cost measurement system. They can be computed on a replacement cost or realizable value basis as well as on an inflation-adjusted historic cost basis, each ratio varying according to the measurement basis used. In other words, when assessing the liquidity of a company by means of its working capital ratio, the analyst must understand that, as with the entire accounting measurement process, such data are extremely flexible. Thus, liquidity cannot be assessed in any absolute sense. What is vital is that working capital ratios be measured on a comparable and consistent basis to allow the analyst to compare them over time as well as between companies.

Thirdly, as liquidity is such an important aspect of the financial profile of a company being assessed for decision-making purposes, it is conceivable that company management may attempt to portray it in as favourable a light as possible so as to attract further credit, loans, etc. This can be done either by accelerating current asset/current liability transactions at the end of the reporting period, or, alternatively, by delaying them. For example, assuming the current asset and current liability figures in the illustration on page 186, it can be demonstrated how 'window-dressing' of this type can be made to alter the underlying liquidity position as described by the working capital ratio. If it is assumed that at t_1 management incorporated the return to suppliers of raw materials purchased on credit during the period for £15,000 (the actual return having been made in the following period $t_1 - t_2$), the amended working capital ratio would be:

$$\frac{£94,000 - 15,000}{£85,000 - 15,000} = \frac{£79,000}{£70,000} = 1.13$$

That is, stock and creditors have each been reduced by £15,000, leaving the net current assets figure as before at £9,000; £94,000–85,000 or £79,000–70,000. This improves the ratio from 1.11 to 1.13 at t_1. Similarly, if management at t_2 incorporated the receipt of cash of £15,000 from the sale of part of its land (the actual receipt being made in the next period $t_2 - t_3$), the amended working capital ratio would appear as follows:

$$\frac{£102,000 + 10,000}{£104,000 - 5,000} = \frac{£112,000}{£\,99,000} = 1.13$$

That is, the bank overdraft of £5,000 has been converted into a balance of £10,000. This would alter the net current assets figure from £102,000–104,000 = £(2,000) to £112,000–99,000 = £13,000. It would also require alteration of the fixed assets figure for land and buildings, but that is not a factor affecting the liquidity calculation as such.

In other words, by accelerating the transaction of the sale of land, an adverse working capital ratio of 0.98 could be transformed into a favourable one of 1.13. These are obviously extreme examples of manipulation of accounting data, and hopefully, efficient audit procedures would nullify them, but they remain a possibility which makes the working capital ratio a somewhat imprecise indicator of company liquidity.

The quick ratio

One of the major drawbacks of the working capital ratio is that it does not fully reflect the current ability of a company to meet its financial obligations: the current assets immediately available to cover current liabilities. In other words, the working capital ratio does not, of itself, answer the question of what would happen if all the company's current liabilities had to be met in the relatively near future. The quick ratio has been designed to attempt to do this, and comprises the following relationship:

$$\frac{\text{Current assets} - \text{stock and work in progress}}{\text{Current liabilities}}$$

By ignoring the relatively unrealizable stock and work in progress data, current liabilities are therefore compared with the most realizable of the available current assets. This also avoids the valuation problem which particularly affects stock and work in progress and thereby makes the quick ratio much more comparable than the working capital ratio, both over time and between companies. Using the figures on page 186, the quick ratios in 21m can be derived:

Illustration 21m.

	Time	
	t_1	t_2
	£	£
Current assets — stock and work in progress	31,000	31,000
Current liabilities	85,000	104,000
= quick ratio	0.37	0.30

Thus, as with the working capital ratio, the liquidity position of the company appears to be worsening — by 19 per cent between t_1 and t_2. In fact, the overall position in each period is extremely poor, although it must be remembered that the company would not require to meet all its obligations at the one time, and that there is a continuous flow of stock into debtors into cash. Nevertheless, the company has virtually no cushion available to cope with the repayments of current liabilities and the financing of future transactions, thus indicating possible future liquidity problems. It should be noted that quick ratios are liable to 'window-dressing' treatments in much the same way as working capital ratios.

Other liquidity measures

Working capital and quick ratios constitute the most popular means of assessing company liquidity. However, other statistics can be produced to complete the liquidity profile. These relate, first, to how much stock and work in progress the company is holding and thus having to finance; and secondly, to how quickly it is paying its creditors and how quickly its debtors are paying it back. In other words, the ratios relating to these factors are intended to give the analyst some insight into the quality of financial management in the company, especially in relation to funds tied up in the form of stock and credit terms given and received. They attempt to go behind the aggregate data in the liquidity ratios, and the following paragraphs describe each of them briefly.

Stock turnover ratio

Particularly in manufacturing companies, stock and work in progress is an important financial item. Considerable funds can be employed by the company to finance stock, and it may well be that reductions in stock levels could lead to the release of funds needed for other more pressing purposes. One indication of how much stock is being held can be obtained from the stock turnover ratio which measures the average time stock is held during a period:

$$\frac{\text{Cost of sales for the period}}{\text{Stock at the end of the period}}$$

This ratio attempts to describe the number of times stock has been 'turned over' and replaced during the period, and by dividing the answer into the number of days in the period, it indicates the average holding time for stock. If the cost of sales is not available because of the lack of disclosure in the financial statements, it is usual to use the sales revenue figures as a surrogate. It is also acceptable to obtain an average stock figure for the period to avoid distortions in the calculation should closing stock not be typical of the normal stock level held throughout the period. (In practice, because of lack of information about stock throughout the period, this figure is calculated by averaging opening and closing stock data.) Using the figures in the illustration on pages 185–6, it should be assumed that stock at t_o was £56,000, and the ratios can then be computed as in 21n.

Illustration 21n.

	Periods	
	$t_0 - t_1$	$t_1 - t_2$
	£	£
Cost of sales for the period	240,000	270,000
Average stock for the period	59,000[*]	67,000[†]
= stock turnover ratio	4.0	4.0

$$ [*]\left[\frac{£56,000 + 63,000}{2}\right] \qquad [†]\left[\frac{£63,000 + 71,000}{2}\right] $$

By dividing these ratios into 365 (assuming each period to be one year), it is found that the average holding time for stock in each period is 365/4 = 91 days. This statistic is then available for comparison with similar data for other periods and for other comparable companies and industries. Its reasonableness will depend entirely on the nature of the business; aircraft manufacturers, for example, will obviously require to hold stock and work in progress for far longer periods than, say, a retail food supermarket. It must be realized, however, that its validity depends, first, on a consistency of accounting measurement for both the numerator and denominator over time; secondly, on a similar consistency of treatment between comparable companies and industries to avoid misleading variations arising from the flexibility of accounting practice; and thirdly, on an absence of 'window-dressing' of the type previously mentioned in working capital calculations. For example, taking the first point, if the figure for cost of sales included certain manufacturing overheads which were not proportionately included in stock, this would inflate the numerator at the expense of the denominator, increase the apparent turnover rate and consequently reduce the average stock-holding period. In relation to the third point, if 'window-dressing' had taken place by, for example, including in closing stock an item in fact sold by the end of the period, this would decrease the numerator, increase the denominator, reduce the turnover rate and therefore increase the apparent holding period. In other words, the frailties of the accounting measurement process can significantly affect the 'value' of this statistic, and great care must be taken in its computation and analysis.

Debtor collection

A further indicator of liquidity can be found by measuring the average collection period for debtors: in other words, the average period of credit given by the company to its customers. Obviously, the shorter the period of credit, the speedier will be the receipt of cash to be used in continuing operations. This is particularly important in times of inflation when money is losing its purchasing power over time. The ratio, in its most general form, is as follows:

$$\frac{\text{Sales for the period}}{\text{Debtors at the end of the period}}$$

By dividing the turnover rate into the number of days in the period, the average collection time can be obtained. However, as with the stock turnover rate, it is advisable to use an average denominator for the period so as to avoid a period-end figure which is unrepresentative of the typical figure for the period. Using the figures stated on pages 185–6, and also assuming debtors were £26,000 at t_0 (for averaging purposes), the ratios take the form shown in 21o.

Illustration 21o.

	Periods	
	$t_0 - t_1$	$t_1 - t_2$
	£	£
Sales for the period	300,000	350,000
Average debtors for the period	25,000*	28,000†
= debtors' turnover ratio	11.8	12.5

$$* \left[\frac{£26,000 + 25,000}{2}\right] \qquad † \left[\frac{£25,000 + 31,000}{2}\right]$$

Dividing these ratios into 365 (assuming each period to be a year), the average collection period, or period of credit allowed to customers, is found to be 31 days for period $t_0 - t_1$ and 29 days for period $t_1 - t_2$. This indicates a marginal speeding up in the collection of customer cash in the second period, although the relative merits of the figures will only be established by comparison with those of other past periods, similar companies and comparable industrial statistics.

It should also be noted that the problem of 'window-dressing', by acceleration or delay of transactions affecting credit sales, can affect the validity of debtors' turnover ratios. So, too, can the valuation issue, particularly with regard to the provision of doubtful debts (that is, debts due which are regarded as potentially recoverable). Over-provision of doubtful debts, for example, can reduce the denominator of the ratio, thereby increasing it and decreasing the average collection period. This would therefore portray the company's liquidity profile (of which the debtors' turnover ratio is only a part) in a better light than it deserves, by diminishing the average collection period.

Creditor payments

The above ratio for debtors can be repeated for creditors, giving the average period of credit allowed by suppliers of goods and services to the company. The ratio can take the following form:

$$\frac{\text{Cost of sales for the period}}{\text{Creditors at the end of the period}}$$

However, the denominator, as with other turnover ratios, should be the average creditors for the period to avoid any year-end unrepresentativeness. Taking the figures given in the illustration on pages 185–6, and assuming creditors were £45,000 at t_o, the creditors' turnover ratios in 21p can be produced.

Illustration 21p.

	Periods	
	$t_0 - t_1$	$t_1 - t_2$
	£	£
$\dfrac{\text{Cost of sales for the period}}{\text{Average creditors for the period}}$	240,000	270,000
	42,000*	42,000†
= creditors' turnover ratio	5.7	6.4

$$* \left[\frac{£45,000 + 39,000}{2}\right] \qquad † \left[\frac{£39,000 + 46,000}{2}\right]$$

Thus creditors have turned over nearly six times in period $t_o - t_1$, and over six times in the next period. By dividing these ratios into 365 (again assuming annual periods), the average period of credit given to the company by its suppliers can be ascertained. In period $t_o - t_1$, this amounted to 64 days, and in period $t_1 - t_2$ to 57 days. This indicates a considerable tightening up of credit conditions by suppliers over the two periods, the average payment period being reduced by 11 per cent. This would, of course, require comparison with other comparable statistics, but reveals potential pressures on company liquidity if cash for creditor repayments is to be found much more quickly than previously.

Summary

Summarizing on the above turnover ratios for stock, debtors and creditors, it seems reasonable to suggest that they can give important insights into the liquidity position of the company: the average holding time for stock indicates funds 'tied up' in stock and working in progress; the average collection period for debtors indicates the time taken to collect cash from customers; and the average payment period indicates the time taken to repay suppliers. In the above example, the company holds, on average, about three months' stock throughout the two periods while allowing, on average, approximately one month's credit to customers. The reasonableness of these data, in terms of financial efficiency, would very much depend on the nature and conditions of the trade concerned. However, the significant reduction in the average credit allowed by the company's creditors should cause all users of its financial statements some concern with regard to its future liquidity position: diminishing credit terms of this type are liable to deplete liquid resources, particularly if excessive stock and work in progress levels are being maintained and cash is not being collected quickly enough from customers.

Lastly, from the various comments which have been made at different stages in these sections on liquidity, it is obvious that all such ratios are liable to window-dressing and valuation problems which could distort them and lead to misleading portrayals of liquidity. Obviously, the audit function can alleviate many of these potential problems, but the analyst must understand the frailties of the data and, particularly, the problems of comparison over time and between companies. In other words, they are no more than rough indicators of liquidity and should not be regarded as accurate measurements.

Financial Ratios Indicating Financial Structure and Performance

A company finances itself from a variety of external sources: by issuing shares to investors; by borrowing from lenders, either on a long-term or short-term basis, or both; and by obtaining trade credit from suppliers. The latter source has already been dealt with in the section on liquidity, and on the grounds of simplicity and availability of space, will not be the main issue for discussion here. Trade credit, by its very nature, tends to be a relatively temporary and short-term but extremely important source of finance to any company. However, its availability depends on the conditions of trading, which can vary considerably from period to period, and its cost to the company can generally be regarded as free, unless it is losing substantial cash discounts by not paying suppliers immediately. Even so, assuming the prevailing situation of inflation, it is relatively obvious that the latter 'cost' is, to a considerable extent, compensated for by the gain in 'holding' liabilities in a period when the purchasing power of money is diminishing (the monetary purchasing power of an amount due to a supplier diminishing the longer it remains unpaid).

The main aim of this section is therefore to examine the more permanent sources of finance available to the company (that is, shares and long-term loans), and, by the use of financial ratios, to assess the financial returns to investors and lenders, and the relative degrees of risk taken by these suppliers of capital. Such ratios are consequently of interest not only to investors, but also to lenders, both from the point of view of assessing the risks associated with their investment and the suitability of the returns intended to compensate for such risks.

Capital yields

This is a somewhat complex aspect of investment appraisal and it should be noted at the outset that, within the context of this book, all that can be done is to adopt a 'broad-brush' approach to the subject. However, readers who wish to obtain a more extensive knowledge should refer themselves to a text such as that of Merrett and Sykes.[6]

The yield on capital is, in general terms, equivalent to the financial return expected by the investor or lender on his 'investment'. It is therefore also the cost to the company of financing itself either by shares or long-term loans. At a conceptual level, this can usually be regarded as the yield expected by the investor or lender on the current market value of his shares or loan stock. This, again in general terms, is the approximate relationship between the expected dividend or interest rate and the relevant current market price:

$$r = \frac{c}{p};$$

where r is the yield, c is the expected dividend or interest rate, and p is the current market price of the share or loan stock. However, given that there is a great deal of uncertainty in forecasting future dividends (loan interest rates usually remain constant throughout the period of the loan), the yield computation for shares can be based on a value for c which is equivalent to the current or immediate past dividend rate, with r being increased by a suitable percentage equivalent to the expected rate of increase in future dividends; that is,

$$r = \frac{c}{p} + g;$$

where r and p are as defined above, c is the current dividend rate, and g is the estimated dividend growth rate.

It is these basic models, and adaptions of them, which will now be examined, using data provided in the illustration described on pages 185–6.

Yield on loan capital

This rate of return normally tends to be the easier one to compute. There can be complications when loan stock is not issued at its nominal value. However, for purposes of simplicity, it is assumed that the 8 per cent debentures in the illustration were issued at par, in which case the yield to the lender would be as above:

$$r = \frac{c}{p};$$

where r is the yield, c is the debenture interest rate before tax, and p is the current market price of the debentures. The gross interest rate is taken to avoid the complications of using a net rate which will vary from one lender to another depending on the tax circumstances of the individual. Thus, taking the figures from pages 185–6, the yields at the two points in time would be as in Illustration 21q.

Illustration 21q.

	Time	
	t_1	t_2
Gross interest rate per £1 unit	0.08	0.08
Current market price per £1 unit	£0.90	£0.95
= loan interest yield (x 100)	8.9%	8.4%

These yields therefore represent the financial rewards available to the debenture holders to compensate, at least partially, for the risk attached to their investment in debentures to the company. These data are then available for comparison with yields on alternative investments with lower or higher degrees of risk associated with them: the lower the risk, the lower the acceptable yield. The acceptability of the above yields will depend on such a comparison with prevailing yields on similar loan stock, national and local government securities, as well as ordinary and preference shares.

One further point should be noted. Although the interest numerator in the ratio remains constant through time, the denominator will vary from one point to the next, particularly if the loan stock is marketable. Therefore the yield based on current prices will not remain constant if prices are varying. Future interest yields must depend on the future market values of the loan stock.

Yield on share capital

The calculation of yields on preference shares follows a similar pattern to that for loan stock, the contracted dividend rate remaining constant from period to period. However, the calculation for ordinary shares is somewhat more complex owing to variability of the rate. As mentioned above, to obtain some predictive content to the ratio, it is possible to use the current rate and supplement it with an estimated growth factor. However, the normal procedure is to relate the current dividend rate and market price of the share concerned. In this respect, the dividend rate is usually taken as the dividend per ordinary share, and the ratio is multiplied by 100 to reduce it to a percentage. Again, to avoid the variability of personal taxation, dividends per share would be expressed before deduction of tax, and using the figures supplied on pages 185–6, the yields in 21r would result.

Illustration 21r.

	Time	
	t_1	t_2
Net dividends per financial statements	£16,000	£20,000
Add: advance corporation tax, assumed to be 30% of gross dividends	6,857	8,571
Dividends before tax	£22,857	£28,571
Number of ordinary shares of £1 each	100,000	100,000
Dividends per £1 share unit	22.86p	28.57p
Market price of £1 share unit	£1.75	£2.00
= dividend yield (x 100)	13.06%	14.29%

Therefore, in our example, over the two periods the financial return to ordinary shareholders has increased by 9.4 per cent. The increase seems to indicate a greater uncertainty and risk associated with the ordinary shares, but this would need to be compared with yields of previous periods, similar companies and alternative types of investment (such as loan stock). Estimation of future dividend yields would need to incorporate estimates of future dividends per share and market prices, but calculations based on historic data provide a useful basis for this further exercise.

Earnings yield

An alternative indicator of the financial reward to the ordinary shareholder, which does not limit itself to the distributed dividend returns, is the earnings yield. This ratio relates earnings per ordinary share to the current market price of the shares concerned:

$$\frac{\text{Earnings per ordinary share}}{\text{Market price per ordinary share}} \times 100$$

Alternatively, this is more usually described in its reciprocal form as the price-earnings ratio; that is:

$$\frac{\text{Market price per ordinary share}}{\text{Earnings per ordinary share}}$$

The above ratio includes the distributable earnings per share as a measure of the financial reward for investment in ordinary shares. For this purpose, it is recommended[7] that, because of the complexities of the imputation tax system, earnings should be calculated on the basis of reported income after deduction of corporation tax and preference dividends. Therefore it is not recommended that, as previously demonstrated for return on investment and earnings per share calculations, the earnings denominator in the price-earnings ratio should be grossed up at the advance corporation tax rate.

In essence, the price-earnings ratio reflects the multiple of the latest reported earnings which investors are willing to pay for the ordinary shares — the higher the multiple, the greater the periodic earnings for which investors are willing to pay. Using the data in the illustration on pages 185–6, the price-earnings ratio can be computed as in 21s.

Illustration 21s.

	Time	
	t_1	t_2
Market price per £1 share unit	£1.75	£2.00
Earnings per £1 share unit	22p*	39p†
= price-earnings ratio	7.95	5.13

$$* \left[\frac{£22,000}{100,000}\right] \qquad † \left[\frac{£39,000}{100,000}\right]$$

Therefore, whereas at t_1 (and assuming the periods are annual) investors were willing to pay for almost eight years' earnings, at t_2 they were willing only to purchase five years' earnings. This indicates a falling off in confidence in the company and a reduction in the estimation in which it is held by investors. This can be seen in another way by converting the ratio into its reciprocal: the earnings yield. At t_1 the yield was $100/7.95 = 12.6$ per cent, and at t_2 it was $100/5.13 = 19.5$ per cent. In other words, investors seemed to be seeking a higher financial reward for the degree of risk they were taking, thereby revealing that they regarded an ordinary share investment in the company as more risky at t_2 than at t_1. However, comparisons with other periods and companies would need to be conducted before these conclusions could be built into the financial profile being constructed for the company. As with all these financial indicators, the reliability of the inherent data (for example, with regard to the measurement of periodic income underlying earnings per share) and its variability owing to uncontrollable factors (for example, with regard to market prices for shares), make price-earnings ratios useful if rough guidelines to investment behaviour. In addition, they are mainly historically based, and their users must make some attempt to amend them to allow for predictions of future changes in the basic ingredients.

Finally in this section, it should be of interest to note the difference in orientation between the two main yields: dividend and earnings. Basically this highlights a major difference in investor objectives: some investors are interested mainly in the receipt of income from their investments (thus being concerned with dividend yields); and some are interested mainly in capital growth (thus being concerned with earnings yields as a basis for predicting future earnings and present and future share valuations). The relative emphasis placed on each will therefore depend very much on the objectives investors are attempting to achieve.

Risk indicators

Because they indicate financial returns or rewards, the aforementioned yield ratios also indicate indirectly the relative risks the various providers of finance are taking when investing in a company. A further group of ratios is specifically designed to look at this aspect of its financial structure and performance. These are as follows.

Gearing

Gearing, or leverage, is the term used to denote the relationship between ordinary share capital (with its inherent uncertainty as to dividends and capital repayments) and long-term preference share capital and loan stock (usually with a known and fixed dividend or interest rate and repayment terms). The higher the level of fixed rate capital to that of variable rate capital, the higher the gearing and the greater the risk of ordinary shareholders receiving diminished dividends if available income drops. Conversely, if income levels rise, the greater the chance of ordinary shareholders benefiting through increased dividends. The same sort of argument applies to capital repayments: the higher the gearing, the greater the risk of ordinary shareholders not being repaid on a liquidation. Fixed-rate capital is also affected by these propositions: the smaller the fixed-rate capital, and the lower the gearing, the greater the chance of interest and capital repayments being met when due. In other words, gearing ratios go to the heart of risk evaluation from the point of view of lenders and investors.

Gearing can be computed in two main ways: first, by comparing the relevant capital figures; and secondly, by comparing the relevant income figures. The following sections describe each approach.

The capital approach

Under this method, gearing can be defined as:

$$\frac{\text{Long-term loans} + \text{preference shares}}{\text{Ordinary shareholders' funds}},$$

ordinary shareholders' funds being taken to mean ordinary share capital plus retained income and other relevant reserves.

The numerator can also include bank overdrafts if these have become a permanent source of finance for the company. The ratio can be expressed either in terms of reported data (that is, based on data derived from the historic cost system) or in terms of current market prices of the loans and shares (if available). Given the significant problems of measuring accounting data, the market-based approach seems to have merit (though market-determined prices cannot be said,to be fully reliable unless an efficient market is assumed). In addition, they tend to fluctuate from day to day.

The ratio describes the relationship between funds with a fixed rate of interest or dividend, and funds provided by the ordinary shareholders: the higher the proportion of the former to the latter, the higher the so-called gearing, and the higher the risk ordinary shareholders are taking by investing in the company. If profitability is poor, the chances of income being available for the distribution of ordinary share dividends are diminished because of the high level of interest charges. Similarly, if the company was forced into liquidation, the repayment of a high level of fixed interest capital would equally diminish the ordinary shareholders' chances of capital repayment. The reverse applies if the gearing is low because of smaller interest charges and so forth.

Taking the data supplied in the illustration on page 186, the gearing ratios can be determined, using the capital approach.

Illustration 21t.

(A) *Using reported data*

	Time	
	t_0	t_1
	£	£
Debenture capital	100,000	100,000
Share capital + retained income	159,000	178,000
= gearing (x 100)	62.89%	56.18%

(B) *Using market prices*

	Time	
	t_0	t_1
	£	£
Debenture capital	90,000	95,000
Share capital + retained income	175,000	200,000
= gearing (x 100)	51.43%	47.50%

Whatever data are used, it is clear that this particular company is highly geared at both period ends. Given the relative cheapness of debenture capital in recent years, this is not surprising (debentures issued at 8 per cent effectively cost the company 4 per cent, assuming a 50 per cent rate for corporation tax, for such interest is deductible from taxable income when computing corporation tax). However, the important issue in relation to gearing is the stability of income levels so far as the company is concerned. If income is stable from period to period, then high gearing does not indicate the same degree of risk as in a situation where income levels are liable to fluctuate from period to period. Thus it is important for the analyst to incorporate his gearing ratios into his company profile, particularly in relation to his analysis of income trends. The nature of the latter, coupled with gearing, will provide him with an indicator of the degree of risk associated with ordinary share investment. In addition, the same points apply to assessing risk vis-à-vis preference or debenture capital: the higher the gearing and the more unstable income levels, the greater the risk of fixed interest rate and capital repayments not being met when due.

The income approach

The alternative method of computing gearing is to relate fixed interest or dividend payments to reported income available for such payments. In other words, gearing would be defined as:

$$\frac{\text{Gross interest payments}}{\text{Income before interest and tax}} \text{ (for fixed interest capital)}$$

and

$$\frac{\text{Ordinary dividends}}{\text{Income available for ordinary dividends}} \text{ (for ordinary share capital)}$$

Taking the figures in page 185, this would result for fixed interest capital in the ratios given in 21u.

Illustration 21u.

	Period	
	$t_0 - t_1$	$t_1 - t_2$
	£	£
Debenture interest	8,000	8,000
Income before interest and tax	60,000	80,000
= gearing (x 100)	13.33%	10.00%

This means that, in the periods specified, interest payments were covered 7.5 and 10 times respectively. Therefore, with income at these particular levels, the degree of risk associated with possible non-payment of interest is relatively small. Ordinary shareholders, too, would be interested to see this high interest cover since it indicates that the risk of non-payment of ordinary dividends is small in view of the comparatively high level of distributable income after deduction of interest payments.

The particular 'risk' ratio for ordinary share capital is normally referred to as the dividend cover, and represents the proportion of available income distributed in the form of ordinary share dividends. It therefore also indicates the margin by which available income would have to fall before it leads to a reduction in the current level of distributed ordinary share dividends. Owing to the effects of the imputation tax system in the United Kingdom, it has been recommended[8] that the income denominator in the ratio is grossed up at the effective rate of advance corporation tax, thereby giving an income figure which is the maximum distributable for the period. This would then be compared with the gross dividend before deduction of the relevant advance corporation tax, both numerator and denominator being expressed in 'before tax' terms. The alternative treatment which could be adopted involves using (a) income after deduction of corporation tax, loan interest and preference dividend payments;.and (b) ordinary dividends after deduction of advance corporation tax. Taking the figures from page 185, the ratios in 21v apply for ordinary share capital.

Illustration 21v.

	Periods	
	t_0-t_1	t_1-t_2
	£	£
Ordinary share dividend (gross)*	22,857	28,571
Available income grossed up at the advance corporation tax rate†	31,429	55,714
= dividend cover (x 100)	72.73%	51.28%

*For period t_0-t_1, £16,000 + 6,857; and for period t_1-t_2, £20,000 + 8,571; assuming an advance corporation tax rate of 30 per cent.

†For period t_0-t_1, £22,000 + 9,429; and for period t_1-t_2, £39,000 + 16,714; again assuming a tax rate of 30 per cent.

These ratios reveal that ordinary dividends were covered 1.37 times (1,000 ÷ 0.7273) in the first period, and 1.95 times (1.000 ÷ 0.5128) in the second period. The figures indicate a 'margin of safety' for ordinary shareholders in both periods, the margin increasing substantially in the second one. In other words, available income would need to fall by approximately 27 per cent in period t_0-t_1 (100 − 73 per cent) and by 49 per cent in period t_1-t_2 (100 − 51 per cent) before the ordinary dividends paid for these periods could not be distributed from the available income of the period. It also indicates that 27 and 49 per cent respectively of the available income of the two periods has been retained in the company, thereby aiding its maintenance and development.

A Summarized Profile of the Company

The major ratios which could be used to construct a profile of a company for decision-making purposes have now been explained. It is useful to gather these together so as to comment on any profile which emerges. The ratios selected for this purpose are those measures using recommended practices, to allow for the present system of company taxation. It should also be noted that the profile is a limited one owing to the data being restricted to two periods. For this reason, it would be difficult to apply trend analysis techniques to such a limited series. Illustration 22 contains the summary of ratios computed in the previous sections of this chapter (all figures have been taken to one decimal place).

Illustration 22. *A summarized financial profile.*

	Periods	
	$t_0 - t_1$	$t_1 - t_2$
Profitability		
Return on investment	19.8% (a)	31.3% (a)
Earnings per share	22p (b)	39p (b)
Income margin	20.0% (c)	22.8% (c)
Liquidity		
Working capital	1.1	1.0
Quick ratio	0.4	0.3
Stock turnover	4.0	4.0
Debtors' turnover	11.8	12.5
Creditors' turnover	5.7	6.4
Financial structure		
Debenture interest yield	8.9%	8.4%
Dividend yield	13.1%	14.3%
Price-earnings ratio	7.9	5.1
Gearing − 1	62.9% (d)	56.2% (d)
Gearing − 2	51.4% (e)	47.5% (e)
Debenture interest cover	7.5 (f)	10.0 (f)
Dividend cover	1.4 (g)	2.0 (g)

Notes:
(a) Income after deduction of corporation tax, grossed up at the advance corporation tax rate, and related to shareholders' equity.
(b) Income after deduction of corporation tax, related to ordinary share units.
(c) Income before deduction of interest or corporation tax, related to sales revenue.
(d) Debenture capital related to shareholders' equity as reported.
(e) Debenture capital related to shareholders' equity, both in terms of current market price.
(f) Gross debenture interest related to income before deduction of interest and corporation tax.
(g) Gross ordinary dividend related to income after deduction of corporation tax but grossed up at the advance corporation tax rate.

Given the limitations of the data available, the analyst should be able to discern the following points which could affect the nature of the decisions to be taken.

First, the profitability of the company seems to be improving not only in terms of the returns on investment (indicating the effectiveness of the use made of shareholder funds) and earnings per share, but also in relation to the income margins obtained on sales revenue. Overall, management during the second period appears to have made more profitable use of the company's resources than in the first period. If this progress was maintained, this would auger well for shareholders, lenders, creditors and employers alike, in the sense that increasing profitability is a major factor contributing to the long-term success and survival of the company.

Secondly, despite improving its profitability over the two periods, the company's liquidity position has deteriorated. Although its working capital position at the end of both periods reveals a slight excess of current assets over current liabilities, its quick ratio has decreased by 25 per cent. This should be of some concern to all interested groups, but particularly to existing and potential creditors and lenders. Repayment of their claims depends on the availability of liquid resources to meet them.

The worsening liquidity position can be seen in the more detailed figures, with stock levels being maintained throughout at a fairly high level, debtors being given less time to pay, and creditors having to be paid more quickly. The long-term survival of the company depends on its ability to meet its obligations, and if the position at t_2 continues to deteriorate in the future, there is the danger of the company being less and less able to pay creditors, repay debenture holders, or pay interest and dividends (despite its increasing profitability). In the long-term, creditors may cease to give credit; lenders may cease to lend; and shareholders may cease to receive dividends. The above figures give all concerned some indication of that possibility occurring unless the company can improve its liquidity by, for example, rigorous financial management of working capital or by an injection of new funds from an external source such as shareholders.

Thirdly, the yields on loan and share capitals have changed relatively slightly over the two periods. The significance of these changes and the absolute figures are difficult to comment on since there is a lack of data relating to such yields in general and to interest rates in the economy as a whole. However, the substantial fall by 35.5 per cent in the price-earnings ratio indicates a lowering of the stock market's estimation of the earnings potential of the company; at t_1 it was prepared to pay for earnings of almost eight periods, but by t_2 it was willing to pay for only five periods' earnings. Thus, despite an improving profitability record, it seems that investors have taken the deteriorating liquidity position of the company into consideration in their collective determination of the share price at t_2.

Alternatively, either the company's shares may have been over-priced at t_1, for reasons other than its financial condition (and the t_2 price reflects a correction of this), or the shares may be underpriced at t_2 for similar reasons. Readers are reminded of earlier comments about investor behaviour and stock market prices (in Chapter 8) which tend to make indicators, such as the price-earnings ratio, somewhat difficult to interpret. Movements in it, as well as the absolute figures, would require to be compared with ratios for comparable companies – as for the interest and dividend yields.

Fourthly, somewhat in contradiction to the price-earnings situation, the degree of risk being taken by debenture holders and shareholders in the company seems to have been somewhat reduced over the two periods. Interest and dividend cover has improved significantly, providing indications of substantial 'cushions' of income to maintain existing levels of interest and dividend distributions in the future. Similarly, the high gearing position (whether in historic cost or market value terms) has been reduced, thereby reducing shareholders' risk. However, the latter factor still remains at a relatively high level at t_2 and can be presumed to be a contributing factor to the decreasing price-earnings ratio (which, when looked at in its reciprocal form, is the earnings yield: the earnings return on the market value of the shares). That is, a decreasing price-earnings ratio indicates a higher earnings yield, which, in turn, indicates that investors are looking for a higher return on their investment to compensate for the increasing degree of risk they are taking.

And fifthly, in summary, the company appears to be a relatively profitable one with a deteriorating liquidity position and a high degree of risk associated with ordinary share investment. These factors, assuming they are examined over a longer period of time and compared with those of other similar companies, would appear to provide useful data for incorporation in the decision models of shareholders, lenders and creditors, as well as being of interest to other users of the company's financial statements.

An Alternative Approach to Financial Ratios

The previous paragraphs have attempted to illustrate and describe certain of the main ratios which can be derived from the published financial statements of companies. They can be gathered together in convenient groupings related to broad aspects of a company's financial profile. As such, they are intended to be useful for a variety of decisions; that is, for the prediction and monitoring functions in decision-making. However, as any search of the relevant literature reveals, very little attention is paid to designing financial ratios for specific decisions, and to proving their usefulness.

The traditional (and current) approach to financial ratios seems to be one of producing as many as possible, with an implied assumption that the individual decision-maker can then select those ratios in which he is particularly interested and finds useful. This is simply an extension of the general-purpose approach to company financial reporting already looked at in the first part of this book up to Chapter 8: provide a variety of data and leave the user to choose what he believes will be useful to him. Little attempt has been made to investigate which ratios are useful to whom, and the validity of the utility assumption remains relatively untested at the present time. This is contrary to the early history of financial ratio usage,[9] which reveals that a particular decision area was identified for ratio analysis (a banker deciding whether or not to lend or continue to lend to a company) and a particular ratio was used for this purpose (the working capital ratio to assess liquidity, the ratio to be no less than 2.0 if loans were to be given). However, as company and investment activity grew more complex, financial ratios tended to proliferate without much regard for their specific usefulness. The result has been the previously mentioned lack of attention to utility in general, and to predictive ability in particular. Fortunately, in very recent times, more attention is being paid to testing the usefulness of traditional ratios and deriving alternative indicators of company performance designed in accordance with the nature of the decision concerned. These issues will now be discussed in more detail.

The usefulness of traditional financial ratios

Decisions imply prediction, and it is not surprising that the empirical testing of traditional indicators of financial performance and condition have concentrated solely on this aspect of decision-making. The monitoring or control aspect has hitherto been largely neglected. The favourite empirical study appears to be that concerned with assessing the predictive ability of the earnings per share ratio, this being assumed to be a vital ingredient in the investment decision because of its use in the price-earnings ratio (or earnings yield) and in predicting future dividend per share data for incorporation into the share valuation model. Previously mentioned studies such as those of Green and Segall,[10] Brown and Niederhoffer,[11] Coates,[12] and Brown and Kennelly[13] have, for example, looked at the predictive ability of interim earnings per share announcements, mainly in relation to predicting annual earnings per share data. Other studies, such as those of Little[14] and Little and Raynor,[15] have examined time series of ratio data as a basis for prediction; that is, the annual growth rates of earnings per share of companies. Most of these studies have produced evidence to suggest that company income, as expressed in earnings per share terms, tends to contain a random element over time which makes it difficult to use past data to predict future data. This tends to cast doubt on the overall usefulness of such ratios for decision-making, particularly when the problems associated with measuring income, and thus earnings per share, are remembered. This is not to refute the usefulness of income measures in decision-making; it is simply to point out the difficulties of using them for such purposes.

One of the most fruitful areas for the use of traditional financial ratios seems to be that of predicting company failure. This latter factor is crucial to all persons concerned with the future of a company: if it fails, then its investors, lenders, creditors, employees and customers are all affected. This has been recognized by researchers for a number of years, and several studies, from the early 1930s to the present, have attempted to determine financial ratios which tend to be good predictors of failure.[16] The typical approach has been to compare financial ratios of failed and non-failed companies over a number of years prior to failure. Usually it has been found that the financial ratios of failed companies tend to deteriorate for several years prior to failure, the period varying from study to study but averaging out at about five years (that is, failure could be detected, on average, five years prior to it happening). For example, in a very early study, Fitzpatrick[17] was able to produce evidence to suggest that return on shareholders' investment and capital gearing ratios were good indicators of failure at least three years before it occurred.

The early studies on financial ratios tended to lack statistical precision and were limited in scope. However, in recent times, Beaver has removed much of this criticism in his studies of the predictive ability of traditional financial ratios and company failure. For example, he has concluded[18] that it is possible to predict failure up to five years before the event, and that long-term indicators, such as return on total assets, tend to be better predictors of failure than short-term indicators, such as the working capital ratio. He also found in a more recent study[19] that, by examining the share price movements of failed companies prior to failure, it appears that investors were forecasting failure sooner than was indicated by financial ratios produced from reported information, indicating that they were using more up-to-date sources of information for this purpose.

All in all, therefore, it seems that financial ratios have a predictive value vis-à-vis company failure; non-liquidity ratios are more useful than liquidity ratios for this purpose (which is surprising, given the usual literature descriptions of the latter indicators); but no firm concensus of opinion exists as to what are the best indicators in this area.

One further area which has received some attention with regard to the predictive ability of traditional financial ratios is American in origin, but reveals factors of interest to the non-American reader. This is in relation to the rating of bonds, or medium and long-term loans, to companies. Such loans are rated in the United States according to possible default in repayment of capital and/or interest to the lenders. In other words, this is a problem of assessing loan risk, and the aspect of interest in the context of this chapter is the usefulness of financial ratios in such assessments. Horrigan,[20] in a recent study, concluded that the most important ratio in this respect is the capital gearing one, though working capital and income margins were other important ingredients.

In summary, therefore, it seems that traditional financial ratios can be used for predictive purposes in a variety of decision-making areas. But there is no conclusive evidence as yet to suggest that certain ratios are better predictors than others of particular aspects of a company's financial profile. It is for this reason that Lev[21] has suggested an alternative approach to the problem of making best possible use of available financial accounting information.

The suggestion of an alternative approach to accounting information analysis is a largely new and relatively untested one. Therefore, although it would be unfair not to examine it within the context of using accounting information, it is not intended to cover it in great detail. Originally conceived by Theil,[22] and later developed by Lev,[23] this particular approach to the analysis of company financial statements is based on the relatively complex subject of information theory.

The main aim is to produce informational measures with values which describe the proportionate development of individual items of reported accounting information over time. In particular, the measures are intended to indicate the relative stability or instability of these items over time, a zero value indicating complete stability, and increasing values indicating increasing instability. The technique can be applied to accounting groupings such as assets, liabilities, income and funds flow, and concentrates on the composition of each of these groupings (as well as changes in composition) rather than on the specific relationship of individual items in different groupings (as in traditional financial ratio analysis). That is, the analyst using informational decomposition as a technique would be concerned with the periodic change in the relative shares of fixed assets and current assets to total assets over time, rather than with the relationship of fixed assets to sales revenue or current assets to current liabilities at one particular point of time. The decomposition measures, once computed, can be compared over time between companies or with industrial averages.

The usefulness of this approach to the analyst concerned with decisions and prediction is hard to assess at present. Certainly it is designed to investigate structural changes in the company over time, and this would appear to be something which the decision-maker should be interested in, particularly in relation to questions such as 'what proportionate changes in the financial structure of the company are likely to result in its continued life and what changes are likely to indicate impending failure?' Lev[24] has demonstrated in recent empirical work that informational decomposition measures indicate some ability to discriminate between failing and non-failing companies some time before failure takes place. At the very least, and given further proving research, this appears to suggest that the decomposition approach, because of its emphasis on company stability and instability over time, could be a useful addendum to the existing array of analysis techniques available to the user of company financial reports.

Suggested Discussion or Essay Topics for Chapters 9 and 10

1. The main aim of financial ratio analysis is to construct a financial profile of the company being examined. What is the general nature of this profile; what are its constituent parts; and why is it so important to the analyst?

2. If, as Henry Ford stated, 'all history is bunk', why should decision-makers find financial ratios useful when, as is generally the case, they are based on historical data?

3. The use of a single indicator of company profitability, liquidity or financial structure for investment or other decision-making purposes could be extremely misleading. Explain, and outline an alternative approach to the use of financial ratios.

4. Financial ratios are only as good as the accounting information upon which they are based. Discuss.

5. The return on investment is an example of the difficulty of attempting to assess company profitability by using financial ratios. What are the main problems involved in relation to such returns?

6. Assuming return on investment ratios as comparisons of income before deduction of tax and loan interest with total assets, you are required to comment on the significance of the following comparative returns (all figures are percentages), particularly with regard to those of the individual company:

Period	Individual company	Manufacturing companies[*]	
		Quoted	Unquoted
$t_0 - t_1$	22	15	19
$t_1 - t_2$	29	17	20
$t_2 - t_3$	20	17	18

*These data would be averages taken from government statistics.

7. Current investment practice places considerable emphasis on company earnings per share. Discuss why this should be so, indicating the problems associated with its computation.

8. The price-earnings ratio of a company increases from 8 to 10. Explain the significance of this change to the potential investor, and its possible impact on his investment decision. Also comment on these matters if the ratio had fallen from 8 to 5.

9. Indicators of company liquidity are of vital interest to all concerned with assessing company performance. Discuss.

10. The working capital ratio was the sole indicator of company performance during the early part of the twentieth century. Discuss the use to which it was put; its limitations (if any); and the reasons why it has not remained as the primary indicator.

11. A company can be profitable and yet become bankrupt because of lack of liquid resources. Explain how this can be so, and the relevance of financial ratio analysis in providing indicators of such a potential situation.

12. A company's working capital ratio at three successive points of time has been 1.0, 0.6 and 0.2 respectively. Explain the meaning of these ratios; the significance of the trend; the possible reasons for the trend; and the implications of the figures for the investor, lender and creditor.

13. What is meant by the term 'yield' in relation to share and loan investment, and what significance does it hold for the investor and lender?

14. The dividend yield on the ordinary shares of a quoted company was 9 per cent at a time when the yield on its debenture stock was 12 per cent and the average yield on irredeemable government loan stock was 15 per cent. Explain the possible reasons for the differences in these yields, assuming that they were not untypical of differences in similar investments at the time.

15. Your stockbroker advises you that a company you are contemplating investing in is highly geared. Discuss what he means by this statement, and what influence it should have on your investment decision, assuming this would be in ordinary shares. What difference would it make to your decision if the company had a low gearing?

16. The decision-maker is as much interested in using financial ratios to predict company failure as he is to predict company success. Comment and discuss.

17. The data given below relate to a company in which a client has invested.

	Periods	
	t_0-t_1	t_1-t_2
	£	£
Income from trading	40,000	50,000
Less: loan interest paid	1,000	4,000
	39,000	46,000
Less: corporation tax	23,000	20,000
	16,000	26,000
Less: dividends on		
Preference shares	1,120	1,120
Ordinary shares	4,500	5,250
	5,620	6,370
Income retained	10,380	19,630

	Time	
	t_1	t_2
	£	£
Share capital:		
Preference shares: £1 units, fully paid	20,000	20,000
Ordinary shares: 50p units, fully paid	50,000	50,000
	70,000	70,000
Retained income	75,710	95,340
Loan capital: debenture stock	10,000	40,000
	155,710	205,340

From this data the client has produced the ratios noted below, using the figures as stated.

	Periods	
	t_0-t_1	t_1-t_2
(A) *Return on investment*	—	—

Income after deduction of tax, interest and dividends
———————————————————————————
Share and loan capital employed

$$= \frac{10,380}{155,710}; \frac{19,630}{205,340}; (\times 100) =$$

	6.7%	9.6%

(B) *Earnings per share*

Income from trading
———————————
Ordinary share capital

$$= \frac{40,000}{50,000}; \frac{50,000}{50,000} =$$

	80p	£1

(C) *Dividend yield*

Total dividends
_____

Total share capital and retained income

$$= \frac{5,620}{145,710} \; ; \; \frac{6,370}{165,340} \; ; (\text{x } 100) =$$

3.9%	3.9%

(D) *Earnings yield*

Earnings per share (as above)
_____

Total ordinary share capital and retained income per share

$$= \frac{0.8}{1.3} \; ; \frac{1.0}{1.5} ; (\text{x } 100) \qquad =$$

61.5%	66.7%

He further comments from these computed data that it is difficult to assess the investment potential of the company; its return on investment, despite a significant increase over the two periods, remains relatively low; earnings per share have improved, but dividend yield remains stable and low; and the earnings yield, apparently at a high level, appears to be inconsistent with the other indicators of potential.

You are asked to comment on his figures, and to point out any changes to them which you believe to be necessary. (Assume any other data to them which you believe to be relevant.)

Notes and References

1. R. T. Sprouse and R. J. Swieringa, *Essentials of Financial Statement Analysis*, Addison-Wesley, 1972.

2. e.g. 'The Treatment of Taxation Under the Imputation System in the Accounts of Companies', *Statement of Standard Accounting Practice 8*, 1974.

3. Society of Investment Analysts, 'ED12. . . The Treatment of Taxation Under the Imputation System in the Accounts of Companies Including Effect on Earnings per Share', *Investment Analyst*, December 1973, pp. 30-31; and 'The Society's Recommendations and Comments on Earnings Per Share Under the Imputation System', *Investment Analyst*, December 1972, pp. 31-3.

4. See L. Revsine, *Replacement Costing Accounting*, Prentice-Hall, 1973, pp. 170-88, for a description of financial ratios based on replacement cost accounting.

5. Society of Investment Analysts, op. cit.

6. A. J. Merrett and A. Sykes, *The Finance and Analysis of Capital Projects*, Longmans, Green, revised edition 1974.

7. Society of Investment Analysts, op. cit..

8. ibid.

9. See J. O. Horrigan, 'A Short History of Financial Ratio Analysis', *Accounting Review*, April 1968, pp. 284-94.

10. D. Green and J. Segall, 'The Predictive Power of First-Quarter Earnings Reports', *Journal of Business*, January 1967, pp. 44-55.

11. P. Brown and V. Niederhoffer, 'The Predictive Content of Quarterly Earnings', *Journal of Business*, October 1968, pp. 488-97.

12. R. Coates, 'The Predictive Content of Interim Reports — A Time Series Analysis', *Empirical Research in Accounting: Selected Studies*, 1972, pp. 132-44.

13. P. Brown and J. W. Kennelly, 'The Informational Content of Quarterly Earnings: An Extension and Some Further Evidence', *Journal of Business*, July 1972, pp. 403-15.

14. I. M. D. Little, 'Higgledy Piggledy Growth', *Bulletin of the Oxford University Institute of Economics and Statistics*, November 1962, pp. 389-412.

15. I. M. D. Little and A. C. Raynor, *Higgledy Piggledy Growth Again*, Basil Blackwell, 1966.

16. For coverage of these various studies, see S. Dev, 'Ratio Analysis and the Prediction of Company Failure', in H. Edey and B. S. Yamey, *Debits, Credits, Finance and Profits*, Sweet & Maxwell, 1974, pp. 61-74.

17. P. J. Fitzpatrick, 'A Comparison of Ratios of Successful Industrial Enterprises with Those of Failed Firms', *Certified Public Accountant*, October, November and December 1932, pp. 598-605, 656-62 and 727-31.

18. W. H. Beaver, 'Financial Ratios as Predictors of Failure', *Empirical Research in Accounting: Selected Studies*, 1966, pp. 71-111.

19. W. H. Beaver, 'Market Prices, Financial Ratios, and the Prediction of Failure', *Journal of Accounting Research*, Autumn 1968, pp. 179-92.

20. J. O. Horrigan, 'The Determination of Long-Term Credit Standing with Financial Ratios', *Empirical Research in Accounting: Selected Studies*, 1966, pp. 44-62.

21. B. Lev, *Financial Statement Analysis: A New Approach*, Prentice-Hall, 1974.

22. H. Theil, 'On the Use of Information Theory Concepts in the Analysis of Financial Statements', *Management Science*, May 1969, pp. 459-80.

23. Lev, *Financial Statement Analysis*.

24. B. Lev, 'Financial Failure and Informational Decomposition Measures', in R. R. Sterling and W. F. Bentz, *Accounting in Perspective*, South-Western Publishing, 1971, pp. 102-11.

Selected Bibliography for Chapters 9 and 10

Past writings on financial ratios have tended to concentrate on the mechanical aspects of the topic under discussion in these two chapters, and therefore it has proved exceedingly difficult to provide a suitable bibliography to support their content. The following publications are regarded as being the most suitable; readers interested in pursuing individual points should find useful readings in the list of references.

R. J. Briston, *The Stock Exchange and Investment Analysis*, Allen & Unwin, revised edition 1974. The analysis of financial statements (pp. 287-330); a useful discussion of gearing (pp. 331-46); and the nature and computation of yield and cover ratios (pp. 347-70).

S. Dev, 'Ratio Analysis and the Prediction of Company Failure', in H. Edey and B. S. Yamey, *Debits, Credits, Finance and Profits*, Sweet & Maxwell, 1974, pp. 61-74. A very readable analysis of the use of financial ratios as predictors of failure, giving brief accounts of the existing empirical evidence in this area.

J. O. Horrigan, 'A Short History of Financial Ratio Analysis', *Accounting Review*, April 1968, pp. 284-94. Content as indicated by title.

B. Lev, *Financial Statement Analysis: A New Approach*, Prentice-Hall, 1974. The most authoritative study to date of the nature and use of financial ratios; compares the traditional approach to the decomposition approach; and examines areas to which financial ratios can be applied, including predicting future income and company failure, loan risk evaluation and credit evaluation by banks.

R. H. Parker, *Understanding Company Financial Statements*, Penguin Books, 1972, pp. 46-83. An elementary introduction to traditional financial ratio analysis.

K. V. Peasnell, 'The Usefulness of Accounting Information to Investors', *ICRA Occasional Paper 1*, 1973. Another look at a publication which discusses the problems of using historical accounting information to predict future company performance.

D. Weaver, *Investment Analysis*, Longmans, Green, 1971, pp. 26-84. A detailed, and expert, account of traditional ratio analysis.

Epilogue

Introduction

The aim of this text has been to provide the reader with a detailed understanding of the nature, production and use of company financial reports, particularly those which are published annually. This has been done without the conventional approach of involving him in the detailed mechanics of accounting for reportable data. The emphasis has therefore been deliberately biased towards the users of financial reports, this, in the opinion of the writer, being the most neglected area of financial accounting. There is little point in providing students of financial reporting with endless explanations and descriptions of accounting procedures, designed to cope with identifiable reporting problems, if the consumer of the information is ignored. The information must be relevant to his needs; he must be able to understand it and have confidence in its relevance and quality; the limitations of the data because of measurement problems should be appreciated by him; and he ought to be able to appreciate the various ways in which the data can be analysed to be of use to him.

Each of these points has been covered in the preceding chapters. The environment has necessarily been the United Kingdom, and therefore includes descriptions of UK company legislation and taxation. However, these have been kept to a minimum as the issues and problems involved are international in nature and of interest to a much wider audience than simply readers in the United Kingdom. Readers will also have noticed that the text has consistently discussed the various issues and problems, both from a measurement and behavioural point of view. Accounting information has to be measured and analysed, and this raises measurement problems and difficulties. In addition, its specific purpose is to influence the behaviour of its users, and this creates the requirement to examine what these influences might be.

The User of Company Financial Reports

From what has been stated above, it should be relatively obvious that a text such as this must identify the users of financial reports, and describe their apparent requirements for relevant data. Chapter 4 provides the foundations for this exercise by looking at the objectives of financial reporting in relation to users and uses. Chapter 7 continues the theme by describing the problems of attempting to satisfy user requirements by providing relevant accounting and other information. And Chapters 8 to 10 specifically outline the function of using financial reports in a variety of decision-making activities.

However, the user and use of financial reports cannot be discussed properly without reference to three subjects: the nature of financial reports and the corporate and legal environment in which they are produced (this is covered, in both historical and contemporary terms, in Chapters 1, 2 and 3); the measurements and communication problems associated with their production (Chapters 5, 6 and 7 attempt to describe these); and the function of analysing their data content for use in decision-making (Chapters 9 and 10 provide the reader with relevant material on this). In other words, it is hoped that the reader has been provided with a sufficient knowledge of the function of financial reporting to be able to appreciate equally the function of using financial reports.

The Present State of Play in Financial Reporting

Despite its long, honourable and useful history, company financial reporting has remained a remarkably unchanging function over the years. Largely regulated by legal or governmental provisions, its emphasis has been one of producing annual financial statements of past profitability and financial position measured on an extremely conservative basis with the minimum explanation of reported data. In recent years, to be fair, the disclosure of data has increased, and annual statements have, on occasion, been supplemented by interim statements of profitability and, even more occasionally, by income forecasts. Nevertheless, the system has largely been historical and cautious in outlook; and surprisingly little attention has been paid to changes in the consumer population.

Certainly, the legal and accountancy professions have consistently recognized existing shareholders as the primary users of company financial reports, despite the rather obvious increase in their use by other interested persons and organizations. In addition, the conventional wisdom has been to regard annual financial reports in particular as primarily for the purpose of making company management accountable to existing shareholders. This view is well summarized in a quite recent legal opinion approved by the Institute of Chartered Accountants in England and Wales.

'. . . the object of annual accounts is to assist shareholders in exercising their control of the company by enabling them to judge how its affairs have been conducted.'[1]

In other words, the system has been relatively rigid in its outlook over the years, with the function of stewardship as its major objective. In addition, it has largely been based on a number of assumptions which have remained untested; for example, that existing shareholders are the primary user group; that stewardship is the primary information function; and that reports of past profitability and financial position are the most relevant sources of information for this purpose.

Fortunately, opinion within and outside the accountancy profession appears to be changing at the present time, with professional bodies actively examining the objectives of financial statements, the identity and informational needs of potential users, and the alternative types of information which might satisfy these needs. For example, in the United States there has been the Trueblood Study Group;[2] and in the United Kingdom, the Accounting Standards Steering Committee is presently examining the scope and aims of financial statements. These are revolutionary moves which could change the entire complexion of financial reporting practice and use in the developed world in the next decade. The major changes would appear to be in the recognition of a variety of potential users of company financial reports other than existing shareholders, and the importance of decisions in relation to the use of these reports by these various users. For example, no more than a decade after the afore-mentioned statement on the stewardship aim by the English Institute, it has published the following statements:

'It follows therefore that the fundamental objective of periodic financial statements is to provide the investor with information useful for predicting his expected return from the investment, evaluating the risk involved and comparing with the return expected from other investments, in order to assist him in making rational investment decisions.

'[And, in relation to other users] . . . we can frame a second objective as the need to provide the user with information which is useful for predicting the company's cash flow and potential earning power, to enable him to make rational decisions regarding his own relationship with the company.'[3]

The preceding chapters have attempted to describe this contemporary approach, contrasting it, where relevant, with the traditional stewardship approach. In the opinion of the writer, this makes the text much more relevant to students of the financial reporting function than it would have been otherwise. The intention has been to highlight the major measurement, communication and analysis problems facing the producer and consumer of financial reports today and in the years to come.

Suggested Discussion or Essay Topics

1. You are employed as a professional accountant, and one of your clients approaches you with a problem. He has a reasonably large portfolio of shareholdings in quoted companies, and he reads fairly regularly the financial press. He has become concerned about the increasing press comments on the weaknesses and inaccuracies attributable to reported accounting information, and writes to you as follows:

'I have always attempted to take an active interest in company affairs and, for this purpose, I have read company financial reports with a view to improving my knowledge of the activities of individual companies. I have not always been successful in my investment decisions but, on the whole, I believe I have benefited from making use of available information, despite its complexity and despite my lack of a formal accounting education.

'Now I am informed by certain financial journalists that published accounting information can be inaccurate and misleading. They write that it omits more data than it contains; and is not likely to be understood by the so-called unsophisticated investor. If this the case, why is this information being produced by companies? Why should it continue to be legally required to be published? And what is the auditor doing when he signs his report? Frankly, I am confused and uncertain.'

You are required to describe the various points you would make in reply to this client, explaining the various advantages and disadvantages attributable to the present type of information. In other words, prepare a reasoned case for his continuing (or not continuing) to make use of company financial reports.

2. Accounting information published by companies can only be of use to the qualified expert; that is, someone with a knowledge and experience of accounting and reporting practices which will enable him to appreciate its strengths and weaknesses, as well as the meaning of reported data. Discuss.

3. It is relatively obvious that bankers and institutional investors, because of the significant part they have to play in the provision of finance to companies, are in a privileged position vis-à-vis the companies in which they have an existing or potential financial interest. This mainly takes the form of obtaining 'inside' information about company activity not usually available to other interested parties such as private shareholders. Comment on the ethicacy of this situation, given

the known weaknesses of the present type of published accounting information.

4. Investment and similar decisions can be affected by so many different factors which cannot be predicted with any degree of certainty that it appears that the provision and use of formal accounting information by companies is a largely meaningless exercise. Discuss.

5. 'Theodore Sturgeon, an excellent science fiction writer, was once asked by an interviewer why so much science fiction is bad. "Well", replied Sturgeon, "ninety per cent of science fiction is rubbish because ninety per cent of everything is rubbish".' Comment in relation to company financial reports.

References

1. 'Accountants' Liability to Third Parties', *Statement V8,* 1965, p. 2.
2. 'Objectives of Financial Statements', *Report of the Study Group on the Objectives of Financial Statements,* American Institute of Certified Public Accountants, 1973.
3. 'The Fundamental Objectives and Principles of Financial Statements', *Investment Analyst,* September 1974, p. 27.

Appendix: Analysis of Disclosure Provisions Affecting Company Financial Reports

Contributed by T. Robertson, University of Edinburgh

A.   **The Companies Acts 1948 and 1967.**

B.   **Statements of Standard Accounting Practice.**

C.   **The London Stock Exchange and City Code.**

This appendix has been prepared with the intention of giving readers an outline of the various detailed provisions (legal and otherwise) which companies are required to comply with, where appropriate, when producing their financial reports. In other words, it summarizes the minimum disclosure requirements of the present time which government, the City and the professional accountancy bodies believe to be necessary to allow investors and other users of financial reports a reasonable description of company activity.

A. THE COMPANIES ACT 1948 AS AMENDED BY THE COMPANIES ACT 1967

Disclosures to be made in financial statements or in notes thereto where appropriate. Comparative figures must be disclosed.

Balance sheet

1. Authorized share capital – summary. Also: options on unissued shares – number, description, amount, price, option period.
2. Issued share capital – summary. Also: shares held by subsidiaries or nominees – number, description, amount.
   Redeemable preference shares (mandatory or optional) – state earliest date, latest date, premium on redemption.
3. Reserves: including excess depreciation or other provisions. Show movements on reserves if not shown in retained income figures of annexed income statements.
4. Capital redemption reserve fund: amount equivalent to nominal value of shares redeemed other than out of proceeds of new issue. Source: income otherwise available for dividend.
5. Share premium account (see S.56, Companies Act 1948).
6. Other reserves under appropriate headings.
7. Liabilities and provisions: a provision shall mean either (a) any amount written off or retained by way of providing for depreciation, renewals or diminution in value of assets; or (b) any amount retained by way of providing for any known liability the amount of which cannot be determined with substantial accuracy.
8. Debentures: (a) nominal amount and book value of company's debentures held for the company by a nominee. (b) Company's debentures beneficially held by subsidiaries (number, description, amount). (c) Redeemed debentures which may be reissued (S.90, Companies Act 1948).
9. Secured liabilities: assets need not be specified.
10. Charges to secure third-party liabilities.
11. Tax equalization account (where applicable, amount used for other purposes).

12. Current liabilities including: (a) borrowings; if repayable (wholly or in part) more than five years from balance sheet date. (b) Bank loans and overdrafts; disclose total. (c) UK corporation tax; state basis on which computed; include ACT on proposed dividends. (d) Recommended dividend excluding related ACT.

13. Contingent liabilities: state general nature and amount (if material). Future capital expenditure: state, where practicable, (a) contracted but not provided; and (b) authorized but not contracted.

14. Assets: fixed assets, current assets, and assets which are neither, are to be separately identified.

15. Fixed assets: (a) state aggregate amounts of assets acquired, disposed of or scrapped during period. Show separately freehold land, land on long lease (more than fifty years to run), land on short lease (land includes buildings thereon). Where fixed assets at valuation, state year(s) of valuation: if current period, state names of valuers (or their qualifications) and bases of valuations. (b) Show aggregate depreciation relating to (a). (c) Show net amount (a) − (b) and treat net amount of pre-1948 assets (the original cost of which cannot be ascertained without unreasonable expense) as though at valuation. (d) Assets on renewals provision or direct revenue charge basis; state means by which provision is made and aggregate amount of provision.

16. Goodwill, patents and trade marks aggregate.

17. Quoted investments aggregate.

18. Unquoted investments aggregate.

19. Unquoted investments in equity share capital − either directors' estimate of value or (a) aggregate income for the year ascribable to the investments; (b) shares of profits less losses before and after tax, arising in financial year; (c) accumulated share of undistributed profits less losses since date of acquisition; (d) the manner in which any losses have been dealt with in the company's financial statements.

   If shares are held in excess of 10 per cent of the equity share capital of another company, or if shares in a company (not a subsidiary) are held where the amount of such shares is in excess of 10 per cent of the investing company's total assets, then, (a) the name of the company must be disclosed; (b) the country of incorporation (if other than Great Britain); or the country of registration (England or Scotland) if the investing company is not registered in the same country; (c) description and proportion of nominal value of issued shares; and (d) like particulars of each holding in the other classes held, whether or not equity shares.

20. Shares in subsidiaries − aggregate. Note of identities of holding company and subsidiaries − a subsidiary must state in its statements the name of the company its directors consider to be the holding company. A holding company must state the names of its subsidiaries.

   In the case of the holding company's financial statements, state the subsidiaries' countries of incorporation (if other than Great Britain) or country of registration (England or Scotland) if the holding company is not registered in the same country.

21. Subsidiaries indebtedness − aggregate; and also, separately, aggregate amounts owing to subsidiaries, holding company and fellow subsidiaries. Distinguish debentures from other indebtedness.

22. Shares in fellow subsidiaries − aggregate.

23. Current assets. State: if realizable value less than book amount (directors' opinion); basis of conversion of foreign currencies; and basis of valuation of stock and work in progress. Show separately: (a) loans to employees for purchases of shares in company or its holding company: and (b) loans to directors and officers of company and repayments during year.

24. Amounts not written off − show separately (a) preliminary expenses; (b) share or debenture issue expenses; (c) commission on shares or debentures; (d) debenture discount; and (e) share discount.

Income statement (or profit and loss account)

1. Turnover and method by which it is arrived at (exemptions in the case of banking and discounting companies, or if not a holding or subsidiary company and turnover ≤£50,000).

2. Group trading income.

3. Income from rents of land (if substantial part of total revenue).

4. Income from (a) quoted; (b) unquoted investments.

5. Directors' emoluments.

State separately (a) chairman or chairmen acting during the year (unless duties wholly or mainly discharged outside the United Kingdom); (b) highest paid other director(s) (if in excess of chairman or chairmen); and (c) the remainder of the number of directors in a scale by steps of £2,500:

Number of directors	Emoluments
	Up to £2,500
	£2,501 – £5,000, etc.

Exemption to company which is not a holding or subsidiary company and total of director's emoluments ≥£15,000.

Number of directors and aggregate amount of waived remuneration. Show in respect of all directors amount of (a) aggregate emoluments for services as directors; (b) aggregate emoluments for other services; (c) aggregate directors' and past directors' pensions; (d) aggregate payments for loss of office; and (e) prior year adjustments.

6. Employees in receipt of emoluments of £10,000 (or more unless employed wholly or mainly outside the United Kingdom) in a scale by steps of £2,500:

Number of employees	Emoluments
	£10,000 – £12,500
	£12,501 – £15,000, etc.

7. Auditors' remuneration, including expenses.

8. Interest payable (a) on bank loans etc., and on loans repayable within five years; and (b) on other loans.

9. Plant and machinery hire charges (if material).

10. Provision for depreciation (not applicable to shares in subsidiaries) distinguishing between depreciation and renewal provisions. State (a) basis of depreciation provision if not based on assets in balance sheet: (b) method of depreciation provision or renewal if not by above charge; and (c) if no provision made.

11. UK corporation tax.

Overseas taxation.

See also *Statement of Standard Accounting Practice 8*, 'The Treatment of Taxation under the Imputation System in the Accounts of Companies'.

12. Provisions for redemption of (a) share capital; and (b) loans.

13. Transfers to or from reserves.

14. (a) Transfers to provisions other than depreciation, etc.; and (b) transfers from provisions not applied to original purposes.

15. Dividends at amount paid or payable to shareholders.

16. Charges and credits relating to prior years. See also *Statement of Standard Accounting Practice 6*, 'Extraordinary Items and Prior Year Adjustments'.

17. Exceptional items. See *Statement of Standard Accounting Practice 6*, 'Extraordinary Items and Prior Year Adjustments'.

18. Show, as a note, the amount, rate per cent and details of the share capital upon which interest has been paid during the financial year.

Directors' report

Where items are shown in the directors' report instead of in the annual financial statements, comparative figures must be disclosed.

1. Directors' names, including the names of other persons who were directors during the financial year.
2. Principal activities of the company and subsidiaries, including significant changes during the financial year.
3. Significant changes in the fixed assets of the company or subsidiaries during the year.
4. The market value of interests in land held as fixed assets where this is materially different from the book amount (interests in land include the buildings thereon).
5. The number (shares) or amount (debentures) of each class issued during the financial year. State the relevant consideration received and reasons for making issues.
6. Interest of director(s) in contracts with the company, including contracts which subsisted at any time during the year. State names of parties; director(s) nature of contract; and interest of director. Exclude a director's contract of service and where the director's only interest is that of being director of both contracting companies.
7. Directors' interests in shares or debentures in the company or any other body corporate where the company is a party to the arrangement. Explain the arrangements and the names of all persons involved. Includes arrangements which subsisted during the year.
8. Directors' interests in shares or debentures in the company or any other company in the group giving comparative figures for beginning and end of financial year (or date of becoming a director if during the year) of number, amount of shares and debentures; specifying each company. Detail as in company register. Under Statutory Instrument 1968 (1533), sec. 1, para. 1(a) and (b), certain exemptions relating to wholly owned subsidiaries are granted (a) to a director from notifying a wholly owned subsidiary of a body corporate incorporated outside Great Britain; and (b) to directors of a holding company from notification to wholly owned subsidiaries of which they are also directors, where the holding company itself is required to maintain a register under S29(1), Companies Act 1967.
9. Analysis of turnover by substantially different classes of business; show the effect on profit or loss of each class on company (or group, if a holding company) financial results.
10. Company with more than 100 employees and if not a wholly owned subsidiary and excluding employees ex UK.
    (a) Average number of employees per week calculated by dividing the sum of the numbers employed each week by the number of weeks in the financial year.
    (b) Aggregate of wages and bonuses paid.
11. Separate totals, if together greater than £50, of political and charitable contributions. In the case of an individual political contribution of over £50, give name of recipient or party. (Not applicable to wholly owned subsidiaries.)
12. Where turnover exceeds £250,000, the value of goods exported is to be stated or a statement of *nil* exports is to be made. If the company is acting only as agent, this provision can be disregarded.
13. The amount, if any, of (a) recommended dividend; and (b) proposed transfer(s) to reserves.

Auditor's report

To be read before the company in general meeting.

General form

Opinion as to whether the financial statements comply with the Companies Acts 1948 and 1967 and give a true and fair view as concerns the member of the company of the state of affairs and of the profit or loss for the financial year.

Where applicable, a statement that the financial statements of certain subsidiaries have been audited by other auditors.

Particular points

1. Opinion as to whether financial statements have been properly prepared.
2. Investigation adequate to form opinions as to –
   (a) whether proper books and records have been kept, and proper and adequate branch returns have been received; and
   (b) whether the balance sheet and income statement are in agreement with the books, records, and returns.
3. Statement, where appropriate, that 2(a) and (b) above have not been complied with.
4. Auditors' right of access at all times to books, records, vouchers and to such information and explanations as auditors think necessary to perform their duties.
5. Statement, where appropriate, of failure to obtain all necessary information and explanations.
6. Auditors entitled to receive notices and communications relating to all general meetings at which part of the business concerns them as auditors.

Statements of Standard Accounting Practice

1. Significant departures to be referred to *whether or not* disclosed in notes to the financial statements. If a true and fair view thereby results, auditor's statement of concurrence is required.
2. Express qualified opinion, disclose necessary information, quantify financial effect, refer to notes to the financial statements (if any):
   (a) When departure is not considered justified, and a true and fair view is thereby impaired; or
   (b) where adherence to a standard has impaired a true and fair view.

B. STATEMENTS OF STANDARD ACCOUNTING PRACTICE (as relating to disclosure)

These statements do not remove disclosure exemptions available under the Companies Act 1967, e.g. to banking or discount companies and, in certain instances, wholly owned subsidiaries.

1. *Associated companies*

Names and interests in companies treated as associates and others in which not less than 20 per cent of equity voting rights held. Where an associate's financial statements not co-terminous, or unaudited, disclosure of facts and year-end dates.
(a) Income statements (including comparative figures for preceding period):
   (i) Investing company's financial statements to include dividends received to the accounting date and declared dividends receivable in respect of prior accounting periods.
   (ii) Group financial statements to include the investing group's share of profits less losses.
   (iii) Where group financial statements do not apply, an adapted income statement is required which includes the investing company's share of profits less losses.
(b) Balance sheets (including comparative figures for preceding period):
   (i) Investing group's interests shown either at valuation or at cost less amounts written off plus the group share of post acquisition income and reserves. Where group financial statements are not applicable, show as note to balance sheet of investing company.
   (ii) Information regarding associates' assets and liabilities; if materially relevant to appreciation of nature of investment.
   (iii) Distinguish between income retained by the investing company, subsidiaries and associated companies (potential liability to tax, if overseas associates' retained income subsequently distributed, to be disclosed).
   (iv) Movements on associates' other reserves.

2. *Accounting policies*

(a) Clear, fair and brief explanation of accounting policies followed in preparation of financial statements.
(b) Statement, where appropriate, that the financial statements have been prepared on bases materially different from any or all of the four fundamental concepts of 'going concern',

'accruals', 'consistency' and 'prudence', together with an explanation of the facts. The absence of such a statement implies that these concepts have been observed.

3. *Earnings per share (EPS)*

(a) Earnings per share on 'NET' basis on face of audited income statement, together with comparative figures for previous period (where materially different it is desirable that EPS on 'NIL' basis also be shown).
(b) Basis of calculation shown with (a) or as note (particularly earnings amount and number of equity shares).
(c) Disclosure of possible dilution of future EPS resulting from the issue of equity or agreement to issue further shares, debentures or loan stock convertible into equity, the effect of which would be experienced after the current period. State basis of calculation where fully diluted EPS is material (i.e. 5 per cent or more of basis EPS) giving equal prominence to basis and fully diluted EPS. Comparative fully diluted EPS for previous period not required unless assumptions upon which based still apply.

Notes:

(i)
$$EPS = \frac{\text{Profits before extraordinary items} - \text{tax, minority interests, and preference dividends}}{\text{Number of issued equity shares ranking for dividend.}}$$

(ii) 'NET' basis (i.e. taking into account all tax liabilities) = as in (i) where tax includes (a) corporation tax; (b) tax attributable to dividends received; (c) unrelieved overseas tax because of higher overseas rate; (d) irrecoverable ACT; and (e) unrelieved overseas tax arising from dividends paid or proposed.
(iii) 'NIL' basis (i.e. as though distributions were 'NIL') as in (ii) where tax is (a), (b) and (c) only.

4. *The accounting treatment of government grants relating to fixed assets*

Either (a) deduct the amount of the grant from the fixed asset or (b) treat it as a deferred credit, transferring annually an appropriate proportion of it to revenue. If amount of deferred credit is material, show separately in the balance sheet.

5. *Accounting for value added tax (VAT)*

No separate disclosure is required. Where purchase tax (or sales tax in Republic of Ireland) was customarily disclosed, VAT may be shown for purposes of comparison in initial years as a deduction from gross turnover in arriving at the required disclosure of turnover exclusive of VAT.

6. *Extraordinary items and prior year adjustments*

(a) The nature and size of material, infrequent, irregularly occurring events or transactions outside the ordinary activities of the business, less attributable taxation, are to be disclosed separately in the income statement as extraordinary items. Income before and after such extraordinary items are also to be disclosed.
(b) Material adjustments relating to prior years and arising from changes in accounting policies, or from the correction of fundamental errors, to be accounted for and disclosed by restating prior years, thus adjusting the opening balance of retained income.
(c) Items of abnormal size and incidence deriving from the ordinary activities of the business should be included in arriving at income before tax and extraordinary items and their nature and size are to be disclosed.

Items representing normal recurring corrections and adjustments of accounting estimates made in prior years should be included in the income statement, and nature and size disclosed if material.

7. *Provisional standard – accounting for changes in the purchasing power of money*

Note: Provisional standards are not mandatory.
(a) Financial statements showing the financial position at the year end and the results for the year in reasonably summarized form, to which have been applied a general index of prices, are to be presented in a supplementary statement supporting the published annual statements laid before members of listed companies in general meeting.
(b) Where applicable only consolidated financial statements need be dealt with in this way.
(c) The method of conversion from historical to current purchasing power pounds is to be outlined in a note, including the treatment of financial statements originally prepared in foreign currencies.
(d) Comparative figures are to be updated in terms of the current index.

8. *The treatment of taxation under the imputation system in the accounts of companies*

Income statement
(a) Where material, show separately:
    (i) Corporation Tax on current income, including transfers to/from deferred taxation account; tax on franked investment income; irrecoverable ACT; and overseas taxation relief.
    (ii) Total overseas taxation (including that part arising from the payment of dividends).
(b) Where the rate of corporate tax is not known for the whole or part of the period, the latest known rate should be used.
(c) Outgoing dividends to be shown at amount paid or payable to shareholders, and incoming dividends at the amount of cash received or receivable plus tax credit.

Balance sheet
(a) Dividends proposed (or declared and not yet payable) to be included in current liabilities at the cash amount payable. ACT on proposed dividends to be included in current tax liability.
(b) ACT recoverable on proposed dividends either shown as deduction from deferred taxation account (if available) or as deferred asset.
(c) Where a class of shares issued before 6 April 1973 includes in its title a fixed rate of dividend, the new rate should now be incorporated in the description in the balance sheet.

C. THE LONDON STOCK EXCHANGE, QUOTATIONS DEPARTMENT

1. *Dividends or financial results*
In advance, disclose the date fixed for any board meeting at which it is expected a dividend will be recommended, declared or determined for payment, an announcement of profits or losses for any period is to be approved and, *immediately after* the above meeting, the following are to be disclosed: (a) preliminary income announcements for any period (including earnings per share); (b) dividend and other distributions recommended; (c) decisions to pass any dividend or interest payment; and (d) proposals for change in capital structure or redemption of securities.

2. *Particular matters to be notified without delay*

(a) Particulars of material acquisitions or realization of assets.
(b) Specific disclosure provisions of the City Code:
    (i) Lapse, extension, closure of offer or its becoming unconditional, with total number of those shares held before, those acquired (or agreed to be acquired) during the offer period, and those for which acceptances have been received (rule 24).
    (ii) In the case of a takeover or merger (other than partial offer) transaction, daily disclosure by 12 noon on the dealing day following the transaction, of total shares of offeror or offeree company purchased or sold by them or their associates on any day during the offer period and the average price of such shares (rule 31).
(c) Changes in the directorate and/or proposed changes in the general nature of the company or group.
(d) Acquisition, changes in, amounts of and disposal of substantial individual shareholding in shares carrying unrestricted voting rights. A substantial individual holding is 10 per cent or more of the nominal value of such shares.
(e) Any other price-sensitive information (including a change of status of a company under the

close company provisions) which is necessary to enable an appraisal of the company and avoid the establishment of a false market in its securities.

3. *Financial reports* (including preliminary announcements)
(a) Explanation of any delay (in excess of six months after the end of the financial period) in issue of annual report and audited financial statements together with statement of expected publication date.
(b) Half yearly or interim reports to be circulated to holders of securities or published in two leading daily newspapers and containing (where* = not applicable to a company which is not a holding company):
   (i) (Group*) turnover; (ii) (group*) income after tax; (iii) taxation deducted in (ii); (iv) (amount of (ii) attributable to members of holding company* and) extent to which (ii) affected by special debits or credits; (v) rates and amounts of dividend(s) of (holding*) company; (vi) earnings per share (in pence) for year or other full accounting period; (vii) comparative figures covering (i) to (v) inclusive; (viii) any other information relevant to a reasonable appreciation of the results or material changes in retained income and other (group*) reserves.

4. *Directors' annual reports*

(a) An explanation, where applicable, of why trading results differ materially from any published forecast.
(b) A statement of reasons for any departure from *Statements of Standard Accounting Practice*.
(c) A broad geographical analysis of turnover and contribution to income of trading operations *extra UK* in figures or percentages.
(d) Principal country of operation of each subsidiary.
(e) If shares in excess of 20 per cent of the equity share capital of another company (not a subsidiary) are held, disclose in respect of the other company its principle country of operation, particulars of issued share and loan capital, the percentage of each class of loan capital attributable to the group's interest and, except where that interest is dealt with in the consolidated balance sheet as an associated company, the total amount of its reserves.
(f) A note of any change (or, if appropriate, statement of 'no change') in directors' interests both beneficial and non-beneficial in the share capital, occurring between the end of the financial year and a date not more than one month prior to the date of the notice of the meeting.
(g) Particulars and amount of any interest in a substantial ($\geqslant 10$ per cent) part of the voting share capital by any person other than a director. Applies to same time period as in (f); where appropriate, a statement of 'no change' must be made.
(h) A statement of whether or not the company is a close company and of any change in status since the financial year end. Similar provisions apply in respect of an investment trust.
(i) Director(s) interest in contracts with company (or negative statement if applicable). *Includes:* contract with a subsidiary; contracts which in aggregate represent >1 per cent of company's (or group's where applicable) total purchases, sales, payments or receipts; capital transactions, including those a principal purpose of which is the granting of credit >1 per cent of the net assets of the company (or group where applicable).
   Interest is extended to include a discretionary object or reversion or remainder under a trust except where derived through a body corporate such interests amount to <10 per cent of its equity and voting power.
(j) Particulars of waiver or agreement to waive emoluments (director) and dividends (shareholder).

5. *Prospectuses – accountants' reports*

(a) Profits and losses:
   (i) Period covered – each of the five financial years preceding publication. Application may be made to cover shorter period where earlier years irrelevant or misleading.
   (ii) Sales to third parties specifying method of calculation.
   (iii) Cost of sales showing, separately, depreciation, etc., charges against fixed assets, and financial expenses.
   (iv) Share of associated companies' profits.
   (v) Income before taxation and extraordinary items.

   (vi) Taxation on income and basis.
   (vii) Minority interests.
  (viii) Extraordinary items.
   (ix) Income attributable to shareholders.
    (x) Preferential dividends.
   (xi) Income attributable to equity.
   (xii) Dividends on equity, rate for each class, details of waivers.
  (xiv) Increase in retained income for year.

Where the nature of the business and special legislation require extra disclosure in annual reports, the accountants' report must make equivalent disclosure.

(b) Balance sheets to be provided in respect of:
    (i) The company and the group at the end of the last accounting period.
   (ii) The group (or company if no subsidiaries) at the end of each previous accounting period *and* at the beginning of the first period.
  (iii) Statement of accounting policies used.
  (iv) Any other relevant matters.
(c) The latest financial period reported on must end less than six months before the prospectus date.
(d) Statement of reasons for any significant departure from *Statements of Standard Accounting Practice.* Companies exempt, because not incorporated in the United Kingdom or Ireland, should give clear statement of accounting policies adopted.
(e) Indication of bases adopted in computation of profits or losses.
(f) Where a report is qualified and contains reservations, the extent and materiality of such reservations to be indicated.
(g) An explanation of the trend of income to be included in body of prospectus (dealing particularly with changes in financing, acquisitions of subsidiaries, etc.).
(h) Where the opinions of other experts are used, the names, addresses and professional qualifications of such experts to be disclosed together with statement of their written consent to use the reports, valuations, etc., in the form and context in which they are included.
(i) Statements of adjustments (relating to each of the two financial years preceding the publication of the prospectus).
Section A
Net increase/decrease in balance of retained income (derived from comparison of opening and closing balance sheets). Add/deduct items required by disclosure provisions of the Companies Acts 1948 and 1967. Material revenue not dealt with in income statements and other extraordinary items including prior year adjustments. Final figure = income before interest, etc.
Section B
Final figure as in Section A. Detail and give reasons for adjustments to reconcile with accountants' report.
(j) Where applicable, a statement reconciling the final balance sheets with the corresponding published audited balance sheets.
(k) Detailed reports on the following matters are to be submitted in a letter to the Quotations Department: stock and work in progress; depreciation and amortization; deferred taxation; accounting policies.
(l) Material overseas interests: indicate amount, situation, or source of assets and income; basis on which currencies and taxation are dealt with. Explanations, where appropriate, of any restrictions affecting remittances.
(m) Long-term ($>$ one year) hire of plant – details to be disclosed.
(n) Any other information or variation in the above which the Department may from time to time require.

Author Index

Accountants International Study Group, 75
Accounting Objectives Study Group, 50, 52,
    59, 61, 62, 69, 145, 146, 177, 223
Accounting Standards Steering Committee,
    57, 108, 112
American Accounting Association, 50, 62, 63
American Institute of Certified Public
    Accountants, 16, 33, 57, 95, 96, 120,
    132, 136
Andersen, Arthur, & Co., 21, 51, 69, 90
Anthony, R. N., 176
Asebrook, R. J., 123
Atkinson, R.C., 62, 63
Axelson, K. S., 132

Bailey, F., 22, 75
Baker, H. K., 56, 69
Ball, R., 7, 54, 55, 78, 124, 170
Barr, A., 60
Barry, R. G., Corporation, 58
Beaver, W. H., 54, 143, 149, 216
Becker, S.W., 110
Beckman, R., 168
Bedford, N. M., 79, 86, 113, 114, 120
Bell, P. W., 58, 91
Benishey, H., 180
Benston, G. J., 54
Bevis, H. W., 22
Bierman, H., 86
Bigg, W.W., 36
Bird, P., 24, 26
Birnberg, J. G., 78
Bonbright, J. C., 91
Brearley, R. A., 150, 169
Brenner, V., 57
Briston, R. J., 22, 153, 156, 157, 173, 221
Brown, P., 7, 54, 55, 78, 124, 148, 149, 170,
    215
Brummet, R. L., 58, 130
Bull, R. J., 86
Burget, R., 122
Buzby, S. L., 78, 86, 120

Carey, J. L., 22, 83
Carmichael, D. R., 123, 124, 140
Carsberg, B., 51, 54, 59, 69, 147, 148, 173
Chambers, J. C., 125
Chambers, R.J., 49, 58, 64, 75, 77, 86, 92,
    102, 122

Choi, F. D. S., 53
Cilliers, H. S., 77
Clark, J. J., 59, 124
Coates, R., 215
Coen, P. J., 156
Committee to Prepare a Statement of Basic
    Accounting Theory, 49, 69, 90, 91
Copeland, R. M., 56
Copeman, R. C., 78
Cooper, V. R. V., 80
Cooper, W. W., 59, 123
Cowan, T. K., 128
Cutler, R. S., 98

Dailey, R. A., 125
Dascher, P. E., 56
Davidson, S., 72
Desai, H. B., 56
Dev, S., 123, 125, 216, 221
Dickerson, P. J., 91
Dockweiler, R. C., 120
Doherty, W. O., 83
Dohr, J. L., 182
Dolphin, R. D., 56, 116
Dopuch, N., 59, 78, 123
Dyckman, T., 57

Earl, V., 22
Edey, H. C., 26, 27, 32, 36, 72
Edwards, E. O., 58, 91
Elgers, P., 59, 124

Falk, H., 56
Fama, E. F., 173
Fawthrop, R. A., 178
Fertakis, J. P., 56, 63
Fisher, I., 90
Fitzpatrick, P. J., 216
Flamholtz, E. G., 58, 130
Flint, D., 135, 140
Foley, B. J., 145
Foulke, R. A., 176
Fraser, I. G., 60
Freear, J., 147, 148
Freeman, P., 173

Gans, M. S., 143, 173
Gibson, R. W., 36
Gleim, I. N., 78

Gomme, E. D., 156
Grady, P., 62, 80
Granger, C. W. J., 169
Green, D., 147, 215
Greenball, M. N., 53, 57, 143
Gynther, R. S., 57, 64, 95, 122, 132

Hannah, L., 28, 29
Haslem, J. A., 56, 69
Hawkins, C. J., 90
Hendriksen, E. S., 79, 120, 181
Hicks, J.R., 90
Hilgard, E. R., 62, 63
Hope, A., 51, 54, 59, 69
Horrigan, J. O., 215, 216, 221

Ijiri, Y., 90
Institute of Chartered Accountants in England
    and Wales, 33, 43, 51, 57, 72, 76, 77, 80,
    81, 96, 98, 102, 105, 109, 111, 112, 113,
    114, 120, 121, 124, 125, 133, 134, 136,
    181, 182, 187, 223, 224
Institute of Chartered Accountants of Scot-
    land, 43, 75, 103, 135
Issuing Houses Association, 45, 47, 60, 61

Jahoda, M., 63
Johnson, O., 130
Jordan, J. R., 77, 79, 86

Keller, T. F., 59, 123
Kendall, M. G., 156
Kennelly, J. W., 55, 143, 149, 170, 215
Kiger, J. E., 55, 170
Kircher, P., 86
Kirkpatrick, J. L., 51
Kitchen, J., 36
Knapper, C., 114
Kohler, E. L., 90

Lawson, G., 58, 59, 128
Lee, G. A., 22, 24, 25, 26, 27, 86, 142
Lee, T.A., 16, 19, 22, 36, 49, 57, 58, 59, 61,
    69, 70, 75, 81, 83, 86, 91, 92, 94, 98, 99,
    105, 106, 107, 120, 126, 129, 131, 132,
    133, 135, 136, 141
Lev, B., 58, 130, 216, 217, 221
Lillie, J. A., 1
Little, I. M. D., 53, 147, 215
Littleton, A. C., 23, 32, 36, 86, 90, 109
Lorenson, L., 136
Lynch, T. D., 60

MacNeal, K., 90, 92
Marley, C., 33, 60, 102, 120, 133
Mathews, R. L., 95
Maunders, K. T., 145
Mautz, R. K., 70, 132, 141
May, G. O., 49, 145
May, R. G., 55, 170
McDonald, G. A., 92, 94, 120

McLean, A. T., 106
McMonnies, P. N., 75
McRae, T. W., 7
Merrett, A. J., 205
Moonitz, M., 9, 10, 22, 73, 76, 78, 91, 178
Morison, A. M. C., 22, 70
Mueller, G. G., 77, 86
Mullick, S. K., 125

Naylor, G., 22
Nichols, D. R., 181
Neiderhoffer, V., 148, 215

O'Connor, M. C., 149
Ophir, T., 56

Panitpakdi, P., 26, 27, 32, 36
Pankoff, L. D., 57
Parker, R. H., 22, 77, 221
Parker, W. E., 95
Paton, W. A., 86
Pearce, D. W., 90
Peasnell, K. V., 53, 69, 143, 173, 221
Pollins, H., 23, 24, 25, 36
Popoff, B., 128
Pyle, W. C., 58, 130

Rae-Smith, D. D., 51
Rayman, R. A., 58, 128, 141
Raynor, A. C., 53, 147, 215
Renshall, J. M., 136
Revsine, L., 58, 91, 120, 191
Roberts, C., 168
Ronen, J., 174
Rose, H. B., 26, 29, 51, 69
Rosen, L. S., 95
Rosenfield, P., 136, 143
Ross, H. I., 32, 75, 90
Rossouw, S., 77

Salmonson, R. F., 81, 133
Scapens, R. W., 51, 54, 59, 69
Schattke, R., 123, 132
Schwartz, A., 58, 130
Securities Exchange Commission, 57
Segall, J., 147, 215
Shannon, R. M., 143, 173
Sharaf, H. A., 132, 141
Sharp, R. A., 123
Shwayder, K., 115
Singh, A., 53, 147
Singhvi, S. S., 56
Skousen, K. F., 123
Slater, J. D., 4
Small, J., 147
Smith, A., 132
Smith, C. H., 77, 86
Smith, D. D., 125
Smith, J. E., 56, 79, 116
Smith, N. P., 56, 79, 116
Snaveley, H. J., 49

Society of Investment Analysts, 190, 194, 208, 212
Solomons, D., 126
Soper, F. J., 56, 116
Sorter, G. H., 58, 110, 130, 143, 173
Spacek, L., 61, 75, 102, 120
Sprouse, R. T., 9, 10, 91, 176, 184
Stallman, J. C., 56
Stamp, E., 33, 60, 64, 75, 76, 102, 109, 120, 122, 133, 135, 179
Staubus, G. J., 48, 49, 53, 61, 69
Sterling, R. R., 49, 58, 73, 92
Stock Exchange, 44, 47, 60
Still, M. D., 116
Stone, D. E., 69
Streit, R. G., 143, 173
Sutherland, A., 60
Swieringa, R. J., 176, 184
Sykes, A., 205

Theil, H., 217
Throgmorton Publications, 78
Tolman, R. K., 123

Tomkins, C. R., 59, 123, 141

Virgil, R. L., 57
Vos, J., 122
Voss, W. M., 143

Wallis, R. W., 86
Warr, P. B., 114
Warren, N., 63
Watzlaff, R. H., 23
Weaver, D., 174, 221
Webb, M., 123, 125
Welsch, G. A., 176
Westwick, C. A., 98
Weygandt, J. J., 120
Whittington, G., 53, 147, 150
Williamson, J. P., 169

Yeomans, K. A., 157, 159, 161

Zeff, S. A., 109
Zimmerman, V. K., 23, 36

Subject Index

Accountability,
  as financial statements objectives, 3-4, 4-6,
    18, 23-32, 49, 51-2, 121, 145, 146, 223
Accounting income,
  criticisms of, 75-6, 87-90, 94, 121-2, 179
  nature of, 7, 13-14, 30-2, 72-3, 87-8
Accounting Principles Board Opinion, 33
Accounting records,
  legal requirements for, 24, 26, 37, 71, 230
Accounting Research Studies, 33
Accounting standards,
  development of, 32-4, 100-1, 109
  flexibility problem and, 75-6, 108-12
  nature of, 32, 108, 109
  need for, 32-4, 75-6, 99-108, 179
  problems with, 33, 109-12
  professional requirements for, 33-4, 43,
    109, 230-32
  *see also Statements of Standard Accoun-
    ting Practice*
Acquisition and merger accounting, 18, 28-9,
  100-1, 105-7
  see also goodwill accounting
Advance corporation tax, 187
Aggregation problem, 76-7
Allocation problem, 73-4
Ammonia Soda Co. v. Chamberlains 1918, 31
Analysis of financial data,
  see financial ratios
  see also financial reports
Annual financial reports,
  see financial reports
Articles of association, 3, 26, 27, 153
Assets,
  current, 9-10, 198-200
  defined, 9, 199
  fixed, 9
Atlantic Acceptance Corporation case, 135
Attitudes,
  and financial reporting, 63
Audit function,
  legal requirements for, 24, 26, 27, 29, 40-2,
    81, 83, 133-6, 229-30
  nature of, 7, 19-20, 80-83
  professional requirements for, 43, 82, 136,
    137, 230
Audit report,
  legal requirement for, 5, 20, 26-7, 81, 229-
    30
  nature of, 20, 82
  professional requirements for, 43
  qualification, 82
Auditor,
  legal rights of, 29
  qualifications for office of, 24, 29, 83,
    131-2
  responsibilities of, 20, 29, 133-7

Balance sheet,
  defined, 8-13
  disclosure, 226-7
  for group of companies, 12-13
Bolton v. Natal Land Colonisation Co. Ltd.
  1892, 30
Bond v. Barrow Haematite Steel Co. Ltd.
  1902, 31
Bubble Act 1719, 23
Budgeted financial data,
  see forecasts

Candler v. Crane, Christmas & Co., C.A. 1951,
  134
Capital,
  and income, 7-8
  nature of, 8
  and value, 8
Capital turnover ratio, 197
Capital yields, 205-9
Case law developments, 30-2, 134-6
Cash flow statements, 58, 128-9
Chairman's report, 4-5, 156
City Code on Take-overs and Mergers, 3, 4, 45
Cohen Committee on Company Law Reform,
  29
Communication,
  and financial reports, 51, 61, 62, 77-80, 113-
  problems in, 78-80, 113-6
Companies,
  defined, 1, 2
  regulation of, 3, 23-30, 37-46
  sources of finance for, 1-2
Companies Act 1862, 27
Companies Act 1907, 28
Companies Act 1908, 28
Companies Act 1929, 29
Companies Act 1948,
  accounting records, 37, 71
  audit function, 29, 40-1, 81, 83

disclosure of information, 29, 38, 226-30
financial statements, 4, 29, 37-9, 39-40, 60, 70, 134-5
prospectuses, 42
Companies Act 1967,
audit function, 41-2, 81
disclosure of information, 38, 78, 226-30
financial statements, 4, 38, 39, 40, 60, 134-5
Companies Clauses Consolidation Act 1845, 24
Comparability concept, 61-2, 75-6, 144, 150, 178-9, 184
Conservatism convention, 6, 73, 108, 110, 179
Consistency concept, 61-2, 76, 144, 145, 150, 161, 178-9, 184
Control,
and investment decisions, 50, 51-2, 53, 54-5, 60, 144, 146
and prediction, 54-5, 144, 149
Creditors turnover ratio, 203
Current assets, 9-10, 198-200
Current values,
defined, 90-93
need for, 58, 88-90, 93-4

Data processing, 71-2
Debtors collection ratio, 203
Decisions,
and financial report analysis, 142-63, 175-6, 185
and financial statements, 50, 52-3, 54-6, 57-9, 61, 62, 64, 121-2, 223-4
and investment analysis, 150-63
nature of, 143-4
types of, 145-6
Deferred shares, 2
Depreciation of fixed assets, 30, 74-5, 104-5
Directors' report, 5, 229, 233
Disclosure,
in annual financial reports, 26, 27, 28, 29, 38, 52-3, 56, 78, 226-30
in prospectuses, 42, 233-4

Earnings per share, 191-4, 196, 231
Earnings yield, 208-9
Economic value and income, 90-1
Equity capital, 10-11
Escott et al v. BarChris Construction Corp. et al 1968, 136
Events accounting, 58, 130-31
Exchange Telegraph Co. Ltd., 19, 154
Extra-ordinary items, 180-81, 231

Fairness concept, 61
Finance Act 1965, 59-60
Financial information,
need for, 3-4, 23-30, 48-64, 142-50
Financial ratios,
and company tax, 186-8, 190-1, 193-4, 195

computation of, 184-217
criteria for, 177-82
and investors, 177
and lenders and creditors, 177
nature of, 175-82, 176
objectives of, 176-7
usefulness of, 149, 179-80, 215-16
Financial reports,
alternative forms of, 57-9
analysis of, 142-71, 184-214
annual, 4-6, 49-52, 54, 226-32
communication and, 51, 61, 62, 77-80, 113-6
criteria for, 6-7, 61-3
history of, 23-34
interim, 18, 55
and investment, 49, 52-9, 146, 147-9, 150-52
nature of, 4-7, 18
objectives of, 25, 26, 27-8, 29, 48-64, 121-3
production of, 70-83
quality of, 24, 25, 26, 27, 28, 29, 31, 32-4, 61-3, 144, 149, 154, 179-80
Financial report analysis,
criteria for, 149-50
and decisions, 142-63, 175-6, 185
fundamental analysis and, 175
and investment analysis, 146-50
investment decisions and, 146, 147-9, 150-2
loan and credit decisions and, 147
objectives of, 144-5, 175
process of, 184-214
Financial statements,
annual, 5-6, 37-9, 39-40, 49-52, 54
decisions and, 50, 52-3, 54-6, 57-9, 61, 62, 64, 121-2, 223-4
general purpose approach to, 49-50, 63-4
government and, 59-61, 146
interim, 18, 55
investors and, 23-30, 51-9
legal requirements for, 23-30, 37-9, 39-40, 70, 71, 78, 81, 83, 226-30
lenders and creditors and, 6, 25-8, 59
management and, 50, 145
nature of, 5-6
objectives of, 25, 26, 27-8, 29, 49-64, 121-3
prediction and, 53-6, 121-5
professional requirements for, 32-4, 43, 75-6, 78, 96, 109, 111, 230-32
relationship between, 18
Stock Exchange requirements for, 44-5, 233
taxation and, 59-60, 146, 232
Financial structure and performance ratios, 185, 205-12
Fixed assets, 9
Flexibility problem,
accounting standards and, 75-6, 108-12
effects of, 75-6, 101-2, 179, 191

evidence of, 102-8
nature of, 75-6
origins of, 99-101
Forecasts, 59, 122-5
Foster v. The New Trinidad Lake Asphalte Co. Ltd. 1901, 31
Fundamental analysis,
    financial ratio analysis and, 175
    nature of, 152-63
    random walk theory and, 152, 170
    sources of information for, 153-5
    technical analysis and, 152, 153, 163-4, 168-9
    trend analysis and, 155-6, 157-63
Funds statements, 6, 16-17, 57, 107-8, 128

Gearing,
    capital approach, 210-11
    income approach, 211-12
    nature of, 209
General purpose financial statements,
    nature of, 49-50
    v. specific purpose financial statements, 63-4, 143, 144, 149
Gerrard, Thomas, & Son Ltd. 1968, 135
Goodwill accounting, 12, 30-1, 105-6
Governmental use of financial statements, 59-61, 146
Group financial statements,
    legal requirements for, 29, 38-9
    nature of, 5, 12-13, 15-16, 76-7
Hedley Byrne & Co. Ltd. v. Heller & Partners Ltd. 1964, 134
Historic cost financial statements,
    alternatives to, 58, 90-94
    arguments against use of, 90
    nature of, 6, 72-7
    realisation convention and, 6, 72-3, 87-9, 179
    usefulness of, 90, 179
History of financial reporting,
    accounting standards development, 32-4
    case law developments, 30-2
    legislative developments 1844-1900, 25-7
    legislative developments 1900-1948, 27-30
    pre-limited company era, 23
    railway example, 23-5
Holding companies, 3, 39
Human resource accounting, 58, 129-30

Imputation tax system, 186-8, 190, 193, 232
Income,
    alternatives to, 127-31
    and capital, 7-8
    defined, 7, 127
    economic, 90-1
    problems of defining, 127
    problems of measuring, 126
    realizable, 58, 92-3
    relevance of, 7, 126-31
    replacement cost, 58, 91-2

shareholder behaviour and reports of, 54-5
    trends, 148, 150, 156, 158-60
    and value, 8
Income margins, 194
Income statement,
    defined, 13-16
    disclosure in, 227-8
    for group of companies, 15-16
Independence of auditor,
    auditors as shareholders, 24, 132
    concept of, 83, 131-3
    management services and, 132-3
    third parties and, 133
Inflation accounting,
    financial statements, 96-8, 232
    nature of, 94-9
    need for, 57, 94-8
    usefulness of, 98-9
Information processing, 72-80
Informational decomposition measures, 217
Interim reports,
    nature of, 18
    shareholder behaviour and, 55, 148-9, 215
    Stock Exchange requirements for, 4, 44, 233
Investment analysis,
    decisions and, 150-63
    financial report analysis and, 146-50
    fundamental analysis and, 152-63
    technical analysis and, 163-9
Investment decisions,
    control and, 50, 51-2, 53, 54-5, 60, 144, 146
    financial ratios and, 177
    financial report analysis and, 146, 147-9, 150-2
    financial statements and, 52-9
    fundamental analysis and, 152-63
    nature of, 147-8
    prediction and, 148, 149, 156, 157-63
    risk and, 148, 151-2, 156
    technical analysis and, 163-9
    valuation and, 150-52
Irish Woollen Co. Ltd. v. Tyson & Others 1900, 135

Joint Stock Companies Act 1844, 26
Joint Stock Companies Act 1855, 26
Joint Stock Companies Act 1856, 26

Kingston Cotton Mill Co. (No. 2) 1896, 135

Lee v. Neuchatel Asphalte Co. Ltd. 1889, 30
Legal requirements,
    for accounting records, 24, 26, 37, 71, 230
    for annual financial statements, 23-30, 37-9, 39-40, 70, 71, 78, 81, 83, 226-30
    for audit function, 24, 26, 27, 29, 40-42, 81, 83, 133-6, 229-30
    for group financial statements, 29, 38-9
    for prospectuses, 42

Legislative developments in financial reporting,
    1844-1900, 25-7
    1900-1948, 27-30
    1967, 38, 39, 40, 41
Liabilities, 10, 198-9
Limited liability, 1
Liquidity ratios, 185, 197-205
Loan and credit decisions,
    financial ratios and, 177
    financial report analysis and, 147
    financial statements and, 6, 25-8, 59
Loan capital yield, 206-7
London and General Bank (No. 2) 1895, 134
*London Oil Storage Co. Ltd. v. Seear Hasluck
    and Co.* 1904, 134
Lubbock v. The British Bank of South America
    1892, 30

Mainstream corporation tax, 186
Management,
    decisions, 145
    responsibility for financial statements, 70
    use of financial statements, 50, 145
Management letter, 83
Materiality concept, 61, 77, 182
Measurement criteria, 61-2
Memorandum of association, 3, 153
Merger accounting,
    see acquisition and merger accounting
    see also goodwill accounting
Monetary unit problem, 57, 94-9, 179, 191,
    232
Moodies Services Ltd., 19, 154

Objectives of financial statements,
    see financial statements
    see also financial reports
Objectivity concept, 7, 90
Ordinary shares, 2

Pacific Acceptance Corporation case, 135
Perception and financial reporting, 62-3, 114-5
Prediction,
    and analyzed data, 149-50, 156, 216
    and control, 54-5, 144, 149
    financial statements and, 53-6, 121-5
    investment decisions and, 148, 149, 156,
        157-63
    trend analysis and, 157-60
Predictive financial reports,
    nature of, 18, 122-3, 233-4
    problems with, 123-5
Preference shares, 2
Presentation of financial information, 79,
    115-6
Price-earnings ratio, 209-10
Production of financial reports, 70-83
Professional requirements,
    for accounting standards, 33-4, 43, 109,
        230-32
    for annual financial statements, 32-4, 43,

75-6, 78, 96, 109, 111, 230-32
    for audit function, 43, 82, 136, 137
    for profit forecasts, 124-5
Profit forecasts,
    City Code on Take-overs and Mergers and,
        45
    Professional requirements for, 124-5
    Stock Exchange requirements for, 44,
        233-4
Profitability ratios, 185, 188-97
Prospectuses,
    legal requirements for, 18, 42
    Stock Exchange requirements for, 44,
        233-4

Quantity of financial information, 56, 78-9,
    115, 179
Quick ratio, 200-201

Railway financial reporting, 23-5
Random walk hypothesis,
    defined, 169
    financial reporting and, 169-70
    fundamental analysis and, 152, 170
    investment analysis and, 170
    investment decisions and, 169-70
    technical analysis and, 169
Realizable value accounting, 58, 92-3
Realizable convention. 6, 72-3, 87-9, 179
Recommendations on Accounting Principles,
    33
Regulation of Railways Act 1868, 25
Relevance concept, 49, 61, 149
Replacement cost accounting, 58, 91-2
Responsibility of auditor,
    activities responsible for, 41, 71, 134-6
    persons responsible to, 81, 134
Retained income, 10-11
Returns on investment, 188-91, 195-7
Rex v. Kylsant & Morland 1932, 31
Risk,
    decisions and, 148, 151-2, 156
Risk indicators, 209-12

Selection of data, 71
Share capital, 1-2, 10
Share capital yield, 207
Shareholder behaviour,
    income reports and, 54-5
    interim reports and, 55, 148-9, 215
Shareholders,
    financial statements and, 6, 23-32, 51-9
Sources and application of funds statements,
    see funds statements
Specific purpose financial statements,
    v. general purpose financial statements,
        63-4, 143, 144, 149
*Squire, Henry, (Cash Chemists) Ltd. v. Ball,
    Baker & Co.* 1921, 135
Stapley v. Read Bros. Ltd. 1924, 31
Statement of Intent on Accounting Standards

in the 1970s, 33
Statements of Standard Accounting Practice,
    general coverage, 33-4, 43, 75-6, 78, 82,
    109, 136, 137
    Statement 1, 112, 230
    Statement 2, 43, 230-31
    Statement 3, 112, 231
    Statement 4, 231
    Statement 5, 231
    Statement 6, 231
    Statement 7, 96, 111, 232
    Statement 8, 232
Statements on Auditing, 43
Stewardship accounting,
    see accountability
Stock Exchange requirements,
    Admission of Securities to Listing, 44
    directors' reports, 233
    financial statements and, 44-5, 233
    general coverage, 232-4
    interim reports and, 4, 44, 233
    Listing Agreement, 44
    profit forecasts and, 44, 233-4
    prospectuses, 44, 233-4
Stock turnover ratio, 201-2
Stock and work in progress accounting, 75,
    102-4, 199
Subjective judgement, 74, 113, 150
Subsidiary companies, 3, 39

Taxation,
    financial ratios and, 186-8, 190-1, 193-4,
    195
    financial statements and, 59-60, 146, 232
Technical analysis,
    fundamental analysis and, 152, 153, 163-4,
    168-9
    investment decisions and, 163-9
    nature of, 164-8
    and random walk hypothesis, 169

trend analysis and, 164-6
Terminology problem, 56, 79, 116
Timeliness concept, 62, 80
Trend analysis,
    defined, 157-60
    fundamental analysis and, 155-6, 157-63
    and prediction, 157-60
    technical analysis and, 164-6
True and fair view, 5, 38, 39, 41

Understandibility concept, 61, 79, 113-4
Uniformity and comparability, 61-2, 75-6,
    110
United States v. Simon 1968, 136
Usefulness,
    of current value financial statements, 58,
    88-94
    of financial ratios, 149, 179-80, 215-16
    of historic cost financial statements, 90,
    179
    of inflation-adjusted financial statements,
    98-9
Users of financial statements,
    criteria for, 62-3
    decisions of, 52-61, 145-9, 223-4
    degree of use by, 55-6
    empirical evidence of, 54-5
    identification of, 48-50, 145-9, 222-3
    satisfying, 121-3
Utility concept, 49

Valuation problems, 74-5, 87-94, 191
Value,
    capital, income and, 7-8
Verification, 7, 80-82
*Verner v. General and Commercial Investment
    Trust Ltd.* 1894, 30

Wilmer v. McNamara and Co. Ltd. 1895, 30-1
Working capital ratio, 198-200